De Valera and The Ulster Question
1917–1973

DE VALERA
AND THE
ULSTER QUESTION
1917–1973

JOHN BOWMAN

CLARENDON PRESS · OXFORD
1982

Oxford University Press, Walton Street, Oxford OX2 6DP

London Glasgow New York Toronto
Delhi Bombay Calcutta Madras Karachi
Kuala Lumpur Singapore Hong Kong Tokyo
Nairobi Dar es Salaam Cape Town
Melbourne Auckland
and associates in
Beruit Berlin Ibadan Mexico City Nicosia

Published in the United States by
Oxford University Press, New York

British Library Cataloguing in Publication Data
Bowman, John
De Valera and the Ulster Question, 1917-1973.
1. De Valera, Eamon   2. Partition — Ireland
I. Title
320.5'4'09415   DA959
ISBN 0-19-822681-0

Library of Congress Cataloging in Publication Data
Bowman, John, 1942-
De Valera and the Ulster question, 1917-1973.
Bibliography: p.
Includes index.
1. Ireland — Politics and government — 1910-1921.
2. Ireland — Politics and government — 1922-
3. Northern Ireland — Politics and government.
4. De Valera, Eamon, 1882-1972.   I. Title.
DA690.B65 1982   941.5082   82-12597
ISBN 0-19-822681-0

Set by Hope Services, Abingdon
Printed by Mackay Ltd Chatham

For Eimer
and in memory of my parents

Acknowledgements

I am indebted to the following individuals and wish to record my thanks: Frank Aiken, the late Ernest Blythe, F. H. Boland, Kevin Boland, the late Lord Brookeborough, Noel Browne, Mike Burns, Dan Bryan, Patrick Buckland, Jack Carroll, Michael Carroll, the Late Erskine Childers II, M. J. Costello, Cornelius Cremin, Bernard Crick, Conor Cruise O'Brien, Paddy Devlin, Ted Dolan, James Dillon, T. Ryle Dwyer, Robin Dudley Edwards, the late Brian Faulkner, Gerard Fitt, Donal Flanagan, Alexis FitzGerald, Garret FitzGerald, Douglas Gageby, George Gilmore, the late Joseph Groome, Kevin Healy, Kerry Holland, Patrick Hillery, Patrick Keatinge, John M. Kelly, Brian Lenihan, the late Sean Lemass, Lord Longford, Jack Lynch, Charles Lysaght, Edward MacAteer, Sean MacBride, the late Frank MacDermot, the late Malcolm MacDonald, Peter McEvoy, Fred McEvoy, Sean MacEntee, the late Liam MacGabhann, Brendan MacGiolla Choille, the late Patrick McGilligan, Patrick MacGill, the late Michael McInerney, Edward MacLysaght, Deirdre MacMahon, Tom Manning, Jack Miller, Maurice Moynihan, Edward Mulhall, Brigid Mullins, John A. Murphy, the late Sean Nunan, Dermot O'Bryne, Patricia Grennan O'Byrne, Martin O'Donoghue, Peader O'Donnell, Ronan O'Donoghue, Cornelius O'Leary, T. P. O'Neill, Bernadette O'Sullivan, William O'Sullivan, Eamonn Phoenix, Brian Quinn, Brian Reynolds, Liam Robinson, the late David Thornley, James Tully, Elizabeth Turner, and J. H. Whyte.

I also wish to record my thanks to the directors, librarians, keepers, and staffs of the following record offices and archives: Manuscripts Department, Birmingham University Library; Department of Western Manuscripts, Bodleian Library, Oxford; British Library; Public Records Division, Public Archives of Canada, Ottawa; Department of Western Manuscripts, University Library, Cambridge; Manuscripts Division, Library of Congress, Washington; Freeman Library, Department of Geography, Trinity College, Dublin; House of Lords Record Office, London; National Archives, Washington; Department of Manuscripts, National Library of Ireland; Manuscripts and Archives Division, New York Public Library; Archives of the Department of External Affairs, Ottawa; Public Record Office, London: Public Record Office of Ireland, Dublin: public Record Office of Northern Ireland, Belfast; Radio Telefis Eireann; Roosevelt Library, Hyde Park, New York; State Paper Office, Dublin; Manuscripts Room, Trinity College, Dublin; Archives Department, University College Dublin. I am especially indebted to the staff of the Library, Trinity College, Dublin.

As my 'Note on sources' below underlines, there has been a dearth of good source material for the writing of contemporary Irish history. Consequently, Irish historians are indebted to the families of Ernest Blythe, Erskine Childers, Frank Gallagher, Patrick McGilligan, Mary MacSwiney, Richard Mulcahy, and others who have made their papers available for research. I gladly add my thanks here. I am grateful to Lord Craigavon for permission to photocopy his mother's diary; and to Mrs Dingwall for permission to read her father, W. B. Spender's papers at the Public Record Office of Northern Ireland in Belfast. I feel a special debt to the political reporters on Irish newspapers for their accurate and fair-minded chronicling of Irish politics: this is especially noteworthy in the case of the *Irish Press* — founded after all by de Valera — and so often pilloried as the 'kept paper' of the Fianna Fail party.

I am especially indebted to the late Francis MacManus, T. W. Moody, and T. Desmond Williams for their encouragement at important moments. I gladly record my thanks to Professor Basil Chubb of Trinity College, Dublin, my supervisor for the original Ph.D. thesis on which this book is based, for providing the right mixture of cajolement, approval — and coercion. I am indebted to the staff of the Oxford University Press for their courtesy and guidance.

To my family the completed typescript and, earlier, the thesis on which it is based, must have seemed like Billy Bunter's postal order — much discussed, a perennial excuse for trespassing on their generosity, and constantly imminent if always to-morrow. I wish to record my special thanks to them: to Jonathan and Emma — and, more recently, Abie — Philbin Bowman, for their insistence that I finish and for their practical help towards that end; to Eva Philbin for her help, direct and indirect; to John M. Philbin for his comments on an earlier draft, his generous help at proof stage, and especially his advice on points of style and syntax; and to my late father John Bowman for never joining the doubters. Finally my thanks to Eimer Philbin Bowman who — now that the postal order has arrived — has plans to be repaid for all the hours spent at my typewriter which she believes ought to have been spent in the garden.

Dublin,
28 July 1982.

Contents

Abbreviations

DE	*Dail Eireann, Official Debates*
DEA Ottawa	Archives of Department of External Affairs, Canada
DGFP	*Documents on German Foreign Policy*
FRUS	*Foreign Relations of the United States*
HC	*House of Commons, Westminster, Official Debates*
MEA	Ministère des Affaires Etrangères: Archives Diplomatiques: Paris
NA	National Archives of the United States, Washington
NI	Northern Ireland
NIHC	*Northern Ireland House of Commons, Official Debates*
NLI	National Library of Ireland, Dublin
PAC	Public Archives of Canada, Ottawa
PRO	Public Record Office, London
PROI	Public Record Office of Ireland, Dublin
PRONI	Public Record Office of Northern Ireland, Belfast
SE	*Seanad Eireann, Official Debates*
SS	United States, Secretary of State
SPO	State Paper Office, Dublin

NB Readers should note that a capital U for Unionist or Unionism denotes organized unionism, i.e. the Ulster Unionist Party or the Northern Ireland cabinet which throughout the period of this study was formed from the ranks of this party; use of lower case, unionist opinion, etc., refers to those citizens of Northern Ireland who wished to maintain the Union between Great Britain and Northern Ireland. Likewise a capital N for Nationalist refers to the Nationalist

Party in Northern Ireland, nationalist to the population who opposed the Partition of Ireland.

Biographical notes make no claim to being complete being confined to the role of the individual in this study.

Introduction

An enigma or an 'open book'? A revolutionary nationalist who
defined his goal in the 1916 Easter Rising in Dublin and spent
the rest of his long career working for the achievement of a
united, sovereign Irish Republic; or, the first of the revisionists,
a complex, secretive, essentially conservative politician who
often concealed his political strategy from his colleagues and,
consciously, from history? Which of these views best en-
compasses the career of Eamon de Valera?

The former view is the most widely held. It is the popular
legend among Irish nationalists — and, one might add, the *un-*
popular legend among Ulster unionists. Outside Ireland it is
widely believed,[1] and it is reflected in the Longford and
O'Neill 'authoritative' biography based on de Valera's papers
and written with his co-operation.[2] The present writer believes
that this de Valera legend needs revision; that it fails to do
justice to the truth, or, indeed, to de Valera himself; and that,
far from being an 'open book', de Valera presents the historian
with a paradox: must his career, given his avowed aims, be
considered a failure, or should he be credited with stabilizing
democracy in the aftermath of the Civil War, albeit in a partitioned Ireland?

De Valera himself, although preoccupied by the verdict of
history,[3] has not facilitated the historian's task: his own papers
still remain closed to researchers and in conducting his political work — whether in cabinet, ministry, or party — he was

---

[1] Obituaries of de Valera, *The Times, Sydney Morning Herald*, 30 Aug. 1975.

[2] Lord Longford and T. P. O'Neill, *Eamon de Valera* (London: 1970), pp. xv–xvi.
The publication of this biography was approved by de Valera; it was written with
his co-operation, based on his papers, but still lacked the imprimatur of an official
biography. Lord Longford told the author that de Valera might have given it a
nihil obstat, but not his imprimatur.

[3] De Valera, 'The New Ross speech', in *National discipline and majority rule*,
Fianna Fail pamphlet, 1936; DE: 152: 552, 12 July 1955; *Irish Times*, 15 Oct.
1962.

invariably shy of committing a full record to paper. Often, the most cursory mention of the topic under discussion is all that is recorded in the official minutes of de Valera's cabinet, and for some historic meetings no record may be extant.[4] He struck colleagues and negotiators as obsessively secretive. In America in 1920, John Devoy complained that de Valera 'keeps his plans secret and we shall not know what they are until he springs them on us.'[5] Republican fundamentalist, Mary MacSwiney considered de Valera to be 'a very difficult man to get a definite answer from. He would like to get a *carte blanche* and will give no undertakings.'[6] Malcolm Mac-Donald and David Gray both gathered the impression during the Second World War that de Valera did not confide in his own ministers.[7] Consistent with such a political style was de Valera's preference to 'minimise written records', the policy of his wartime government being to do their work 'orally as far as possible'.[8]

This instinct not to commit the most sensitive material to paper, the rumoured destruction of some files,[9] the occasional removal of papers by some ministers,[10] the failure to employ professional archivists within government departments, and the generally tardy policy concerning access — all of these factors result in serious problems for the historian of Irish politics since independence. Moreover, as a leader, de Valera did not easily delegate responsibility. He always remained — to his supporters — 'The Chief', and in power he tended to

---

[4] Note for instance complete dearth of information in Irish cabinet minutes during Anglo-Irish negotiations, Jan.-Apr. 1938, SPO G1/1-31; also during Mac-Donald-de Valera talks, June 1940, ibid., G2/155-70; for further disappointment, see 'Meeting of Special Committee of the Cabinet', 20 Apr. 1938, ibid., S 10631.

[5] John Devoy to Gov. E. F. Dunne, 9 Sept. 1920, Cohalan papers, MS 15,416(4). John Devoy (1842-1928), from his exile to the US in 1871, conspired against British rule in Ireland; proprietor-editor, *Gaelic American*; vituperative dislike of de Valera from 1919; supported 1921 Treaty.

[6] Mary MacSwiney to Eamon Ua Brian, 25 Apr. 1926, MacSwiney papers, P48/C/30. Mary MacSwiney, sister of Terence who died on hunger strike, 1920; a diehard republican activist, she monitored what she saw as Fianna Fail's sell-out of the republic until her death in 1942.

[7] MacDonald, report (via Maffey) to DO, 27 June 1940, PRO CAB 66/9 WP (40)233 annex I; Gray to Roosevelt, 28 May 1941, Roosevelt papers, PSF 56.

[8] De Valera to Richard Mulcahy, 12 Feb. 1941, Mulcahy papers, P7a/215.

[9] Confidential source.

[10] Interview Sean Lemass re 1932 change of government.

take initiatives which, in any 'open' system of government, would have been the result of collective cabinet decisions. Reinforcing a natural instinct for privacy and secrecy was a personal sense of self-justification which dated from the Treaty and Civil War period. Not only had his opponents' propaganda simplified the issues involved and attempted to attribute culpability entirely to him, but on the anti-Treaty side of that division de Valera was sometimes suspected of moderation, or, worse, opportunism. Deflecting such criticism was important to him, not only for party purposes but also in terms of self-esteem and self-justification for his rejection of the Anglo-Irish Treaty of 1921.

The rest of his long career was devoted to reconciling, on the one hand, the aspiration to an independent, sovereign, separatist republic for the entire island of Ireland, with, on the other, his appreciation that, strategically, Irish defence was inseparable from that of Britain, and that in the north-east of the island, a local majority was determined to resist Irish unity on the nationalists' terms. Aware of the formidable difficulties in reconciling the aspirations of Irish nationalism with British interests and Ulster's antipathy, de Valera clearly felt the need to explore potential solutions without being scrutinized by the fundamentalist republican school. As a former member — indeed a founder member — of this school in his own generation, he knew only too well how vulnerable any mooted compromise was to the criticism most tellingly expressed in Pearse's admonition that

The man who, in the name of Ireland, accepts as 'a final settlement' anything less by one fraction of one iota than Separation from England . . . is guilty of so immense an infidelity, so immense a crime against the Irish nation, . . . that it were better for that man . . . that he had not been born.[11]

For many nationalists after 1916 Pearse's admonition was their guiding principle; and for those for whom it was not, few spoke out against this example of what Paine has categorized as the 'most ridiculous and insolent' of tyrannies — 'the vanity

---

[11] *Collected works of Padraic H. Pearse: political writings and speeches*, (Dublin: 1924) pp. 231-2. Pearse (1879-1916), poet, revolutionary; leading martyr of 1916 Rising.

and presumption of governing beyond the grave'.[12] Although de Valera was adept at using the imprimatur of the 'dead generations' when it suited his purpose, he was also capable — and on the most important occasions — of siding with Paine rather than Pearse.[13]

Nor is the task of the student of de Valera's politics made easier — although it may be rendered more interesting — by his cast of mind. Those who politically disagreed with him often thought him pedantic and vacillating, incapable of decisive action. Hugh Kennedy, Attorney-General in the first Free State government, characterized de Valera's mind as 'adept in futile ingenuity and metaphysics, loving to examine problems of concrete life in a vacuum exhausted of the atmosphere of fact.'[14] Richard Mulcahy jested that on the day of general judgement, before the last bugle was sounded, de Valera would plead for time for 'just one more explanation';[15] a more sympathetic witness, Kevin Boland, confirms, from his own and his father Gerald's experience, this capacity for scrupulous indecision on de Valera's part;[16] and, most significantly, de Valera's own republican nominee on the Treaty delegation, Robert Barton, accused him, at the crucial meeting when his cabinet divided on the Treaty, of vacillation throughout the period of negotiations.[17] Lloyd George considered him a man of narrow views and limited vocabulary, and Smuts, Craig, C. P. Scott, Tim Healy, Lord Cranborne, and Ramsay MacDonald — all from their widely differing perspectives — do not contradict this impression.[18] Baldwin considered him 'impossible to deal with' — only one of three such men in his

---

[12] Thomas Paine, *Rights of man* (Dublin: 1792), p. 7.

[13] Frank Gallagher, typescript, 'De Valera', Gallagher papers, MS 18,375(6).

[14] Hugh Kennedy to W. T. Cosgrave, 13 Aug. 1923, Kennedy papers, P4/B/30.

[15] Mulcahy, speech, news clipping (*c.* 1925).

[16] Interview, Kevin Boland.

[17] Erskine Childers, diary 8 Dec. 1921, Childers papers, MS 7814.

[18] For Lloyd George, see Thomas Jones, *Whitehall diary, III: Ireland: 1918–1925*, Keith Middlemas (ed.) (London: 1971), p. 90; for Smuts see p. 50 below; for Craig, pp. 47–8 below; for Scott, p. 50, n. 14 below; Healy to William O'Brien, 2 Mar. 1926, O'Brien papers, MS 8,556(31); Cranborne, note 1 Feb. 1941. PRO DO 35/1109/W.X.11/24; MacDonald to archbishop of York, 13 Sept. 1932, MacDonald papers, PRO 30/69/2/35.

experience.[19] Not surprisingly, the researcher, in attempting to trace the formulation of de Valera's policy on a specific issue, particularly an issue as sensitive, intractable, and central as Partition, may be forgiven if he sometimes shares the view attributed to Lloyd George that grappling with de Valera's thought is akin to trying to pick up mercury with a fork.[20] Nor is the difficulty lessened by the discovery of de Valera's confession to Mary MacSwiney that he had made it 'a habit to talk to our own people almost as if I were an opponent' — this the better to educate his supporters to the complexities of an issue in question!'[21]

De Valera was not only preoccupied by the need to justify himself to his contemporaries; he was also concerned with the verdicts of historians and he lived long enough to be in a position, when President, of telephoning them at the conclusion of a broadcast lecture to impress upon them his version of events. It did not seem to have occurred to him that this 'rather transparent anxiety' on his part, might be construed by them as 'evidence of a very different kind'.[22] De Valera was preoccupied by the Irish past. This was a standard joke among British politicians concerned lest they find themselves at the receiving end of a discourse on Irish grievances over the centuries. Such lectures did have a ready audience from public platforms in Ireland and de Valera's idealization of a Gaelic past and his mastery of a rhetoric suited to what was, after 1916, an extreme nationalist phase in Irish history was the basis of his political popularity.[23] Even his critics conceded this role: to O'Faolain he was the 'Irish nationalist oracle';[24] to McCartan, 'nationalism is de Valerism'.[25]

De Valera's political motivation was to redress past wrongs and refashion society, drawing, in part, on his view of an Irish

[19] W. P. Crozier, *Off the record: political interviews: 1933–43*, A. J. P. Taylor (ed.), (London: 1973), p. 27.

[20] Lord Longford, *Peace by ordeal* (London: 1972 edn.), p. 74.

[21] De Valera to MacSwiney, 14 Nov. 1922, Childers papers, MS 7835/21.

[22] F. S. L. Lyons, 'De Valera revisited', *Magill*, Mar. 1981, p. 59.

[23] For a discussion of the sources of charisma in nationalist leaders, see Martin E. Spencer, 'What is charisma?', *The British Journal of Sociology*, vol. 14, 1973, pp. 341-54.

[24] Sean O'Faolain, *De Valera* (London: 1939), p. 19.

[25] Patrick McCartan to W. J. Maloney, 2 Oct. 1925, Maloney papers, box 21.

golden age. In 1932 the then British Prime Minister, Ramsay Macdonald, deplored de Valera's style as a negotiator:

He begins somewhere about the birth of Christ and wants a commission of four picked solely to give individual opinions to explore the past centuries and all he demands is a document, a manifesto, a judgement as from God himself as to how the world, and more particularly Ireland, should have been ruled when they were all cutting each others' throats and writing beautiful missives at the same time. It makes one sick. Behind it is the romance of force and of arms — shooting, murdering and being murdered. It is a gay adventure of the fool put into a china shop in hobnail boots with liberty to smash.[26]

Although London then hoped that de Valera would prove 'a transient apparition',[27] he had no intention of ceding control of mainstream nationalist politics as had happened after the Treaty split a decade before. In fact he remained the central figure in Irish public life until 1959, and then he did not retire but was elected President of the Republic, a position he held until 1973. Having first come to prominence in the era of Asquith and Woodrow Wilson, it was almost sixty years later in the age of Heath and Nixon that he retired to private life.

It was the threat of Partition which had first prompted de Valera's involvement in politics;[28] once it had been enacted, it is no exaggeration to state that he spent the remainder of his long public life preoccupied by it. He confided to an American diplomat that 'he would consider his career a failure' if during his lifetime Ireland was not united.[29] From 1917 until his retirement from active party politics in 1959, he made some thousands of speeches on Ulster. Thereafter, as President until 1973, although the office was above politics, the issue was one on which he was questioned by historians and journalists. Moreover, his views were of more than academic interest during these years, in the course of which his successors as

[26] Ramsay MacDonald to Abe Bailey, 22 July 1932, MacDonald papers, PRO 30/69/35. MacDonald (1866-1937), first British Labour Prime Minister; later as Prime Minister in National Government (1931-5) failed to find an accommodation with de Valera; member Irish Situation Committee, 1932-7.

[27] Smuts's prediction, PRO CAB 27/525 ISC(32)23.

[28] Longford and O'Neill (1970: 470).

[29] John Cudahy (US Minister) to Secretary of State (hereafter SS) 20 Apr. 1938, NA, R.G.59, 741.41D/69.

leader of Fianna Fail — Sean Lemass until 1966 and Jack Lynch thereafter — faced formidable challenges on the Partition question. The belief that de Valera was the only Irish leader who could end Partition — a consistent claim by his followers down the years — encouraged his successors, Lemass, Lynch, and, from December 1979, C. J. Haughey — at least, to claim that their policies were consistent with his.[30] Not only were they leading a party whose *raison d'être* was the abolition of Partition, but if they took an initiative on Northern Ireland which could be represented as inconsistent with what was presumed to have been de Valera's traditional approach, they were vulnerable within the party to a charge of being heretics. This was true despite the fact that those who saw themselves as the custodians of de Valera's version of republicanism often knew little of the complexity of his policy on the Ulster question.

What was this policy? How consistent was it? How pragmatic? How revisionist? To what extent did he reveal his full mind in public? To what extent must his policy be inferred from his actions or inaction? To what extent did he accept

[30] See speeches at unveiling of de Valera memorial, Ennis, *Irish Times*, 12 Oct. 1981; Jack Lynch, *Irish unity, Northern Ireland, Anglo-Irish relations* (Dublin: 1971), pp. 65-6; interview, Sean Lemass. Sean Lemass (1900-71), founder member and organizing genius of Fianna Fail; member of all de Valera governments 1932-59 and unopposed as his successor as party leader and Taoiseach, 1959-66; never an enthusiastic supporter of de Valera's ideal of a Catholic, Gaelic, rural utopia. In January 1965, surprised country, party and cabinet colleagues with his historic visit to NI Prime Minister, Terence O'Neill; initiated and later served on all-party committee to review de Valera's Constitution which recommended that territorial claim on Northern Ireland be rephrased as an aspiration. Jack Lynch (1917-), TD, 1948-81, Taoiseach, 1966-73, 1977-9; a compromise choice in 1966 when he succeeded Lemass as Fianna Fail leader; at first continued north-south *rapprochement* initiated by Lemass; after civil disturbances in Northern Ireland in 1969, resisted party hawks and attempted throughout the 1970s — not always with success — to dampen southern expectations on Partition issue; dismissed Charles Haughey from his government in 1970 on suspicion of arms smuggling to defend northern nationalists; failed to deliver party leadership to his preferred successor, George Colley, in December 1979 when Haughey became fourth leader of Fianna Fail. Charles Haughey (1925-), TD, 1957-, Taoiseach, Dec. 1979-June 1981, Mar. 1982-; both his parents fought with northern IRA, pre-Treaty; son-in-law of Lemass; minister in all Fianna Fail governments from 1961 to 1970 when he was dismissed by Lynch on suspicion of smuggling arms to northern nationalists; charged and acquitted in Arms Trial, 1970; remained in Fianna Fail, succeeding to front bench, 1975, to government, 1977, and to party leadership, 1979; insists that Northern Ireland is a 'failed political entity'; advocate of Dublin-London talks to agree Irish unity.

the myths about Ulster which were popularly believed by
Irish nationalists? To what extent did changing circumstances
encourage him to modify his policy towards the north? In
Part 2 of this work we consider de Valera's record on the
Ulster question throughout his public career from 1917 to
1959 and in Part 3 consider his impact on the issue and the
legacy he left to his successors. As an introduction, Part 1
examines the geography of Partition. The argument here
presented is that *images* of Ireland were profoundly important
in determining approaches to politics, and of particular significance were *map-images*.

Indeed, de Valera himself had a very specific map-image of
Ireland. He always kept a map of the partitioned island close
at hand to impress his views on visitors. Sir John Maffey, the
first British diplomatic representative in Ireland, noted how
one of his first meetings with de Valera, in September 1939,
concluded: 'As I left the room he led me to his black map of
Eire with its white blemish on the North East corner and said:
"There's the real source of all our trouble." He could not let
me go without that.'[31] Many years earlier, in the course of
his American tour in 1919–20, de Valera outlined what he
saw as the spurious map-image of 'Ulster' then prevalent in
the United States:

When the word 'Ulster' occurs to the average American there springs
immediately to his mind the concept of an Irish province with fixed,
well-defined historical boundaries, within which there is a solid, homogeneous, political or religious block such as this 'Ulster' which British
propaganda has suggested to Americans. There is no such racial block.
This Ulster is a thing of the mind only, non-existent in the world of
reality.[32]

[31] Maffey to DO after meeting with de Valera, 20 Sept. 1939, PRO DO
35/1107/W.X.1/5.
[32] *Gaelic American*, 24 Jan. 1920.

PART I
THE POLITICAL GEOGRAPHY OF PARTITION:
THE CASE OF IRELAND

'If we could frame the world to our own desire, we would place the small States in their ancestral territories — and I know all the difficulties there are about that.' (Eamon de Valera, speech at the College Historical Society, Trinity College, Dublin, *Irish Press*, 2 Nov. 1944.)

'the so-called "nations" or "peoples" of which the nationalists dream do not exist.' (Karl Popper, 'The history of our time: an optimist's view', in *Conjectures and refutations* (London: 1963), p. 368.)

'Ulster will be a . . . geographical fact.' (Edward Carson in 1914, quoted in Richard Rose, *Northern Ireland: a time of choice* (London: 1976), p. 7.)

1. A Line on the Map

(i) IRISH NATIONALISM'S NATIONAL IMAGE

(a) *The geographical dimension*

The partition of the island of Ireland in 1921 exercised a profound, complex, and largely misunderstood effect on the course of Irish nationalism: profound, because it has since remained the fundamental issue in Irish politics; complex, both because of its continuing reverberations within nationalist ranks and because of its impact on north-south and Anglo-Irish relations; and misunderstood because so few of the nationalists whose efforts resulted in political independence for the twenty-six southern counties acknowledged that part of the price of independence was Partition itself. This latter point has been obscured, not only because it was uncomfortable to accept, but also because of a prevailing consensus among nationalists in their opposition to Partition, a consensus which remained unquestioned because of the plausibility of the case against the border *as drawn*. Bitterly resenting an unfair border — itself the result of Ulster Unionist leverage — nationalists could easily ignore any merits in an Ulster unionist case for *some* border.

Essentially then, Irish nationalism, concerned with territorial tidiness or completeness, has done little to develop a political culture capable of uniting the population of the entire island. Unlike landlocked nationalist movements elsewhere, Irish nationalism can admit of no compromise on where any new boundary line might be drawn. 'Ireland cannot shift her frontiers. The Almighty traced them beyond the cunning of man to modify.'[1] The special importance to Irish nationalists

[1] Arthur Griffith, holograph draft, 'On nationality', S. T. O'Kelly papers, MS 8496(2).

of the territorial bond may be due to the fact that, unlike, say, the Poles, they have always thought of the 'homeland' in terms of a discrete geographical entity. Hertz emphasizes the significance to every nation of the 'national territory' which is considered 'an inalienable sacred heritage'; moreover,

its independence, integrity, and homogeneity appear bound up with national security, independence and honour. This territory is often described as the body of the national organism and the language as its soul. In the ideology of almost every nation, therefore, its historical territory is looked upon almost as a living personality which cannot be partitioned without destroying it altogether.

Further, he suggests that in the case of smaller countries the *integrity* of what is perceived as the national territory is of especial importance.[2]

Every state, argued Febvre, has 'its germinal, its geographical starting-point'.[3] Political geographers have since distinguished two broad categories: states which 'have been created arbitrarily to fill some preconceived geographical frame' which Pounds and Ball term *arbitrary* states; and 'those which have grown slowly and over a long period of time from some nuclear, germinal, or core-area' which they categorize as *organic* states.[4] Using this typology the twenty-six-county state which has resulted from the efforts of Irish nationalists is essentially an organic state but with the arbitrary aspiration to encompass the entire island.

The Irish preoccupation with a 'preconceived geographical frame' may be attributed to the fact that the Irish *map-image* is so sharply delineated. Political geographers have come increasingly to acknowledge the importance of map-images. Hartshorne describes the state as 'a geographic feature which we visualise on the political map, the most common map in educational and general daily use'; the tendency is for citizens to identify the state in their minds, 'primarily in its external morphology, notably its size and shape'. Hartshorne, a prolific

[2] Frederick Hertz, *Nationality in history and politics* (London: 1944), pp. 150–1 and ch. 5 *passim.*

[3] N. J. G. Pounds and S. S. Ball, 'Core areas in the development of the European States system', *Annals of the Association of American Geographers*, vol. 54, Mar. 1964, pp. 24–40; reprinted in H. J. de Blij, *Systematic political geography* (London: 1973 edn.).

[4] Pounds and Ball (1964: 87).

and influential political geographer, retrospectively regretted that he had given 'but scanty attention' to map-shape in his earlier work.[5] Boulding agrees that the map-image of a country is of central importance: 'the shape of the map that symbolizes the nation is constantly drilled into the minds of both young and old, both through formal teaching in schools and through constant repetition in newspapers, advertisements, cartoons, and so on.'[6]

This constant exposure to the map-shape is particularly prevalent in Ireland, whose external morphology, being an island, is sharply delineated.[7] Moreover, along with its constant repetition in all the ways mentioned by Boulding, the Irish map is also recognized as a *symbol* of the nation being commonly incorporated into the mastheads of nationalist newspapers, and, notably being used as the design for the most common postage stamps in the first half-century following independence.[8] Given that the state occupies such a large part of the island, it is scarcely exceptional that the map used is that of Ireland. What may have significance, especially in the context of the south's irredentist claim to 'reintegrate the national territory', is the constant omission of the boundary line, especially in a map being used to symbolize the state. Indeed, few citizens of the twenty-six-county state can have a clear map-image of their *state*. The Irish case then is complicated by the fact that the state is not coterminous with what is popularly, and — since the enactment of the 1937 Constitution — formally, regarded as 'the national territory'. Nor is resentment of such discontiguity peculiar to Irish nationalism:

[5] Richard Hartshorne, 'Morphology of the state area: significance for the state', in C. A. Fisher (ed.), *Essays in political geography* (London: 1968), pp. 27–32.

[6] K. E. Boulding, 'National images and international systems', *The Journal of Conflict Resolution*, vol. 3, 1959, pp. 120–31; reprinted in J. N. Rosenau, *International politics and foreign policy* (New York: 1969 edn.), pp. 422–31.

[7] De Valera speech, SE: 22:980, 7 Feb. 1939.

[8] For newspapers, see mastheads of the Fianna Fail weekly, *The Nation*, 1927–31, and *Irish Press*, at least throughout the 1930s. A map of Ireland was the feature on one of four designs which comprised the definitive series of Irish postage stamps from 1922 to 1968, Liam Miller, *Postage stamps of Ireland: a checklist: 1922–76* (Dublin: 1976). Maps were also used by cartoonists: *Dublin Opinion*, Feb. 1969, Aug. 1970; *Irish World*, 5 and 12 Dec. 1925; cartoon 'de Valera's home again!', in Golden papers, NLI MS 13,141(1)a. Maps were widely used in advertisements, *Irish Independent*, 7 May 1921. The map was used as a symbol of Ireland, as in the presentation medal to de Valera, see *Irish Press*, 14 Apr. 1941.

Jones writes of a general and 'almost mystical' dislike of discontiguity;[9] Smith suggests that '"Incompleteness" is not merely an insult, it is a negation of the "nation"';[10] Boulding notes an uneasiness with map-shapes which show 'strong irregularities, enclaves, detached portions, and protuberances or hollows';[11] Pounds concludes that the 'bond between people and place, between nation and state, is a close one and is sometimes exaggerated and exalted into a kind of spiritual union. The land itself comes to be thought of as divinely shaped, and any proposal to partition or truncate it becomes sacrilege.'[12]

Such nationalist instincts must be all the more strongly felt in a case where the 'geographical frame' is as clearly perceived as is the map-shape of Ireland. Indeed Heslinga suggests that to many Irishmen 'it is almost a dogma that the Creator has predestined Ireland to be a national and political unit, because it is a perfect geographical entity.'[13] From the time when it was first mooted, Irish nationalsts have condemned Partition as essentially unnatural, John Redmond believing the very idea 'an abomination and a blasphemy'.[14] Once enacted, the exclusion of the six counties was deeply resented: 'That portion of Ireland was the very head of the island in more senses than one, but it is beheaded now'.[15]

The partition of Ireland has been particularly controversial because of the political greed of the Ulster Unionists when the boundary line was decided. Originally based on the historic nine counties of Ulster, the Ulster Unionist Council, fearing that any devolution of power to such a province would leave their majority vulnerable to nationalist erosion, opted instead for a 'clean cut' of six counties. In these counties they enjoyed a two-to-one majority but the territory chosen also included

    [9] S. B. Jones, 'Boundary concepts in the setting of place and time', *Annals of the Association of American Geographers*, vol. 49, 1959, pp. 241–55; reprinted in H. J. de Blij, *Systematic political geography* (London: 1973, 2nd edn.), pp. 162–75.
    [10] A. D. Smith, *Theories of Nationalism* (London: 1971), p. 223.
    [11] Boulding (1959: 426).
    [12] N. J. G. Pounds, 'History and geography: a perspective on partition', *Journal of International Affairs*, vol. 18, 1964, pp. 161–72.
    [13] M. W. Heslinga, *The Irish border as a cultural divide* (Assen: 1962), p. 41.
    [14] Quoted in Nicholas Mansergh, *The Irish Question: 1840–1921* (London: 1965; 2nd edn.), p. 206.
    [15] Tom Hales, TD, DE: 67: 123, 11 May 1937.

significant areas with nationalist majorities which were contiguous to the proposed border. Political geographers while highly critical of the border as drawn[16] dissented from what nationalists believed was a corollary: that the only admissible political boundary was the 'natural' boundary of the sea. Indeed, political geographers seem unanimous in their rejection of what they see as a doctrine of geographical predestination: Febvre,[17] Sieger, Maull, Solch,[18] Broek,[19] Minghi,[20] and Jones[21] all reject the theory of natural boundaries, a term which should, in Hartshorne's view, be 'banned from scientific literature'.[22] Prescott, reviewing the arguments, concludes that natural boundaries have now 'no academic currency. Their worthlessness has been demonstrated by a generation of political geographers since Fawcett' in 1918.[23] Gilfillan, reviewing the political boundaries of Europe in 1924, also dismissed the theory of natural boundaries, faulting, in particular, the 'propagandist historian' who invariably found 'an unlimited quantity of heroic actions, great patriots,

[16] Heslinga (1962: 22); M. A. Busteed, *Northern Ireland* (Oxford: 1974), p. 23; N. C. Mitchel, 'Ireland: divided island', *Geoforum*, vol. 8, 1971; E. E. Evans, 'The personality of Ulster', *Transactions, The Institute of British Geographers*, no. 51, Nov. 1970, p. 2; A. R. Orme, *The world's landscapes: 4: Ireland* (London: 1970), p. 249.

[17] Lucien Febvre, *A geographical introduction to history* (London: 1925), pp. 308-9.

[18] Sieger, Maull and Solch, all in Richard Hartshorne, 'Geographic and political boundaries in Upper Silesia', *Annals of the Association of American Geographers*, vol. 23, 1933, p. 196.

[19] Broek, quoted in J. V. Minghi, 'Boundary studies in political geography', *Annals of the Association of American Geographers*, vol. 53, 1963, reprinted in R. E. Kasperson and J. V. Minghi, *The structure of political geography* (London: 1970), pp. 140-60, quotation p. 144.

[20] Minghi (1963: 160).

[21] S. B. Jones (1959: 167).   [22] Hartshorne (1933: 193).

[23] J. R. V. Prescott, *Political geography* (London: 1971), pp. 69-70. See also Prescott, *The geography of state policies* (London: 1968), pp. 34-5; N. J. G. Pounds, *Political geography* (New York: 1972), pp. 83-4; S. B. Cohen, *Geography and politics in a divided world* (London: 1964), pp. 190-1; Bernard Crick, *In defence of politics* (London; 1964, 2nd edn.), pp. 80-1. Pounds (1964: 169-70) does cite Ireland as one example of a discrete territorial entity, 'so distinctive and so separate from their neighbours that they almost demand to be administered as units', but does not himself support this view. For a rare expression of support for natural boundaries from a political geographer, see Roderick Peattie, *Look to the frontiers: a geography for the peace table* (Port Washington, NY: 1970 re-issue; first published in 1944), p. 19.

picturesque incidents and all the other matter that, whether false or true, makes up what is essentially each nation's mythology. How much talk there is of "when Ireland was a nation", though she never was."[24] Encouraging this trend in Ireland is the fact that throughout its recorded history, Ireland has been a discrete geographical space,[25] the 'map-image' or 'geographical frame' facilitating an unhistorical belief — de Valera himself being a most persistent offender[26] — in a continuous 'Irish nation'.

(b) The historical dimension

Although the geographical realities and myths contribute substantially to the national image, it remains essentially in Boulding's words an

> *historical* image — that is, an image which extends through time, backward into a supposedly recorded or perhaps mythological past and forward into an imagined future. The more conscious a people is of its history, the stronger the national image is likely to be . . . It is no exaggeration to say that the function of the historian is to pervert the truth in directions favourable to the images of his readers or hearers.[27]

Kristof, the political geographer, has called for a distinction between the *national culture* and the *national idea*, the latter 'essentially, an idealized self-image of the nation, the *acceptable* part of the national culture, the heritage, true or imaginary, of which the nation is proud, which is to be emulated.'[28] He argues that 'the iconography of the fatherland' is constantly adjusted to harmonize 'with evolving aspirations, with the anticipated future . . . According to which idea and what image of the fatherland is cherished, appeal is made to different

---

[24] S. Column Gilfillan, 'European political boundaries', *Political Science Quarterly*, vol. 39, 1924, pp. 458–84, quotation pp. 477–8.

[25] A. T. Q. Stewart, *The narrow ground* (London: 1977), pp. 34–5.

[26] *Gaelic American*, 12 July 1919, 3 Jan. 1920; Maurice Moynihan (ed.), *Speeches and statements by Eamon de Valera: 1917–1973* (Dublin: 1980), pp. 247–50, 466–9. Hereafter, De Valera speeches: 1980.

[27] Boulding (1959: 424).

[28] L. K. D. Kristof, '"The Russian image of Russia": an applied study in geopolitical methodology', in Charles A. Fisher (ed.), *Essays in political geography* (London: 1968), ch. 19, quotation p. 347.

cultural and geohistorical heritages, and different ideals and geopolitical identities are seen in the future.'[29]

Once established, these images have considerable resistance to rational criticism; Deutsch and Merritt emphasize the influence of early socialization as a guide to subsequent behaviour, men being willing to 'distort many of their perceptions and deny much of reality, in order to call their prejudiced souls their own.'[30] Nor are political leaders immune; indeed, they must broadly share the national image to survive. Boulding concludes that like the ordinary citizen, the powerful statesman holds 'naïve, self-centered, and unsophisticated images of the world' in which his own nation moves.[31]

Irish politicians have not proved exceptions to these norms, and in particular to the propensity of nationalists to hold a selective view of their nation's past. Arnold Toynbee found in the history of Ireland a 'hypnotization of a living self by a dead self';[32] James Joyce complained of the nationalists' emphasis 'on the old pap of racial hatred';[33] George Russell railed against the exclusion from membership of the nation of those not preoccupied by the 'dreams of worn-out yesterday'.[34] Sean O'Faolain argued that the dominating problem facing Irish politicans post-independence was 'what to do with their lovely Past'.[35] The historian, Mansergh, reckoned that the minds of the living were overshadowed by the 'rigid, inflexible doctrines of the "martyred" dead.'[36] In particular, Pearse's warning of the immense infidelity of accepting anything less than full separatism were words which served to undermine the possibility of constitutional compromise and his 'irreconcilable spirit still haunted, or inspired, the minds of the Sinn Fein leaders. That was their tragedy . . . The 1916

[29] Ibid., p. 356.

[30] K. W. Deutsch and R. L. Merritt, 'Effects of events on national and international images', in Herbert C. Kelman (ed.), *International behaviour: a social-psychological analysis* (New York: 1965), pp. 130-87, quotation pp. 182-3.

[31] Boulding (1959: 423-4, 430).

[32] Arnold Toynbee, *A study of history: IV* (London: 1939), p. 291.

[33] His specific target was Arthur Griffith in September 1906, quoted in Richard Ellmann, *James Joyce* (London: 1959), p. 246.

[34] Poem, 'On behalf of some Irishmen not followers of tradition'.

[35] Sean O'Faolain, *The Irish* (London: 1969 edn.), p. 145.

[36] Nicholas Mansergh, *The Commonwealth and the nations: studies in British Commonwealth relations* (London: 1948), pp. 167-8.

rising was above all a challenge to those Irishmen who believed
in compromise. It was a challenge which they could not meet.
History was against them.'[37]

Nor is the exaggeration of the role which violence may
have played in the formation of the state, unique to Irish
nationalism. Boulding asserting that 'there is hardly a nation
which has not been cradled in violence and nourished by
further violence', emphasizes that war is an experience which
is dramatic, important, and shared by everybody. In the
formation of the national image

> the consciousness of great *shared* events and experiences is of the utmost
> importance. A nation is a body of people who are conscious of having
> 'gone through something' together. Without the shared experience, the
> national image itself would not be shared, and it is of vital importance
> that the national image be highly similar.[38]

The admixture which incrementally formed the Irish
national idea also included notions about race, language, and
religion. With concepts of racial distinctiveness fashionable in
the early decades of this century, the notion of a separate
'Irish Race' was, for some, an important strand. Racial theories
are now generally dismissed as pseudo-scientific, a 'parasite of
nationalism';[39] nevertheless, in Ireland, as Stewart argues, 'the
theory of a racial distinction between planter and "Gael"' is
still dominant. Given the various population movements
recorded throughout Irish history and the scientific evidence
now available, 'the idea of an unmixed racial group ought to
have been laughed out of court at the outset.' However, it has
proved 'unshakeable' given the peculiar nationalist approach
to historical evidence.[40] On language, the widely held theory
that it determined nationality had its advocates in Ireland —
any dilemma posed by the fact that Gaelic was no longer the
spoken language of those to be included in the nation, being
solved by the espousal of a restoration policy. De Valera, in
particular, constantly recorded his own conviction that Irish
nationality would wither if the language revival failed.[41]

Perhaps the most misunderstood factor in the Irish national

[37] Ibid., p. 167.   [38] Boulding (1959: 424-5).
[39] Crick (1964: 83).   [40] Stewart (1977: 26-7).
[41] SE: 22: 988-9, 7 Feb. 1939.

idea is religion, so often 'the shibboleth of the contending parties' within Ireland,[42] although the *substance* of their disagreement concerns ethnic identity and national allegiance. Even the most self-conscious republican such as de Valera — avowedly dedicated to uniting north and south — consistently promulgated the notion that Ireland was a Catholic nation: 'Since the coming of St Patrick 1,500 years ago, Ireland has been a Christian and a Catholic nation. All the ruthless attempts made down through the centuries to force us from this allegiance have not shaken her faith. She remains a Catholic nation.'[43]

(c) *The state-idea*

Along with all of these factors which went to form the national idea — what Kristof terms 'the carrier of the heritage of the past' — can be added 'the dynamic, forward-looking and future-oriented element', what he terms, after Ratzel, the *state-idea*. In evolving its own image, argues Kristof, the nation is helped by the state-idea:

> looking through its prism the nation draws strength from a sense of being *pushed* by history and *pulled* by an ideal — from a sense of past fulfilment and a duty to fulfil the future destiny. By linking that which was with that which is to be, the nation develops an image of what it itself is and what it *should become*.[44]

Van Gennep suggests that 'nationality is never in other than an unstable equilibrium. It is always *becoming*.'[45] Francis in his consideration of the ethnic factor in nation-building, also places emphasis on the future, writing in terms of a common solidarity, destiny, purpose, mission — all future-oriented terms.[46] The post-independence rhetoric of Irish nationalism — again with de Valera to the fore — reflects similar preoccupations. There is a constant emphasis on what the nation

---

[42] Stewart (1977: 180).
[43] Quoted in Richard Rose, *Governing without consensus* (London: 1971), p. 247.
[44] Kristof (1968: 345).
[45] Quoted in Alfred Cobban, *The nation state and national self-determination* (London: 1969, revised edn.), pp. 126–7.
[46] E. K. Francis, 'The ethnic factor in nation-building', *Social Forces*, vol. 46, no. 3, Mar. 1968, pp. 338–46, quotation p. 342.

ought to be: and along with the customary exhortations and
expectations found in all nationalist movements, there is the
additional obsession of 're-uniting the national territory'. Indeed, Heslinga suggests that the distinguishing characteristic of
an Irish nationalist is a belief in the 'necessity of the abolition
of Partition' — a definition rooted in a future contingency.[47]
Specifically referring to the alienation felt by nationalists
when nation and state are not coterminous, Kristof suggests
that if this alienation is not overcome by idealizing the past,
then nationalists may instead imagine 'an idealized future —
the paradise, the Utopia that is to come.'[48]

(ii) A SEPARATE ULSTER IMAGE

(a) *A second nation?*

To attempt to arbitrate on whether the Ulster unionists
comprise a separate nation is beyond the scope of the present
study. What is manifest is that Irish nationalists — as one of
them admitted — often excluded northern unionists from the
Irish nation: 'We have had a habit, when it suited a particular
case, of saying they were Irish, and when it did not suit a
particular case, of saying they were British or planters or the
seed of planters.'[49] Such ambivalence prompts Miller to write
of Irish nationalists as being capable of reaffirming their own
group 'not only as it was — a sectarian nationality — but also
as it "ought" to be — an Irish nation transcending the sectarian
division of Irish society.'[50] Political geographers refute any
nationalist assumption of one nation: Semple,[51] Holdich,[52]
Mackinder,[53] Unstead, [54] Johnson,[55] and Prescott[56] all

[47] Heslinga (1962: 53).   [48] Kristof (1968: 355).
[49] Michael Hayes, SE: 22: 882, 26 Jan. 1939.
[50] David Miller, *Queen's rebels* (Dublin: 1978), p. 86.
[51] E. C. Semple, *Influence of geographic environment on the basis of Ratzel's
system of anthropo-geography* (London: 1911), p. 435.
[52] Thomas Holdich, replying to a paper on 'Race and nationality', read to the
Royal Geographical Society, 7 May 1917, *Geographical Journal*, vol. 50, p. 329.
[53] H. J. Mackinder, *Britain and the British seas* (Oxford: 1930, 2nd edn.),
pp. 301-2.
[54] J. F. Unstead, *A world survey from the human aspect: III* (London: 1957),
5th edn.), pp. 263-5.
[55] James H. Johnson, 'The political distinctiveness of Northern Ireland', *The
Geographical Review*, vol. 52, no. 1, pp. 78-91.   [56] Prescott (1970: 379).

recognized the distinctiveness of the north, Orme concluding that the province became 'the powerful bastion of people whose speech, habits, traditions, unwavering loyalties and resolute Protestantism differed totally from native ways.'[57] Isiah Bowman wrote of two 'totally unlike nations'.[58] Estyn Evans suggested that in 'anthropological terms, there are two endogamous communities, nursing different historical myths.'[59] Political geographers concerned with theories have also added their evidence: Pounds and Ball identify two *core-areas* in Ireland;[60] Jefferson notes the existence of two *primate cities*, Dublin and Belfast, each the focus for the crystallization of a nationalism;[61] and Pounds argues that if the ethnic distance between Protestant and Catholic were to be measured in Northern Ireland, it would result in a 'yawning gulf'.[62]

Theorists of nationalism also refute the Irish claim to one Irish nation:[63] Hertz notes 'the alienation of Ulster from the Irish cause';[64] Schmitt suggests that 'the core issues involve ethnic and national identities';[65] Toynbee wrote of the two communities behaving towards one another 'like oil and vinegar in a salad';[66] and Crick clearly has the Ulster unionists in mind when, in questioning irredentist enthusiasms, he asks: 'What if . . . there are fellows who pass a nationalist examination on race, fail on religion, are passed on geography, but fail on wanting to join in?'[67] Cobban, in his historical survey, *The nation state and national self-determination*', concludes that the 'essential price' paid by Irish nationalism for its success was the partitioning of the island.

In Ireland, the fatal logic of the nation state . . . had triumphed. Except where a community is culturally homogeneous, the principle of the nation state means that the success of a majority in achieving self-

[57] Orme (1970: 123).
[58] Isaiah Bowman, *The new world* (New York: 1928, 4th edn.), p. 60.
[59] Evans (1970: 4).   [60] Pounds and Ball (1964: 97).
[61] Mark Jefferson, 'The law of the primate city', *Geographical Review*, vol. 29, no. 2, 1939, pp. 226-32; reprinted in W. A. Douglas Jackson, *Politics and geographic relationships* (Englewood Cliffs, New Jersey: 1964), pp. 172-5.
[62] Pounds (1972: 21).
[63] Hertz (1944: 243); Royal Institute of International Affairs, *Nationalism* (London: 1939), p. 111.
[64] Hertz (1944: 175).
[65] David E. Schmitt, *The irony of Irish democracy* (Lexington: 1973).
[66] Toynbee (1939: IV: 293).   [67] Crick (1964: 80).

determination will involve the assimilation, extinction, or exclusion of the minority. The Ulster Orangemen, with Great Britain behind them, were able to insist on the third of these possibilities.[68]

(b) Ulster's map-image

The rhetoric and metaphors of Ulster unionists confirm the self-image of a besieged garrison, defending, as their ancestors did, the Ulster Plantation.[69] This was facilitated not only by their own reading of their community's past, but also by the circumstances prevailing when organized Ulster Unionism gathered its resources to fight Home Rule. The geographical base of the Ulster Unionists — whether it encompassed the whole of Ulster or only a part — would be a 'last redoubt' for all *Irish* unionists.[70] Whenever Home Rule for Ireland looked probable, Ulster's veto came into play, the self-confidence of loyalists being expressed by their leader, Carson, in 1914: 'The difficulty will remain, and Ulster will be a physical and geographical fact.'[71]

That it was eventually a six-county rather than a nine-county fact, left some unionists within the new state with a sense of guilt and grievance over the boundary line: its arbitrary nature, with even its most glaring anomalies unrectified, resulted in some dissatisfaction on the part of six-county unionists with the map-shape of Northern Ireland. J. R. Fisher — eventually to be the north's representative on the Irish Boundary Commission — expressed his conviction, when Partition was first enacted, that 'Ulster [*sic*] can never be complete without Donegal.' In a letter to Craig, he advised him to lobby for the inclusion of Donegal and a safer boundary with the south: 'With North Monaghan *in* Ulster and South Armagh *out*, we should have a solid ethnographic and strategic frontier to the South, and a hostile "Afghanistan" on our north-west frontier would be placed in safe-keeping.'[72] Once the six-county state

---

[68] Cobban (1969: 163-5).
[69] Carson, *The Times*, 14 July 1919; Craigavon, ibid., 20 Jan. and 3 July 1934; N. J. G. Pounds, *An historical and political geography of Europe* (London: 1947), p. 462; Mitchel (1971: 60); Rose (1976: 11).
[70] Miller (1978: 88).   [71] Quoted, Rose (1976: 7).
[72] Quoted, D. R. Gwynn, *The history of Partition: 1912-1925* (Dublin: 1950), pp. 215-6.

was established and particularly after the threat posed by the Boundary Commission had receded, Ulster unionists developed a map-image of their state, which, to an increasing extent, as the years passed, was depicted in the press and, later, on television as a six-county map.

(c) *The historical dimension*

Although complicated by the fact that their union with Britain made the development of a local nationalism irrelevant, it would be a mistake to believe, as so many southern nationalists tended to do, that the Ulster unionists were, therefore, assimilable into the Irish nation. Taking Boulding's model, two distinct *national images* on the island of Ireland can be identified: Ulster unionists manifestly do not share with Irish nationalists, a 'consciousness of great shared events . . . of having "gone through something" together.' Few communities have as keen a sense as they of their own history, a factor which places them firmly within Boulding's theoretical framework for a group with a distinctive national image: 'it may be an experience shared long ago but constantly renewed by the ritual observances and historical memory of the people.' [73] Not only were Ulster unionists non-participants in the Irish struggle for independence — 'the great shared event' of contemporary Irish nationalism — but their very resistance to that phenomenon forms their own, most recent, 'great shared event'. If, in Renan's celebrated aphorism, a nation lives 'by a daily plebiscite', [74] then the Ulster unionists have consistently renewed at least their minimum allegiance not to be assimilated into the Irish nation. In his study of Ulster loyalism, Miller suggests that although thinking of themselves, in the decades immediately preceding Partition, as the loyal Irish, they were also 'being driven to think of themselves as Ulstermen, a designation which they were reluctantly prepared to put forward as a "nationality" if that was a necessary ploy in the game of self-determination they were, perforce, playing.' [75]

[73] Boulding (1959: 424-5).
[74] Quoted in D. A. Rustow, *A world of nations: problems of political modernisation* (Washington, DC: 1967), pp. 20-1.
[75] Miller (1978: 119).

(d) *Northern Ireland's state-idea*

Once Partition had been enacted, the Unionists' slogan, 'What we have, we hold', neatly encapsulated the *state-idea* of Northern Ireland as perceived by the majority community. But a one-third minority within its borders opposed the very existence of the state: the consequent, permanent, polarization of politics on such a fundamental issue precluded the development of a *unified* state-idea in Northern Ireland.[76] Unionism, however, had its own exclusive state-idea, confirmed by all the slogans of its leaders: 'A Protestant Parliament for a Protestant people', 'Not an Inch', 'No surrender!'. Indeed the Northern Ireland state-idea was nothing less than the antithesis of the state-idea espoused by the south: the south wanted Partition abolished; the north insisted on its retention. Furthermore, taking the other two concepts discussed above, it seems clear that as a community, Ulster unionists at least excluded themselves — and were, in practice, largely excluded by Irish nationalists — from the Irish national image and national idea.

(iii) BRITAIN'S MAP-IMAGE OF IRELAND

One other map-image is relevant: Britain's perception of her western flank. For some centuries the strategic unity of the British Isles had become 'a fundamental principle'; Ireland was thought of as 'a back-door to England through which more than one great power had endeavoured to pass.'[77] If anything, the strategic issue was even more acute when the British government came to consider the Irish settlement in 1920 — a bargaining point not forgotten by the Ulster Unionists. Having recently, successfully, withstood the U-boat menace of the Great War, Britain was apprehensive that Ireland was, in Churchill's words, 'intriguing with foreign enemies against her'.[78] Churchill's image of Ireland as an island 'lapped about by British sea-power' was widely shared by strategic

---

[76] Mitchel (1971: 60).

[77] C. Barnett, *The collapse of British power* (London: 1972), pp. 184-5.

[78] Quoted in Martin Gilbert, *Churchill IV: 1916-1922* (London: 1975), pp. 668-9.

theorists. Although offensive to Irish nationalists, such statements expressed fundamental strategic realities: not only
would geography render Britain and Ireland, whatever their
respective naval strengths, strategically interdependent, but in
the period under review, Irish nationalists, *in government*,
accepted that they could not undertake the naval defence of
the Irish coasts.[79] This, however, was emphasized privately.
In public, a more orthodox, separatist rhetoric was heard. As
George Orwell remarked in just this context, the 'intellectual
decencies' could 'vanish' and the 'plainest facts' could be
'denied' when an Irish nationalist refused 'even in his secret
thoughts' to admit that 'Eire can only remain independent
because of British protection.'[80] A central British consideration when the Government of Ireland Act was being prepared
in 1920, this strategic dimension remained important, at least
throughout the period of de Valera's leadership of Fianna
Fail, and formed part of the context in which the Partition
question was considered in Dublin and Belfast, as well as
London.

[79] Minister for defence to Executive Council, 22 July 1925, Blythe papers,
P24/107; de Valera at conference between the representatives of the UK and Eire,
23 Feb. 1938, PRO CAB 27/642 IN(38)6; also Lloyd George to King, 21 July
1921, Lloyd George papers, F/29/4/60.
[80] George Orwell, 'Notes on nationalism' (1945), in *Collected essays* (London:
1961), pp. 284-5.

PART II
DE VALERA'S ULSTER POLICY:
1917–1959

'In almost every exchange, formal or informal, between [de Valera] and his British counterparts,
there recurs, like the clanging of a bell, one theme;
Partition, Partition, Partition! Every argument came
back to it, every decision was affected by it.' (Sean
MacEntee, 'De Valera: the man I knew', *Iris Fianna
Fail*, Winter, 1975.)
'Mr de Valera is always 100 per cent stiff and 100 per
cent right and that is discouraging.' (Sir John Maffey
to Anthony Eden, [c.25 Jan.] 1940, not sent, PRO DO
130/10/79/40.)

2. 'A Rock in the Road': 1917–1925

(i) NATIONALIST MYTHS ON PARTITION

'No man has the right to set bounds to the onward march of the nation.' Probably no political slogan was more often incanted from Fianna Fail platforms than these words of Charles Stewart Parnell.[1] Throughout de Valera's years as leader of the party, they constantly recur, underlining Fianna Fail's belief that they were, in their generation, in the vanguard of Irish nationalism, the inheritors, not of Parnell's policies, but of Parnell's promise.[2] Ironically, it was this generation of politicians who, at the 1918 election, effectively eclipsed the party which Parnell had first made effective. As the victorious Sinn Fein MPs well knew, part of the reason for the old Irish Party's defeat was nationalist disenchantment with what was seen as their appeasement of Ulster Unionism.[3] Yet by voting Sinn Fein in 1918, the electorate was supporting a policy even more extreme than that which had proved unacceptable to Ulster: in this, the southern voters were at one with their politicians, who, preoccupied by the relationship with Britain,

---

[1] Charles Stewart Parnell (1846-91), constitutional nationalist. His dominance in the 1880s helped effect a revolution in land ownership, but failed to win Home Rule; his controversial private life and early death left a vacuum in Irish politics. Known as 'the uncrowned king of Ireland', his influence continued after his death and he was the dominant figure in Irish politics during de Valera's boyhood. De Valera believed that his own generation of nationalists 'marched to victory on the shoulders of that great generation. . . Our "eyes have seen the glory" which Parnell and his comrades longed for and strove for but did not see.' De Valera: speeches (1980: 491-3).

[2] See, for instance, *Irish Press* reports of de Valera's last general election campaign in 1957: speeches at Clonmel, reported 18 Feb., at Ennis, 25 Feb., at Bandon, 4 Mar., and at the final rally, GPO, Dublin, 5 Mar. 1959.

[3] Dr William Fogarty (Bishop of Killaloe) to Redmond, 3 June 1915, Redmond papers, MS 15,188(5); George Gavan Duffy to F. J. O'Connor, 20 Oct. 1916, Gavan Duffy papers, MS 5581; J. J. Horgan to Serjeant Sullivan of Irish Recruiting Council, 19 July 1918, Horgan papers, P 4645.

seriously underestimated the Ulster dimension to the Irish Question.

The new generation of nationalists held highly subjective views on Ulster. Six key ideas which were common currency in their speeches and propaganda can be identified. Conventional nationalists presumed

  (i) that the people of Ireland comprised one nation;

 (ii) that Britain had partitioned Ireland solely from self-interest;

(iii) that an independent, politically 're-united' Ireland was inevitable;

(iv) that even if Britain had to coerce the Ulster unionists into unity — as she was, in honour, if necessary, bound to do — the resulting united Ireland would be economically prosperous and politically stable;

 (v) that if Britain unilaterally broke the link with Northern Ireland, the Ulster unionists would be obliged to accept an accommodation with the south;

(vi) that Britain had the necessary resources — military and/or economic and/or political — to coerce the unionists into accepting a united Ireland.

De Valera, as will be seen presently, is on public record in the early part of his career, as espousing all six of these ideas. The concluding chapter will examine whether, and to what extent, he modified or discarded any of these myths. The chapters which follow analyse de Valera's record on Partition from 1917 to 1959. From the twenties to the fifties he was pre-eminent on the Irish political stage; even his political opponents acknowledged that he embodied Irish nationalism to the majority of the people. What does the record tell us of his Ulster policy during the first forty years of Partition?

(ii) COERCION OR EXPULSION? DE VALERA'S POLICY TOWARDS THE ULSTER UNIONISTS: 1917-18

De Valera's initial involvement in politics had been prompted by the success of Ulster's veto of the 1914 Home Rule Bill.[4]

---

[4] Longford and O'Neill (1970: 470).

Following the 1916 Rising, his fellow-prisoner, Sean MacEntee, records de Valera as being 'firm in the conviction' that the troubles in Ulster were 'due to British guile and nothing else'.[5] Such a simplistic perspective on Ulster is also reflected in de Valera's speeches during the eleven months between his release from gaol in June 1917 and his re-arrest in May 1918, an eventful period during which he became abstentionist MP for East Clare, campaigned in other by-elections, was elected President of Sinn Fein, opposed conscription, and conducted a Sinn Fein organizing drive in the north-west of Ulster, in counties Derry, Tyrone, and Donegal, soon to be bisected by the boundary. His biographers, Longford and O'Neill, in their chapter covering this period quote his constantly repeated theme that 'Ulster was entitled to justice and she should have it, but she should not be petted and the interests of the majority sacrificed to please her.'[6] They also complain that de Valera's views on Ulster were distorted by the press, a viewpoint which he shared: having been 'emasculated and distorted' by the censor, one speech had then, he complained, been 'doctored by another hand' to suit the policy of the *Freeman's Journal.*[7]

It is not always clear whether specific grievances against the newspapers concern omission, distortion, or editorial hostility.[8] The latter may be discounted here, as our concern is to trace de Valera's thinking on Ulster. Undoubtedly some of his views were omitted, either by timid or hostile editors, or by the censor, but from a reading of the newspaper files of the period there is no evidence to suggest that even with the journalists' and censors' interventions between de Valera's speeches and the following morning's press the words which were published had not been spoken. Nor, given the consistency with which key ideas recur, could the charge be sustained that

[5] MacEntee (1975: 1). Sean MacEntee (1899-), active with de Valera in Ulster by-elections, 1917-18; one of the few TDs to predict that the 1921 Treaty would entrench Partition; founder member of Fianna Fail and member of all Fianna Fail governments, 1932-65; retired, 1969, but remained a contributor to public debate on Partition issue.

[6] Longford and O'Neill (1970: ch. 6 *passim*, quotation p. 63).

[7] *Irish Independent*, 23 Jan. 1918; Longford and O'Neill (1975: 75).

[8] See, for instance, editorials in *Freeman's Journal*, 1 Feb. 1918 and *Irish News*, 23, 25, and 28 Jan. 1918.

de Valera's words were quoted out of their context. So repetitious are the newspaper reports that they can be accepted as the best evidence of de Valera's views on Ulster at this period.

These speeches invite the question: did de Valera envisage *any* future for the Ulster unionists within Sinn Fein's Irish Republic? And, if they were to have a future, on whose terms could they remain? De Valera variously described the Ulster unionists as a 'foreign garrison' and 'not Irish people';[9] he had 'never used any argument with unionists except this — are you Irishmen first or Englishmen first?'[10] He threatened them that if they rejected Sinn Fein's solution 'they would have to go under';[11] that if they stood 'in our way to freedom we will clear you out of it';[12] that they must decide to 'either be in Ireland or out of it'.[13] He also stated that the Irish Question would be settled quickly if England 'cleared out her troops';[14] that he was not a pacifist;[15] that 'ten foot pikes' in the hands of Irish Volunteers 'were a far greater guarantee that they would not be conscripted' than were eighty MPs in London;[16] and that the 'methods of their striving were to be bound by no constitution but that of the Ten Commandments.'[17] He repeatedly asserted his belief that no theological argument could be sustained against the use of force.[18] While defending the Church's 'right to interfere' on moral questions, he challenged any theologian to deny Ireland's right to prepare for 'a just revolt'.[19]

There was nothing in any of this to reassure the Ulster unionists that de Valera was offering them what he was shortly to call 'their share in Ireland's glorious traditions'[20] which, to de Valera, included Ireland as 'an Irish-speaking nation'.[21] Sinn

[9] *Freeman's Journal*, 12 Nov. 1917.

[10] At an election meeting in Newry during the South Armagh by-election, reported in *Irish Independent, Freeman's Journal, Irish Times*, 1 Feb. 1918.

[11] *Irish Independent*, 6 July 1917.

[12] *Freeman's Journal*, 20 July 1917.   [13] Ibid., 19 Jan. 1918.

[14] *Irish Times*, 13 Feb. 1918.

[15] *Kilkenny Moderator*, 11 Aug. 1917.

[16] *Irish Independent*, 29 Jan. 1918.

[17] *Irish News*, 9 Apr.; also, *Freeman's Journal*, 19 Feb. 1918.

[18] *Freeman's Journal*, 3 Nov. 1917.

[19] Ibid., 5 Nov. 1917. For the Catholic Church's role in Irish politics at this critical juncture, see David W. Miller, *Church, state and nation in Ireland: 1898–1921* (Dublin, 1973), pp. 329–496, *passim*.

[20] *Freeman's Journal*, 30 Jan. 1918.   [21] Ibid., 5 Nov. 1917.

Fein supporters, he claimed, were the 'vast majority' and
stood for separation: 'If he felt that the best thing for Ireland
was not separation he would fall in with the Unionists. But if
the Union were maintained it would mean the destruction of
the Irish language.'[22]

However, as the Ulster by-elections were to show, both
Ulster communities proved difficult missionary terrain for de
Valera. He described Sinn Fein's defeat in the South Armagh
by-election as 'a disaster and a defeat for Ireland'.[23]

Immediately following this reversal, de Valera undertook,
with MacEntee, a ten-day tour of the north-west, speaking in
Donegal, Derry, and Tyrone: 'Ulster cut from Ireland would
leave her without her head — without her heart.'[24] His declared
strategy was to fight sectarianism, win Ulster's nationalists to
Sinn Fein 'because their nationality was the same'[25] and
then unite

under the same banner of equality . . . a large number of the deluded
followers of the capitalist class of Belfast. He believed the people of
Ulster aspired for freedom as much as the people of Munster, Leinster
or Connaught. Ulster's hard-headedness was like the cat that would like
to get the fish, but would not wet her paws to get it. Whilst they were
struggling for their freedom they meant to concentrate the minds of the
Irish people on their own nation. If they did that — even if their struggle
went on for forty years — they would have advanced materially.

In contrast, MacEntee, from the same platform, implied that
the Republic would be won within twelve months.[26] To
attempt this, thought John Dillon,[27] would result in 'horrible
bloodshed and disaster', a fear which he thought was now
'dawning' on de Valera's mind, hence his reference to a
possible forty-year wait.[28] De Valera's moderation in comparison to his colleagues was already a matter for comment

[22] *Irish Times*, 13 July 1917.   [23] *Freeman's Journal*, 19 Feb. 1918.
[24] *Anglo-Celt*, 16 Feb. 1918.   [25] *Freeman's Journal*, 15 Feb. 1918.
[26] *Irish Independent*, 11 Feb. 1918.
[27] John Dillon (1851-1927); MP, 1885-1918; leading nationalist MP on land,
and Home Rule questions; succeeded Redmond as leader Irish Parliamentary
Party, March 1918; led the party in the December 1918 general election when it
was eclipsed by Sinn Fein, de Valera taking Dillon's seat, thus ending thirty-three
years in House of Commons; astute observer of the Irish revolution despite being
one of its victims; father of James Dillon, future Fine Gael TD and leader.
[28] Letter to *Freeman's Journal*, 14 Feb. 1918.

although Dillon feared that de Valera's fate 'would be like that of Mr Kerensky in Russia.'[29]

Politicians, priests, and editors hostile to Sinn Fein constantly drew a parallel with the Russian Revolution. It was a scare which de Valera seems to have been particularly keen to defuse: 'They were called by certain people the Revolutionary Party. Were they called the Conservative Party they would be more correctly named. They would conserve the spirit of true Irish nationality.'[30]

Sinn Fein's opponents commented on de Valera's comparative moderation. The Irish Unionist Alliance noted, in November 1917, what they saw as conflicting views on Ulster by Sinn Fein's leaders. They quoted Arthur Griffith as saying that the Ulster unionists 'must make up their minds either to throw in their lot with the Irish nation or stand out as the English garrison. If they did the latter the Irish nation must deal with them.' They contrasted this with de Valera's invitation to the Ulster unionists to be 'loyal to Ireland and to be true and honest to their flag. He would not like to see any man who was loyal as an Irishman, be he Unionist or Separatist, coerced.'[31] De Valera often struck such a note but he had also outlined an extremist policy towards the north: 'Ulster must be coerced if she stood in the way';[32] her case for self-determination was merely that of 'the robber coming into another man's house, and claiming a room as his';[33] again, he said 'As far as the Unionists were concerned he had nothing more to say to them than that they represented only English interests, and as they were in the minority they had nothing to do but give way to the majority. (Cheers.)'.[34]

---

[29] *Dublin Daily Express*, 22 Feb. 1918; A. F. Kerensky (1881–1970), Russian political leader and head of the provisional government, July to November 1917; that he was ousted by the Bolsheviks made his name synonymous with a leader used as a front by extremists who intended usurping power once it had been entrusted to him. His conservative critics sometimes likened de Valera to Kerensky, at least until the 1930s: Thomas Bodkin, typescript speech [1932], Bodkin papers, MS 6918/54; also, *Round Table*, Dec. 1932, p. 126.

[30] *Anglo-Celt*, 4 May 1918.

[31] 'Sinn Fein and Ulster — conflicting views of leaders', *Notes from Ireland*, vol. 26, no. 4, p. 74, 1 Nov. 1917, Irish Unionist Alliance, Dublin.

[32] *Sligo Champion*, 28 July 1917.   [33] *Irish Times*, 9 Feb. 1918.

[34] *Sligo Champion*, 28 July 1917.

At an election meeting during the South Armagh by-election de Valera suggested that the

> Unionists of the North must make up their minds whether they were going to be a British garrison or Irishmen. If they are content to be a British garrison we have only one thing to do and that is not to try to conciliate them. They had seen the effect of conciliation in Ulster's attitude towards the Convention.

Such an approach has only made 'the Unionists sit tight and contribute not a single suggestion to a settlement of the Irish Question.' De Valera 'recognised the Unionists as a rock in the road'. He recognized the position they took up and said that

> that position must be stormed from at home, and they must make up their minds not to be peddling with this rock. They must if necessary blast it out of their path. They must face[35] this problem, and if the choice offered to them was the choice of Solomon they would reject it. They would not accept that choice. The child was theirs: this was their land, and there was no parity of reasoning in those who said that Ulster's secession from Ireland was the same as Ireland's secession from the Empire.[36]

John Dillon, a persistent critic of Sinn Fein's threats to Ulster, publicly rebuked de Valera for threatening force against Ulster within six months unless she accepted the Republic. De Valera replied in an open letter to Dillon published in the *Irish Independent* two days after the reports of his Bessbrook speech. Specifically, de Valera denied that he had prophesied 'in terms of months' as it was 'unwise': 'That you should make me give six months to Ulster is for you, seemingly very natural. I never was guilty of such stupidity. If your other "quotations" are as genuine as those attributed to me they are three-fourths fabrications. What is the good of all this filthy lying?'[37] It will be noted that this strongly worded refutation of Dillon's speech limits its specific denial to the stupidity of prophesying 'in terms of months'; although it also has the clear effect of calling into question the veracity

[35] *Freeman's Journal*, 28 Jan. 1918 reports de Valera as saying that Sinn Fein 'must *force* this problem'.

[36] Based on reports in *Freeman's Journal, Irish Times, Dublin Daily Express, Irish News, Northern Whig, Belfast Newsletter*, all 28 Jan. 1918.

[37] Open letter to John Dillon, *Irish Independent*, 30 Jan. 1918.

of his critics and the accuracy of all press accounts, it does
not specifically deny or withdraw the threat of force; it may
well have been written to shield de Valera from those of his
critics who believed what they read of his speeches in the
press.

At the close of the campaign in South Armagh, de Valera
expressed general dissatisfaction with press reports that his
policy amounted to no conciliation of the Ulster unionists.
On 30 January the *Freeman's Journal* announced that it had
received a letter from de Valera too lengthy to publish in full
— it would have taken up three full columns. However, the
paper did publish de Valera's 'corrected' views on Ulster. His
position was that no 'compromise' rather than no 'conciliation'
was possible with the unionists. One tradition in Ireland must
prevail. 'Any half-way position is bound to be unstable. That
the Unionists should come over to us is both reasonable and
just, sanctioned by nature, justified by precedent . . . We offer
them, too, their share in Ireland's glorious traditions. If they
refuse, they're an "alien garrison". With such there can be no
peace.' Moreover, de Valera suggested that Ulster would
appreciate his 'straight dealing'; his was a 'plain, blunt, manly,
honest statement and fair'.[38] It was also ambivalent and confused. Having chided the *Freeman's Journal* for suggesting
that his policy rejected 'conciliation' with Ulster, de Valera
explicitly contradicts this within days both in a letter to
Patrick McCartan[39] and in a public speech in Derry where he
defended the use of physical force. The local unionist paper
reports him as saying that 'when the opportunity presented
itself they could secure their demands by force of arms.
(Cheers.)'[40]

Even if one relies on de Valera's letter of correction and
clarification to the *Freeman's Journal*, his policy can be fairly
summarized as one of coercion against an 'alien garrison' unless
and until they accepted Ireland's 'glorious traditions' as defined

[38] *Freeman's Journal*, 30 Jan. 1918.
[39] De Valera to McCartan, 7 Feb. 1918, Devoy papers, MS 18,003(4)B. Patrick
McCartan (1878-1966), medical doctor, politician, native of Tyrone, active in
Irish-American and later in Irish politics; although critical of the Treaty, he supported it, refusing to vote 'for chaos'. Author of *With de Valera in America* (New
York, 1935).
[40] *Derry Standard*, 11 Feb. 1918.

by Sinn Fein. It seems fair to suggest that during this period de Valera repeatedly insisted that coercion or expulsion would be the just fate for the unionists of Ulster.

(iii) ASSIMILATION OF THE ULSTER UNIONISTS: DE VALERA ON ULSTER, 1919–20: WHAT HE TOLD AMERICA

Arrested in May 1918, de Valera was effectively silenced until the general amnesty for Sinn Fein prisoners ten months later.[41] On his own initiative, he decided to seek recognition for the Republic in the United States. Much criticized for this decision by some of his colleagues, de Valera was correct in his estimate that the British feared a loss of American support for their Irish policy. 'If America goes wrong we are lost', wrote Lloyd George[42] to Bonar Law,[43] 'I wish Ulster would fully realise what that means. I am afraid they don't.'[44]

From an analysis of what he told his American audiences in the eighteen months from June 1919, it is clear that de Valera's views on Ulster were now more moderate: in these speeches he foresees the assimilation of the Ulster unionists into an Irish-Ireland. What follows is based on a content analysis of all reports of de Valera's speeches in America as

[41] Although he escaped from Lincoln Prison in February 1919, de Valera could not engage in open political activity until the amnesty for Sinn Fein prisoners the following month, Longford and O'Neill (1970: ch. 7).

[42] David Lloyd George (1863–1945), British Prime Minister, 1916–22; after 1916 Rising resolved to settle Irish Question; his Irish Convention of 1917 was a failure as was his attempt to introduce conscription in Ireland, 1918, and his attempt to win a military victory in the Anglo-Irish war, 1919–21; his Government of Ireland Act 1920 partitioned Ireland, established Northern Ireland, but was rejected south of the border; he enjoyed more success at the negotiating table, October–December 1921, in the Anglo-Irish talks which resulted in the Treaty and which settled if it did not solve the Irish Question for at least a half century; enjoyed a legendary reputation in Ireland for negotiating genius and duplicity — both deserved; Ulster Unionists were equally distrustful of him; unimpressed by de Valera in their meetings, July 1921.

[43] Andrew Bonar Law (1858–1923), born in Canada, leader of British Conservative Party, 1911–21, 1922–3; in 1912 pledged unconditional support to any Ulster resistance to the Liberal government's Home Rule policy; Prime Minister, October 1922–May 1923.

[44] Lloyd George to Bonar Law, 12 Jan. 1918, quoted, Patrick Buckland, *Irish Unionism: 1: the Anglo-Irish and the new Ireland: 1885–1922* (Dublin: 1972), pp. 121–2; Redmond to Lloyd George, 13 Nov. 1917, Redmond papers, MS 15,189; Irish file of Governor-General of Canada, June–Oct. 1919, PAC, R.G.7, G.21, vol. 580, file 20,786A *passim.*

reported in one weekly political paper, specially published
for the Irish-American community, the *Gaelic American*. [45]
Although he emphasized in one letter to his cabinet colleagues
in Dublin that 'I do not weigh every word and every sentence
of a speech and of an interview as if it were a treaty I was
actually signing', he also assured them that, in his American
speeches, he said nothing which he 'would not say at home. I
do not believe in the old parliamentarian policy of one sort
of speech for America and another for Ireland.'[46]

Many of the predominant themes in his speeches in America
had relevance to Ulster. His view of Irish history was simple:
he entertained no doubts but that Ireland was, and always
had been, one nation. He told 'the tale of a nation crucified'
during seven centuries of occupation,[47] and, preceding that,
a golden age. He described Ireland as 'a nation before Augus-
tine set foot on English soil';[48] again, as a country which had
'enjoyed sovereign independence for over a thousand years'
before the invasion of the Danes.[49] 'The Irish Nation is *one*
nation, not two', he claimed, it was 'as homogeneous as any
nation upon the earth.'[50]

Britain's responsibility for Ireland's difficulties was another
central theme in de Valera's speeches: he likened the Union
between Britain and Ireland to 'the union of the shark with
its prey';[51] describing nationalism as 'a natural and permanent
system', he suggested that it 'always triumphed' over imperi-
alism.[52]

He also showed himself to be aware of the central preoccupation of the British with regard to Ireland: naval defence.
Ireland, he said, 'with its strategic position at the gate of the
Atlantic Ocean, overlooking 60 per cent of the world's com-
merce' was seen by Britain as her 'key' to be 'mistress of the

[45] See John Bowman, 'De Valera on Ulster: what he told America: 1919–1920',
Irish Studies in International Affairs, vol. 1, no. 1, 1979, pp. 3-18.
[46] De Valera to cabinet (*c*. 27 Feb. 1920), SPO DE 2/245.
[47] *Gaelic American*, 12 July 1919.   [48] Ibid., 6 Sept. 1919.
[49] Ibid., 3 Jan. 1920.
[50] Eamon de Valera, 'Some points from recent speeches by President de Valera',
ibid., 24 Jan. 1920.
[51] Ibid., 17 Jan. 1920.   [52] Ibid., 28 Feb. 1920.

world'.[53] There is also evidence which suggests that, in advance of his more insular colleagues in Dublin, de Valera at this early stage appreciated the potential common interest between Britain and Ireland of an independent Ireland whose neutrality would, in fact but not in law, be guaranteed by British naval supremacy in the Atlantic.[54]

More specifically, on Ulster, de Valera consistently denied that religion was a factor in the Irish Question; it was merely a 'rack on the peg of which England exhibits Ireland's political differences before the world'. Its introduction was 'nonsense',[55] 'an insult',[56] 'unworthy'.[57] Allowing that the 'internal political divisions amongst Irishmen themselves . . . roughly correspond' to the two lines of division of religious belief, he argued that this was 'merely accidental'[58] and was exploited by English statesmen with 'consummate skill to deceive'.[59] He discounted the intransigence of Ulster unionists and repeatedly forecast their imminent conversion to support for Sinn Fein.[60]

The main argument adduced by de Valera to his American audiences was that in accordance with the principle of self-determination, Ireland was entitled to unity and independence. He did not admit that Ulster's objections in any way weakened Ireland's case. He went so far as to claim that if the American parties made the recognition of the Irish Republic an issue in the 1920 Presidential election, it would be 'the most momentous thing that ever happened in the history of the world; because if that is done . . . that is the principle of government by the consent of the governed.'[61] Fundamental to de Valera's argument was the assumption that the *island of Ireland* would be the unit chosen for the application of the self-determination principle. Along with his belief in natural boundaries and the indisputable fact that there was no obvious line which would separate the north-east from the rest of the country, he based his case largely on the result of the 1918 election which Sinn Fein had, after all, fought on the issue of self-determination.

[53] Ibid., 1 Nov. 1919.   [54] Ibid., and *Westminster Gazette*, 6 Feb. 1920.
[55] *Gaelic American*, 24 Jan. 1920.   [56] Ibid., 12 July 1919.
[57] Ibid., 29 Nov. 1919; also ibid., 18 Oct. 1919 and 15 May 1920.
[58] Ibid., 23 Aug. 1919.   [59] Ibid., 11 Oct. 1919.
[60] Ibid., 12 July, 2, 23 Aug., 27 Sept., 11, 18 Oct., 29 Nov. 1919, 10 Jan., 3, 17 Apr. 1920.
[61] Ibid., 15 May 1920.

In terms of seats won, 1918 was a Sinn Fein 'landslide' but in terms of votes won, it was not so impressive. Sinn Fein had won 73 seats to the Unionists' 26 with the old Irish Party reduced to a rump of six. What was significant and was ignored was that within the six counties, the Ulster Unionists had won 22 seats to the Irish Party's four and Sinn Fein's three.

Our concern here is with how de Valera read these election results. It is clear that if the geographical pattern to the distribution of votes could be ignored, the all-Ireland figures could be exploited as a plausible justification for Irish self-determination. Throughout his time in America, this is what de Valera did, constantly citing the election figures and never admitting that within the six counties Sinn Fein had suffered a defeat on a scale similar to the scale of their victory throughout the country. He preferred to claim that 'no people on earth ever agreed so overwhelmingly on a great issue'.[62]

Clearly de Valera considered the topical issue of self-determination one of the most persuasive arguments for his American public. At Washington in January 1920 he claimed that although he had kept his 'ears and eyes open' since coming to the country, for a good argument against Irish self-determination he had heard none.[63] In April he rejected Lloyd George's suggestion that north-east Ulster might also be entitled to self-determination.[64] De Valera had already gone on record that the principle 'if it is not going to be reduced to an absurdity, has to be restricted to some unit, and the unit that was chosen was the Nation, and, therefore, it is not right to say that we are denying self-determination to the people of the North of Ireland.'[65] Lloyd George's 'solid homogeneous Ulster' which he was 'trying to palm off on the world' did not exist. 'He can't take six counties, no, nor four. Why, he can't even take Antrim, because it hasn't a complete Ulster representation. He can't take Belfast, because in Belfast there are more Nationalists than in the City of Cork. Therefore, Lloyd George can't himself find the boundary of his Ulster. His homogeneous Ulster does not exist.'[66]

[62] Ibid., 8 Nov. 1919.   [63] Ibid., 17 Jan. 1920.
[64] Ibid., 15 May 1920.   [65] Ibid., 10 Jan. 1920.
[66] Ibid.

In one speech in America he is reported as favouring four provincial parliaments in an independent Ireland: 'it is certainly a project I would be ready to support — we would divide the island into four little States [sic] so that we might have greater decentralization of government.'[67]

De Valera's conviction that peace and political stability would follow in a united, independent Ireland was another theme in his American speeches. In June 1919 he said that if British troops withdrew 'there is hardly a man or woman in Ireland who will not warmly embrace the Republic.'[68] The following March he claimed that once the British forces were withdrawn 'we'll put a South of Ireland Catholic on a platform in Ulster and an Ulsterman on a platform in the South, and in ten words they will have dispelled the bogy-illusion of religious differences.'[69]

That Ireland's ultimate freedom and unity was inevitable, predetermined by the forces of history and geography, was another of de Valera's claims. 'We are absolutely certain of success; . . . we are not vain dreamers. We are today the one white race inhabiting Europe that has not yet won its freedom.'[70] Nor could Britain's superior force prevail: 'with all England's aeroplanes, poison gas and the rest of it, we shall win, because we have justice on our side.'[71] If necessary, future generations would carry on 'the same holy task that will one day be completed.'[72] Irish freedom, he argued, was not necessarily imminent but it was inevitable.[73] Indeed the peace of the world hinged on the Irish case as 'a test of statesmanship'.[74] Irish aspirations included the re-creation of an Irish golden age: 'all Ireland wants is that the remnant of the Irish race left at home should be permitted to develop and build up the great nation which God intended Ireland to be.'[75]

As for Ulster, de Valera claimed that 'racially' the province 'remains Irish', with the 'great majority of its people' having 'a perspective of Irish history that extends back 2,400 years.'

[67] Ibid.   [68] Ibid., 12 July 1919.
[69] Ibid., 3 Apr. 1920; see also *Irish World*, 25 Oct. 1919.
[70] *Gaelic American*, 15 Nov. 1919.   [71] Ibid., 10 Apr. 1920.
[72] Ibid., 28 Feb. 1920.   [73] Ibid., 2 Aug. 1919.
[74] Ibid., 15 May 1920.   [75] Ibid., 20 Sept. 1919.

On the Ulster plantation, he added that after 'more than 300 years of intermarriage' there were 'few native born Ulstermen or Ulsterwomen today in whom Gaelic blood does not predominate'.[76]

Sinn Fein had no monopoly of propaganda and this must be borne in mind when assessing de Valera's ideas concerning Ulster. The political context in which he was working was not conducive to conciliation: he was struggling for international credibility in the form of recognition for the Republic; in Ireland the War of Independence was being prosecuted; some distinguished, disinterested commentators supported his arguments, and specifically agreed with him that Ulster should not exercise a veto on Irish self-determination;[77] and, of course, the Ulster Unionists themselves were vehemently and influentially opposed to any concessions being made to Sinn Fein. Nor were these the only arguments against conciliation. Mansergh has noted that 'in dependent societies as the time for a transfer, or possible transfer, of power approaches' there is 'an element of political determinism in the working out of majority–minority relations.' Dealing specifically with the dilemma posed by the Ulster question which faced all nationalist leaders from Parnell to de Valera, he suggests that a policy of conciliation had the 'grave liability' of admitting the separateness of the Ulster unionist community and thus encouraging 'a heightening of its claims'. Furthermore, conciliation was unlikely to be effective. 'That being so, was not the wiser course to pursue a policy, not of conciliation, but of undermining the Ulster minority's will to resist and, as a corollary, its means of support?'[78] De Valera had put forward exactly this argument following the collapse of the Irish Convention. 'It was evident to us that with the

---

[76] Eamon de Valera, *Ireland's claim to the Government of the United States of America for recognition as a sovereign independent State* (Washington, 1920), pp. 67-8.

[77] 'The temper of Ireland', *The Nation* (New York), 22 Mar., 'The case for Irish freedom', ibid., 5 Apr. 1919; J. W. Good, *Ulster and Ireland* (London, 1919), *passim*; George Creel, *Ireland's fight for freedom* (New York, 1919), pp. 114-47, *passim*; J. J. Horgan to Stephen Gwynn, 22 Aug. 1918, Horgan papers, P 4645.

[78] Mansergh (1965: 188-9).

"coercion-of-Ulster-is-unthinkable" guarantee, the Unionists would solidly maintain their original position.'[79]

But even allowing for the inevitable overstatement of his position in the context of a propaganda war, it would seem from his American speeches that de Valera had yet to realize how antipathetic the Ulster unionists were to his policies. He does not seem to have appreciated the relevance to Ulster of one of his first speeches made in America. It was on the nature of war and its causes; he predicted that foremost amongst wars in the future would be 'national wars where plain men and women willingly sacrifice themselves to the sentiment of patriotism.' And this sentiment of patriotism, he saw as 'a fundamental fact in human life'. What he did not acknowledge was that there were two 'sentiments of patriotism' in Ireland; further, that they were, not only mutually exclusive, but mutually hostile. He concluded this speech with a claim which he intended to be applied to Irish nationalism but which, with equal force, could be cited as an explanation for Ulster unionism. 'To maintain their nationality', he said, 'men and women will endure as much as to maintain their religion.' As fiercely as the individual would be prepared to fight 'to prevent the assimilation or absorption of his personal individuality' so a 'Nation will fight to prevent the *assimilation* into another Nation.'[80]

(iv) 1921: POSTPONING THE ULSTER QUESTION: DE VALERA'S SEARCH FOR AN ACCOMMODATION WITH THE ULSTER UNIONISTS

After eighteen months of open political campaigning in America, de Valera returned to Ireland at Christmas 1920. The British now perceived him as a moderate:[81] in the words of

---

[79] De Valera to McCartan, 7 Feb. 1918, Devoy papers, MS 18,003(4)B; see also Redmond to Lloyd George, 11 Dec. 1917, Redmond papers, MS 15,189.

[80] *Gaelic American*, 23 Aug. 1920. (Emphasis added.)

[81] British cabinet minutes, 20 Dec. 1920, PRO CAB 23/23 74(20)1; John Dillon believed de Valera 'came home with a view to making peace — if that should prove to be possible', Dillon to C. P. Scott, 18 Jan. 1921, Dillon papers, MS 6843/83.

the Irish Secretary, Hamar Greenwood,[82] de Valera was 'the one man who can deliver the goods'.[83] With no political forum available, de Valera used interviews with the foreign press as a means of publicizing Sinn Fein's viewpoint, and, in effect, communicating it to the British government and to his own supporters. Invariably in these interviews the question of Ulster was raised. If it could be easily overlooked by southern nationalists,[84] outsiders — whether politicians, diplomats, or journalists — saw it as central to any Irish settlement and invariably raised it in any discussions with Sinn Fein.[85] The emphasis which de Valera now placed on the future envisaged for Ulster unionists shows further moderating compared to the policy of *assimilation* expressed in America. In 1921 de Valera's policy can be summarized as that of working towards an *accommodation* with Ulster.

In reply to a questionnaire submitted by American correspondents in January, de Valera said:

The so-called Ulster difficulty is purely artificial as far as Ireland itself is concerned. It is an accident arising out of the British connection, and will disappear with it. If it arose from a genuine desire of the people of the North-east Corner for autonomy the solution proposed would be the obvious one. But it is not due to such a desire — it has arisen purely as a product of British party manoeuvering.

With this paragraph alone de Valera would have reassured his followers that their most cherished views on Partition — one nation, artificially sundered by Britain, but to be united if the British withdrew — were the cornerstone of his policy. He continues with further criticism of the Ulster unionist minority and the partition act — 'an exquisite essay in contrariety'; he then answered the original question which concerned a 'plan

[82] Hamar Greenwood (1870-1948), Chief Secretary for Ireland, April 1920-Dec. 1921; participated in Treaty negotiations.

[83] Greenwood to Craig, 3 May 1921, quoted Lady Craigavon's diary, 3 May 1921. A typescript of Lady Craigavon's diary is in the Craigavon papers in the Public Record Office of Northern Ireland in Belfast, D1415/B/38.

[84] D. S. Johnson, 'Partition and cross-border trade in the 1920s', in Peter Roebuck (ed.) *Plantation to Partition* (Belfast, 1981), pp. 229-46.

[85] Notebook of C. W. Ackerman (London correspondent, *Philadelphia Public Ledger*), London Notes, 1920-1, Ackerman papers; also, reports of Alfred Blanché (Director of political and cultural affairs, French Consulate, Dublin), June 1918-Aug. 1922, Ministère des Affaires Etrangères: Archives Diplomatiques: Europe, 1918-29: Irlande, Z/282/1, vols. 1-2, *passim*.

for the federation of Ireland as a solution to the Ulster difficulty'. De Valera stated that regarding the 'general idea of
decentralisation of administration and devolution of authority,
I am wholly in agreement with it, and I am sure our people
would be.'[86]

These interviews presented de Valera with an ideal opportunity to test Sinn Fein's tolerance for a compromise settlement — a strategy which was clear to Dillon.[87] But specifically
on the north, how would rank-and-file republicans react to
the suggestion of a federal solution? And how much local
autonomy should be granted to what geographical area of
Ulster? As will be seen, throughout 1921 de Valera continued
to keep these questions to the forefront, thereby making
some federal settlement with Ulster more tolerable to fundamental republican opinion.

To the French journal L'Œuvre he said that if England
conceded Ireland's claim to self-determination, 'there would
be no further difficulties, either with her or with the Ulster
minority. If Ulster should claim autonomy, we would be
willing to grant it.'[88] Questioned about Ulster by the Zurich
paper Neue Zeitung, in May, he repeated his assurances that
an independent Ireland would guarantee 'civil and religious
equality' and provided 'the unity and independence of Ireland
is preserved, we are ready to give such local autonomy to
Ulster, or to any other part of Ireland, as would be practicable,
if it would make for the contentment and satisfaction of the
citizens resident there.' In what reads like a scripted interview,
de Valera adds this paragraph:

I feel certain that the Republic would be ready to give to the Six
Counties, for instance, far more substantial powers than those they are
to possess under the British Partition Act, which was designed less to
give local autonomy to Ulster than to foster political and religious
rancour amongst us, and by dividing Ireland into two antagonistic parts
to make both subservient to British interests and purposes.[89]

Later in May to the New York Herald de Valera expresses
a willingness to meet Ulster Unionist representatives to 'see if

[86] Weekly Freeman, 5 Feb. 1921.
[87] Diary note, 2 June 1921, Dillon papers, MS 6582.
[88] L'Œuvre (Paris), reported in New York Evening World, 28 Jan. 1921.
[89] Neue Zeitung, 3 May 1921, reproduced in Macardle (1968: 854-6).

it is possible by negotiation to give such guarantees for the security of their interests as (would) make them loyal and contented citizens'.[90] In July to the same newspaper and to the *Chicago Tribune* he answers a specific question on the 'measure of autonomy' he envisages for the north-east with the reply: 'such autonomy as they themselves desire and is just.'[91]

Meanwhile, 'local autonomy' for the six counties, devolved from Westminster under the 1920 Act, came into effect with elections in May and the official opening of the Northern Ireland parliament in June: this strengthened Ulster's bargaining position, even if it did not, as Winston Churchill suggested, make it 'unassailable'.[92] It certainly changed the context in which any settlement was possible —a point clearly appreciated by de Valera. His understanding, as he wrote to Art O'Brien,[93] was that Britain insisted that the Belfast parliament should retain 'its present powers unless by mutual agreement with the rest of Ireland.'[94] While proceeding with the establishment of the Belfast parliament, the British also sought a *rapprochement* between north and south. With Cope[95] at Dublin Castle the main intermediary, strenuous efforts were made to persuade Craig[96] and de Valera to meet. On 15 April Dr Fogarty,[97] Bishop of Killaloe, wrote to de Valera informing him that a high official in Dublin Castle had suggested that

[90] *New York Herald*, 17 May, quoted in *Gaelic American*, 28 May 1921.

[91] Transcript of interview, circulated by publicity department of Dail Eireann, *Irish Times*, 8 July 1921.

[92] Quoted Macardle (1968: 418).

[93] Art O'Brien (1872–1949), Irish republican representative in Britain, 1919–22; disapproved of the Treaty; remained in London representing anti-Treaty 'government' until deported 1923; later when de Valera came to power in 1930s appointed Irish Minister to France and Belgium, 1935-8.

[94] De Valera to Art O'Brien, 14 June 1921, quoted Macardle (1968: 45-6).

[95] A. W. Cope (1877-1954), Assistant Under-Secretary Ireland 1920-2; on his appointment at Dublin Castle dismissed some civil servants antipathetic to Sinn Fein.

[96] Sir James Craig (1871-1940), abandoned his Westminster career in 1921 to become leader of Ulster Unionist Party and first Prime Minister of Northern Ireland which he later declared to be 'a Protestant state'; died in office, 1940. Created Lord Craigavon, 1927.

[97] Michael Fogarty, Bishop of Killaloe 1904-55; prominent nationalist; supporter of de Valera until Treaty split.

Craig 'would welcome a talk with you' concerning a north-south agreement. 'I think the idea is fiscal autonomy for all Ireland with Partition.' Fogarty urged de Valera to consider it.[98]

On 5 May, in a suburban house in Dublin, the two men who were largely to shape nationalist and unionist politics in the decades ahead, met for the first and only time. It was not a successful meeting. Most of the ninety minutes seems to have been spent on an historical discourse by de Valera. Twenty years later he recalled the meeting.

Craigavon had been told . . . that I had asked to see him and I was told that Craigavon had asked to see me. So we met rather under false pretences. We sat on opposite sides of a table and I said after the first few moments' silence 'Well?' He looked at me and he said 'Well?' I then said 'I'm too old at this political business to have nonsense of this kind: each waiting on the other to begin' and I started putting our case to him. He spoke of the Union as if it were a sacred thing. 'But', said I, 'do you not know how the Union was brought about' and I started telling him about it. After a while he tore a piece from the *Freeman's Journal* which was lying beside him. 'I think', he said, after writing for a few minutes, 'we ought to issue this statement.' He had drafted it to the effect that we had exchanged our respective views on the situation. That ended the talks but I must say I liked him.[99]

The meeting clearly derived its significance, not from what was discussed, but from the fact that it had happened at all. Greenwood described it as 'the most hopeful thing in 750 years',[1] a verdict with which Craig was scarcely in sympathy since his complaint was that de Valera had spent the time 'harping on the grievances of . . . the last 700 years'. It is interesting to compare Craig's retrospective account with de Valera's:

After half an hour he had reached the era of Brian Boru. After another half hour he had advanced to the period of some king a century or two later. By this time I was getting tired, for de Valera hadn't begun to

[98] Fogarty to de Valera, 15 Apr. 1921, SPO DE 2/528; see also C. W. Ackerman, London Notes, 1920-1, Ackerman papers.

[99] De Valera's retrospective account of his meeting with Craig, as 'told to Mr [?] Pyper of the *Toronto Telegram*', 6 Mar. 1940: Frank Gallagher papers, MS 18,375(11).

[1] Greenwood, quoted *Gaelic American*, 14 May 1921. Ulster Unionists took a more sceptical view, Adam Duffin believing London's optimism to be 'rubbish', Duffin to his wife, 10 May 1921, Duffin papers, Mic. 127.

reach the point at issue. Fortunately, a fine Kerry Blue entered the room
and enabled me to change the conversation, and I asked Mr De Valera
what announcement he was going to make to the Press about our meeting.
Finally, I tore off a piece of paper and wrote something down.[2]

The British cabinet on 24 and 25 May discussed the 'probability' of further meetings between the two Irish leaders on
an agenda proposed by Craig: indeed they even expressed
concern lest Britain be left in an 'invidious position' if Craig
and de Valera were to come to some agreement unacceptable
to London.[3] Although both Craig and de Valera denied any
unwillingness to meet, their respective preconditions precluded
a second meeting.

On de Valera's side, his conviction that any satisfactory
settlement must come through negotiations with London not
Belfast dates at least from this period. After his meeting with
Craig he wrote that he saw no hope of ending the Anglo-Irish
quarrel 'through a prior agreement with a Unionist minority'.
Essentially the question was 'an Irish-English one' and the
solution, he thought, 'must be sought in the larger general
play of English interest.'[4]

Whatever political repercussions the meeting may have en-
gendered, there was clearly no business done between the
two principals, who in the decades that followed, were to do
so much to reflect and shape the different political cultures
of north and south. Although Partition, in time, was further
to emphasize the mutual antipathy of these political cultures,
evidence that they were already deeply rooted when Partition
was introduced came in the first elections for the Northern
Ireland parliament held some weeks after the Craig–de Valera
meeting. In this election, de Valera's appeal to 'you plain
people' of 'North-East Ulster' to vote Sinn Fein and thereby
solve the Irish problem 'in a few hours . . . in the quiet and
privacy of the polling booth' was emphatically rejected.[5]

When the suggestion of a truce and an invitation to negotiate
eventually came from London, it was for tripartite talks with

[2] Craig's description 'several years later' in Ervine (1949: 411). For Dublin
Castle reading of the meeting, Mark Sturgis diary, 3–7 May 1921, Sturgis papers,
PRO 30/59/4./
[3] Cabinet minutes, 24 and 25 May 1921, PRO CAB 23/25 41(21)1, –/42(21)1.
[4] De Valera to Judge O'Connor, May 1921, quoted Longford and O'Neill
(1970: 123).   [5] The Times, 24 May 1921.

Craig included. De Valera, believing this would give equal status to the leader of a minority, instead invited Craig to join with Southern Unionists at a Dublin meeting where de Valera 'would like to confer with you and to learn from you at first hand the views of a certain section of our people of whom you are representative.'[6]

For 'sheer impertinence it could hardly be beaten', thought Lady Craig;[7] not surprisingly, Craig, who had already accepted Lloyd George's invitation to London, declined de Valera's blatant offer of demotion.

The South African leader, General Smuts[8] was an important catalyst at this juncture.[9] Acceptable as an intermediary to both sides,[10] Smuts combined a moral commitment to help solve the Irish deadlock — which he considered damaging to Imperial interests[11] — with a belief that South Africa's experience placed him in a position to understand the particular difficulties posed by Ulster; and it was on this aspect of the question, above all, that he lectured de Valera. What de Valera thought of him is not altogether clear. He told the Dail in private session that Smuts had approached the question 'purely as a thinking machine . . . as a professor would approach a problem.'[12] His biographers — perhaps reflecting de Valera's retrospective verdict — record that de Valera 'was genuinely impressed by Smuts', considering him 'the cleverest of all the leaders he met in that period, not excluding Lloyd George.'[13]

[6] De Valera to Craig, quoted Longford and O'Neill (1970: 129).

[7] Lady Craigavon, diary 29 June 1921; Sturgis diary, 29 June, Sturgis papers, PRO 30/59/4.

[8] J. C. Smuts (1870–1950), Boer General, British Field-Marshal, member of the Imperial War Cabinet, Prime Minister of South Africa, 1919–24; highly influential Commonwealth statesman; advocate of concessions to Irish nationalism but convinced of the efficacy of Ulster's veto on a republic encompassing a united Ireland; lectured de Valera on Ulster; de Valera highly impressed by Smuts's ability; Smuts unimpressed by de Valera.

[9] W. K. Hancock, *Smuts: the fields of force: 1919-1950* (Cambridge: 1968), pp. 49-61; Longford and O'Neill (1970: 130-1); Jones (1971: 74-85).

[10] Lloyd George to the King, 23 June 1921, quoted Hancock (1968: 55); Tom Casement, diary extracts, NLI MS 10,723(4); Longford and O'Neill (1970: 130-1).

[11] Smuts to Lloyd George, 14 June 1921, reprinted in Jean van der Poel (ed.), *Selections from the Smuts papers: vol. V: Sept. 1919-Nov. 1934* (Cambridge: 1973), pp. 90-1. Hereafter cited as *Smuts: V: 1973*.

[12] DE: private session: 22 Aug. 1921, p. 28.

[13] Longford and O'Neill (1970: 130).

Such admiration was not reciprocated by Smuts: he did not consider de Valera the 'big man' then needed by Ireland[14] and in his report of his meeting with him to the British cabinet he characterized de Valera as a 'visionary' who lived in 'a world of dreams, visions and shadows'.[15]

Smuts told the British cabinet that de Valera at the Dublin meeting 'continuously harped on the crime of partition.' Smuts had advised him to accept Lloyd George's invitation to a conference with Craig; but this de Valera was unwilling to do because he feared that 'if both of them appeared before the British Government they would be like two bad boys and would start fighting themselves at once and the Government would exploit their differences.'[16]

Smuts jotted down his impressions after his meeting with de Valera. The document headed 'De Valera's position – Dublin meeting' has survived in his papers: 'Ulster having been satisfied, dispute now is (as it has really always been) between British Government and majority in Ireland, and conference should be confined to two. Ulster may be dealt with separately where her interests are concerned.'[17] It was Smuts's belief that he had shaken Sinn Fein's self-confidence in their own analysis;[18] he believed that if a united Ireland were ever to come, it would only be with Ulster's consent; hence his advice to Sinn Fein to tolerate Partition as a temporary necessity and to accept that Ulster had a veto on Irish unity.

(v) THE TRUCE: JULY–SEPTEMBER 1921

During the third week in July both Craig and de Valera were in London for talks with Lloyd George. There was no tripartite meeting nor was any consensus reached, but the truce was maintained and the door to further negotiations was kept

---

[14] Smuts to M. C. Gillett, 23 Feb. 1922, in Smuts (1973: V: 113). See also Jones (1971: 83) and C. P. Scott's diary entry for 13 July 1921, reprinted T. Wilson (ed.), *The political diaries of C. P. Scott: 1911-1928* (London: 1970), p. 391.

[15] Jones (1971: 83).

[16] Smuts's account to the cabinet is recorded by Jones, 6 July 1921, Jones (1971: 82-4).

[17] Smuts: handwritten note, 'De Valera's position – Dublin meeting', reprinted in Smuts (1973: V: 94).

[18] Jones (1971: 82).

open. After the first round of talks Craig informed his cabinet colleagues that de Valera had talked to Lloyd George 'in vague generalities about "self-determination", "right to a Republic", "freedom of a nation"'. Craig advised Lloyd George that the only realistic policy was to put the British proposals in writing to enable the Dail to debate them. 'These proposals were to be embodied in a document full of high-sounding phraseology, which would appeal to the imagination of the Southern Irish, and very highly-coloured lights should be thrown upon the concessions which it was proposed to offer.'

Craig assured his colleagues that 'no coercion of Ulster' was among Lloyd George's non-negotiable commitments.[19] But two days later, on 18 July, at talks in Downing Street, Lloyd George put forward five suggestions to Craig and his ministers as to how they might accommodate de Valera's requirement of Irish unity with local autonomy for the north devolved from Dublin. None was acceptable and the Ulstermen withdrew from London, winning Lloyd George's concurrence for a public statement insisting on the north's right to self-determination.[20] This 'wholly inadmissible claim'[21] angered de Valera[22] and in a protest to Lloyd George he wrote:

I have made it clear in public statements which reflect the views of the Irish people that Ireland, so far from disregarding the special position of the minority in North East Ulster, would be willing to sanction any measure of local autonomy which they might desire, provided that it were just and were consistent with the unity and integrity of our island.[23]

That the Ulster ministers were immovable in their decision not even to discuss such proposals was clear to Lloyd George

[19] PRONI CAB 4/2/3, 16 July 1921; these 'Rough Notes' of the London cabinet meeting of Northern Ireland ministers are incorrectly dated 16 June. They were presumably written up some months later from the cabinet secretary, W.B. Spender's notes.
[20] PRONI CAB 4/3/1, 18 July 1921, 'Rough Notes' of meeting between Northern Ireland ministers and Lloyd George, 18 July 1921. Again, these are incorrectly dated June, see previous note.
[21] De Valera to Lloyd George, 19 July 1921, Lloyd George papers, F/14/6/11.
[22] Childers, diary 19 July 1921, Childers papers, MS 7814.
[23] De Valera to Lloyd George, 19 July 1921, Lloyd George papers, F/14/6/11.

from his meeting with them on the previous day. On 20 July Lloyd George gave de Valera written proposals for a settlement which Tom Jones[24] thought 'one of the most generous acts' in British history: 'Briefly it is "Dominion status" with all sorts of important powers, but no Navy, no hostile tariffs, and no coercion of Ulster.'[25] De Valera reluctantly agreed to place the offer before the cabinet and Dail in Dublin. It was rejected. On Ulster, de Valera replied to Lloyd George, 'We cannot admit the right of the British Government to mutilate our country, either in its own interest, or at the call of any section of our population.' Eight words followed which were to be, for de Valera, among the most important he ever wrote concerning the north: 'We do not contemplate the use of force.' He concluded by reiterating his claim that if Britain stood aside from the Ulster issue, 'we can effect a complete reconciliation'[26] — a claim which Lloyd George found unconvincing.[27] Still anxious to cajole Craig into talks with de Valera, Lloyd George advised the Ulster leader to accept any proffered invitation from Dublin as it might help de Valera to 'realise that Ulster is a fact which he must recognise, not a figment bolstered up by the British government as a counter to Sinn Fein. He does not understand this. Till he understands it, I fear that a settlement will always be unattainable.'[28]

Craig remained wary; whereas he was always open to receive written proposals provided they contained 'no suggestion' of any interference with Northern Ireland's constitutional position, a draft reply to de Valera's expected invitation, reads: 'I repeat, we have nothing left to give away.'[29]

---

[24] Thomas Jones (1870–1955), assistant secretary to the British cabinet 1916–30; confidant of Lloyd George; lectured in Ireland, 1904–5; professor of economics, Queen's University Belfast, 1909–10; influential civil servant on Irish issue in 1921–2.

[25] Jones to Bonar Law, 22 July 1922, in Jones (1971:90–1); also F. S. L. Lyons, *Ireland since the famine* (London: 1971), p. 426.

[26] De Valera to Lloyd George, 10 Aug. 1921, *Dail Eireann: correspondence relating to peace negotiations, June–Sept. 1921* (Dublin, 1921), pp. 10–11.

[27] C. P. Scott, diary 28 July 1921, after breakfast with Lloyd George, Scott (1970: 394–5).

[28] Lloyd George to Craig, 21 July 1921, PRONI CAB 4/10/5.

[29] Draft letter prepared for Craig in anticipation of a request from de Valera for a further meeting, Aug. 1921, PRONI CAB 4/12/5–6.

Smuts tried again, unavailingly, to interest both Irish leaders in talks. Before leaving for South Africa he summarized in a private letter to de Valera his convictions concerning Sinn Fein's Ulster policy. In the short term, he thought 'no solution based on Ulster coming into the Irish state will succeed.' However, he believed that 'over a period of years' the community of interests between north and south would prove 'so great and compelling that Ulster will herself decide to join the Irish state.' For the present

an Irish settlement is only possible if the hard facts are calmly faced and Ulster is left alone. Not only will she not consent to come in, but even if she does, the Irish state will, I fear, start under such a handicap of internal friction and discordance that the result may well be failure once more.

My strong advice to you is to leave Ulster alone for the present, as the only line along which a solution is practicable; to concentrate on a free constitution for the remaining twenty-six counties, and, through a successful running of the Irish state and the pull of economic and other peaceful forces, eventually to bring Ulster into that state.

Smuts acknowledged that such a solution would be 'repugnant' to 'all Irish patriots, who look upon Irish unity as a *sine qua non* of any Irish settlement'; but, he added, 'the wise man, while fighting for his ideal to the uttermost, learns also to bow to the inevitable.' To overcome the facts, there must first be 'a humble acceptance' of them. Written with the knowledge of the British government and broadly sympathetic to their policy, this letter betrayed none of Smuts's impatience with what he saw as de Valera's political *naïveté* on Ulster. An eloquent appeal for pragmatism, it excused its absence: 'A history such as yours must breed a temper, an outlook, passions, suspicions, which it is most difficult to deal with.' On Ulster he concluded:

As I said to you before, I do not consider one single clean-cut solution of the Irish question possible at present. You will have to pass through several stages, of which a free constitution for southern Ireland is the first, and the inclusion of Ulster and the full recognition of Irish unity will be the last. Only the first stage will render the last possible, as cause generates effect. To reverse the process and begin with Irish unity as the first step is to imperil the whole settlement. Irish unity should be the ideal to which the whole process should be directed.

This letter was brilliantly pitched, offering Sinn Fein a plausible escape from the dilemma posed by Ulster's intractability. Reassuringly, it advised de Valera not to give up his ideal, but rather 'to realize it in the only way which seems to me at present practicable. Freedom will lead inevitably to unity; therefore begin with freedom — with a free constitution for the twenty-six counties — as the first the most important step in the whole settlement'.[30]

De Valera may have thought Smuts too detached — a 'thinking machine' as he told the Dail — but, perhaps alone of all his cabinet, he was impressed by this advice from the South African[31] and later that month outlined the most conciliatory policy towards Ulster which he was ever to put on record.

For two days in mid-August, the Dail met in public session to hear de Valera's account of his talks with Lloyd George. Concerning the Ulster question he said that the negotiations had been 'an attempt to get in touch with the people of the North of Ireland and to tell them that for them we had no enmity, and that we would make sacrifices for them we would never think of making for Britain, because they are Irishmen living in Ireland.'[32]

Later when the Dail went into private session he invited TDs to raise 'any questions they had in their minds'. The first question, from J. J. Walsh,[33] asked for a 'full and clear definition of his policy with regard to Ulster'. De Valera once again ruled out force: they lacked the power, 'some of them had not the inclination' and, moreover, the policy would not succeed. Ulster's present position, he said, was that

---

[30] Smuts to de Valera, 4 Aug. 1921, Smuts (1973:V:100–5).

[31] Not only did de Valera think Smuts the most impressive of all the men he met during this period, but a year later, after the outbreak of the Civil War, he admitted that 'if anything could have converted me to acceptance of the Treaty, that letter would. Without hesitation, a united cabinet, however, rejected his recommendations.' Interview with de Valera, 10 Sept. 1922, *Manchester Evening News*, typescript forwarded to McGarrity, McGarrity papers, MS 17,440; Longford and O'Neill (1970: 130).

[32] Quoted in Macardle (1968: 455).

[33] J. J. Walsh, first elected to Dail Eireann, 1918; voted for the Treaty; Minister for Posts and Telegraphs, 1922–7.

she claimed the Six Counties as a constitutional right . . . and did not want to be under the domination of the rest of Ireland whose sentiments, ideals and religion were different. They said they would not give away their established rights and that they were prepared to die for them. The question was how they were to deal with Ulster — peace or war conditions. At the present the Ministry proposed to act as they had done before under war conditions. He could not definitely say further than that their object at present was to get in contact to see what exactly Ulster wanted.

He added that if talks were agreed with the Ulster Unionists, Sinn Fein would be up against

a big difficulty. Ulster would say she was as devotedly attached to the Empire as they were to their independence and that she would fight for one as much as they would do for the other. In case of coercion she would get sympathy and help from her friends all over the world . . . *for his part, if the Republic were recognised, he would be in favour of giving each county power to vote itself out of the Republic if it so wished.* Otherwise they would be compelled to use force.

This speech was met with dissatisfaction, apprehension, and confusion: it won no support from the deputies who revealed a marked antipathy to the Ulster unionists. De Valera remained adamant: he lectured the Dail on the dangers of losing world sympathy if Britain were to argue that one third of the Irish people wanted the British connection and that if Britain left, Sinn Fein would 'smash the sentiments of the minority'. Lloyd George's propaganda, he predicted, would take the line that the Ulster Unionists

had been put into N. E. Ulster and those Sinn Feiners want to stamp upon these people and deprive them of their rights. These arguments he was putting before them were rather fallacious, but the fallacy was not recognised by those to whom they would be addressed. Hence he would like them to realise if they were determined that they would only make peace on the basis of the recognition of the Republic, they were going to face war and therefore he wanted to know . . . would the Dail be ready to take war.

A renewed war, if it came, would be a 'definite attempt at reconquest'; world opinion, he suggested, would be on Britain's side and, in any event, 'she would face the world's odium to crush Ireland to the earth.' Further, echoing Smuts's advice, he told the Dail that the 'building up of Irish unity' would be 'a slow process'.[34]

[34] DE: private session: 22 Aug. 1921, pp. 28-35. Italics added.

On the following day, Walsh, who had initially raised the issue, was granted time to further question de Valera on 'one matter which was agitating the minds' of some members: whether de Valera and his cabinet were 'prepared to consider such a proposal as would amount to a voting out of any county or part of a province of this country from the Free State.' De Valera refused to be 'fettered'; he had not his 'mind made up as to anything'. He insisted on defending what was the most heretical position for any Irish nationalist: that some partition of the island of Ireland could not be excluded. He insisted on freedom

to consider every method. For example, the question of voting out of counties or provinces. That would be a way, if that came up, a way in which a certain result could be obtained. I would be ready to consider that. We should be able to give our reasons. If we are not able to stand on these proposals by the reasons we give, then turn us out. But we must be free to consider and above suspicion to deal with every situation that arises.[35]

One 'certain result' of any county option arrangement would have been the gain by the south of at least Tyrone and Fermanagh at the north's expense. Some weeks earlier an informant of the southern Unionist leader, Lord Midleton, after a meeting with de Valera, believed that the Sinn Fein leadership was especially covetous of Tyrone and Fermanagh. But the suggestion of any transfer would, for obvious reasons, have to be mooted from London. If it were, Midleton was informed, there would be 'no more trouble'.[36]

(vi) THE TREATY NEGOTIATIONS: THE ULSTER DIMENSION

By late September Lloyd George and de Valera had agreed that conference, not correspondence was the most practical and hopeful way to an understanding. While still at the 'talks about talks' stage, a specialist Sinn Fein committee was established 'to collect, compile and arrange . . . statements of fact and argument bearing on the position of Ulster'. Along with collecting evidence to demonstrate the 'impracticability'

[35] Ibid., 23 Aug. 1921, pp. 58-9.
[36] A. Belton to Midleton, 2 Aug. 1921, Midleton papers, PRO 30/67/45. FitzAlan also noted the importance to Sinn Fein of Tyrone and Fermanagh, FitzAlan to Lloyd George, 18 Aug. 1921, Lloyd George papers, F/17/2/8.

of Partition, it was also enjoined to prepare 'the contrary case so far as ascertainable'. This may have been merely to understand the opposition's arguments, but it would also have the beneficial effect of reminding republican purists that any Sinn Fein leaders at the negotiating table had to reckon with the fact that Northern Ireland — with its own parliament, government, civil service, and local security forces — was now a *fait accompli*.

That the leadership was preparing its supporters for something less than a unitary separatist republic is clear from de Valera's statements throughout this year and from the most important of the Ulster Committee's terms of reference: these were to consider the 'effects of alternative future adjustments (i) in the case of the majority in a limited area making option to be excluded from the national government; (ii) in case of a majority making option to come under the National Government but to have some local legislative and administrative powers.'[37] That nationalists must abandon separatism, their hope of 'a clean cut in one shape or other', was a unionist precondition for some north–south relationship.[38] Covetous 'to get all the powers they could' Ulster Unionists were, at this juncture, more open-minded about some north–south relationship than was to be the case hereafter.[39]

Whereas Sinn Fein may have nursed hopes that economic coercion might prove effective against the northern unionists, there was a widespread appreciation of the fact that the military tactics which had been effective in the rest of the country, could not succeed in the north-east. Of the 72,000 men under arms, little more than 4,000 were based in the six counties.[40] The challenge which Ulster posed to the Sinn Fein cabinet was to devise a policy tolerable both to their own supporters and to the British government and which could also be imposed on the Ulster unionists. Given the entrenchment of the

[37] Childers papers, MS 7784/66/8; see also, John Bowman, 'Sinn Fein's perception of the Ulster Question: autumn 1921', *The Crane Bag*, 4, no. 2, pp. 50–6.

[38] Adam Duffin (NI civil servant) to his wife, 10 May 1921, Duffin papers, mic. 127.

[39] George Russell, 'Memorandum on Ulster and Irish Trade policy', record of three hours' talk with H. M. Pollock, J. M. Barbour, and A. Duffin, Oct. 1921, Childers papers, MS 7784/82/2-6; see also Seosamh de Cuipear, 'Financial and economic position of North East Ulster' (autumn 1921), ibid., MS 7784/73/1-17.

[40] Tabulated from Mulcahy papers, P7/A/32/10.

Unionist administration in Belfast, this would have to be some variant of federalism. Not only had de Valera prepared the ground on this since his return from America, but he had also been influenced by both Smuts and Erskine Childers[41] to seek some such solution. While Childers acknowledged that there was some support in Sinn Fein for the 'logically perfect' system of local autonomy to the north devolved from an all-Ireland parliament, he thought 'the advocates for centralization' were 'in the ascendant'. He advised de Valera that they should regard 'the quasi-federal policy as a temporary expedient and trust that before long the arguments for complete unity would triumph on their merits.'[42]

'Painstaking, methodical and brilliant', in de Valera's words,[43] Childers was a particular confidant of the Irish leader, who had brought him into the policital élite of Sinn Fein, included him at cabinet meetings, appointed him as Secretary to the Plenipotentiaries, and — most significantly for the purposes of this research — retrospectively credited him with greater perception on Ulster than he had himself.[44] The most revealing of Childers's writings on Ulster are the incomplete drafts of a paper entitled 'Ulster powers' which he was preparing in London during the course of the Treaty negotiations.

The memorandum first analyses the powers devolved to the Northern Ireland government under the 1920 Act. It then hypothetically considers the consequences for Ulster if the full Irish claim to independence were met by Britain. Childers envisages a subordinate Northern Ireland parliament with no

[41] Robert Erskine Childers (1870-1922), soldier, author, politician; clerk of House of Commons 1895-1910; participated in Howth gun-running 1914; settled in Dublin 1919; elected TD 1921; appointed Minister for Propaganda 1921; principal secretary to Irish delegation at Treaty negotiations; opposed Treaty, took republican side in Civil War, arrested, court-martialled, executed Nov. 1922. Indefatigable worker, confidant of de Valera.

[42] Childers, holograph draft rejecting British proposals of 20 July 1921, Childers papers, MS 7786/4/1.

[43] De Valera to Lord Longford, 25 and 27 Feb. 1963 (copy to Molly Childers), Childers papers, MS 7848/302/2-10. See also de Valera in Dail, DE: private session: 27 Aug. 1921, p. 86.

[44] In later years de Valera often acknowledged his indebtedness to Childers on the Ulster issue. Three of those interviewed by the author mentioned this point: political correspondent, Michael McInerney, secretary to the department of the Taoiseach, Maurice Moynihan, and de Valera's biographer, T. P. O'Neill.

provision for Ulster MPs at Westminster. 'But the question at once arises: Are there to be two or three Parliaments in Ireland?' Childers emphatically prefers two: 'This has been advocated as being the less likely to be permanent and as less complicated and costly.' The framework of the 1920 Act 'which is based on the three-Parliament idea, must be scrapped'. This would preclude Ulster representation at Westminster and also the notion of 'equal representation in any national body taking the place of the Council of Ireland.' Repeating his hypothesis of an independent Ireland with the three-parliament model rejected, he traces the main consequences of the two-parliament system. 'The most important result . . . would be that the "Ulster" Province would not have "security of tenure".' At this point in the *manuscript* draft Childers mentions some 'difficult legal questions' which should not be discussed in this memorandum, adding, 'but it is certain that a simple and literal transference of the reserved powers from Great Britain to a national Irish authority would make a "Ulster" Province a creature of the national authority.' This is scored through in the manuscript and is not included in the typescript version which concludes that Ulster's powers 'could be amended and the province itself be abolished by a simple Act of the All-Ireland Parliament.'

However Childers does not expect 'Ulster' to accept such a fate. '"Ulster" would stand out with reason for a secure status as well as the residuary powers (of government as envisaged in the 1920 Act). Under the two-Parliament system this would probably have to be given her by express provision making her powers and status unalterable except with the consent of her own legislature.' This draft memorandum apparently remained unfinished, being overtaken by events. It was presumably written with de Valera's known tolerances on the question firmly in mind and it may provide a clue to the latter's insistence in the difficult years immediately ahead that some interim, federal solution was the only practical policy on Ulster. Indeed, although popularly associated — and especially by his own followers — as the champion of what undoubtedly was his preferred solution, a united Ireland, de Valera was, throughout his career, to mull over some 'second-choice' policy similar to that discussed in Childers's memorandum: a federal solution, short of a unitary state and vague on whether it was a final or interim settlement.[45]

That de Valera envisaged an outcome from the Treaty negotiations which would fall short of his political ideal was well understood: his goal was to render any outcome *compatible with minimum republican claims* and to allow future generations to complete the work. In one of the many mooted drafts of a possible treaty which the delegates took with them to London, one clause in a draft by de Valera reads

At any time after the first day of January, 1950 [*sic*], the Parliament of Ireland or the Parliament of Great Britain may demand that negotiations be initiated for a revision of this Treaty; and, if, within two years of the date of the first such demand, a new Treaty shall not have been concluded, either the Parliament of Ireland or the Parliament of Great Britain may declare this Treaty to be annulled.[46]

Those republicans who were to reject the Treaty on the grounds that it envisaged less than a unitary, separatist republic often forgot that de Valera's cabinet in preparing their minimum claim for these negotiations had accepted that such an outcome was politically impossible. In particular, de Valera had been responsible for much of the small print in Sinn Fein's attempts to meet the conflicting requirements of their own supporters, the British government and the Ulster Unionists. That de Valera had offended some Ulster nationalists in the process is clear from the complaint of one Donegal TD who objected to de Valera's willingness to cede local autonomy to the Unionists. From them no 'tolerable modern government, or, indeed, any civilised' government at all could be expected: if the Unionists were to be given control of 'police, judiciary and things affecting life, liberty and civil rights (and Mr de Valera has declared he will give more) then we *cannot* submit and our grievance will be against Ireland generally for her desertion of her Highlanders.'[47]

The complex story of the negotiations themselves has

[45] Childers, memo '"Ulster powers" (not complete)', holograph and typescript versions, Childers papers, MS 7786/19/i+1-18.

[46] De Valera draft treaty, 7 Oct. 1921, Childers papers, MS 7785/4/8-13.

[47] J. E. O'Doherty, 'Memo on Partition as it affects the rights and interests of Ulster nationalists', copy in Childers papers, MS 7784/88/1-7.

already been documented in Longford's *Peace by ordeal.*[48] What is of relevance here is the role played by de Valera on the Ulster issue during the course of the negotiations. A central goal for Sinn Fein in their approach to this conference was to re-open the Ulster question. In this they were successful: matters which the Unionists insisted had been settled, became once more matters for negotiation. The Irish tactics were that if the negotiations were to fail, the break should come on Ulster. This was a shrewd ploy and showed an appreciation of what British ministers were saying privately: that as the six-county unit was 'illogical and indefensible', it would be the 'worst ground' on which to attempt to win a battle for public opinion.[49] It was left to Griffith[50] to prepare the Ulster clause in Sinn Fein's draft treaty which they took with them to London. The clause was, however, retained by de Valera for possible revision. Needed urgently in London shortly after the negotiations opened, de Valera forwarded it to Griffith with the comment that it had not 'been submitted to the Cabinet, but I do not anticipate any objection as to the principle — the phrasing is of course open to alteration. I have scarcely changed it at all as you notice.'[51]

As forwarded to London, the Ulster clause provided that all of the constituencies in the six counties or a 'smaller number contiguous and forming a territorially continuous group' could opt out of an All-Ireland parliament and 'be entitled to maintain a legislature' with powers identical to those already exercised by the Northern Ireland parliament. Further, it was envisaged that the MPs who currently went to Westminster would instead be members of an All-Ireland parliament. If, on the other hand, the constituencies opted to forgo their

---

[48] Lord Longford (Frank Pakenham), *Peace by ordeal* (London: 1972 edn.).

[49] Austen Chamberlain to Ivy Chamberlain, 31 Oct. 1921, Austen Chamberlain papers, AC6/1/441. Lloyd George made a similar point to Craig and his ministers at their meeting on 18 July 1921, PRONI CAB 4/3/1.

[50] Arthur Griffith (1871-1922), journalist, politician, nationalist propagandist; resigned presidency of Sinn Fein in de Valera's favour 1917; elected TD, 1918; Minister for Home Affairs and acting President of Dail Eireann, 1919; appointed leader of Irish representatives who negotiated the Treaty, Dec. 1921; President of the Dail in succession to de Valera after Treaty split; died suddenly Aug. 1921. An advocate of passive resistance to British rule in Ireland, he never supported a separatist Republic.

[51] De Valera to Griffith, 14 Oct. 1921, SPO DE 2/304/1.

option of local autonomy, Sinn Fein promised a commission 'to safeguard any lawful interests'.[52]

De Valera watched developments from Dublin but, as the correspondence between himself and Griffith reveals, he did not criticise any of the significant developments on Ulster, including the first mooting of the Boundary Commission.[53] It should be remembered here that Sinn Fein had good reason to believe in the early weeks of negotiation that what they considered their generous offer to Ulster would form the basis of British policy in any settlement. Ulster was not the principal difficulty between both sides. The information available to de Valera from Griffith, Michael Collins,[54] and Childers can fairly be interpreted as broadly reassuring on Sinn Fein's Ulster strategy. And this seems to have been de Valera's reading of it. When Griffith told him of Lloyd George's strategy of coercing Craig, de Valera replied that if a break had to come, it should be on Ulster 'provided we could so manage it that "Ulster" could not go out with the cry of "attachment to the Empire and loyalty to the Throne."' De Valera added that he was aware that the difficulty for the Irish negotiators was

to secure this without jeopardising our own fundamental position.

There can be no doubt whatever that the Delegation has managed to do this admirably, and if a break occurs at this stage, 'Ulster' will be crushed between the public opinion of both countries, as well as the public opinion of the world — if it counts for anything.

De Valera noted that all of this 'is shared by everyone here, so that we shall be quite unanimous on it.' Griffith would understand this to mean that the republican doctrinaires in

---

[52] Enclosed with ibid. The clause is reproduced in Appendix 1.

[53] The de Valera–Griffith correspondence is in SPO DE 2/304/1.

[54] Michael Collins (1890–1922), revolutionary leader; emigrated to London 1916 where he worked as a clerk; returned to participate in 1916 Rising; elected TD in 1918; Minister for Home Affairs, later Minister for Finance, director of organization and intelligence for Irish Volunteers; masterminded de Valera's escape from Lincoln Prison 1919; opposed de Valera's visit to America; on de Valera's return at Christmas 1920, Collins was the dominant figure in the political, military, and intelligence spheres; reluctant member of the Irish delegation at Treaty negotiations; believed signing it was equivalent to signing 'my death warrant'. Chairman Provisional Government to implement Treaty; in June 1922, on the outbreak of Civil War, became commander-in-chief of government forces; ambushed and assassinated, Aug. 1922. Whether as a conspirator, soldier, or politician, Collins demonstrated great energy, leadership, and organizing ability.

the cabinet, Austin Stack[55] and Cathal Brugha,[56] were acquiescing in the compromises already mooted by the Irish delegation in London. De Valera concluded his letter to Griffith with a warning to resist the temptation of making 'any further advances on our side' even though this would have the advantage of putting the Ulster Unionists 'more hopelessly in the wrong'.[57]

This letter crossed with another from Griffith outlining what Jones had called Lloyd George's 'second card against Craig if Craig refused to accept a subordinate Parliament.' This was to be a Boundary Commission to 'delimit the six-county area . . . so as to give us the districts in which we are a majority.' Lloyd George 'would give no further powers than what they possessed under the Partition Act to the area that remained obdurate after the Boundary Commission had completed its work'. However the area would have to 'bear itself its proportion of British Taxation'. Griffith agreed with Jones, his informant for all of this, that the Ulster cabinet would not accept such an offer.

> The move was a tactical one to deprive 'Ulster' of support in England by showing it was utterly unreasonable in insisting to coerce areas that wished to get out.
> He asked us would we stand behind such a proposal. We said that it would be their proposal — not ours, and we would not, therefore, be bound by it but we realised its value as a tactical manoeuvre and if Lloyd George made it we would not queer his position. He was satisfied with this.[58]

It is not within the scope of the present work to evaluate culpability on Griffith's part for any *naïveté* he may have shown regarding this proposal which, at the eleventh hour, Lloyd George was, so decisively, to exploit. What can be said of de Valera's approach is that his absence from the centre of

---

[55] Austin Stack (1880-1929), participated in 1916 Rising; elected TD in 1918; Minister for Home Affairs, 1919-21; declined to join Treaty delegation; opposed Treaty; an uncompromising republican, he remained in Sinn Fein in 1926, after de Valera split that party to found Fianna Fail.

[56] Cathal Brugha (1874-1922), born of Yorkshire immigrants to Ireland, he showed the zeal of the convert to Irish nationalism; elected TD 1918; Minister for Defence, 1919-21. With Stack, a republican diehard in de Valera's cabinet; opposed Treaty; a legendary fighter, killed in action on the outbreak of Civil War, July 1922.

[57] De Valera to Griffith, 9 Nov. 1921, SPO DE 2/304/1.

[58] Griffith to de Valera, 9 Nov. 1921, ibid.

the negotiations allowed misunderstandings to develop and while his presence in Dublin may have enabled him to get what he termed his 'left wing to come up', his 'right', he thought, 'deserted' him.[59] At the last full cabinet meeting held in Dublin on the Saturday before the fateful signing, de Valera objected to the British proposals on the grounds of the Oath and Partition. The official cabinet minute records: 'He personally could not subscribe to the Oath of Allegiance nor could he sign any document which would give N. E. Ulster power to vote itself out of the Irish State.'[60] Longford adds: 'He might understand Griffith giving up independence for National unity, but *"you have got neither this nor that"*.'[61] This seems to suggest a measure of flexibility greater than he was to show when the Treaty was signed. Childers's brief diary entry records that de Valera rejected the document because it was 'very like' that of 20 July: 'in addition to the fact that it gave up conditional character of the settlement (i.e. on Ulster's coming in) and contemplated partition at Ulster's choice. Dispute about this but there was no real doubt that it does so.'

Childers records that there was further discussion of the Ulster clauses later in the day: amendments were suggested but no definite record was made of them. The business was, as Childers recorded, 'too hurried',[62] as the delegates hastened to catch the night boat to return to London where in the early hours of the following Tuesday morning, they signed the Treaty which was to determine the subsequent course of Irish history, re-shaping Anglo-Irish relations, north-south relations, and creating a split in Sinn Fein which precipitated the Civil War and has since determined party cleavage in Irish politics.

(vii) THE TREATY DEBATE: THE ULSTER DIMENSION

On what grounds did de Valera reject the Treaty? Was it solely a question of principle or did tactical considerations complicate the issue? These are questions on which historians

---

[59] Childers, note of de Valera's phrase, 'Rough notes of Dail meetings, 16 Dec. 1921', Childers papers, MS 7804; see also DE: private session: 16 Dec. 1921, p. 192.
[60] Cabinet minutes, 3 Dec. 1921, SPO DE 1/3.
[61] Longford (1972: 209). (Emphasis added).
[62] Childers, diary 3 Dec. 1921, Childers papers, MS 7814.

have disagreed. That de Valera disliked the Treaty's provisions on Partition and allegiance is clear: so did its supporters including its signatories. What is at issue is whether either or both of these provisions was tolerable as the price to be paid for the establishment of the Irish Free State, which, its defenders argued, could be used as a 'stepping-stone' to undo these very aspects of the Treaty. To establish de Valera's position on these questions, concentration on his Ulster policy during these critical weeks is revealing. It seems clear that the proposition that de Valera would reject any agreement which contained *either* the Treaty's Ulster clauses *or* the Oath of Allegiance is no longer sustainable. However, once he had cast his cabinet vote against the London agreement, it was thereafter, perhaps inevitable, that he himself, his followers, and apologists would suggest that he was implacably opposed to the Treaty on *both* of these grounds.

New evidence from Childers's papers emphatically confirms what the analysis of de Valera's speeches throughout 1921 already suggests: that on the issue of allegiance and Partition, which were at the root of the Treaty divide, de Valera should be included among the pragmatists and not the doctrinaires. Childers, who was present at the decisive cabinet meeting on 8 December, noted in his diary: 'President talked at great length. Vehemently pressed to come into line he refused . . . Someone said (:) "*Supposing Ulster came in* on the treaty basis, would you agree to it?*"* he replied that that was the one consideration that might affect his judgement.' Childers added the comment: 'This surprised me.'[63] The clear implication here is that if Ulster were included de Valera would have considered accepting the Oath as worded in the Treaty. Moreover, many of those who had learnt de Valera's views at first hand before the Treaty divide, presumed him to be more moderate than his anti-Treaty stance now suggested.[64]

---

[63] Childers, diary 8 Dec. 1921, Childers papers, MS 7814. See also exchanges between Collins and Brugha, DE: private session, 16 Dec. 1921, pp. 188–9.

[64] Devoy to Cohalan, 9 Sept. 1920, Cohalan papers, MS 15,416(4); F. P. Walsh to Joseph Scott, 17 Jan. 1922, F. P. Walsh papers, box 112; Lloyd George to King, 14 and 21 July 1921, Lloyd George papers, F/29/4/57, 60; Belton to Midleton, 2 Aug. 1921, Midleton papers, PRO 30/67/45.

De Valera's pragmatic approach is also evident in his celebrated alternative to the Treaty — Document No. 2. In its
first draft, circulated to the Dail in private session before
Christmas,[65] de Valera included all the Ulster clauses of the
Treaty prefaced by a declaratory clause asserting the essential
unity of Ireland. At the end of four days of private debate de
Valera defended Document No. 2 as 'a Republican document
. . . as true to the Republic, every line of it, as any document
that I wrote to Lloyd George'. Originally put forward for
possible amendment, this, he said, had not been understood
by the Dail and he had now amended it himself. To a house
which he regretted was not 'more complete' — it was after
11 o'clock on Saturday night — he rather disarmingly said: 'I
have cut out the last clauses myself because I think that it is
very much better that we should make [sic] this question
and that we should simply say as regards Ulster that we offer
to meet them and so on.'[66]

This change entailed no less than the deletion of all of the
Treaty's Ulster clauses from his revise of Document No. 2
when it was eventually circulated in January. The changes so
enraged Griffith that he leaked both versions to the press
who did not share de Valera's verdict that it was merely 'a
slight change of form'.[67] In substitution for all the Ulster
clauses de Valera had expanded the extra 'essential unity'
declaration which had originally been included as a preface to
the Ulster clauses and which was now in the form of a resolution to be proposed to the Dail. While refusing to admit
Britain's *right* to interfere, or the North's *right* to 'be excluded
from the supreme authority of the Parliament of Ireland',
this resolution, to ensure internal peace and to demonstrate
that force was excluded, was prepared to grant to Northern

[65] Circulated to Dail in private session, 14 Dec. 1921; de Valera said: 'It is my
last effort and it is a poor one. It is only a bad best.' DE: private session, 14 Dec.
1921, p. 139. This volume, covering the private sessions of the second Dail,
1921-2, conveniently includes in Appendix 15 (pp. 311-5) the Treaty itself; in
Appendix 17 (pp. 317-20) de Valera's proposed Treaty presented to the Dail on
14 Dec., i.e. Document No. 2; and in Appendix 18 (pp. 321-4), 'The President's
alternative proposals', i.e. the revise of Document No. 2.

[66] DE: private session, 17 Dec. 1921, p. 272.

[67] DE: 5 Jan. 1922, p. 267; see also ibid., 4 Jan. 1922, pp. 258-9. For Griffith's
views, see ibid., 5 Jan. pp. 267-8 and 7 Jan. 1922, pp. 339-40.

Ireland 'privileges and safeguards' not less substantial than those in the Treaty.[68]

There can be little doubt, both at the time and retrospecively, that de Valera felt vulnerable about his handling of Ulster in the Treaty debates and in these documents. Longford and O'Neill in their biography fail to explain the genesis of these changes. They strike a somewhat apologetic note: 'De Valera explained in his speech that his proposals were tentative and designed to form the basis for a document on which they could all agree. They were far from perfect. He was not happy, for example, with the Ulster clauses as they stood.' His biographers add that when he came to explain the Ulster clauses to the Dail, 'he said they were engaged, not in a fight with Ulster, but in a fight with Britain.' He was prepared to grant the north all the rights she received in the Treaty, so long as there was 'a declaratory clause which safeguarded the supreme authority of the Dail over the whole national territory . . . later he amended the Ulster proposals; the basic ideas remained, however, the same.'[69]

Once the first draft of Document No. 2 was circulated, de Valera must have been aware that his critics were not confined to Treaty supporters: the inclusion of the Ulster clauses presumably astonished MacEntee if one is to judge by the powerful — and in many important respects, prophetic — denunciation he was shortly to make of the very clauses to the Dail.[70] De Valera's solution, the omission of the clauses from his second version, was probably the only possible way out of this dilemma: whether this was on his own initiative, or at Childers's prompting,[71] or for another reason, is not clear. In the event, Document No. 2 was never formally put to the Dail: the Treaty was passed, de Valera resigned the Presidency and became the figure around which 'an opposition' party formed.

[68] 'Addendum: North East Ulster', in de Valera's revise of Document No. 2, cited in note 65 above.
[69] Longford and O'Neill (1970: 172-80). See also de Valera's explanation to the Dail, private session, 15 Dec., pp. 149-54, and public sessions 19 and 20 Dec. 1921, pp. 19, 68.
[70] DE: public session: 22 Dec. 1921, pp. 152-8; see also his contribution in private session, 16 Dec. 1921, pp. 200-1. Retrospectively, MacEntee approved of Document No. 2, interview with author.
[71] The *Freeman's Journal* suggested that Document No. 3 — as they termed it — was 'largely the work' of Childers: editorial 5 Jan. 1922.

At one point in the Dail debate de Valera had described Document No. 2 — the first draft — as 'a sort of document we would have tried to get and would not have agreed if we did not get.'[72] The implication was that if it did not prove useful in re-uniting the Dail, he did not feel bound by its compromises. Initially, he resented its publication. It was intolerable that 'the working of one's mind' was 'shown to those with whom we are dealing'.[73] Once public, it became the stuff of pamphlets — from both sides: Treaty supporters used it to remind de Valera that he had once been realistic on the Ulster question; and he himself, as will be seen, may have subsequently found it useful when attempting to maintain some moderation amongst his followers in their policy towards Ulster unionism.[74] With hindsight de Valera could be analytical of what had happened to the Ulster issue during the Treaty period. In 1963, writing to Lord Longford,[75] he justified his record in some detail. He had wanted all documents 'carefully examined' in Dublin 'by legal experts who would themselves not have taken any part in the discussions out of which the documents arose.' This was to avoid the danger

that those involved in the discussions would give to the words and phrases used in any document arising out of them, such special and limited meaning as might have occurred or been attached to these words and phrases in the discussions themselves. . .

Had, for example, this precaution for which I was providing been taken with the Treaty Articles, and were they submitted to lawyers unprejudiced by the discussions, the trap in Article 12 would, I am sure, have been noticed — the trap by which the qualifying phrase 'so far as may be compatible with economic and geographic conditions' was used ultimately to nullify, as a whole, the provision 'in accordance with the wishes of the inhabitants.'[76]

[72] DE: public session: 19 Dec. 1921, p. 25.

[73] Ibid., 5 Jan. 1922, p. 267.

[74] For sympathetic commentaries on Document No. 2, see Erskine Childers, *Clause by Clause: a comparison between 'The Treaty' and Document No. 2* (Dublin: n.d. [1923]); Eamon de Valera, *The Alternative to 'The Treaty': 'Document No. 2'* (Dublin, 1923).

[75] Lord Longford (Frank Pakenham), born 1905; Anglo-Irish politician, banker, publisher, historian; convert to catholicism, socialism, and Irish nationalism; confidant of de Valera; author of definitive history of the Anglo-Irish Treaty of 1921, *Peace by ordeal*, first published in 1935; member of British Labour government, 1948-51; with T. P. O'Neill, joint author of *Eamon de Valera* (London, 1970), written with the subject's co-operation.

[76] De Valera to Longford, 25, 27 Feb. 1963, Childers papers, MS 7848/302/2-10.

This letter to his friend, biographer-to-be, and author of the definitive work on the Treaty itself, is typical of de Valera's sense of self-justification. But it sits unhappily with the record of his own handling of the Ulster issue during the Treaty period. Himself aloof from the discussions, de Valera failed throughout the controversy on the Treaty, to mention 'the trap' in the Boundary Commission clause; indeed, he included it verbatim in his first draft of Document No. 2. It might be argued in de Valera's defence that his point to Longford concerns the scrutiny of the clause before it was signed in London, but this scarcely explains de Valera's subsequent silence on it. Instead, evidence points to a general lack of authority on de Valera's part during this crisis. Against the calm appraisal of his letter to Longford, one must place his confused handling of the Ulster dimension at the Treaty inquest and his indecision at the crucial cabinet meetings of 3 and 8 December. Indeed at this latter meeting when the split became irrevocable, his own 'republican' representative on the Treaty delegation, Robert Barton,[77] criticized de Valera for not himself going to London. Childers's diary records that Barton 'strongly reproached President. Said it [presumably the split] was due to his "vacillations" from beginning.'[78]

(viii) PEACE? JANUARY–JUNE 1922

Although his opponents branded him as a fomentor of civil war — and some of his more bellicose speeches left him vulnerable to such a charge — de Valera's explanation was that his words represented prophecy rather than incitement.[79] It should also be borne in mind that where others had rejected

[77] Robert C. Barton (1881-1975), large landowner, commissioned in the Dublin Fusiliers in 1914 and stationed in Dublin during 1916 Rising. Resigned from British army and joined republican movement; elected to Dail in 1918; Minister for Agriculture, and later Minister for Economic Affairs; a member of the Treaty delegation, he reluctantly signed the Treaty 'as the lesser of two outrages'; cast his cabinet and Dail vote for the Treaty but thereafter supported de Valera; retired from politics 1922. A cousin of Childers.
[78] Childers, diary 8 Dec. 1921, Childers papers, MS 7814.
[79] See de Valera's speech 'Danger of Civil War', 18 March 1922 in De Valera: speeches: 1980: 103-4. For commentaries sympathetic to de Valera see Maurice Moynihan's introductory notes, ibid., 97-103, and Longford and O'Neill (1970: 185).

the Treaty *simpliciter*, he had agonized over his stance and its implications. Charged by Barton with vacillating during the negotiations, his subsequent attempts to reconcile the Treaty with the Republic had damaged his credibility with the doctrinaires.[80] It was clearly the nadir of his political career. He was without executive power, and his authority as 'opposition leader' was ebbing away to the military wing of the republicans, who according to his biographers, felt 'complete indifference' to his views; he was 'in a nightmarish position, with little influence on events'.[81]

Although, in private, the British correctly identified de Valera as among the more moderate of those opposed to the Treaty,[82] Churchill[83] publicly blamed him in the Commons for fomenting sectarian violence in the north[84] and told a delegation of Belfast Catholics that they were 'being tortured' by de Valera.[85] He described him to Collins as a man who might gradually come 'to personify not a cause but a catastrophe'.[86] The British now believed that political stability, if it were to be attained in Ireland, could only come through an understanding between Collins and Craig. The most serious threat to any such north-south understanding was the continuing harassment of the northern nationalists — a factor which tended to unite Collins with de Valera.[87] Both factions in Sinn Fein were being advised by groups of northern nationalists and both had been represented at a special meeting in

[80] McCartan to Maloney, 25 Mar. (1923), Maloney papers, box 21. Incorrectly filed as 25 Mar. 1925 in New York Public Library.

[81] Longford and O'Neill (1970: 187).

[82] Churchill's view, see PRO CAB 43/1/22/N/148/1-5, 23 May 1922.

[83] W. S. Churchill (1874-1965), MP 1900-22, 1924-64; Prime Minister, 1940-5, 1951-5; a signatory of Anglo-Irish Treaty, 1921, his marked antipathy for de Valera dated from the latter's rejection of it; supporter of Ulster Unionism; vehemently opposed Anglo-Irish agreement, 1938 and Irish neutrality, 1939-45.

[84] On 26 June 1922, quoted Gilbert (1975: 735-6).

[85] Ibid., p. 726.   [86] Ibid., p. 708.

[87] Concern that the northern nationalists would be subjected to further pogroms was widespread among southern nationalists: Mulcahy to MacSwiney, 29 Mar. (1922), MacSwiney papers, P48/D/18; anon. 'Events in connection with IRA leading up to attack on Four Courts', n.d. ibid., P48/D/13; Eoin MacNeill, 'Memoir' excerpt, in Michael Tierney, *Eoin MacNeill: scholar and man of action: 1867-1945* (Oxford: 1980), pp. 287-8.

Belfast in early March, de Valera himself attending.[88] Doubtless, in these contacts, de Valera was told of the deep misgivings in these circles concerning southern divisions over the
Treaty.

Collins emphasized another benefit if the south could speak
with 'one voice'. On 2 April he appealed to 'de Valera and his
friends' for southern unity which might give his recent pact
with Craig some chance of replacing suspicion with tolerance
and understanding.[89] But to de Valera, the pact with Craig, in
the light of the continuing pogroms against northern Catholics,
amounted to appeasement. Critical and distrustful of the
northern government and security forces, he was not even
surprised by an alarming rumour detailed to him by the Provisional Government's representative in London, Art O'Brien.
On 6 April, O'Brien forwarded to de Valera — 'to you privately'
— a copy of his report to the Provisional Government outlining
a British political plot about which he had heard from 'a very
reliable informant . . . in the English Government service.'[90]
Its relevance rests not on its veracity but on the fact that to
the necessarily suspicious leaders of both factions in Dublin,
it was not implausible.

Sir Henry Wilson[91] is to act in Ulster with Sir James Craig. The Conservative element of the Coalition is to get rid of Lloyd George as Premier
at any cost. They anticipate being able to get Cabinet control. When they
have gained this object, civil war will break out in Ulster, (preparations for
same being now well in hand,) and to re-establish what is considered
English prestige the reconquest of Ireland will be effected, troops being
kept largely in Ulster, and will later find it necessary to go over the border.
The conversation ended with a laugh from one member of the group, who
stated that they would exterminate the swine this time for good. Further
details can be given to you, personally, at some future time.[92]

---

[88] Provisional Government minutes, 8 Mar. 1922, SPO G1/1. De Valera was
also present at a similar meeting in Derry, Minutes, Six County Advisory Committee, 5 Apr. [1922], PROI 1094/1/17.

[89] *The Times*, 3 Apr. 1922.

[90] O'Brien's sympathies were anti-Treaty but he had yet to be dismissed from
his London post by the pro-Treaty faction.

[91] Field-Marshal Sir Henry Wilson (1864–1922), southern Irish Unionist;
protégé of Lloyd George and his military adviser in First World War; Chief of
Imperial General Staff, 1918; approved policy of repression in Ireland, 1920;
condemned Treaty negotiations as appeasement; appointed military adviser to
Northern Irish government; assassinated by IRA in London, June 1922.

[92] Art O'Brien to de Valera, 6 Apr. 1922, Art O'Brien papers, MS 8424(6).

De Valera replied by return: 'As regards the "political plot" memo, the danger which it foreshadows has already been noticed by us, but it is extremely difficult to find a suitable counter.'[93] De Valera was grateful to have received the information, asked to be kept informed of 'anything of this sort that comes to your notice', and was told by O'Brien on 19 May that on information from British informants, this particular danger had receded.[94]

The Ulster unionists meanwhile feared that a British withdrawal from the south would inevitably encourage the IRA to use it as a base for a guerrilla campaign against Northern Ireland.[95] Although there were some Volunteers who supported such a strategy this was a minority view both because the IRA within the north was poorly armed and seriously outnumbered and because the military context so differed from the recent experience in the south.[96]

It was largely the desperation felt by Sinn Fein supporters in the north which proved to be the catalyst for the temporary *rapprochement* between de Valera and Collins during the spring of 1922. One of the IRA's northern leaders, Frank Aiken,[97] was one of those who were instrumental in impressing on de Valera and Collins what the consequences of a division in the south might be for 'the nation and for Ulster':[98] it would lead, they warned, to the entrenchment of the northern government, 'permanent partition' and the exposure of 'the Catholic and nationalist population' to an element 'only

---

[93] De Valera to O'Brien, 8 Apr. 1922, ibid.

[94] O'Brien to de Valera, 19 May 1922, ibid.

[95] Patrick Buckland, *The factory of grievances* (Dublin: 1979), ch. 8.

[96] See reports on IRA strength in Belfast, especially for July 1922, Mulcahy papers, P7/B/77/1-24 *passim*.

[97] Frank Aiken (b. 1898), native of south Armagh; commandant Fourth Northern Division, IRA, 1921; succeeded Liam Lynch as chief of staff, IRA, at end of Civil War; thereafter considered a hawk on Partition question by Free State army intelligence; very important recruit to Fianna Fail in 1926 as other IRA members followed; appointed Minister for Defence in 1932 in charge of an army which had defeated his own in 1923; member of all Fianna Fail cabinets, 1932-69; TD for Louth, 1923-73; dove during arms crisis which divided Fianna Fail on northern issue 1970; Longford and O'Neill suggest that Aiken 'might be thought of as de Valera's closest friend' (p. 463).

[98] Interview, Frank Aiken.

thirsting to proceed with [their] extermination'.[99] Emphasizing these dangers, the northern delegation helped to close Sinn Fein's ranks through the Collins–de Valera pact which so angered Belfast and London: on 30 May Churchill told the cabinet that Craig 'blamed the supporters of de Valera' for upsetting his agreement with Collins, and that Collins had 'admitted this'.[1]

Attempts by the pro- and anti-Treaty factions to avoid an irrevocable split continued into May. A Committee of Ten, drawn from each side held a series of meetings; among the points of disagreement — Collins believed it was a deliberate ploy to wreck the Treaty — was de Valera's insistence that members for northern constituencies should be free to take their seats in the Dail.[2] There was not necessarily a conflict between this proposal and de Valera's public reiteration the following week of his idea of a local parliament for the north-east. The two ideas were compatible if the northern representatives he envisaged as attending the Dail were to be elected for nationalist areas contiguous to the twenty-six counties while his proposal for 'the largest measure of autonomy' for Ulster would be confined to the unionists' core-area. Interviewed by the international press, he did not specify what area of Ulster should receive devolved powers, but he clearly excluded those border areas with nationalist majorities, when emphasizing that he was against what he termed 'his own people' being coerced.[3]

The subsequent attempts by both factions in Sinn Fein to draft a constitution somehow compatible both with the Treaty and with external association proved abortive. In their joint draft they excluded the Oath, went beyond the already agreed Dominion status, and sought to undermine Northern Ireland's constitutional position.[4] London had no intention of thus accommodating de Valera. The pact, in time, failed to halt

[99] Aiken *et al.*, to Griffith, de Valera, Collins, Brugha, Mulcahy, O'Connor, Lynch, and O'Duffy, on 'six county position in the present national crisis', Mulcahy papers, P7/A/145.

[1] Gilbert (1975: 718-9).

[2] Committee of Ten, 19 May 1922, Mulcahy papers, P7/A/145.

[3] *The Times*, 26 May 1922.

[4] Jones to Hankey, 28 Apr. 1922, quoted Jones (1971: 198-9); see also Collins to Duggan, memo 4 May 1922, Hugh Kennedy papers, P4/E/1.

the slide into civil war in which both sides were engaged by the end of June. The outbreak of hostilities brought to an end whatever influence on the Provisional Government's northern policy may have been due to sensitivity to republican criticism. That that policy had been 'really, though not ostensibly, dictated by Irregulars' was claimed by Kevin O'Higgins[5] in an analytical, revealing, and probably influential, memorandum to his colleagues on 9 August. He advocated a new policy to take account of the changed circumstances of the Civil War: in 'scrapping' the republicans' northern policy, 'we shall be taking the wise course of attacking them all along the line.' Implicit in O'Higgins's detailed advice is the assumption that before the Civil War had commenced in the south, the Provisional Government would have felt unable to fully espouse the northern policies he was now advocating: the 'full acceptance of the Treaty' and the abandonment of all coercive measures against the north, whether of a military or economic character, as well as 'all kinds of minor nagging'.

The only prospect for unity, he argued, was for the south to show a 'friendly and pacific disposition towards the Northern government and people while letting them come up against the full economic logic of Partition.' He also expected through the proposed Boundary Commission that the Free State would gain two and a half counties; he believed, as he wrote, in getting 'the last tittle' out of the Treaty. O'Higgins also held that what he termed 'the outrage propaganda' concerning the six counties, no matter how justified, should be abandoned, as it served only to 'make certain of our people see red which will never do us any good.' He concluded by admitting that his proposed peaceful policy would be vulnerable to the criticism that it allowed 'the Pogromists to have their own way unhindered'. The government's reply should be that the belligerent policy had proved 'useless for protecting the Catholics'; this peaceful policy might, of course, fail; but, at least, 'it has a chance, where the other has no chance.'[6]

[5] Kevin O'Higgins (1892-1927), elected to Dail 1918; assistant Minister for Local Government; strong supporter of Treaty; later Minister for Economic Affairs, Justice, and External Affairs; vice president of the Executive Council; critical of southern *naïveté* on strategy for Irish unity; assassinated, June 1927.

[6] O'Higgins, memo 'Policy in regard to the North East', 9 Aug. 1922, Blythe papers, P24/70.

What distinguished this memorandum — and it was a distinction rarely found in southern approaches to the Ulster issue — was a sense of realism: the policy being advocated considered seriously the obstacles to its attainment. As was clear from the policy he had advocated since his return from America, de Valera was also a comparative realist on the north. But he was also capable of lapsing into a more traditional, sentimental, rhetoric which managed to ignore Ulster's very existence, her obduracy in the face of the republic, her inconvenient insistence on her own sense of identity, and her capacity and will to resist absorption by the south. In his message to mark the sixth anniversary of the 1916 Rising, he called on the nation's youth to

hold steadily on. Those who with cries of woe and lamentation would involve you in a disastrous rout you will soon see rally behind you, and vie with you for first place in the vanguard. Beyond all telling is the destiny God has in mind for Ireland, the fair, the peerless one. You are the artificers of that destiny . . . the goal is at last in sight. Steady, all together, forward, Ireland is yours for the taking. Take it.

The Dublin correspondent of *The Times* noted drily that 'the rhetorical character' of de Valera's style did not conceal 'the vagueness of his policy. He advises the young men to take Ireland but does not suggest how the six north-eastern counties are to be brought into his scheme of things.'[7] Although this rebuke was deserved, it ignored the other side of de Valera's character, the pragmatic realist who alone among opponents of the Treaty had expounded and defended a policy of compromise on Ulster — and this in the midst of his colleagues' passionate espousal of the separatist, united Republic. But having determined his concessions and felt the brunt of his colleagues' misgivings, de Valera was then, it seems, impervious to further change. Tim Healy,[8] presently to be the Free State's first Governor-General, met him secretly in March 1922 and found him 'inexorable and infallible' in refusing to adopt a more conciliatory line on Ulster: ''Twas like whistling jigs to milestones.'[9]

[7] *The Times*, 17 Apr. 1922.
[8] Tim Healy (1855-1931), nationalist MP, 1880-1918; Governor-General of Irish Free State, 1922-8.
[9] Tim Healy to William O'Brien (MP), 3 May 1922, 2 Mar. 1926, both letters

(ix) CIVIL WAR

De Valera himself and his apologists have always exonerated
him from responsibility for the Civil War; in contrast, his
political opponents have exaggerated whatever measure of
responsibility may be rightly his.[10] Decades of claim and
counter-claim, across the floor of the Dail and at chapel-gate
meetings throughout the country, have not helped to sort fact
from myth. The antipathy of the national press to the anti-
Treaty side, combined with the tendency of foreign observers
to oversimplify the issue into one of the government versus
de Valera, has further distorted his role. In particular, those
who were optimistic about the Treaty's prospects for ending
Partition, insisted on his culpability, for fomenting a civil war
whose effects on Ulster unionist opinion they reckoned as
incalculably damaging. Ulster unionists, for their part, with
little concern for the complex details of the war, but a vital
interest in the result, easily accepted any anti-de Valera
propaganda to which they were exposed.

Evidence from his colleagues on the anti-Treaty side
suggests that once his efforts to avert it had failed, de Valera
was an extremely reluctant participant in the war. On 12 July,
two weeks after the Republicans' Four Courts garrison had
been routed, Erskine Childers confided his misgivings about
de Valera's leadership in a letter to his wife.

Dev, I think, has collapsed . . . Frank [?Gallagher][11] and I furious and

referring to a meeting with de Valera in March 1922, William O'Brien papers, MS
8556(29), (31).

[10] Conscious attempts to exaggerate de Valera's culpability are manifest in the
file covering his arrest and imprisonment in 1923, SPO S 1369/15; see also O'Duffy
to Executive Council, 5 July 1924, Blythe papers, P24/233; file, 'Messrs de Valera
and Stack: imprisonment: 1923-4', SPO S 1369/15, *passim*; Intelligence file,
'De Valera: newspaper cuttings and press reports', 25 July 1922-1925, Desmond
FitzGerald papers.

[11] Frank Gallagher (1898-1962), journalist, historian; worked as publicist
with Erskine Childers from 1919, editing *Irish Bulletin*; took anti-Treaty side in
Civil War; confidant and supporter of de Valera; first editor *Irish Press* 1931;
appointed deputy director Radio Eireann, 1936; director Government Information
Bureau, 1939-48. 1951-4; author of *The indivisible island: the history of the
partition of Ireland*, a tract against Partition published by Gollancz in 1957 but
secretly funded by all-party Mansion House Committee as part of their anti-
Partition campaign; an early draft of a de Valera biography is included in his
papers in the National Library of Ireland.

fear general cave in. Trying to get them to form a normal government. At least act strongly. No one leader alas! There is a truce in one district already but details very vague. Dev. says we 'should surrender while we are strong', I believe. Have not seen him.[12]

Three months later Free State army intelligence received information that de Valera's status with the Irregulars had been eroded by further unsuccessful peace initiatives.[13] Nor was de Valera inciting republicans north of the border to become involved in military activities: rather, he advised them to concentrate on 'civil organization without further delay'.[14] In a letter to Joseph McGarrity, he confided that he was 'almost wishing [he] were deposed' because he was obliged to take responsibility for a programme which was not his own. 'The programme "Revise the Treaty" would be mine and I could throw myself into it heart and soul. I am convinced it is the only way for the present to keep the Republican idea alive.' Yet again he defends the terms of Document No. 2: it represented 'the farthest possible that Republicans could go to meet the claims of England and the North without sacrificing the Republic.' He hypothesized about possible victory for the Free State and the political course which he would then follow: it is a remarkable prophecy of what was to be the course of Fianna Fail's subsequent policy under his leadership. De Valera saw 'no programme by which we can secure independence but a revival of the Sinn Fein idea in a new form. Ignoring England. Acting in Ireland as if there was no such person as the English King, no Governor-General, no Treaty, no oath of Allegiance.' This, as de Valera explicitly claimed, amounted to 'acting as if Document No. 2 were the Treaty.' Later, he assured McGarrity, they could act with still more

[12] Erskine to Molly Childers, 12 July 1922, Childers papers 7855/1269; see also tone of de Valera's last letter to Cathal Brugha, 6 July 1922, MacSwiney papers, P48/B/41. Longford and O'Neill, while emphasizing de Valera's despair on the outbreak of Civil War, claim that he 'plunged wholeheartedly into the war'. Longford and O'Neill (1970: 197).

[13] Wireless message from intelligence officer, 2nd Southern Command to GHQ, 9 Oct. 1922 (stolen and now in) O'Malley papers, P17/F/38; also, copy, extract, Maurice Healy to Tim Healy, sent 19 Oct. 1922 to Director of Intelligence, suggesting that when de Valera proposed that arms be laid down, he was outvoted on Lynch's motion and told that 'henceforth E[rskine] C[hilders] as their leader.' ibid.

[14] De Valera quoted by P. O'R. to E/D, 27 Dec. 1922, PROI 1094/2/1.

independence. 'Whilst the Free state were in supposed existence [sic] would be the best time to secure the unity of the
country. That is my one hope out of the situation. If we can
get a single state for the whole of the country, then the future
is safe.'[15]

However for McGarrity, Document No. 2 was an unacceptable 'starting point'. He replied to de Valera that 'As a united
Ireland is essential, your minimum must include that — a
united Ireland. By that I mean all of Ulster in [,] with the
same rights and privileges as any other part — nothing more,
nothing less.'[16]

Despite such criticism and a propaganda campaign launched
by the Free State government based on the compromises of
Document No. 2, de Valera persisted in publicly defending its
terms. In a personal rebuke, the IRA's leader, Liam Lynch,[17]
complained that de Valera's move had had 'a very bad effect'
on the morale of his men because generally 'they do not
understand such documents.' De Valera, in his reply to
Lynch, refused to apologize for what he considered a realistic
political programme and threatened to resign rather than be
expected to account for what he had to say 'to people who
have not given a moment's thought to the whole question.'[18]

As the republicans' military position became weaker, de
Valera's criticisms of the efficacy of military opposition to
the Free State, finally made some impression on Lynch.
After a clandestine conference with the IRA generals, Lynch
asked de Valera how he thought the 1916 signatory, Tom
Clarke, would regard the understanding they had reached.

[15] De Valera to McGarrity, 10 Sept. 1922, McGarrity papers, MS 17,440.
Joseph McGarrity (1874-1940), revolutionary; born in Co. Tyrone, emigrated to
Philadelphia at 16; devoted his life to aiding physical force republicanism in Ireland;
sided with de Valera in 1919-20 when other Irish-American leaders censured de
Valera; believed de Valera the greatest Irishman of his generation and was willing
to give his constitutional methods conditional support in 1920s; McGarrity finally
broke with de Valera in 1933 when IRA members were gaoled; believed in 'the
fanatical thing' and masterminded and funded the IRA's bombing campaign in
Britain in 1939; willing to enlist Nazis' help, 1939-40; died August 1940.
[16] McGarrity to de Valera, 27 Sept. 1922, ibid.
[17] Liam Lynch (1890-1923), soldier, prominent in War of Independence,
1919-21; chief of staff, IRA in Civil War; reluctant to accept hopelessness of
republican position in spring, 1923; killed April 1923.
[18] Lynch to de Valera, 28 Feb. and reply 27 Mar. 1923, quoted Longford and
O'Neill (1970: 215-6).

De Valera suggested that the question was irrelevant; they were the living Irish generation and had to make their own decisions.[19] Consistently such evidence accumulates attesting to de Valera's pragmatism. Above all, although no pacifist, he had shown himself pacific when confronted with the formidable odds which he could now see were arraigned against the Republic: the war-weariness of the general population, the military superiority of the Free State, and the persistent intransigence of the north; nor could British re-intervention be ruled out in the event of a republican victory over Free State forces.

Notwithstanding Cumann na nGaedhael's portrayal of him as a war-lord, the historical evidence attesting to de Valera's pacific role within republican circles is overwhelming. In addition to the evidence, already cited, of his efforts to avert, deflect, and then to end the Civil War, his correspondence with the Clan na Gael organizer in Philadelphia, Joseph McGarrity, also suggests that consistently de Valera's strategy was to subvert the militarists and focus republican attention on a realistic discussion of the best means to undo the Treaty settlement.[20]

(x) POLITICS: WAR BY OTHER MEANS: 1923-5

The Civil War may have ended with the military defeat of the republicans: but, at its close, they had been persuaded to accept, not a surrender, but a ceasefire.[21] De Valera's efforts to convince the defeated republicans that they should become political, rather than military, opportunists was not helped by his internment for twelve months by the Free State authorities following his arrest in August 1923.[22] In the absence of his moderating presence, considerable attention was paid — if Free State army intelligence reports are any

[19] Frank Gallagher, 'De Valera', typescript, Gallagher papers, MS 18,375(6). Tom Clarke (1857-1916), revolutionary; oldest of executed 1916 leaders and symbol of continuity of republican movement.
[20] See n. 81, p. 105 below. See also series of memoranda, de Valera to A.L., 16 May-11 June, 1923, PROI, 1094/8/1-9 *passim*.
[21] Lyons (1971: 462); Longford and O'Neill (1970: 222-3); see also Aiken's statement in Sinn Fein's *Daily Sheet*, 24 May 1923, Mulcahy papers, P7/B/229/159.
[22] T. P. O'Neill, 'In search of a political path: Irish Republicanism, 1922-1927', *Historical Studies*: X, G. A. Hayes-McCoy (ed.), (Dublin: 1976), pp. 156-8.

guide — to the possibility of attacking the north. By May 1924, Eoin O'Duffy,[23] in collating this intelligence material for the cabinet, reported that there was 'no doubt that Aiken was strongly in favour of such a move';[24] it had been brought before the republican 'cabinet' with Aiken present: 'The whole question was gone into very minutely and after a lengthy and heated discussion, Aiken was turned down on the grounds that his scheme was impracticable and impossible.'[25] That there was still a lobby for a campaign of force against the north was understood by the Cosgrave[26] government.[27] Another concern was that any error in their policy towards the boundary controversy might result in political gains for de Valera. On this point, though, they were willing to use the prospect of their replacement by a 'strong Die-hard Government', as leverage to win a sympathetic hearing in London.[28]

Such was the political context in which de Valera found himself when he was released from gaol in July 1924. Within Republican circles he found that less conciliatory voices than his own had prevailed in his absence.[29] His comparative moderation was again clear when, attending the first clandestine meeting of republican deputies since his release, he was questioned about policy towards Ulster. If deputies were hoping that he had abandoned his pre-Civil War stance, they were to be disappointed. He defended his earlier policy that the Treaty's Ulster provisions should be fulfilled. Although the record does not make his meaning explicit clear, he seems to be suggesting that as the boundary clauses were

[23] Eoin O'Duffy, although a hawk on the Ulster question, he supported the Treaty; first police commissioner, Irish Free State; collated intelligence reports to Cosgrave government; dismissed by de Valera, 1933.

[24] For O'Duffy's own views of using force against northern unionists see the Treaty debates, DE: public session: 4 Jan. 1922, pp. 224-7.

[25] O'Duffy to Executive Council, 29 May 1924, O'Malley papers, P17/F/49.

[26] W. T. Cosgrave (1880-1965), participated 1916 Rising; TD 1918-45; Minister for Local Government in de Valera's pre-Treaty cabinet; supported Treaty; after deaths of Griffith and Collins assumed leadership of those supporting Treaty; President Executive Council (Prime Minister) Irish Free State, 1922-32; lost power to de Valera's Fianna Fail 1932; leader of the opposition until retirement, 1945. Boasted 1940 that he had not spoken privately to de Valera since Treaty split.

[27] O'Duffy to Executive Council, 30 Sept. 1924, O'Malley papers, P17/F/49.

[28] Kevin O'Shiel to cabinet (Nov. 1922), Mulcahy papers, P7/B/288.

[29] Longford and O'Neill (1970: 235).

'ridiculous', their inherent contradictions would be manifest if they were acted upon. It is clear that he believed time favoured the Republicans; and among the issues which would, eventually, justify their opposition to the Treaty would be the boundary question: 'The object of the Free State was to make it appear that we by our opposition had smashed the possibility of the North coming in. We will have to be very careful as to that. The Ulster problem will remain for us and it will be a very difficult problem.'

Yet again he invoked the 1921 republican cabinet's imprimatur for the notion of local autonomy for the north-east. They were, he insisted, not admitting the Ulster unionists' right to a local parliament but offering it as a concession. If it were refused, Sinn Fein would feel free to withdraw the offer. Moreover, the parliament in Belfast would be 'subordinate' and its jurisdiction would be confined to 'those areas where the people would vote definitely for such a parliament'. Even this circumscribed offer was unacceptable to MacEntee who bluntly expressed the hope that 'we were not going to commit ourselves to a settlement of the Northern question as outlined in Document No. 2. The people in the North could not see how it was going to be settled on that basis.' Indeed they considered Document No. 2 as 'being no better' than the Treaty. 'Heart and confidence would have to be restored to these people. There ought to be issued a strong unequivocal declaration that Republicans would not accept any solution based on Partition.' Obviously stung by MacEntee's characterization of his policy as partitionist, de Valera denied that there was anything in Document No. 2 'which was contrary in any sense to our position as the established government of the Republic. The two fundamentals were the unity and sovereignty of the nation and these he would always endeavour to get.'[30]

This exchange revealed the embarrassment and controversy which still rankled among republicans over Document No. 2. MacEntee's argument on this occasion, for instance, implicitly denies the claim of the Sinn Fein election leaflet in 1923,

---

[30] Minutes of *Comhairle na dTeachtai* (clandestine meeting of abstentionist, republican, elected representatives), 7 Aug. 1924, MacSwiney papers, P48/C/8.

which had insisted that Document No. 2 made 'no recognition of the Partition of Ireland'.[31]

Free State publicists were well aware of these differences within Sinn Fein. They had been manifest since the initial publication of Document No. 2 with its inclusion of all the Treaty's Ulster clauses, and de Valera's revised version in which he deleted them and substituted an addendum covering the Ulster question. In October 1924, when de Valera had already made the boundary issue a theme in his political speeches throughout the country, 10,000 copies of a pamphlet were published comparing in detail both versions of Document No. 2 with the Treaty. The pamphlet was prefaced with the suggestion that 'When Mr de Valera states on a public platform what he will do if the Ulster Unionists will accept the national authority, ask what he will do *if they won't*. That is the question Ireland has had to face, and that was the question Mr de Valera faced when he put forward his alternative to the Treaty—Document No. 2.' Claiming that de Valera's original solution to the Ulster question was *'precisely the same as that of the Treaty'*, this leaflet accused him of endeavouring 'to make political capital out of the Boundary problem.' Moreover, the fact that his altered version of Document No. 2 had been re-adopted by him in February 1923, threw 'into still bolder relief' the inconsistency of his 1924 attacks on the Treaty's Ulster clauses. In support of this claim, the author of the pamphlet reminded de Valera that in his revised version of Document No. 2 he had included a promise that the Dail would be willing to grant to the six counties 'privileges and safeguards not less substantial' than those provided in the Treaty, such a policy being justified 'in order to make manifest our desire *not to bring force or coercion* to bear upon any substantial part of the Province of Ulster, *whose inhabitants may now be unwilling to accept the national* authority'; in contrast, by 1924, de Valera was insisting that Ulster must accept the national authority, Sinn Fein's preparedness to grant local autonomy to the north-east being now *'"on condition that that minority will give loyal allegiance to this nation as a single State"'*. The pamphlet

---

[31] 'The Document No. 2 lie', Sinn Fein election leaflet, 1923.

concluded that de Valera's efforts 'to convince his own ad-
herents and the Nationalists of the North East, that he never
accepted the Ulster clauses of the Treaty are absurd in face of
his own printed proposals.'[32]

While concentrating on what they saw as the contradictions
in de Valera's policy, another theme in Free State propaganda
was the moderation of de Valera's Ulster policy compared to
the extremist rhetoric of some Sinn Fein speakers, notably
that of Mary MacSwiney.[33] In contrast, the unionist press in
Belfast still saw him as an extremist, emphasizing his 'trucu-
lent' opposition to Partition and his promise that republicans
would 'use every available means by which determined men
would win their freedom.'[34] De Valera's speeches were scrutinized on all sides. O'Duffy in his intelligence reports to Free
State ministers, thought that de Valera's references to a 'military defeat, and his secondary statement that, while he proclaimed himself a moderate man, he still refused to exclude
the utilization of any and every means to secure this object,
seems a pretty fair indication of the pains he is at to try and
discover a middle course.' O'Duffy questioned whether de
Valera had the qualities necessary to unite the two extreme
republican factions, Stack's constitutionalists and Aiken's
'Ultra-Militarist Section', the latter 'by no means keen to
throw their politicians into the limelight.'[35]

If de Valera had already shown greater awareness than his
colleagues concerning the difficulties which the north posed
to any party aspiring to unite Ireland, there was nothing in
his experience of the north in the months ahead which could
have given him any reason for optimism. In the October 1924
Westminster election, Sinn Fein nominated abstentionist anti-
Partitionist candidates in eight constituencies, all of them
safe Unionist seats with the exception of Fermanagh–Tyrone,

[32] 'The Treaty and Document No. 2', Dublin, 1924; also 'Document No. 2:
clauses expunged by Mr de Valera when it became necessary to submit the document to public inspection', n.d. NLI LOP 117/41/1.
[33] See draft of speech by ?Mulcahy, entitled 'Miss MacSwiney v. Mr de Valera',
Mulcahy papers, P7/C/96.
[34] See emphasis in report of de Valera's Ennis speech, Aug. 1924 in *Belfast
Weekly News*, 21 Aug. 1924.
[35] O'Duffy to Executive Council, 8 Sept. 1924, Blythe papers, P24/223.

then a two-seat constituency with a comfortable, if narrow, nationalist majority. MacSwiney's acceptance that the results were 'none too good'[36] was an understatement: the elections proved to be a débâcle for Sinn Fein and a triumph for the Unionists, particularly in the counties of Fermanagh and Tyrone then in dispute because of the impending Irish Boundary Commission. The French consul in Dublin reported that the results had caused 'perfect consternation' among all political parties in the south.[37] They also prompted a review of de Valera's policy towards the north. Chastened by this experience, he was hereafter wary of attempting to determine from Dublin any detailed strategy for northern nationalists.[38]

Nor were de Valera's personal interventions in six-county politics very fruitful. In September 1924 he announced that he would be visiting the north: he wrote to Joe Devlin[39] hoping to meet him 'for a short talk' believing it 'a pity that the full anti-partition strength cannot be registered at this time.'[40] His visit when it transpired was only successful on the level of personal publicity following his arrest by the RUC. He was first deported on the instructions of the northern government. Then amidst considerable public speculation, he re-entered Northern Ireland to speak at Derry where he was arrested, and brought before a Belfast court which he refused to recognize. It may safely be presumed that he also failed to make himself understood, his non-recognition, like all his interjections in court, being in Gaelic. He was gaoled for one month and found the conditions worse than he had experienced in either Free State or British custody.[41]

Although there may have been propaganda gains from this visit, there were limited opportunities to make contacts with

[36] MacSwiney to de Valera, 24 Apr. 1925, MacSwiney papers, P48/B/2.

[37] Blanché to Edouard Herriot, 2 Nov. 1924, MAE Z/282/1 vol. 5.

[38] M. J. Costello to Chief of Staff, 'Sinn Fein in N.E. Ulster', 20 Mar. 1925, Sinn Fein policy: Secret Police Reports 1924–6, FitzGerald papers.

[39] Joseph Devlin (1871-1934), nationalist, journalist, politician; first elected as MP 1902; defeated de Valera in Falls division of Belfast, 1918; defended interests of northern nationalists in London and Belfast parliaments in those years when abstentionism was abandoned in favour of participation; unofficial leader of northern nationalists.

[40] De Valera to Devlin (1924), H. J. Moloney papers, T2257/1; quotation taken from calendar entry as original not in file, May 1979.

[41] Longford and O'Neill (1970: 238-9).

local anti-Partitionists, still less to attempt any ambitious plan to unite them. Not only were they fragmented; they were ambivalent about southern interference. O'Duffy reporting to the Cosgrave cabinet on advance preparations for de Valera's visit suggested that 'Irregular sympathisers . . . have not been as eager as was expected to make the necessary arrangements, excusing themselves on the grounds that any such meeting would be proclaimed . . . and would result in having many more of their supporters arrested.'[42]

Although his followers may have appreciated the publicity which accrued from his imprisonment in Belfast, the incident did little to expedite de Valera's main objective: the reunification of nationalist ranks. He came under increasing attack from the Cumann na nGaedhael government. O'Higgins specifically pilloried his Ulster policy.

Mr de Valera hates facts like a cat hates water, and we have got to rub these facts into him in the next few weeks . . . we cannot just live in a world of make-believe. If we denounce the Treaty and tear up the Constitution . . . it is certain to mean the loss of the North-east.[43]

Already, or so it was believed by pro-Treaty supporters, the Civil War had meant the postponement of the opportunity enshrined in the Treaty of a quick decision by a Boundary Commission to grant large stretches of Northern Ireland to the Free State. Further, there was the cost of reconstruction following the Civil War which delayed what O'Higgins saw as the 'building up [of] a worthy State that would attract and, in time, absorb and assimilate' the Ulster unionists. Instead 'we preferred the patriotic way' of practising 'upon ourselves worse indignities than the British had practised on us since Cromwell and Mountjoy and now we wonder why the Orangemen are not hopping like so many fleas across the Border in their anxiety to come within our fold and jurisdiction.'[44]

Where possible, government propaganda pinned culpability on de Valera. Meanwhile the Boundary commissioners had begun their work; whatever their arbitration it was likely to have a profound impact on politics throughout Ireland.

[42] O'Duffy to Executive Council, 30 Sept. 1924, Blythe papers, P24/223.
[43] *Irish Independent*, 9 Feb. 1925.
[44] O'Higgins to McCartan, May 1924, quoted Terence de Vere White, *Kevin O'Higgins* (Tralee: 1967 edn.), pp. 206-7.

(xi) SINN FEIN ARD FHEIS, 1925

What would have been de Valera's moderating influence was absent from the 1923 Sinn Fein Ard Fheis because he was in Free State custody, and from the 1924 conference because it fell during his month in gaol in Belfast.[45] The 1925 Ard Fheis was, then, the first which he had attended since the Civil War; it was also to be his last, since the launching of his new party, Fianna Fail, was, presently, to split Sinn Fein. Two persistent rumours of considerable significance to Sinn Fein were in circulation at this time: one was that some of the more restless abstentionists among the party's TDs were about to enter Leinster House;[46] the other was that the Boundary Commission, far from delimiting Northern Ireland to the point of unviability, might instead, merely rectify anomalies in the boundary and even cede some areas of the Free State to the north.[47]

Addressing a reception on the eve of the Ard Fheis,[48] de Valera attacked the latter possibility and once again put on record that republicans were willing to cede a local parliament 'to all those areas in the north' which could 'prove they had a majority'; but they 'never contemplated giving their sanction to the cutting off of any portion from Ireland' and claimed that 'in justice' the Ulster unionists 'could not ask for anything more'. Also, although 'they did not like it', Sinn Fein were prepared to tolerate external association with the British Empire as a further gesture to the north. All of this, concluded de Valera, 'was a great concession for national Ireland.'[49] Some of his audience obviously thought the concessions too great. When the Ard Fheis itself was convened, a northern resolution 'respectfully' suggested that Document No. 2 be withdrawn as it would not now represent an 'equitable' settle-

---

[45] See, for instance, de Valera 'Headings of topics', notes for Ard Fheis speech (not delivered as he was in Belfast gaol), 26 Oct.1924, MacSwiney papers, P48/D/10.

[46] Discussed in private session, Sinn Fein Ard Fheis, *Irish Independent*, 19 Nov. 1925; see also intelligence report to Executive Council, 15 June 1925, Blythe papers, P24/223.

[47] The inspired forecast of the Commission's decision had been published in the *Morning Post*, 7 Nov. 1925; see also *Irish Independent*, 19 Nov. 1925.

[48] One thousand attended this meeting, while Ard Fheis delegates numbered two hundred, *Irish Independent*, 18 Nov. 1925.

[49] Ibid.

ment. De Valera, in reply, emphasized that external association
and local autonomy for Ulster were 'the kernels' of his policy,
predicting that they would prove acceptable to the electorate.
The circumstances might have changed since he had first promulgated this policy, but 'the fundamental problem had not
changed' and any future republican government would face
the same dilemma as faced the 1921 cabinet. His policy as
enunciated in Document No. 2

> was an attempt to give expression in a final form to that policy of ex-
> ternal association with England [*sic*] Canada and Australia and with
> autonomy for the North-East corner.
>
> There was no use in their denying the fact that there were people in
> the country who had certain sentimental regard for the nations called
> the British Empire.
>
> The view of the Republican Cabinet at that time — and it still remained
> his view — was that the views of that section were entitled to full con-
> sideration.
>
> In the action they took at that time they thought they would secure
> a united Ireland. The same problem would have to be faced again, and he,
> for one, could not agree to have the idea of possible External Association
> for a United Ireland completely ruled out of court.

Care should be taken, he added, 'before they did anything
which would limit any honourable settlement of the question',
adding, characteristically, that 'the rights of Ireland were
complete and absolute independence'. And, perhaps with
Cumann na nGaedheal's propaganda in mind, he reminded
the delegates that the Document had originally been put forward during the Treaty debate as 'a rough draft', and added
that 'it probably contained some things against which he himself would vote.' But he did not specify what these might be
and to those delegates who had formally initiated this debate,
the objectionable parts of Document No. 2 were clearly its
'kernels' of external association and local autonomy for Ulster
which de Valera had just defended. Thus did de Valera manage
to nurse his Ulster policy past the sniping of its critics, including MacEntee, who followed him to the rostrum to argue
that he did not agree that the Ulster unionists 'were entitled
to the consideration which the President was prepared to give
them'. However, he asked the delegates to give the strategy
conditional support: 'they should give the policy a chance.' [50]

[50] Ibid., 19 Nov. 1925.

Although tepid, this endorsement was valuable to de Valera. His concessions on Partition, in possible danger of lapsing through lack of attention, had been challenged and then endorsed by the Ard Fheis. In the four years since he had first advocated these concessions to Ulster, he had persuaded his followers to tolerate rather than champion this policy; other republicans who spoke on the subject either ignored de Valera's concessions, or, if moved to comment, expressed misgivings or open hostility. Obviously his own persistent repetition of the policy, along with his description of it as 'the Republican position'[51] and his constant emphasis on the approval it had won from the pre-Treaty Sinn Fein cabinet, can be taken as further evidence of an early awareness on his part of the endemic intractability of the Ulster question and his expectation that he would need the flexibility embodied in this policy if he were ever to hope to deliver a political settlement. Where other republican speakers indulged in simplistic anti-Partition rhetoric, de Valera was clearly bent on curbing republican expectations on Ulster. Such an emphasis was particularly significant at this juncture, on the eve of the Boundary Commission crisis, which was shortly to change the entire context in which Partition was considered.

On the day following the Ard Fheis, the boundary crisis deepened with the shock announcement of the resignation of the Free State's Commissioner Eoin MacNeill. In the weeks which followed, as it became clearer throughout nationalist Ireland that the hopes vested in the boundary clauses of the Treaty had been misplaced, it must have seemed to the republicans that their hour had come. Perhaps the political ground lost in the Civil War might be regained. Might it even be that retrospectively their stand against the Treaty itself would be vindicated?

[51] Ibid., 18 Nov. 1925.

3. The 'Slightly Constitutional' Opposition: 1926–1931

'Could anybody find the effective way of ending Partition? The man who could and who succeeded in it would be the saviour of the country.'[1] (Eamon de Valera to Fianna Fail Ard Fheis, 1931.)

(i) BOUNDARY COMMISSION RESULT: SINN FEIN SPLIT: FORMATION OF FIANNA FAIL

In 1923 de Valera had claimed privately that he had 'always told Griffith he would be euchred' on the Boundary Commission clause of the Treaty, a clause on which de Valera himself would not have placed 'a particle of dependence'.[2] While there was disappointment in all parties, inside and outside the Dail, at the outcome of the Boundary Commission, public opinion was acknowledged to be relatively apathetic.[3] Indecision marked Sinn Fein's response: some supporters believed that de Valera should lead his abstentionist TDs into the Dublin parliament and attempt to muster a majority of members on an anti-Partition platform; others rejected this as apostasy, insisting that republicans should boycott any parliament based on Partition which included an Oath to the King of England.[4] De Valera responded with some caution; he told a meeting in his own constituency in Clare that he had not come 'to shout "I told you so"', but rather to insist on the

[1] *Irish Press*, 28 Oct. 1931.
[2] De Valera to prominent cleric, 23 June 1923, quoted D. Keogh, 'Ireland, the Vatican and Catholic Europe: 1919–1939', Ph.D. thesis, European University Institute, Florence, 1979, p. 224. Derived from an American card game, 'to euchre' means to gain advantage over an opponent.
[3] O'Kelly to Art O'Brien, 24 Nov. 1925 and reply, 17 May 1926, Art O'Brien papers, MS 8,461; McCartan to Maloney, 4 Dec. 1925, Maloney papers, box 21.
[4] [MacSwiney] to abstentionist TDs, 15 June 1926, MacSwiney papers, P48/D/13.

importance of a unified approach to the Boundary Commission controversy.[5] He emphasized this theme repeatedly during the critical two-week period between MacNeill's[6] resignation and the eventual acceptance by the Free State of the existing border.

Many nationalists had naïvely expected the Commission to cede so much of Northern Ireland's territory to the Free State that the north would prove economically unviable. Following the leak in the *Morning Post* and the resignation of MacNeill, it became obvious that the Commission, far from undermining the border, now seemed likely merely to modify it, thereby legitimizing and entrenching Partition. Irish government ministers confirmed to the British Prime Minister, Stanley Baldwin[7] that they faced 'certain defeat' if they attempted to implement such an award by the Commission.[8]

The political unrest, particularly in border areas, at this juncture would be difficult to exaggerate. Once *published*, the Commission's decisions would be immediately binding; contingency plans had been drawn up by the security forces north and south to take over any territories to be transferred. The possibility of armed resistance by dissidents in the affected areas was feared by both Dublin and Belfast governments.[9] Moreover, whilst MacNeill's resignation had raised some hopes in the south that it would preclude any arbitration being enacted, constitutional experts seemed agreed that the remaining two Commissioners could publish their report and

[5] *Clare Champion*, 5 Dec. 1925.

[6] Eoin MacNeill (1867–1945), born Co. Antrim; co-founder Gaelic League; professor Early Irish History, UCD; formed Irish Volunteers, 1913; as chief of staff, unsuccessfully attempted to stop 1916 Rising; supported Treaty; Minister for Education, 1922–5; IFS representative on Irish Boundary Commission, 1924–5; resigned from Commission, from the government, 1925, and retired from politics, 1927.

[7] Stanley Baldwin (1867–1947), Prime Minister for third time, 1935–7 when he tolerated but did not initially support Malcolm MacDonald's policy of seeking a settlement of the Anglo-Irish economic war; believed de Valera to be 'impossible'.

[8] Notes of meeting between O'Higgins, McGilligan, O'Byrne, and Baldwin at Chequers, 28 Nov. 1925, Baldwin papers, vol. 99. That republicans believed the boundary issue would prove an electoral asset is manifest in the file, 'Secret Police Reports: Sinn Fein policy: 1925–6', FitzGerald papers.

[9] 'L.M.' to Director of Intelligence, 8 May 1924, O'Malley papers, P17/F/48; Minister of Defence to Executive Council, 22 July 1925, Blythe papers, P24/107; Administration of transferred boundary areas: temporary file', McGilligan papers, P35/B/140; Northern Ireland cabinet meeting, 16 Sept. 1924, PRONI CAB 4/121/16; *Irish Independent*, 18 and 27 Nov. 1925.

thereby alter the border.[10] De Valera's response was typically constructive. Whilst others scorned MacNeill's performance, [11] he complimented him: 'The only redeeming feature of the whole business was Eoin MacNeill's resignation . . . no Irishman could be allowed to put his signature to an instrument which meant the Partition of his country.' De Valera was also anxious to preclude any resort to force: 'They might not be able to go and rescue the people, but there was one thing they could do — not be a party to the Partition of their country.' It may have been a moment of intense national disappointment but it was also one of opportunity. De Valera's aim was to achieve what had been possible in 1918: to bury party differences on an issue as fundamental as opposition to conscription had been then.

Although implacably against Partition, believing any boundary 'indefensible and ruinous to all concerned', de Valera now argued for a fairer boundary than that of 1920.

But if the Treaty, which as Republicans we have resisted and will continue to resist, no matter what happens, gives us Partition, then in the interests of the nation and of justice to the people [*sic*] of the North-East whose lives and fortunes are immediately affected, I want to see that that Partition will not be a worse Partition than the Partition contemplated by the Treaty.

De Valera was even prepared to offer Cosgrave advice on how to handle the crisis, though he prefaced it with the necessary disclaimer: 'I am not a Free Stater and the Treaty policy is not my policy.' His advice was to abandon those elements in the Treaty — the Oath and the Crown — which Griffith had been persuaded to tolerate because of British promises regarding the outcome of the Boundary Commission.[12] This advice was not disinterested. If followed by Cosgrave, such a course would, at a stroke, have done much to resolve. Sinn Fein's internal problems; without the Oath, many of the abstentionist TDs could have entered a Leinster House where party alignment would no longer be predictably pro- and anti-Treaty.

---

[10] Baldwin, Cosgrave, and Craig all express their concern in PRO CAB 61/16 CP 503(25).

[11] Brian O'Higgins, speech, *Clare Champion*, 5 Dec. 1925.

[12] *Clare Champion*, 5 Dec. 1925.

The government had no intention of adopting de Valera's policy. On 3 December they accepted the existing boundary and waived their claims under Article 12 of the Treaty in return for financial concessions. Cosgrave's claim that it was a 'damned good bargain' did little to assuage the feelings of northern nationalists who felt betrayed if not bartered.[13] Nationalists and republicans believed the settlement 'a farce',[14] 'terrible',[15] 'a debacle';[16] worse still, some described it as a 'sale'.[17] De Valera's response was more moderate. A public meeting was called for Dublin:

Advertisement: No Partition; Demonstration to voice the NATION'S PROTEST against the DISMEMBERMENT of our Country and the BETRAYAL OF THE NORTH. EAMON DE VALERA and representatives from the provinces.[18]

De Valera bemoaned the futility of verbal protest at this 'meditated crime'. Again his concessions to the Ulster unionists of 1921 were instanced; he had been willing to go very far — 'I hardly like to think how far' — but 'against any proposal for cutting Ireland in two we would have held out to the death.'[19]

Significantly this public demonstration was not organized by Sinn Fein. Already de Valera was aware of the need to establish a broader political base. The futility of Sinn Fein's abstentionist strategy was manifest to many republicans and de Valera had annoyed MacSwiney during the previous twelve months by not denying rumours that some Sinn Fein TDs were 'coquetting with the idea' of entering the Free State Dail.[20] MacSwiney, vigilant in her role as custodian of republican

[13] 'Protest adopted at a conference of Border nationalists', 7 Dec. 1925, MacSwiney papers, P48/D/20.
[14] E. Coyle to Blythe, 15 Sept. 1925 commenting on rumours that the southern government might accept the existing boundary, Blythe papers, P24/498.
[15] Stack to de Valera, 4 Dec. 1925, quoted O'Neill (1976: 166).
[16] Dr McHugh (Bishop of Derry) to Fr E. Coyle, 5 Dec. 1925, Maloney papers, Box 22.
[17] Donnelly to William O'Brien, 13 Feb. 1926, William O'Brien papers, MS 7,998.
[18] Display advertisement, *Irish Independent*, 5 Dec. 1925.
[19] *Irish Independent*, 7 Dec. 1925.
[20] MacSwiney to de Valera, 24 Apr. 1925, MacSwiney papers, P48/B/2.

orthodoxy,[21] was well placed to note the loss of self-confidence among republicans in their strategy of boycotting all Free State institutions.[22] Even before the débâcle of the Boundary Commission, republican ranks were in 'a muddle'.[23] Impotent politically, to avert this consolidation of Partition, de Valera now feared a further resort to arms. That some factions contemplated such a move was widely rumoured. Free State army intelligence feared an attempt on the lives of some government ministers and also monitored a group of 'dangerous lunatics' interested in winning political support for terrorist incursions into Northern Ireland. Despite his never being given the benefit of the doubt, de Valera emerges from these special branch intelligence files as a moderate.[24] Moreover, McCartan reported that 'on good authority' he had learned that de Valera had, in the aftermath of the signing of the Boundary Agreement, 'prevented the assassination of MacNeill, Blythe and O'Higgins.'[25]

Since the Civil War de Valera had been committed to transferring the republican struggle 'to another plane'.[26] More than other opponents of the Treaty — including those who were to be prominent in Fianna Fail — he was resolutely opposed to force.[27] In these critical months which followed the Boundary Agreement, he took soundings on support for a more flexible and less doctrinaire opposition to the Free State. By March 1926 at a specially convened Sinn Fein Ard Fheis, his resolution that if the Oath were to be removed from the Dublin and Belfast parliaments 'it becomes a question not of principle but of policy' whether republicans should attend,

[21] See exchange of letters between Aiken and MacSwiney, Oct. 1926, MacSwiney papers, P48/C/10.
[22] MacSwiney to O'Kelly, 28 Nov. 1924, MacSwiney to de Valera, 27 June and 24 July 1925, MacSwiney papers, P48/B/2.
[23] O'Kelly to MacSwiney, 1 Oct. 1925, MacSwiney papers, P48/B/1.
[24] Director of Intelligence to Minister for Defence, and B. Donegan to Director of Intelligence, both 11 Dec. 1925; also Sinn Fein policy: Secret Police Reports 1924-6, FitzGerald papers.
[25] McCartan to Maloney, 16 Mar. 1926, Maloney papers, box 21. Ernest Blythe, northern Protestant, convert to Irish nationalism; minister in Cumann na nGaedheal governments, 1922-32.
[26] De Valera to McGarrity, 31 May and 4 June 1923, ibid.
[27] See for instance speeches by Aiken and O'Kelly, reported *Irish World*, 23 Jan. 1926.

was narrowly defeated thereby giving him the opportunity to break with the doctrinaires and found Fianna Fail.[28] Initially he was careful not to alienate the Sinn Fein rump: during the following decade he would win further recruits from their ranks.

De Valera outlined the fundamental aims of Fianna Fail — launched in May 1926 — foremost among which were the unification of the country and the restoration of the Irish language. Important support came from northern nationalists who after the disastrous collapse of Cumann na nGaedheal's anti-Partition strategy now switched their allegiance and hopes to Fianna Fail.[29] Such support helped to offset the frequently voiced criticism that because of the Civil War, de Valera had been, as Tim Healy put it, 'more responsible for the sufferings of Northern Catholics than any man alive. Ingredients of blame belong it is true, elsewhere, but on him the guilt is blackest.'

Healy writing to his former Home Rule colleague, William O'Brien, complained of the political capital which de Valera had made out of the Boundary Commission disappointment. De Valera had characterized Cosgrave's settlement as 'a crime' but now made 'a stock topic' of the desertion of the northern nationalists.[30] Healy believed the Republicans 'practically finished'.[31] O'Brien agreed: although a supporter of de Valera, especially on Partition,[32] he believed de Valera had 'largely failed'.[33] Art O'Brien was equally pessimistic, believing de Valera 'quite hopeless as a leader'. Since he had 'exercised personal sway he [had] ruined everything.'[34] In America, Devoy's judgement was that Irish unity 'can only come about

---

[28] Longford and O'Neill (1970: 242-3).

[29] E. Phoenix, 'Introduction and calendar of the Cahir Healy papers', MA thesis, Queen's University Belfast, 1978.

[30] Healy to William O'Brien, 2 Mar. 1926, O'Brien papers, MS 8,556(31). William O'Brien (1852-1928), nationalist MP, 1883-1918; abhorred Partition; endorsed Fianna Fail, 1927 elections.

[31] Healy to sister-in-law, 14 Apr. 1926, Healy papers, P6/A/155.

[32] Leaflet, 'Mr William O'Brien on the forthcoming election' [1927], O'Brien papers, MS 7998.

[33] Wm. O'Brien to Healy, 3 Mar. 1926, Wm. O'Brien papers, MS 8,556(31).

[34] Art O'Brien to O'Kelly, 17 May 1926, Art O'Brien papers, MS 8,461. Another prominent opponent of the Treaty, L. H. Kerney was also sceptical of de Valera's abilities as a leader, Kerney to Hannah Sheehy Skeffington, 15 Apr. 1924, Hannah Sheehy Skeffington papers, MS 24,095.

by the complete elimination of de Valera.'[35] The press, too, was sceptical concerning de Valera's new departure.[36] There was little indication from opponents, supporters, or commentators that Fianna Fail would transform Irish politics. Yet not since Parnell's ascendancy in the 1880s would Irish aspirations be so coherently pursued by a national leader dominating a great political machine — at once, a party and a movement. De Valera himself wrote to McGarrity: 'What will be the fate of this new venture, I do not know. I have at any rate done my duty and launched the ship on the sea of fate. If favourable winds blow, I may bring her safely to harbour. If not, well I am prepared to go down trying.'[37]

(ii) FIANNA FAIL IN OPPOSITION

In launching Fianna Fail de Valera had been scrupulous not to alienate those who remained in Sinn Fein.[38] At the party's first Ard Fheis in November 1926 he spoke of the 'heart-wrench' of breaking with his former comrades whom he regarded 'as a redoubt on the left wing of the Republican forces' who feared that 'the operations Fianna Fail were performing were too dangerous for them to risk.' He asked them 'to do nothing further than not to fire on them as they were advancing from their trenches into the open.'[39] Senior Fianna Fail politicians were pleased to have left some of their former colleagues in the trenches: they saw them as cranks who were determined to remain strangers to political reality.[40] An attempt was made in the spring of 1927 — largely prompted by Eamonn Donnelly — to work out a basis of agreement between the two parties.[41] Donnelly feared that 'a deal' on

[35] Devoy to Maurice Moore, 29 Jan. 1924, Moore papers, MS 5,500.

[36] *The Times*, 10, 11, and 12 Mar., *Irish Times*, 11 Mar. 1926.

[37] De Valera to McGarrity, 13 Mar. 1926, McGarrity papers, MS 17,441.

[38] See collection of de Valera's replies to American press queries concerning the formation of Fianna Fail, J. J. Hearn papers, MS 15,987; also, de Valera's contributions in minutes, *Comhairle na dTeachtai*, 18–19 Dec. 1926, FitzGerald papers.

[39] *Irish Independent*, 25 Nov. 1926.

[40] Interviews, Joseph Groome, Sean Lemass.

[41] E[amonn] D[onnelly], 'Basis for discussion', [Mar. 1927]; MacSwiney to Donnelly, 2 Apr. 1927, MacSwiney papers, P48/B/21b. Donnelly, abstentionist MP, NIHC, 1925–9, 1942–4, Fianna Fail TD, 1933–7; Armagh nationalist, preoccupied

Partition was being suggested from London and that the Cosgrave government might secure a spurious but 'superficial unity'.[42] But his efforts to persuade Sinn Fein and Fianna Fail to agree on a joint approach to the Ulster question failed and within months the assassination of the deputy Prime Minister, Kevin O'Higgins, along with the government's response, changed the entire context of parliamentary politics. The government introduced legislation obliging elected TDs to take their seats in the Dail or forfeit them. This ended Fianna Fail's abstentionist policy; they took their seats and the hated Oath of allegiance as 'an empty formula'.[43]

Fianna Fail's presence in the Free State parliament no matter how much emphasis they placed on being a 'slightly constitutional' party[44] rendered them outcasts to the rump of republican purists who scorned 'the song of compromise so sweetly sung by Mr de Valera'.[45] And from the other end of the political spectrum de Valera was also ridiculed for his acceptance of the oath. Described as the 'political Houdini' of his generation, voters were invited by Cumann na nGaedheal to admire his 'escape from the political strait-jacket of the Republic'.[46] In fact the voters admired in sufficient numbers to strengthen Fianna Fail's position in the election of September 1927 when they virtually eclipsed Sinn Fein and came close to office. Their entry to the Free State Dail tested party unity and prompted the delegates to the next Ard Fheis to insist that 'the furthermost limits in compromise had been reached.'[47]

by one issue — Partition; joined Fianna Fail, 1927; remained impatient with de Valera's strategy on Partition until his death, 1944.

[42] Donnelly to MacSwiney (Mar.–Apr. 1927), MacSwiney papers, P48/C/7; see also McCartan to Maloney, 4 Mar. (1926, incorrectly filed 1922 in New York Public Library), Maloney papers, box 21; also, copy de Valera to McCartan, 15 Apr. 1926, ibid.

[43] Longford and O'Neill (1970: 250-8); J. A. Murphy, *Ireland in the twentieth century* (Dublin: 1975); Donal O'Sullivan, *The Irish Free State and its Senate* (London: 1940), pp. 214-30; Lyons (1971: 491-4); for de Valera's attitude to the Oath issue when Fianna Fail was being founded, see his statement on Clann Eireann, 18 Apr. 1926, F. P. Walsh papers, box 112.

[44] Lemass's description, DE: 22: 1615-6. Mar. 1928.

[45] Sean C. O'Riada, open letter to Clan na Gael and IRA clubs (in USA), 12 Feb. 1932, Irish Race Convention (New York) Aug. 1932 papers, MS 7363/3.

[46] Cumann na nGaedheal election poster, Sept. 1927.

[47] Agenda, Fianna Fail Ard Fheis, 1927.

In general — and particularly on the Partition issue — the party rank and file tolerated rather than supported de Valera's pragmatic lead. Initiatives from delegates at the annual conferences during the early years of the party included a call, unanimously carried, that 'at the earliest practicable opportunity' the Boundary Agreement of 1925 be repudiated;[48] that a 'more fighting and militant' policy on Partition be adopted in the Dail; and that economic boycott of the north be tried.[49] De Valera's response was invariably a call for realism: 'It is long ago since I first said that I was not a Republican doctrinaire, and it was clear that I meant that I was a realist. And I hold that I have always been a realist in politics.' The delegates must not forget that the party 'could not perform miracles'.[50]

Concerning the party's strategy on Partition, Fianna Fail seemed divided between those who considered that while in opposition, propaganda against its injustice was all that could usefully be accomplished and others who thought this too inactive and sought every opportunity to intervene on the question. That unilateral initiatives could achieve very little was de Valera's answer to the interventionists. However, one initiative, strenuously advocated by the latter, did lie completely within the party's discretion: to organize Fianna Fail in the six counties and contest elections there. Given that the 'parent' party, Sinn Fein, was so organized and given that Fianna Fail's first aim was to unite the country, the apparent hesitation, indeed reluctance, of the leadership on this question clearly came as a surprise and disappointment to many.

The first Secretaries' Report admitted that the general organizing committee 'had not attempted actively' to organize the party in the north. They had however 'established contact' with republicans in many centres but being anxious to avoid 'unnecessary division' the 'existing organization had not been interfered with.' De Valera invited support for this approach: he compared the position north and south. In the twenty-six counties, the nationalists, 'Republicans at heart', were in a

[48] *The Nation*, 3 Dec. 1927.
[49] Resolutions, 7 and 51, agenda, Fianna Fail Ard Fheis, 1928.
[50] *The Nation*, 10 Dec. 1927.

majority and it would be 'their own fault' if they did not
'take over the Government'; in the north the position was
'entirely different'.[51] Fianna Fail, said de Valera, was 'intended
to be an All-Ireland organization.' But it should 'take cog-
nisance' of important differences north and south: 'The time
to start organizing in the six counties would depend on the
conditions there.'[52] The delegates expressed impatience with
this strategy but the compromise of referring the issue to the
National Executive allowed the party hierarchy to resume
their cautious approach.[53]

Obviously highly vulnerable if a serious organizational
drive did not establish the party as leaders of the northern
nationalists, Fianna Fail was still willing to accept the affili-
ation of local branches provided the initiative came from
within the six-county area. As will be seen this issue was to
remain a live one for a minority within the party who argued
— very plausibly, it must have seemed — that it was paradoxical
for a movement whose *raison d'être* was the winning of the
north not to be organizing there.

Before the crisis of August 1927 which precipitated Fianna
Fail's entry to the Dail, de Valera gave a series of interviews
to British newspapers in which he was closely questioned on
Ulster. He assured the *Daily Mail* that 'If we in the twenty-six
counties built up a sound national economy, raised standards
of living and generally made the country a place to be proud
of, I believe that the people of the six counties would be
anxious to join us.' 'Even though you were a Gaelic state?'
asked the questioner: 'Yes, I believe they would,' replied
de Valera. He had prefaced his remarks on attracting the
north, by insisting that 'Irish unity can be achieved only on
the basis of complete freedom from English interference in
our affairs.'[54]

The *Daily Express* questioned this analysis, pointing to the

[51] *Irish Independent*, 25 Nov. 1926.
[52] *Irish Times*, 26 Nov. 1926.
[53] Minutes, Fianna Fail National Executive, for inaugural, second, and fifth
meetings, 25 Nov., 2 and 30 Dec. 1926.
[54] *Daily Mail*, 22 June, reprinted *The Nation*, 2 July 1927. This interview was
not found in the British Library's edition of the *Daily Mail*; it may have been confined to the early overseas edition.

'fact that cleavage in ideas and ideals' already existed between north and south. De Valera, however, was adamant that the responsibility for Partition rested with Britain: there were 'acute political differences' in 'every country and in every State. Is secession and partition suggested as the remedy?' Partition had 'introduced two minority problems where there was only one.'[55] His interview in the *Manchester Guardian* was more detailed: he claimed that northern nationalists were 'virtually disfranchised' being without 'political freedom'; that the unionist 'ascendancy' was 'digging itself in deeper every day. It does not even trouble to pretend that it desires or aims at an ultimate reunion. It distrusts and despises the rulers of the Free State as men who say one thing and mean another.' He added that 'Ulster has more respect for the honest Republican, and is more likely to come to terms with a Republican Government than with the Free State. But the prospect is bad.' When asked if a Fianna Fail government would 'recognise the accomplished fact and have friendly relations with the Northern Government?', he replied: 'No, I cannot exactly say that. We must, of course, recognise existing facts, but it does not follow that we must acquiesce in them.' Partition was a 'hideous mutilation'. At present they might be 'powerless to undo what has been done, but Ireland must reserve her right to act as and when opportunity presents itself.'

Nor was de Valera's next point reassuring to Ulster. The unionists there who *'have wilfully assisted in mutilating their motherland can justly be made to suffer for their crime.'* He approved of economic coercion of the Ulster unionists: They had

chosen separation. Let them feel what separation means. Public opinion in Ireland will insist on high protection. If Ulster chooses to remain outside our political system she can have no special right of access to our markets. But we do not rely only or chiefly on pressure. When Ireland flourishes as a Republican Ireland would flourish, Ulster will be attracted and will seek reunion.

The interviewer put a final point: 'I wish you could accept the Northern Ireland settlement, bad as it is, and take the

[55] *Daily Express*, 15 June, reprinted *The Nation*, 25 June 1927. Again, quotations taken from *The Nation* reprint; not found in British Library's final London edition of the *Daily Express*.

position we find ourselves in for a basis on which to rear your spiritual edifice.' De Valera replied: 'There is no wisdom in building on unsound foundations.'[56]

All of these interviews were reprinted in the Fianna Fail newspaper, *The Nation*, a certain indication that de Valera was here communicating with his own supporters as well as with international opinion. He was scarcely communicating with — he was certainly not convincing — the Ulster unionists when he reassured the *Daily Mail* that even a 'Gaelic state' would attract Ulster. One pattern in de Valera's politics is already clear: whether on the language question, or the Oath, or economic protectionism, he believed in expediting his cultural, constitutional or economic policies irrespective of the preferences of Ulster unionists.[57]

One point on Ulster in these newspaper interviews became a matter for controversy. De Valera's threat that the Ulster unionists who had 'wilfully assisted in mutilating their motherland' could 'justly be made to suffer for their crime' was condensed to the phrase: 'we must punish Ulster'. Although this was not a direct quotation from the original interview, it was a fair summary and it was the phrase which was used by opposition critics. The verb 'punish' is used four times in one Cumann na nGaedheal advertisement in the September 1927 election, a campaign in which the governing party was anxious to make the link between Fianna Fail and the IRA.[58] The advertisement ridiculed de Valera who 'proposes to establish this perfect peace by enlisting its gunmen in the people's army, by smashing the Treaty, by destroying the Constitution, by having "another round" with England, by "punishing Ulster"'. Elaborating on the last point, the advertisement explained what 'punishing Ulster' entailed: 'by sending Mr Frank Aiken northwards with his "army" to bring in by force the six counties, to "punish Ulster" with all

[56] 'An interview with Mr de Valera', *Manchester Guardian*, 27 June 1927. Italics added. This interview was also reprinted in *The Nation*, 9 July 1927: quotations taken from *Manchester Guardian* original.

[57] See also de Valera's responses to a questionnaire submitted by P. J. Barry of New York, *The Nation*, 2 July 1927.

[58] For Cumann na nGaedheal's advertisements, *Irish Independent*, 3, 12 Sept., Fianna Fail's response, ibid., 10, 12 Sept. 1927.

the consequences the "punishment" would bring to Ulster Nationalists.'[59] In this, the Cumann na nGaedheal government was exploiting the confidential information received from their own intelligence branch which had constantly portrayed Aiken — with no support from de Valera — as lobbying within the Sinn Fein movement of 1924-5 for a policy of force against the six counties.[60] De Valera's moderation, also reported in these files, was ignored by the Cumann na nGaedheal publicists.

By this stage, de Valera may have regretted his indiscretion in the *Manchester Guardian* interview: the threat to 'punish Ulster' had become one of the issues in the election. He was attacked for it in the press[61] and a series of questions was posed by Professor E. P. Culverwell of Trinity College Dublin:

1. Does your intention of punishing the six counties include only an economic war with them?
2. If the economic war does not succeed in getting the six counties to join the Free State will your policy be to allow them to stay out, i.e. to remain as they are?
3. Or will it be to declare war on them as a last resource [*sic*]?[62]

It was de Valera who secured widespread publicity for Culverwell's challenge to Fianna Fail's Ulster policy.[63] In his reply, de Valera argued that the south lacked the power to force Ulster into unity. 'They were not in a position to declare war on the six counties with England behind them, and they were more concerned with the safety of their own country than with the safety of English interests.'

It is even possible that de Valera prompted Culverwell to raise these questions.[64] He certainly seems to have welcomed

[59] Boxed alongside this quotation was the sentence: '"We must punish Ulster" — Mr de Valera in the *Manchester Guardian* interview', *Irish Independent*, 5 Sept. 1927.

[60] Intelligence reports to Executive Council, *passim* but especially 29 May 1924, Blythe papers, P24/233.

[61] Editorial, *Irish Independent*, 15 Sept. 1927.

[62] *Irish Independent*, 13 Sept. 1927. E. P. Culverwell, academic, Trinity College Dublin; possible acquaintance of de Valera through university Irish language debating society.

[63] The controversy was, for instance, the lead story in *The Times*, 14 Sept. 1927.

[64] Culverwell had attempted mediation in Sept. 1922 during the Civil War,

the opportunity to remind the voters — and indeed his own 'wild men' — that the party eschewed force. An election advertisement proclaimed:

What Fianna Fail Does Not Stand For: Attacking the North East: Fianna Fail does not stand for attacking 'Ulster'. It will accept EXISTING REALITIES, but will work resolutely to bring Partition to an end.[65]

International opinion was not forgotten by de Valera. He took every opportunity to propagate his belief in the inherent injustice of Partition. As a delegate to the Inter-Parliamentary Union conference in Berlin in August 1928 he told the *Telegrafen Union* that there would be an 'overwhelming majority' throughout Ireland for independence; moreover Britain could 'still do whatever she wanted' in Ireland. British troops could reach Dublin from the 'strongly occupied' Northern Ireland within a few hours.[66] During Fianna Fail's opposition years de Valera made three visits to America, spending, in all, nine months in the country.[67] Here, he was obliged to defend his Ulster strategy to audiences which were potentially sceptical — they might favour the Free State government or the Sinn Fein position. He insisted that Partition was not essentially a religious question;[68] that it resulted wholly from British policy which through Clause 12 of the Treaty had been designed 'to make it permanent'; that Irish public opinion had accepted the Boundary Agreement of 1925 only because of their mistaken belief that 'there would be a complete wiping off of all further payments to England';[69] and that an all-Ireland plebiscite would give 'an overwhelming majority' for unity,[70] their being, at most, only two counties which would favour Craig's government.[71]

being then 'able to communicate with Mr de Valera', Hugh Kennedy papers, P4/F/15.

[65] Fianna Fail advertisement, *Irish Independent*, 14 Sept. 1927; see also de Valera speech, ibid., 13 Sept. 1927.

[66] De Valera interview with *Telegrafen Union*, Berlin, reported *The Times*, 23 Aug. 1928.

[67] This section is based on all speeches, statements, and interviews by de Valera, as reported in the *Irish World*, during his American visits. Sympathetic to Fianna Fail, this paper claimed to publish 'exclusive statements and reports' of de Valera's 1927 tour, ibid., 26 Mar. 1927.

[68] *Irish World*, 23 Apr. 1927.   [69] Ibid., 16 Apr. 1927.
[70] Ibid., 7 May 1927.   [71] Ibid., 16 Apr. 1927.

His utopian streak also found expression in America: on his 1927 tour he stated: 'We can support in Ireland not merely the four and a quarter millions we have, but we can support the sixteen millions we should have. Economists have calculated that Ireland can support a population of from sixteen to twenty millions of people.'[72] He believed Ireland potentially self-sufficient and insisted that a Fianna Fail government would pursue a rigorous protectionist policy.[73] Ireland could feed, clothe, and house her population, adding in a revealing phrase, that this could be achieved 'even if a wall a thousand feet high were put around our island and I believe there is hardly another country that could do it.'[74]

Among the Irish-Americans there was a strong lobby for the use of force against Northern Ireland: and at a first reading, de Valera's speeches in America seem to classify him as a hawk. But a more careful examination usually shows him insisting on a distinction between the moral justification for force — an argument he approved — and the rejection of force on the grounds that it would be counter-productive. In 1927 he asked a Boston audience: 'Do you think that the Irish people are so mean that after all this fighting for seven and a half centuries they are now going to be content to have six counties of their ancient territory cut off?'[75] The press reported '"No" and "Never" coming from thousands of throats.' A New York audience heard his familiar metaphor: 'We have a point in front of us that the enemy cannot strengthen. We are strong enough in Ireland to break it down (applause) and when we have broken it down are you going to tell me that the conquering army is going to stop at that point? It is not!'[76] In seven speeches of his 1927 tour he stated or implied that peace could not be established as long as Partition lasted.[77] Yet these quotations, while bellicose, did not advocate force. The unstoppable 'conquering army' after all was composed of the 'Soldiers of Destiny' — the Fianna Fail party. A Chicago

---

[72] Ibid., 6 May 1927.
[73] Ibid., 30 Apr. 1927.
[74] Ibid., 6 May 1927.
[75] Ibid., 26 Mar. 1927.
[76] Ibid., 26 May 1927.
[77] Speeches at Boston, ibid., 26 Mar.; Rochester, Minn., and Butte, ibid., 16 Apr.; Oakland, ibid., 23 Apr.; Chicago, ibid., 30 Apr.; New York, ibid., 7 May 1927.

audience on the same tour was told that British troops garrisoned in Northern Ireland, were 'within an hour's march of our capital.' If foreign troops were within an hour's march of Washington, he asked: 'an hour's march with their armo[u]red cars and their tanks, would you permit a foreign power to maintain their troops there? You would not as long as you were able at all to drive them out! So it is with Ireland today.'[78]

Three years later on his next extended American tour, de Valera's speeches on Ulster have changed little; but if anything he is even more explicit about the threat to the Free State posed by the British troops in Northern Ireland. Britain wanted 'a safe base — a bridgehead across the Irish sea — from which her troops could pour over the entire island at will.'[79] That Partition left Irish nationalists with an interest in Britain's downfall was another theme in his American speeches:

As long as a British soldier remains in Ireland . . . as long as our country is partitioned, no Irishman can say that this is the final settlement of Ireland's claim to nationhood . . . Every Irishman worthy of the name, no matter where he may be, lives in the hope that there will be a battle of Clontarf for the British as there was for the Danes.

Earlier in the speech he had claimed that the Irish victory at Clontarf had 'smashed the Danish Empire'. Later he added that British troops were still in the north 'because at the present time we are not able to put them out.'[80]

It must be remembered that these speeches were being made to audiences whose support for de Valera's particular approach to establishing the Republic was conditional and relatively fickle. Furthermore, de Valera knew that if the dollars collected by this community for the republican cause did not come to him, they would, in all probability, be diverted to the IRA. As McGarrity's letters to him reveal, there was already considerable resentment against de Valera's use of such funds for political propaganda, for fighting elections, even for Irish language lessons. The subscribers whilst accepting that republicans in Ireland must decide how best to spend the dollars, clearly preferred what was popularly termed 'one

---

[78] Ibid., 30 Apr. 1927.   [79] Ibid., 3 May 1930.
[80] Ibid., 22 Mar. 1930.

more round with John Bull'.[81] If his American rhetoric rendered him indistinguishable from an IRA fellow-traveller in
the eyes of Ulster unionists, his strategy was, in fact, rooted
in a pacific approach. He wrote to the IRA's principal supporter in the United States, McGarrity:

Take this as an axiom: in the present circumstances, unless those who
stand for the Republican cause can get a majority of the elected representatives of the people on their side, there can be no success for force.
A successful Civil War, with England on the side of those opposed to
the Republic, cannot be waged. Those who think it can had better be
brought down to the hard facts of the situation.[82]

The sixth Ard Fheis of Fianna Fail held in October 1931
was known to be the last before Cumann na nGaedheal would
be obliged to call an election. In fact, Fianna Fail were to be
in government within three months. Consequently, the Partition debate at this Ard Fheis is a useful indication of the
range of opinion within the party on Ulster at this juncture.
Again, de Valera's concern was to curb the expectations of
the more naïve faction in the party while reassuring the voters
that Fianna Fail was not the revolutionary party of gunmen
portrayed in Cumann na nGaedheal publicity. Any incoming
government, de Valera informed the Ard Fheis, needed plans
when facing serious problems:

The first step is to get a clear understanding of the data in each case,
and to face all the facts without blinking. To ignore the data, to adopt
an ostrich policy in regard to any of them, to be content with phrases
applicable to past conditions only, is to court failure.

Given his ascendancy in the party, it cannot have been easy
to criticize de Valera on the Partition issue at a party conference; yet, in 1931, tentatively, but consistently, speakers
did voice their doubts. One TD characterized de Valera's
approach as akin to that of the Free State government. Seven
speakers, including two TDs and three members of the National

[81] Based on McGarrity to de Valera, 23 June 1923, McGarrity papers, MS
17,440, also letters of 5 June 1925, 23 Dec. 1927, 10 Jan., 25 Sept. 1928, 2 Oct.
1933, ibid., MS 17,441; also de Valera to McGarrity, 6 July 1923, Maloney papers,
box 21; and letters of 30 Apr., 28 June, 20 Dec. 1927, McGarrity papers, MS
17,441; also McGarrity to Aiken, 1 Sept. 1926, ibid., MS 17,421; O'Kelly to Mac-
Swiney, 18 Mar. 1926, MacSwiney papers, P48/D/5.
[82] De Valera to McGarrity, 30 Apr. 1927, McGarrity papers, MS 17,441.

Executive, are reported in the *Irish Press* as expressing broad
sympathy with the IRA, then the target of emergency legislation by the Cosgrave government. Dr Con Murphy of the
National Executive said the IRA

> had a moral right to resist foreign domination, and in that they were
> one with Fianna Fail, but it should be pointed out to them that the
> means they were adopting would never bring about success in their
> object. Their only hope was to put in power a Dail representing the
> Irish people.[83]

De Valera, in his reply to this debate, spent considerable
time explaining on what grounds he denied the IRA the right
to take life. The arms dumped after the Civil War were never,
he said, intended for

> class warfare or for civil war — they were for the one purpose of sup-
> porting a Republican State if the people decided to establish that state
> (applause). If the Republican State is again established it will be done
> by Dail Eireann and the majority will be behind it and in that event he
> did not think they would lack the necessary weapons.

De Valera was speaking here at a time of apprehension by the
Catholic bishops and others that the IRA's links with com-
munism were a new threat to the status quo. Cast as a Kerensky by some republicans, and so described by others to his
right, de Valera rejected such a role, denying that a Fianna
Fail government 'would be a mere stalking horse for some
other people'; nor would a Fianna Fail government fail in its
duty to maintain order, though he added a specific promise
that, in office, his government would repeal the 'recent Coercion Act'.[84] His strategy encompassed winning power,
abolishing the Oath and then calling a further election at
which those republicans with scruples about the Oath would
have an 'opportunity for securing representation'.

His tone — didactic and persistent — at this Ard Fheis
emphasized the need for realism: 'We must be very careful or
we will let our sympathies run away with us on matters of
right and wrong'; 'It is just as well that there should be no
loose thinking . . . We are not play-acting in this organization';
specifically on Partition, he could 'see no immediate solution

[83] Irish Press, 28 Oct. 1931.   [84] Ibid., 29 Oct. 1931.

of that problem'; and, replying to the criticism of his Ulster policy, he said he was trying to get the party 'to face the situation as it was'. If he could point to no effective way to end Partition, he wanted to point to 'ways which most certainly would not end it'. Force was 'out of the question. Were it feasible, it would not be desirable.' De Valera contented himself with a vague aspiration: 'The only hope that I can see now for the re-union of our people is good government in the twenty-six counties and such social and economic conditions here as will attract the majority in the Six Counties to throw in their lot with us.'

In the meantime, Fianna Fail's tariff policy would be coercive towards Northern Ireland. It was intended, said de Valera,

to make certain that no outsider would live upon them as long as their own people were not able to get a living for themselves (loud applause). Clearly, if the people of the Six Counties continued to separate themselves, that policy would have to operate against them as it would against the British and other peoples.[85]

There was nothing in any of this to reassure the Ulster unionists, already wary of the possibility that Fianna Fail might win power at the forthcoming Free State election.[86] At this Ard Fheis the party revealed antipathy, even hostility, towards Ulster: de Valera might see himself as the realist attempting to educate an ill-informed party on the complexities of the Ulster question but his own Ulster policy was seen by the unionists as naïve, hostile, and, above all, irrelevant. Nor would they have been impressed by his repetition at one controversial point in the proceedings that his fundamental touchstone remained what it had been in 1917: 'I declared that, if all came to all, I was a Catholic first [applause].'[87]

Although the Partition question had become relatively quiescent since the Boundary Commission débâcle, Fianna Fail had, by now, established themselves as the leading advocates

[85] Ibid., 28 Oct. 1931.
[86] David Harkness, 'Unionist reaction: bitterness and hostility', *Irish Times*, 19 May 1976.
[87] *Irish Press*, 29 Oct. 1931.

of Irish unification. Although anxious to place the electoral emphasis on more immediate, attainable goals, the party consistently argued that they alone could undo Partition; de Valera tended to be less certain about *when* this might be accomplished and consistently attempted to quieten the party rank and file on the question. Essentially, Fianna Fail's anti-Partitionism was now *aspirational* in character. Frankel has usefully divided the policies of political parties, especially in the foreign policy context, as expressing essentially *aspirational* or *operational* interests. His characterization of aspirational interests provides a succinct and, it seems, accurate summary of Fianna Fail's unification policy at this important juncture, the eve of the party's accession to power. Indeed Frankel generalizes that aspirational interests 'command more attention from an opposition free of the restraints of, and the preoccupation with, the tasks of governing than from the actual government'. Although the incoming Fianna Fail government in 1932 was to open the Partition question with Britain, shortly after assuming office, it can retrospectively be seen — and, in particular, it was true of de Valera's own emphasis — that the experience of office made the party more quiescent and realistic on the issue. While in opposition, Fianna Fail's goal of Irish unity seems to 'fit' Frankel's typology of aspirational interests. For Fianna Fail, Irish unity was a 'long-term interest', 'rooted in history', of particular concern to the extremist faction within the party 'concerned with ideological purity': moreover, the aspiration provided 'purpose or direction, or at the least, a sense of hope'; it contained contradictions and it was not 'fully articulated and co-ordinated'; it could be believed in without being costed or being the subject of a 'feasibility study'; and it meets Frankel's concluding point that aspirational interests are determined

by political will rather than by capabilities — ideology is a strong determinant. The influence of power is ambivalent: while an ambition may be due to the people's awareness of the power of their state, it can be likewise due to their awareness of their powerlessness and their escape into day-dreams.[88]

[88] J. Frankel, *National interest* (London: 1970), pp. 32-3.

4. 'The Play of English Interest': 1932–1937

(i) ASPIRATIONAL OR OPERATIONAL POLITICS: DE VALERA'S CHOICE IN OFFICE

Only once during his long public career did Eamon de Valera discuss the Irish Question with the leader of Ulster Unionism: that was at his ninety-minute meeting with James Craig in May 1921. After it he wrote: 'I do not see any hope of ending the struggle with England through a prior agreement with a Unionist minority. At bottom the question is an Irish-English one and the solution must be sought in the larger general play of English interest.'[1] It was de Valera's constant assertion that Britain had originally fomented religious tensions in Ulster in order to divide Irishmen; that the culmination of this policy was Partition; and that her motive throughout was to secure her strategic interests in the Atlantic. His conviction was that this policy was counter-productive and that Partition, in fact, led to instability within Ireland which could be exploited by Britain's enemies. Once in power, in 1932, his avowed aim was to convince the British government that their strategic interests would be best served by a stable, peaceful, independent, and united Ireland.

As has been shown, de Valera prized the pre-Treaty concessions to Ulster which he had won from his cabinet in 1921. He had managed in the decade which followed to retain the essentials of this Ulster policy — local autonomy devolved from Dublin and external association for the whole island. Although intent on a radical realignment of Anglo-Irish relations, de Valera appreciated the intractability of Partition; explicitly he stated that unity was not attainable in the short term. Moreover, there were, in his view, many aspects of Anglo-Irish

[1] De Valera to O'Connor, May 1921, Longford and O'Neill (1970: 123).

relations which needed revision, and these — unlike Partition — permitted initiatives which could be taken *unilaterally*. For two such changes — abolition of the Oath of allegiance to the Crown, and non-payment of the land annuities — he could claim a mandate at the polls. Indeed, he had, with some deliberation, limited the mandate he sought from the electorate to these two issues. In conflict with the British government within weeks of his election victory and in talks with them by July, de Valera was anxious to debate 'fundamentals' including Partition. But if the latter proved, at least for the moment, non-negotiable, he was content to pursue a gradualist approach to the Republic.[2]

(ii) ANGLO-IRISH RELATIONS

The British government was alarmed at de Valera's victory in the 1932 election. They saw him as the bogeyman of Irish nationalism who, having militarily failed to overthrow the 1921 Treaty, was now determined to achieve this goal by a radical revision of Anglo-Irish relations according to his alternative to that Treaty — Document No. 2. Such a prospect discomfited British officials who had enjoyed the respite from the Irish Question which had followed the 1921–2 settlement. Moreover, as a political adversary and negotiator, British ministers found de Valera incomprehensible: Baldwin thought him 'impossible';[3] Thomas and Hailsham considered him 'a complete dreamer';[4] Ramsay MacDonald found his mentality baffling 'in its lack of reason'.[5] Nor was this picture modified by the informants on whom Whitehall relied for intelligence

[2] Thomas and Hailsham, ISC memorandum, 8 June 1932, PRO CAB 27/525, ISC(32)26. Sterling to SS, 4 Feb. 1932, NA, R.G. 84, American Legation Dublin papers, 1932, vol. 4. J. H. Thomas; as Dominions Secretary 1930–5, he was not a success, being disliked by Dominion politicians and not respected by the officials within his own department who thought him 'the greatest blatherer living'; he underestimated de Valera and unlike his junior minister and successor, Malcolm MacDonald, enjoyed no success in Anglo-Irish relations. Joseph Garner, *The Commonwealth Office*, (London: 1978) p. 18. Douglas Hogg, Viscount Hailsham, Secretary of State for War, 1931–5; unsympathetic to Irish nationalism.

[3] Crozier (1973: 27).

[4] Thomas and Hailsham, note covering preliminary discussions in Dublin, 8 June 1932, PRO CAB 27/525 ISC(32)26.

[5] MacDonald to Archbishop of York, 13 Sept. 1932, Ramsay MacDonald papers, PRO 30/69/2/35. Sankey considered de Valera an 'impossible fanatic', diary, 15 July 1932, Sankey papers, Eng. hist. e. 286.

from the Irish Free State. Lord Granard reported to London that he found de Valera 'a most curious personality' and 'certainly not normal'. He suggested that de Valera was

on the border line between genius and insanity. I have met men of many countries and have been Governor of a Lunatic Asylum, but I have never met anybody like the President of the Executive Council of the Irish Free State before. I hope that the Almighty does not create any more of the same pattern and that he will remain content with this one example.[6]

Despite this view of him as an impractical eccentric, the British were obliged to take de Valera seriously. There was a keen awareness in London of the interdependence of the two countries and of the potential damage which an unstable Free State could do to Britain's trade, to her strategic interests, to the nature of dominion status, and, not least, to Ulster.[7] Indeed in some quarters, there seems to have been a fear that the incoming Dublin government might sanction force against Northern Ireland, a possibility which de Valera was careful to deny in two press interviews.[8] Nevertheless, 'Defence of the Border' was soon tabled for discussion by the Northern Ireland cabinet[9] and British ministers discussing the change of government in Dublin noted that 'An armed attack on Ulster was not, however, anticipated' — a comment which suggests that it was considered, at least, in the realm of the possible.[10]

Reluctantly, but inexorably, the British were obliged by de

[6] Granard, note of conversation with de Valera, 25 Aug. 1934, PRO CAB 27/526, ISC(32)86, annex II. Eighth Earl of Granard (1874-1948), member Irish Convention, 1917; member Irish Free State Senate, 1921-34; member of House of Lords; Master of the King's Horse; prominent in racing circles, Britain and Ireland; acted as intermediary between de Valera and British government during economic war.

[7] Ramsay MacDonald, memo, 'Situation arising from Mr de Valera's pronouncements', 30 Mar. 1932, PRO CAB 27/525 ISC(32)4. De Valera's challenge to the British government was also keenly monitored in the Dominions. The US State Department was informed that in New Zealand, it was 'of absorbing interest'. Copy report No. 37, 31 Mar. 1932, NA, R. G. 84, American Legation Dublin papers, 1932, vol. 4. For Canadian interest, see Sir George Perley to Prime Minister, Canada, 10 Apr. 1932, R. B. Bennett papers, reel 889, J. 150, vol. 1, f162857-8. For Smuts's response, see Smuts papers, vol. 49, reel 252, no. 769, July 1932.

[8] *News Chronicle*, 17 Feb. 1932; *Irish Press*, 17 Mar. 1932.

[9] Cabinet minutes, 22 June 1932, PRONI/CAB 4/303/31.

[10] Cabinet minutes, 22 June 1932, PRO CAB 23/71 37(32)2.

Valera to reconsider questions which they had presumed to
be closed by the agreements of 1921 and 1925. Shortly after
his accession to power they felt it necessary to establish a
powerful specialist cabinet committee, chaired by the Prime
Minister, the Irish Situation Committee, which had the responsibility of 'coming to terms with Mr de Valera's Government on the various outstanding issues — constitutional,
financial, defence and economic.'[11] Partition, although the
most intractable problem in Anglo-Irish relations, was not
included in the committee's terms of reference. De Valera
consistently argued that any settlement which ignored it could
not result in the 'friendly neighbour' policy which he sought:
but then, having recorded his fundamental objection, he
acquiesced in its postponement.

With some deliberation he had placed little emphasis on
Partition during the 1932 election campaign:[12] at its close,
when asked by the *News Chronicle* if a Fianna Fail government would 'take immediate steps to a[b]olish the Boundary',
he reiterated his abhorrence of Partition but added that 'we
can only protest', admitting that there were 'no effective
steps that we can take to abolish the Boundary. Force is out
of the question.'[13] And at the press conference which followed
his election victory, when asked if he intended making any
representations to Ulster he admitted that he did not 'see
any way in which we can make them effectively. There are
no steps so far as I can see, which we can take to change a
situation which I regard as disastrous.'[14]

De Valera did constantly remind London of his fundamental
rejection of Partition: for Ireland, he argued the Treaty
had 'meant the consummation of the outrage of Partition,
and the alienation of the most sacred part of our national

[11] Explanatory note, Irish Situation Committee (ISC), PRO CAB 27/522.

[12] But at New Ross, de Valera suggested that an incoming Fianna Fail government 'would not be satisfied with the Partition of the country', *Irish Times*,
25 Jan. 1932. At Kanturk he criticized the extravagance of having two governments in Ireland and promised a tariff barrier against the north, ibid., 18 Jan. 1932.
In the main, his emphasis was on the Oath and land annuities issues, Sterling to
SS, 1 Apr. 1932, NA, R. G. 59, 841D.00/1000.

[13] *News Chronicle*, 17 Feb. 1932.

[14] *Irish Press*, 17 Mar. 1932.

territory with all the cultural and material loss that this unnatural separation entails.'[15]

Again, when Thomas and Hailsham went to Dublin for
talks in June, they heard de Valera expound on the need for
agreement on 'fundamentals' if true friendship between Britain
and Ireland was to be established. 'We asked him if he would
tell us what he meant by the "fundamentals"', reported
Thomas and Hailsham to their colleagues.

He said — 'Certainly.' They were two — first the reunion of the six
counties as to which, he said, Mr Lloyd George seemed to him in 1921
to have been anxious only to secure the partiton of Ireland, and secondly
the recognition of the position of Ireland as a Republic.

De Valera went on to detail his theory of external association;
both British ministers had to resist the temptation to interrupt
and enter a protest. Instead they asked de Valera to expound
on his alternative to a tackling of 'fundamentals': this was
what he termed a 'modus vivendi' by which he meant 'the
acceptance by the United Kingdom of the abolition of the
unjustified payments.' Futher, any such agreement 'would
only last until a fresh mandate had been secured at another
election.'

Further talks in London that same month proved equally
futile. De Valera having indicated that he presumed 'that no
useful purpose could be served by his discussing the two
"fundamentals"',

nevertheless . . . proceeded, for about a quarter of an hour, to develop
his ideas as to these, on the same lines as in Dublin.
    After he had finished, the Prime Minister said that, in his view, no
useful purpose could be served by discussing these 'fundamentals' since
the British Government could not possibly entertain either.[16]

Although cordial, these discussions failed, as did a further
attempt to reach some understanding in talks in October. The
British were reassured, possibly at de Valera's prompting, by

[15] De Valera to Thomas, 5 Apr. 1932, PRO CAB 27/525 ISC(32)7. A holograph
draft in de Valera's hand dated 23 March is in Gallagher papers, MS 18,375(12). This
includes a further charge: 'the cutting off of six of our counties from the motherland', omitted from the official letter.
    [16] Thomas, note, 'Discussions in London', 14 June 1932, PRO CAB 27/525,
ISC(32)31.

J. W. Dulanty in June,[17] and by J. P. Walshe in October,[18] that the experience of office had greatly altered de Valera.[19] Sir John Simon noted de Valera's insistence that he 'was a realist and not a theorist' and would always have men on his left;[20] Hailsham, whose views on de Valera were 'rabid',[21] remained sceptical, believing that, having failed to get a slogan from the London talks, de Valera was now looking for an election issue.[22] Partition was not on the agenda during the four sessions of negotiations in October. As they concluded in failure, de Valera reminded the British that the issue would be central to any overall settlement. For as long as Partition lasted 'the majority of Irishmen would take advantage of any opportunity to re-open that question.'[23]

That Irish unity was a distant prospect — and distinctly less likely, given the trend of de Valera's policies — was unquestioned in London. Although their files included cuttings of de Valera's main speeches, there was other evidence which enabled the Dominions Office to read between the lines of his public condemnations of Partition. In two instances they were literally enabled to read between the lines when transcripts, corrected by de Valera, of two comprehensive interviews

[17] Thomas, ISC memorandum, 4 June 1932 'Developments in the IFS situation', ibid., ISC(32)25.

[18] PRO CAB 27/523, ISC(32)15th meeting, 25 Oct. 1932.

[19] Dulanty and Walshe may well have been prompted by de Valera to reassure London. Similar points were made by de Valera himself to Peters, PRO DO 35/397/11111/36; and to a visitor from the Conservative Party's research department, unsigned note of an interview with de Valera, 30 Mar. 1932, Baldwin papers, vol. 101. J. W. Dulanty, a Cumann na nGaedheal appointment in 1930 as Irish High Commissioner in London, de Valera was under pressure to replace him; in fact, Dulanty remained in this post until 1949; Garner describes him as 'not a powerful figure in any sense of the term and de Valera frankly admitted his deficiencies to Maffey.' Churchill thought him 'a general smoother' and believed him to be 'thoroughly friendly to England'. J. P. Walshe (1886-1956), Secretary, Department of External Affairs, 1922-46; close working relationship with de Valera.

[20] As note 18 above. Sir John Simon held the key posts of Foreign Secretary, Home Secretary, Chancellor of Exchequer, Lord Chancellor from 1931 to 1945; member of Irish Situation Committee, 1932-8; participated Anglo-Irish negotiations, 1938.

[21] Interview, Malcolm MacDonald.

[22] As note 18 above.

[23] Conference between representatives of UK and IFS, IN(32)4th meeting, 15 Oct. 1932, PRO CAB 27/525, ISC(32)70.

were passed to them for their information. The Dominions
Office clearly welcomed details of the 'not uninteresting'
interview which the European Correspondent of the *Christian
Science Monitor* brought to Whitehall on his return from
Dublin; but the 'most interesting part' was de Valera's amendments in which he had 'considerably toned down' some statements, which, however, their informant had 'no doubt' had
been made at the original interview.[24] De Valera, claiming
that he had not changed his views on Ulster '"at all"', since
his interview for the same newspaper in 1918,[25] emphasized
that the boundary was 'entirely artificial, fostered by British
money and British influence in the alleged interest of "mino-
orities".' Having emphasized the importance and indeed the
inevitability of unity, de Valera was asked whether the Ulster
question might not be better

settled by degrees — the North [being] gradually brought back into the
southern fold, as it were?
     'Sometimes it is better to do these things all at once,' riposted the
President without committing himself to saying that this was one such
time.
     'Are you going to take this question up with the British Govern-
ment[?]
     'I think it would be unwise for me to say what I am going to do
about that.'

In correcting the interview for publication, de Valera was
clearly satisfied with this non-committal note. He seems to
have been keen to emphasize that Partition was subsidized by
Britain. Claiming that without the southern market, the north
would eventually find itself economically 'strangled', he added
the qualification that this would be so 'in the absence of foreign
aid'; and, in a later addition to the text, he revealed the same
preoccupation by suggesting that if '"British influence and
British financial contributions"' were withdrawn, 'the force
of common interest, the natural interdependence of the two
parts of the country and the sentiment of nationality would

---

[24] C. G. L. Syers to Thomas, 3 Mar. 1933, commenting on Lias, note of interview with de Valera, corrected by de Valera, Feb. 1933, PRO DO 35/398/11111/
399.
[25] *Christian Science Monitor*, 15 May 1918.

work irresistibly for the restoration of the unity destroyed by British policy in 1920.'[26]

There was no suggestion here that Britain could forthwith terminate Partition. Likewise, there was nothing to offend a Fianna Fail supporter, confident that such a solution was available to Britain. In October 1934, when questioned about 'the very serious difficulty of Ulster' by a Welsh mine-owner, de Valera replied in terms of north and south protecting their respective minorities; and, making special criticism of Stormont's abolition of proportional representation, he added the comment that 'he had no room for dictatorships'. His only two amendments to the typescript on this occasion both emphasized his willingness to grant local autonomy to the north.[27]

Despite the public impasse in Anglo-Irish relations — not without its advantages to de Valera in domestic politics — indirect contacts were not discouraged by either side. As early as the summer of 1933, P. J. Fleming 'a friend and intimate' of de Valera and acting with his knowledge but 'without any express authority', paid two visits to the Dominions Office in Whitehall. Assuring Harding that it would not be 'a waste of time' for Britain to consider his proposals, Fleming sought a settlement of the economic war, repeatedly pressed for the replacement of the Treaty by Document No. 2, and suggested that it should be publicly declared that, if the north consented, Britain would not veto a united Ireland. In response Harding argued that there could be no useful discussion of Irish unity 'except on the basis of a satisfactory settlement of the constitutional position in the Irish Free State.'[28] Invariably, Dublin's response to such arguments was also to insist on linking Partition with the wider questions in Anglo-Irish

[26] Lias, note of interview with de Valera, Feb. 1933, op. cit.
[27] A. E. Jones, note of interview with de Valera, 18 Oct. 1934, PRO DO 35/890/X.1/15.
[28] Harding, note of conversations with P. J. Fleming, 28 July and 17 Aug. 1933, PRO DO 35/398/11111/463, and —/473. Sir E. J. Harding (1880-1954), civil servant; Permanent Under-Secretary of State for Dominion Affairs, 1930–40; somewhat irritated by Irish failure 'to play the game according to strict D.O. rules'. Garner (1978: 112). P. J. Fleming, fought in Civil War on republican side; de Valera supporter.

relations; constantly, London was reminded in these years that, for as long as British policy rested on the Treaty and included Partition, there would remain in Ireland, as Walshe put it privately to Batterbee, a 'slumbering revolt'.[29]

Against this, it must also have become clear to the British government that de Valera himself — for all his rhetoric — was willing to proceed cautiously on the Partition question. While his aspirations for a united Ireland baffled some of the informants of the Dominions Office,[30] there was also on their files sufficient reliable evidence to allow the British to appreciate the difficulties inherent in de Valera's position as the leader of a party pledged to remove the Border. Justice Wylie, on official business in London, representing the Free State's Customs authorities, was confidentially asked by Batterbee, if de Valera 'really believed that he could win over Ulster to the idea of an all-Ireland republic.' Wylie felt certain that 'in his own heart Mr de Valera must know that the idea was absurd. In view, however, of the promises he had held out to his followers, it was impossible for him to make any such admission.'[31] Nor was there anything in Dulanty's communication with the Dominions Office to seriously contradict this impression. This, however, is not to suggest that de Valera's High Commissioner in London was not constantly seeking some 'movement' on Partition. However, the modesty of Dublin's short-term expectations is revealed in Harding's note of a conversation with Dulanty in February 1934. Dulanty urged the British to prevent a 'drift' to the Republic, by publicly ruling out a British veto on a united Ireland within the Commonwealth provided that this 'were Northern Ireland's own wish'. At another stage in the conversation, as Harding notes, Dulanty 'went rather further' hinting at the possibility of a flat statement of approval by Britain for a united Ireland within the Commonwealth but without mentioning a veto for

[29] Walshe to Batterbee, 11 Nov. 1933, PRO DO 35/398/11111A/93. Sir Harry Batterbee (1880–1976), Assistant Under-Secretary, Dominions Office, 1930–8; the 'honest broker' of the DO, Garner (1978: 27).

[30] Batterbee, note of conversation between MacDonald and Henry Hall, 'the Australian historical [sic] student', July 1933, PRO DO 35/398/11111/454.

[31] Batterbee, note of conversation with Justice Wylie, 3 Aug. 1933, PRO DO 35/398/11111/466.

Ulster; however he then realized that 'any statement of this kind was not within the realms of practical politics.'[32]

Some months later, after another conversation with Dulanty who had just returned from Dublin, Harding noted that, to the Irish High Commissioner, de Valera now seemed to have

what might be described as a dual outlook. The first was that which he had always had — belief in a Republic of Ireland as his ultimate political aim.

The second was that of a man who believed that a Republic of 26 counties was not a satisfactory solution, who felt that a Republic of 32 counties was unlikely during his lifetime, and who, as a responsible political leader, was determined to do his utmost to avoid a civil war.[33]

It was some time before this pragmatic and pacific side to de Valera was appreciated in London, although for his own part he seems to have been anxious to bring it to their earliest attention. Within days of winning the 1932 election he had called in the most senior British official in Dublin, the United Kingdom trade commissioner, William Peters, who had duly reported to the Dominions Office that he well understood de Valera's 'real object' in talking to him: 'to disabuse H.M.G. of the idea that he was a firebrand looking for a second round with England'. Furthermore, on Partition, de Valera had then confided that there was 'no question of an immediate settlement' and although the issue 'stood at the back of everything it had to be left out of account so far as immediate relations with Great Britain were concerned.'[34]

One detailed proposal for a settlement of Partition was mooted towards the close of Thomas's tenancy of the Dominions Office. In forwarding the scheme to London, Granard informed the Dominions Secretary that two delegates, one of whom was 'in touch with Mr de Valera and is a personal friend of his', had asked him 'to put it into the hands of a [British] Cabinet Minister' and had also hoped that the King would see it. The delegates had claimed to Granard that their scheme

[32] Harding, note of talk with Dulanty, 19 Feb. 1934, PRO DO 35/398/11111A/55.

[33] Harding, note of talk with Dulanty, 13 June 1934, PRO DO 35/398/11111A/94.

[34] Peters to Batterbee, 14 Mar. 1932, PRO DO 35/397/11111/36. William Peters, UK trade commissioner in Dublin.

'would have the approval of the Irish Government . . . and
would settle the Irish deadlock provided that the British and
the Northern Governments would assent to it.'[35] The proposals
advocated the establishment of a sovereign, federal, *Irish*
Commonwealth, composed of two Dominions, north and
south, both externally associated with the British Commonwealth. Such a 'new arrangement' was imperative because the
1921 Treaty had 'failed to establish Anglo-Irish peace and
friendship; and the timing of such an initiative was opportune,
it was argued, because of Britain's desire for a settlement, the
worsening 'commercial dispute', the drift in the Free State
'towards a Republican form of Government', and Ulster's 'constitutional difficulties . . . and loss of Free State trade.' Urging
'sacrifice by all sides', the authors advocated 'a settlement by
goodwill' trusting that time would 'soften some features which
arise from the tragic past.' They contended that their solution
would meet the fundamental requirements of all three parties,
the British, the Ulster unionists and the Irish nationalists:
Britain would secure her strategic and commercial interests;
Ulster would secure 'political peace', and trade with the
south, and would also 'give England a present of an Irish
settlement'; and for Irish nationalists, such a solution would
meet 'the unquenchable Irish desire for nationhood'.

The requirements of these three parties would be 'brought
into one frame' by the proposed settlement which the authors
then detailed:

(a) The establishment of an Irish Commonwealth, acknowledged by
     Great Britain to possess Sovereign authority,
(b) The Commonwealth to be federal, so that the Northern Irish
     Parliament and the Free State respectively will continue to
     exercise their present powers in their own territories.
(c) A Treaty of Association between the Irish Commonwealth
     and Great Britain designed to meet British interests and yield
     benefits to all Ireland.
     N.B. Terms (a), (b) and (c) would satisfy the bare requirements
     of the parties concerned. Each one of the three is essential to
     a settlement.

Reciprocal citizenship between Ireland and Britain would

---

[35] Granard to Thomas, 11 Mar. 1935, PRO DO 35/399/11111A/163.

follow as would preferential trade agreements and a defensive and military alliance 'recognising the strategic unity of these islands' but with Irish forces occupying all ports.

While the 'State Parliaments' in Dublin and Belfast would retain their present powers, their members would also elect an Irish Commonwealth parliament which would 'control the transferred powers of North and South and also such other common services as the North and South may decide to surrender to it, e.g. agriculture[.]' This Commonwealth parliament would also elect a President, who would be an Irish citizen, preferably a non-political personage, who would be elected for a term equal to the normal term of three parliaments: assent to Bills of the Commonwealth and state parliaments would be delegated to the President. The authors urged the British government to 'approach and endeavour to persuade the North'; claiming that Dublin was 'willing', they added, 'it happens that London is willing too. Is Belfast?' If agreement was reached, the proposals would then be submitted for ratification to a Constituent Assembly with representatives of north and south 'elected at an *ad hoc* general election'. Such ratification was deemed

necessary to secure the concurrence of the Irish nation; and so eliminate the objections which have been taken by extremists in the past.

We are satisfied that the Government of the Free State will accept these proposals if the assent of the Northern Government is obtained.

For the first time in history, all the parties would appear to have a common interest, and a settlement should therefore be possible.[36]

This proposal appears to have been, initially, at least, of some interest to the Dominions Office: a note was prepared on the financial relations between Northern Ireland and Great Britain; the Home Office was alerted; then, through an intermediary, Granard sent the proposals back to Dublin, to de Valera. Some gamesmanship can be presumed in this move, as it reads like London asking de Valera for an opinion on what they must have presumed was his own kite! De Valera, in his response, was not tempted to make a firm proposal: what went back to London was still a kite. His intermediary

[36] Anon., 'Protocol of an Irish Settlement', forwarded by Granard to Thomas, 11 Mar. 1935, ibid.

informed Granard that the scheme would form a satisfactory basis for settlement for the great majority of the Irish people if initially advocated by the British government; in such circumstances, the intermediary assured Granard, de Valera 'would talk business'.[37] As the Irish Situation Committee was dormant at this juncture — it did not meet at all during 1935 — it is difficult to assess the seriousness with which the proposal was considered in London. Although expressing disbelief that Northern Ireland would give her assent, and noting that the scheme envisaged Irish forces holding the Treaty ports, the main misgivings noted in the Dominions Office file concern the role envisaged for the Crown and unease about the proposed functions of the President; apart from these issues, however, Harding's note continues, 'the principles set out . . . as the basis of the scheme would seem generally to afford a basis for negotiations.' This, however, may merely have been Harding's 'first sight' response; that these words are scored through on the file suggests that he had second thoughts on them; his basic view is more probably expressed in the less optimistic covering memorandum to Thomas: 'It is, I fear, clear that the proposals . . . do not really carry us any further. They are only a rather elaborate variant on Mr de Valera's original idea of "external association".'[38]

It was this view which, in time, prevailed and no bilateral, still less trilateral talks with Belfast included, took place on the proposal. The Ulster Unionists' antipathy to a comparable proposal advocated in the *Irish Times* was already on record.[39] Published under the pseudonym, 'Pacificus', this was written by Aodh de Blacam, one of those senior members of Fianna Fail who were preoccupied by Partition. Denby, the American Minister in Dublin, reported to the State Department that while de Blacam's scheme was 'interesting and stimulating' to some Fianna Fail ministers, it had not been officially inspired.[40] The article had praised de Valera's recent 'magnificent

[37] PRO DO 35/399/11111A/163, *passim*.
[38] Harding to Thomas, enclosing note on 'Protocol of an Irish Settlement', 14 Mar. 1935, ibid.
[39] *Irish Times*, 1 Jan. 1935.
[40] Denby to SS, 4 Jan. 1935, NA, R.G.59, 741.41D/20. Aodh de Blacam (1890-1951), journalist, born London of Ulster parents; publicist for Sinn Fein during War of Independence; member Fianna Fail sub-committee on Partition,

conception' of the Commonwealth as 'a smaller League of Nations' and had mooted the possibility of the United States becoming a member of a wider Anglo-Celtic Commonwealth. Although widely publicized and appealing to pluralists in Ireland at the time, the scheme was faulted for being academic, utopian, and romantic.[41] The importance of these proposals lies not in any success they achieved, but rather that, taken together, they may be presumed broadly to reveal the form which de Valera would then have thought tolerable for his fundamental ideas of external association and local autonomy for the north. Such concessions would not have satisfied the small core of diehard republicans: MacSwiney had warned de Valera in 1932 that such a solution would represent a 'betrayal beyond all forgiveness'.[42]

Vulnerable to such diatribes, Fianna Fail, in these years, was invariably more sensitive to its republican critics than to those few who argued that it should, despite the indifference of the Ulster unionists, ensure that it did not further alienate that community. Yet such alienation was the effect of Fianna Fail's consolidation of its power base with nationalist voters: along with the abolition of the Oath, and the non-payment of land annuities, there was the virtual eclipse and then the abolition of the Governor-General's office, the withdrawal of the right to appeal to the Privy Council, and the unilateral repudiation of British citizenship. Nor could Ulster unionists ignore the abolition of the Free State Senate, explicitly set up to defend the interests of southern unionists. And they were unlikely to be impressed by de Valera's prosecution of the economic war, more particularly since de Valera envisaged it as part of his 'drastic experiment in economic nationalism',[43] one of whose bonuses he believed might be the economic

---

1938-9; author of propagandist tract, *The Black North* (Dublin: 1938) foreword by de Valera; member Fianna Fail National Executive until December 1947 when he defected to rival republican party, Clann na Poblachta.

[41] See also 'Ireland and the Commonwealth', written by an Irish citizen 'of distinct nationalist sympathies' in *Round Table*, vol. 25, pp. 21-43, Dec. 1934; and a reply by 'an Ulster Protestant' in ibid., pp. 249-65, Mar. 1935; *The Times, Belfast Newsletter*, 2 Jan. 1935.

[42] MacSwiney to de Valera, 7 June 1932, MacSwiney papers, P48/B/19.

[43] W. K. Hancock, *Survey of British Commonwealth affairs, vol. 1, Problems of nationality, 1918-1936* (London: 1937), p. 350.

persuasion, if not coercion, of Ulster into a new relationship with the south. But his entertainment of such hopes contradicted the syndrome — well understood by de Valera[44] —which Gellner has identified as the capacity of ethnic groups to ignore rational self-interest if the 'call of blood or group loyalty or territoriality' is awakened. That such might be the north's response to economic pressure should have been clear to de Valera. Was not the acceptance by many of his own supporters of their losses in the economic war consistent with Gellner's theory?[45]

It was not only Fianna Fail's policies on Anglo-Irish relations which alienated the Ulster unionists. Other constitutional issues, church–state relations, cultural and language policies, must all be considered in the context of de Valera's declared strategy of fashioning a society capable of attracting the north to, at least, a federal embrace. Another critical area — where the Belfast government had, perhaps, its most direct interest — was de Valera's handling of internal security, his government's relationship with extremist groups, and, in particular, the IRA.

(iii) DE VALERA'S PARTITION STRATEGY: THE IRISH CONTEXT

De Valera saw Fianna Fail as a broad 'national front' party which he hoped would unite Irish nationalists. In particular, he was eager to persuade 'physical force' republicans to forswear military, and adopt constitutional, methods. Throughout the 1930s he was still winning such recruits to Fianna Fail. Among those who would not join, some saw Fianna Fail as trimmers who had usurped the republican cause, while others welcomed the party's success in the 1932 election believing that a de Valera-led government would be lenient towards the IRA.[46] In fact Fianna Fail was lobbied to reach

---

[44] John Cudahy to SS, 5 Dec. 1938, NA, R.G.59, 841D.00/1146. John Cudahy, (1887-1943), American of Irish descent; not a career diplomat, he supported Roosevelt in 1932 election and was appointed Ambassador to Poland, 1933-7; at his own request, Minister to Ireland, 1937–40; unlike his predecessors, very active in seeking de Valera's views.

[45] Ernest Gellner, 'Scale and nation', in Gellner, *Contemporary thought and politics*, ed. I. C. Jarvie and J. Agassi (London: 1974), p. 150.

[46] McGarrity to de Valera, 22 Oct. 1933, McGarrity papers, MS 17,441.

an understanding with the extremists. McGarrity believed this
to be a 'national necessity' and wrote to de Valera from
America:

> They can do the things you will not care to do or cannot do in the face
> of public criticism . . . You both profess to desire the same goal, why in
> God's name do you hesitate to sit down and try to find a working agree-
> ment. It is the extreme, the fanatical thing as the English call it, that
> frightens them and causes them to seek for peace. We denounced Collins
> and his friends for stopping the boycott on Ulster, and why now stop it
> by those who have the courage to carry it on.[47]

De Valera agreed that some understanding was necessary with
the IRA,[48] though his version of what an acceptable understanding would be differed from McGarrity's: 'You talk as if
we were fools and didn't realise all this. My God! Do you not
know that ever since 1921 the main purpose of everything I
have done has been to try to secure a basis for national unity.'
But the 'need and desire' for unity, added de Valera, should
not lead Fianna Fail into an alliance with a group 'too stupid
or too pigheaded' not to see that a disaster would follow if
Fianna Fail's approach were to be replaced by a policy of
force. De Valera did not believe 'the wit of man' would discover any alternative to his strategy. If the country was to
avoid becoming 'a Mexico or a Cuba' there was no alternative
to order being imposed by the elected majority: 'We have
undertaken a responsibility to the people at present living, to
the future, and to the dead. We will not allow any group or
any individuals to prevent us from carrying it out.'[49]

De Valera used similar arguments to the IRA leader, Sean
MacBride, in five meetings held in the first eighteen months
of Fianna Fail rule. MacBride reported to McGarrity that at
the last meeting de Valera had 'got excited and said that he
would maintain law and order even if it cost him his life.'
Partition was the outstanding difficulty, de Valera told Mac-
Bride; but in MacBride's lengthy letter outlining many hours
of talks, no discussion of strategy on Partition is noted. The
understanding between Fianna Fail and the IRA, which
MacBride clearly thought probable because of 'great pressure'

[47] Ibid.
[48] S. T. O'Kelly to McCartan, 22 Mar. 1932, Maloney papers, box 21.
[49] De Valera to McGarrity, 31 Jan. 1934, McGarrity papers, MS 17,441.

from within Fianna Fail, was for 'a united front in the economic war crisis'.[50] Given the ambivalence of the Fianna Fail rank and file towards the IRA — it was little more than a decade since many of them had fought together for the Republic — de Valera had to tread warily in handling what he clearly saw as the IRA's threat to the status quo.[51] IRA leaders were offered posts in the Free State army;[52] a new volunteer force was inaugurated which the IRA correctly realized was 'a political instrument for the seduction' of their members.[53] De Valera's strategy was to attempt to 'get the IRA lads to see a little bit of sense':[54] the failure of many of them to comply finally prompted him to deploy against them the same anti-subversion laws which he had castigated when in opposition. That he had first used these laws against the quasi-fascist Blueshirts[55] made their invocation against the IRA more tolerable to the Fianna Fail rank and file; but to the MacSwiney faction his final outlawing of the IRA in June 1936 was bewildering, contemptible and, they believed, inevitably futile. 'Poor, foolish, foolish Dev. How are the mighty fallen!', wrote MacSwiney to him in a private letter. She found his reply 'cheap, impertinent, insincere', attacking him as 'a fool, a criminal fool'.[56]

By now, such criticism was heard from a vociferous but increasingly marginal rump of republicans. Through astute

[50] MacBride to McGarrity, 19 Oct. 1933, McGarrity papers, MS 17,456. Sean MacBride (b. 1904), son of executed 1916 leader, John MacBride and Maude Gonne; participated in War of Independence and Civil War on republican side; sometime political secretary to de Valera; disapproved of formation of Fianna Fail, 1926; remained in IRA, becoming chief of staff, 1936-7; prominent barrister defending IRA prisoners; in 1946 formed rival constitutional republican party, Clann na Poblachta; Foreign Minister, 1948-51. Winner Nobel Peace Prize, 1974.

[51] Frank MacDermot to W. Ormsby Gore, 9 Jan. 1934, Baldwin papers, vol. 101; Leslie E. Woods (US consul, Cork) to Sterling, 7 Jan. 1932, NA R.G.84, American Legation Dublin papers, 1932, vol. 4; for further evidence of Fianna Fail's care to maintain leadership of Irish republicanism at this juncture, see Irish Race Convention (New York) August 1932 papers, MS 7363, *passim.*

[52] Interviews, Frank Aiken, Sean MacBride.

[53] Denby (US Minister, Dublin) to SS, 26 Mar. 1934, NA, R.G.59, 841D.20/5.

[54] De Valera to O'Kelly, but probably written for McGarrity's attention, 6 Sept. 1933, McGarrity papers, MS 17,441.

[55] For the history of the Blueshirts, see M. Manning, *The Blueshirts* (Dublin: 1970).

[56] MacSwiney to de Valera, 20 and 30 June, de Valera to MacSwiney, 22 June 1936, MacSwiney papers, P48/C/20.

timing and a keen awareness of the tolerances of public opinion, de Valera had eroded support for Sinn Fein and the IRA and had established Fianna Fail as the principal vehicle of the republican tradition. His rhetoric was brilliantly pitched towards this end. Characterizing Fianna Fail as 'the resurrection of the Irish nation',[57] he posed the choice to the party's Ard Fheis in 1933 in these terms: 'We either march forward as a disciplined people with a recognised and accepted headship, or we are going to be a rabble and get nowhere. Which is it to be? Voices: "Forward".'[58]

De Valera repeated this metaphor at the next Ard Fheis in a speech counselling patience: 'Each step in advance henceforth ought to be a step taken when they had brought up all the necessary reinforcements from the rear to enable them to take it and hold it.'[59]

On the same theme in 1935 he told the delegates 'to wait and not to seize something before it was ripe.'[60] In 1936 he asked them to ensure that there would be 'no retreat' remembering that 'when you have a position like this, your opponents will do their utmost to storm the position.'[61]

The assumption was general at these conferences that the party was the custodian of the nation's destiny,[62] which it defined as 'a free, self-contained, united Gaelic Ireland'.[63] De Valera himself in reassuring successive conferences about the ultimate goal of the party, seems to have contradicted his proposed concessions to the Ulster unionists: certainly to that community, obsessively suspicious of all Irish nationalists and especially of de Valera, his Ard Fheis speeches can have brought no reassurance. In 1933 he emphasized the difficulties of 'restoring' the north to the nation:[64] in 1934 he talked of a 'completely united . . . independent republic';[65] in 1935 he foresaw a 'unified State' where a majority would inevitably opt for 'complete independence' taking 'the republican form'.[66]

---

[57] De Valera, quoted *Irish Press* editorial, 9 Nov. 1932.
[58] *Irish Press*, 9 Nov. 1933.   [59] Ibid., 14 Nov. 1934.
[60] Ibid., 4 Dec. 1935.   [61] Ibid., 4 Nov. 1936.
[62] Secretaries' Report to Ard Fheis, ibid., 13 Nov. 1934.
[63] Secretaries' Report to Ard Fheis, ibid., 9 Nov. 1932.
[64] *Irish Press*, 9 Nov. 1933.
[65] Ibid., 14 Nov. 1934.   [66] Ibid., 4 Dec. 1935.

De Valera was in the mould of those nationalist leaders who wish to refashion society. On education, morality, materialism, agriculture, industrialization, even on women's fashions, and especially on the language issue, de Valera believed in change.[67] The direction and scale of the changes he envisaged imply a confidence on his part that human behaviour could be significantly altered; and, that if leadership proved inadequate, then state intervention would be justified and effective. For instance, he suggested that to save the Irish language it would be necessary to give jobs — he instanced technical jobs — to less qualified applicants who had the 'essential national qualification of the language'.[68] Indeed he often suggested that the restoration of the language was a more urgent national issue than Partition, arguing that while Irish unity was inevitable, the language had to be saved in his generation. Once restored, he foresaw it spreading across the border.[69]

Characteristically he argued that the economic war with Britain would lead to 'the foundation here of the sort of economic life that every Irishman who thought nationally in the past hoped for':[70] his new order would be modelled on an idealized Gaelic past.[71] Acknowledging as a 'central difficulty' the affection of Irish unionists for the Crown,[72] he allowed for no plurality of views on this question, insisting that in the name of democracy majorities should decide — and the majority for which he spoke was 'the historic Irish nation'. As narrowly defined by de Valera, this nation could only include unionists through assimilation which, he predicted, was inevitable: 'I have no doubt as to the direction you will have to go in the end.'[73]

In all of this, de Valera — as opposition deputies constantly pointed out in the Dail — was entrenching Partition. The 1937

[67] De Valera: 1980: speeches, pp. 145–8; 150–3; 233–5; 425–33; 466–9; 522–6; *The hundred best sayings of Eamon de Valera* (Dublin: n.d.) *passim*; *Irish Press*, 9 Nov. 1933.

[68] *Irish Press*, 9 Nov. 1933.

[69] In particular in his addresses to annual conferences, see *Irish Press*, 10 Nov. 1933, 14 Nov. 1934, 4 Nov. 1936. Longford and O'Neill (1970: 459-60).

[70] Quoted in Longford and O'Neill (1970: 281).

[71] *Gaelic American*, 17 Jan. 1920; SE: 22: 988–9, 7 Feb. 1939.

[72] *Irish Press*, 8 Nov. and *The Times*, 10 Nov. 1934.

[73] *Irish Press*, 8 Nov. 1934.

Constitution was the most formal expression of the contra-
diction at the core of Fianna Fail's strategy on unification:
their attempt at nation-building on a specifically republican,
Catholic, Gaelic model in an island where such values were
not shared or tolerable throughout the putative 'nation'. De
Valera at the 1936 Fianna Fail Ard Fheis had promised that
the forthcoming Constitution would be 'in accordance with
their traditions, their aspirations, and their philosophy of
life.'[74] Scholars and politicians might argue about whether
there were, or were not, two *nations* in Ireland: but who could
deny that there were two traditions, two aspirations, two
philosophies of life? The concept of political culture best
demonstrates the cleavage: were there not two 'intelligible
webs of relations' on the island of Ireland? Further, was not
de Valera's Constitution as finally passed emphatically the
expression of one of these political cultures; and far from
being suited to a united country was it not antipathetic to the
traditions of Ulster unionist society, 'the spirit of its public
institutions, the passions and the collective reasoning of its
citizenry, and the style and operating codes of its leaders.'?[75]

The most persistent contemporary critic of the contradictions in de Valera's policy was one of the most independent-
minded members of the Dail in the 1930s, Frank MacDermot.
He characterized Fianna Fail's initial 'onslaught on Commonwealth symbols' as a policy which 'might have been specially
designed to consolidate Partition.' De Valera rejected Mac-
Dermot's arguments that the south should shape its policies
bearing Ulster's interests and sensitivities in mind. If they
were to do this, the unity of Ireland would not follow. Consequently when the southern public heard 'talk about the
unity of Ireland' being dependent on 'our attitude', they had
'sufficient sense . . . not to bother their heads about it.'[76]

---

[74] Ibid., 4 Nov. 1936.
[75] L. W. Pye and S. Verba, *Political culture and political development* (Prince-
ton: 1965), p. 7.
[76] DE: 55: 2256-86, 10 Apr. 1935. Frank MacDermot (1886-1975), politician,
journalist, Anglophile; contested West Belfast in Westminster election 1929; won
Dail seat as independent 1932; formed National Centre Party, 1932, dedicated to
rapprochement with north and Britain merging with Cumann na nGaedheal to
form Fine Gael, 1933; resigned from Fine Gael 1935 and from Dail, 1937; advocating a pluralist society, he was a persistent critic of de Valera's northern policy

MacDermot railed against what he termed 'the stale claptrap and the weary fallacies of Fianna Fail propaganda'; and claimed that 'some very prominent politicians on both sides of the House' had suggested to him that 'the North would be an embarrassment to us . . . and that we were better off without them.'[77]

If the trend of southern politics was inimical to northern interests, this seems to have been a matter of indifference to de Valera. Under assault from MacDermot, he admitted that no member of the Dail could point 'to any plan which will inevitably bring about union. We do not pretend to be able to do it.' Partition may have been 'a disaster and a shame but we cannot by any action of ours remedy that. All we can do is to try our best to bring about union but no one can say how it can be inevitably done. The question for us is how far we should deny ourselves in order to bring it about.' He reminded the Dail of Ulster's lack of interest in his 1921 concessions but claimed that Fianna Fail would always leave 'the door open'. Developments in the south's constitutional status *vis-à-vis* Britain, he believed, would eventually prove a 'help' rather than a 'block or a barrier' to the north: 'We cannot get them in; Deputies yonder cannot get them in and our policy is to go ahead in our own way.'[78]

De Valera's defence of his strategy on unity clearly reveals that his primary instinct was to defend his party's republican flank, irrespective of the consequences on Ulster opinion. It could, of course, be argued that no policy to weaken the border short of an application by the Free State to rejoin the United Kingdom, would have won a hearing from the Ulster unionists.[79] Traditionally suspicious of the south, they reserved a particular antipathy for de Valera and his policies and when, in 1932, Fianna Fail came to power, their reaction was one of apprehension, if not foreboding, particularly

and of his 1937 Constitution; appointed a Senator by de Valera, 1938; later, New York and Paris correspondent of *Sunday Times.*

[77] DE: 59: 196-210, 30 Oct. 1935.
[78] DE: 56: 2112-6, 29 May 1935.
[79] There was some Ulster Unionist interest in a customs union of the British Isles, Buckland (1979: 71).

among loyalists along the border. At a cabinet meeting to discuss the changed security situation in June, the northern government noted that in view of 'the excitement, amounting almost to frenzy', which had been caused by the Eucharistic Congress then being held in Dublin, 'it was generally felt that certain incidents might occur on the Border which would lead to bloodshed.' Although the cabinet heard reports that drilling was taking place along the southern side of the border, home affairs minister, Dawson Bates, did not expect 'anything in the nature of a major operation' but thought some 'tip and run' attacks a possibility.[80] The emphasis at this cabinet meeting on the Eucharistic Congress is revealing. Craigavon's government — itself subjected to nationalist attack for its espousal of the epithet 'Protestant' — clearly thought of Partition as an expression of religious divisions in Ireland. At Stormont, in reply to his critics, Craigavon claimed that 'in the South they boasted of a Catholic State . . . All I boast of is that we are a Protestant Parliament and a Protestant State.'[81]

Fianna Fail's security and tariff policies may have been matters for intense suspicion in the north, but when it came to eliciting the siege reflex, on which, after all, organized Unionism thrived, de Valera's programme was exactly suited to Craigavon's book. All nationalists were unreliable, but here, at least, was an acknowledged enemy of Ulster in power in Dublin. Some comfort from this development seems to have been drawn by the former Northern Ireland Minister, by now a member of the British government, Lord Londonderry, when he confided to Craigavon that, in Britain, they were 'now faced by the more or less open opposition of a De Valera government instead of the somewhat doubtful friendship' of a government led by Cosgrave whose goodwill would probably have depended 'entirely upon the concessions they could get from us.'[82]

---

[80] Cabinet minutes, 22 June 1932, PRONI CAB 4/303/31; also Lady Craigavon, diary 12 and 14 Apr. 1932, Craigavon papers, D1415/B/38. Richard Dawson Bates, NI Minister of Home Affairs, 1921–43.

[81] Quoted Buckland (1979: 72); see also cabinet discussion on whether a religious question should be included in the Northern Ireland census to obtain information 'pertinent to the State as a whole'. 30 Oct. 1934, PRONI CAB 4/331/24.

[82] Quoted Buckland (1979: 71). Lord Londonderry (1878-1949), NI Minister of Education, 1921-6, later British Secretary of State for Air, 1931-5, Leader House of Lords, 1935-6, antagonistic to Chamberlain's Irish policy, 1937-9.

One concession coveted by the northern government was some amelioration of the south's tariff policy. Recognized as inimical to northern interests under Cumann na nGaedheal, it was now, as amended by the new government, significantly harsher and was thought, in Belfast, to be coercive in intent.[83] Envious of the south's fiscal powers, frustrated by their own impotence in such matters, and constantly harassed by northern industrialists who were losing markets and profits in the south, this remained an abiding grievance with the Stormont government.[84] As early as June 1932, Andrews expressed his concern to Craigavon that the witholding of the land annuities by de Valera's government, if successful, would result in the continuation of the lower income-tax rate, and the establishment of better social services in the Free State, a trend which, he thought, was already apparent. If this were to continue, he warned, 'it will ultimately have a very unsettling effect upon some of our people. We can absolutely trust, as you know, the older members of our community, but among the younger ones is where a danger lies.'[85]

Consistently, throughout this period, Unionists were immune to any hints from Britain that they should make concessions to Irish unity to prevent the drift in the south to a republic. Northern Ireland's answer to such pressures, said Craigavon, 'would always be the same — "Nothing doing".'[86] Moreover, Craigavon warned his followers to be particularly vigilant lest a British government with 'antipathy' towards Ulster might be open to persuasion by Dublin's lobbying: attempts, he predicted, to have Ulster brought under an All-Ireland parliament would persist 'for all time'.[87]

[83] That the Ulster Unionists were apprehensive about this policy is clear, Pollock to Baldwin, 20 July 1932, Baldwin papers, vol. 98; moreover, this had always been well understood by Irish nationalists, Redmond to Lloyd George, 19 Nov. 1917, Redmond papers, MS 15,189.

[84] Buckland (1979: 73-7).

[85] Quoted ibid., p. 76. John M. Andrews (1871-1951), MP NIHC, 1921-49, Minister of Labour, 1921-40; succeeded Craigavon as Prime Minister, 1940, but lost support of Ulster Unionist MPs in 1943 when he was replaced by Basil Brooke.

[86] *The Times*, 27 Aug. 1934; see also Sir Kingsley Wood, ibid., 20 Jan. 1934; J. Davison and Craigavon, ibid., 13 July 1934. Unionists were also concerned that southerners would 'infiltrate' the north, see Cabinet discussion throughout 1934, PRONI CAB 4/320/5, −/321/6, −/331/24.

[87] *The Times*, 13 July 1934.

Virtually powerless in Northern Ireland, and suffering the gross and petty discriminations of Ulster Unionist rule, the northern nationalists tended to look southwards for their salvation. Notoriously fragmented,[88] they had, in the main, supported Collins's most optimistic reading of the outcome of the Boundary clauses of the Treaty;[89] it was only when their expectations had been disappointed with Cosgrave's 'damned good bargain' in signing the 1925 Boundary Agreement, that they switched their hopes to de Valera. Fianna Fail's accession to power in 1932, brought with it a quickening of expectations.[90] De Valera, however, while sympathetic to their plight, and invariably a publicist for their grievances, was reluctant to share an anti-Partition strategy with their leaders; consistently, to the chagrin of one faction within Fianna Fail, he kept the party aloof from political alliances which might erode his strict personal control of Fianna Fail's Partition strategy. He informed Cahir Healy that whereas Fianna Fail was 'ready to co-operate in any movement which is likely to bring Partition to an end', it would not intervene 'in differences of opinion, among Six County anti-Partitionists'.[91] Although his successful candidature as abstentionist MP for South Down in 1933 gave, to some, the contrary impression, most of the evidence, public and private, suggests great inhibition on de Valera's part in his relations with northern nationalists.

Any republican organization, and particularly a political party whose *raison d'être* was to unite Ireland, yet which confined its base to the south, left itself vulnerable to criticism. The orthodox policy for such a party, would be to organize throughout the thirty-two counties and adopt an abstentionist policy in six-county elections. Within Fianna Fail, one faction persistently demanded such an approach, arguing that Fianna

[88] M. Coyle to Healy, 10 Nov. 1937, Healy papers, D2991/A/50.

[89] See Kevin O'Shiel to Executive Council, 17 Nov. 1923, Mulcahy papers, P7/B/287. O'Shiel became director of the North-East Boundary Bureau, preparing the Irish case for the Boundary Commission.

[90] Buckland (1979: 72-3).

[91] Sean Moynihan (on de Valera's behalf) to Healy, Jan. 1934, Healy papers, D2991/A/17B. Cahir Healy (1877-1970), leading anti-Partitionist among border nationalists; supported 1921 Treaty but switched his hopes to de Valera after Boundary Commission collapse, 1925; MP NIHC, 1925-65, MP Westminster, 1922-4, 1931-5, 1950-5, dates inclusive of abstentionist phases; interned, 1922-4, 1941-2.

Fail should 'throw its mantle over Ulster'.[92] There was even the suggestion — reportedly discussed in the spring of 1933 — that the Nationalist Party in Northern Ireland should, *en bloc*, rename themselves Fianna Fail.[93] Donnelly, fertile with ideas on Partition, thought the south quiescent, even polite, on the subject, and remained 'incensed' at de Valera's refusal to extend Fianna Fail across the border.[94] At the 1933 Ard Fheis,[95] he heckled de Valera on Partition which prompted the party leader to defend his northern record in a speech which met with such 'extraordinary enthusiasm' in the north, that the *Irish Press* shortly published a 'sensational report' detailing an invitation to the entire Fianna Fail cabinet to stand as abstentionists throughout the north.[96] Although de Valera accepted a nomination for South Down, no other minister stood, Fianna Fail's aim being 'to consolidate . . . not to divide' the northern nationalists.[97] Nothing of what emerged from a week of rumour and consultation contradicts what must remain speculation: that the original *Irish Press* scoop was in fact a kite being flown by Donnelly.[98]

A more significant initiative favoured by the interventionist faction was to open Leinster House to elected representatives from the six counties. At a stroke, this would have 'legitimized' Dail Eireann for republicans, by putting it on the same basis on which it had been founded after the 1918 election: the all-Ireland parliament established by a majority of elected representatives from south and north. The subsequent exclusion of six-county representatives, after the Treaty, had rankled with northern nationalists and de Valera who had then protested at their exclusion,[99] now had the power to admit them to the Dail.

In February 1933 the two leading constitutional nationalists in the north, Devlin and Healy, privately approached de Valera

---

[92] Eamonn Donnelly's phrase, *Irish Press*, 4 Nov. 1936.

[93] Lucien Memminger to US Ambassador, London, 25 Mar. 1933, NA, R.G. 84, Records of American Legation Dublin, 1933, vol. 4.

[94] E. Rumpf and A. C. Hepburn, *Nationalism and socialism in twentieth century Ireland* (Liverpool: 1977), p. 185.

[95] *Irish Press*, 9 Nov. 1933. [96] Ibid., 11 Nov. 1933.

[97] Ibid., 18 Nov. 1933. [98] Ibid., 11–18 Nov. 1933, *passim.*

[99] Minutes, Comhairle na dTeachtai, 7 Aug. 1924, MacSwiney papers, P48/C/8.

seeking seats in the Dail as the elected representatives of northern constituencies. De Valera refused; he even declined to offer them any advice on whether they should return to Stormont.[1] To de Valera's discomfort, this tactic continued to have its advocates. Some republican fundamentalists went further, threatening to call for a boycott of both Stormont and Leinster House and the convening instead of an all-Ireland parliament: 'the effect would be tremendous. Fianna Fail could not refuse to co-operate.'[2]

Yet two more northern-based organizations prepared strategies to force the Partition question: the National Unity Organizing Committee was pledged not to 'take part in the proceedings of any partition Parliament, or any Parliament other than the sovereign independent legislature of all Ireland';[3] and a rival Irish Union Association, inspired by Healy, which pledged its members to fight Partition but, to Fianna Fail's comfort did not prohibit membership of 'partitionist parliaments'.[4] But even this latter organization, although obviously the most moderate of these groupings, was preparing to put further pressure on de Valera — the orchestrator being, again, the indefatigable Donnelly. In October 1936 Healy confided to a fellow MP that he received 'a letter from a well-known Fianna Fail TD, from which I gather that *they* think we are likely to let the national spirit die here'.[5] Donnelly had written: 'Partition is now in operation fifteen years and we are worse today than when it began. If the present position lasts for another ten years we may chuck in.' This generation would only be remembered 'as a lot of weaklings who saw what to do and who didn't do it.' Donnelly's advice to northern MPs was to act independently, 'No more delegations and resolutions'. They should leave Stormont ¯and demand admission to the Dail: 'We'll carry all Ireland on this.' Donnelly outlined his talks with politicians north and south and felt certain that the policy advocated would 'pull together all the

---

[1] Healy to de Valera, 19 June 1956, Phoenix (1978); not calendared, but cited in his chapter on 'The Nationalist Party in Northern Ireland, 1921-55', p. 6.
[2] George Gilmore to Healy, 25 Oct. 1935, Healy papers, D2991/A/31A.
[3] Press cutting, Healy papers, ibid., —/37D.
[4] Copy of draft Constitution, 16 Sept. 1936, ibid., —/39E.
[5] Healy to J. J. McCarroll MP, 23 Oct. 1936, ibid., —/41E.

various elements', would generally 'force the pace' and make the re-unification question 'practical politics again'.[6]

Critical of Healy's more circumspect approach, Donnelly later enthused about the 'grand' Ulster resolutions due for debate at the 1936 Ard Fheis. In particular, he was elated by a resolution which, he believed, contained 'the solution'.[7] This read: 'This Ard Fheis demands that a clause be inserted in the new Constitution enabling the elected representatives of North East Ulster to sit, act and vote in Dail Eireann.'[8] But despite the imprimatur of Healy's anti-Partition grouping,[9] this seems to have presented little difficulty to de Valera at the Ard Fheis. After some debate, it was, at his suggestion, withdrawn on the grounds that it would be premature to pass any resolutions concerning the new Constitution.[10]

Despite such caution, de Valera was assured by Healy in October 1935 that the 'vast majority of the Nationalists here would be supporters of Fianna Fail.'[11] From de Valera's own viewpoint, Partition represented a continuing threat to the political stability he was seeking in the south — a new equilibrium through which he hoped to assimilate extreme republicans to constitutional methods. His particular fear was that IRA violence might erupt in the north.[12] He would have agreed with what Frank MacDermot had told Westminster MPs at a private meeting in 1936: 'Whatever assurances Mr de Valera or anybody else may give you about our attitude in time of war, there is nothing to guarantee you against violent outbreaks by the Nation[al]ist minority in the north, which would produce overwhelming reactions in the Irish Free State.'[13]

On the international stage too, consistent with the cautious policy already revealed, de Valera did not place any great emphasis on Partition during these early years in office. In

---

[6] Donnelly to Healy, 25 Sept. 1936, ibid., —/42A.

[7] Donnelly to Healy, 30 Oct. 1936, ibid., —/42C.

[8] Resolution 4, agenda, 1936 Ard Fheis.

[9] Irish Union Association, *Irish Press*, 2 Nov. 1936.

[10] *Irish Press*, 4 Nov. 1936.

[11] Healy to de Valera, 23 Oct. 1935, Healy papers, D2991/A/29A.

[12] De Valera to Healy, 20 July 1935, ibid., —/25A.

[13] Frank MacDermot to the 1922 Committee at House of Commons, 20 July 1936, noted in PRO DO 35/399/11111A/257.

particular, he withstood all lobbying to raise it at the League of Nations.[14] By 1936, Donnelly was writing to Healy: 'Rule out Geneva. This is dead or dying. The chance was lost and apparently "statesmen" like Joe Connolly knew more about Bolivia, Paraguay, China ... than about Ballinamallard or Tempo.'[15]

Occasionally de Valera did remind the League about Partition, usually emphasizing the importance of evolving methods for the solution of such international problems. Participating in a debate on possible methods of guaranteeing minority rights, he suggested that 'the greatest common measure of the rights of minorities might be distilled by a conference and given universal application. But he admitted that the greatest difficulty was to agree upon the problem, "What is a minority?"'[16]

Arguably it was off-stage at Geneva, during informal talks with British ministers, that de Valera made whatever progress was possible on Partition;[17] his aim was to make it a negotiable issue between himself and the British government; his strategy was to link it to a defence agreement; his argument was that without such a comprehensive settlement, Partition brought endemic instability to Ireland leaving both islands vulnerable in a Europe drifting towards war. His pessimism about the prospects for international peace clearly gave an impetus to these diplomatic dealings with London. Although it was in the interest of both countries to end the mutually damaging 'economic war', the threat of another major war also formed part of the context in which the Anglo-Irish negotiations of 1938 took place. These negotiations represented de Valera's long-awaited opportunity to question the basis of the 1921 Treaty, a document which unilaterally he had already rewritten in his first six years in power. As has been seen, he spent these years virtually ignoring the Ulster unionists, deflecting any unwelcome liaison with the northern nationalists and curbing the excesses of southern extremists of all hues. His ascendancy in the Free State was established but republican

---

[14] DE: 44: 1164-7, 4 Nov. 1932.
[15] Donnelly to Healy, 25 Sept. 1936, Healy papers, D2991/A/42A.
[16] The Times, 22 Sept. 1934.
[17] Interview, Malcolm MacDonald.

support on which it depended was conditional on his making progress on the national aim: establishing Irish unity.

(iv) ANGLO-IRISH RELATIONS: THE THAW: MALCOLM MACDONALD AS DOMINIONS SECRETARY

In November 1935, in a British cabinet re-shuffle, Malcolm MacDonald succeeded Thomas as Secretary of State for the Dominions. During the three following years his impact on Irish policy was immense. A young, gifted politician, son of the former Prime Minister, Ramsay MacDonald, he had two advantages over his more senior colleagues: he believed in the Commonwealth rather than the Empire and, on Ireland, he was young enough not to have typecast de Valera in 1922 as the wrecker of the Treaty settlement. His dealings with de Valera were to be characterized by 'tact, goodwill and above all by an almost sublime patience.'[18] There was an empathy between both men which de Valera had never managed to establish in his earlier relationships with British politicians. MacDonald found de Valera 'a transparently honest and sincere man who never concealed, or even half-hid, his beliefs and aims.'[19]

MacDonald was a diligent negotiator, a prolific writer of memoranda to his colleagues, and a persistent advocate of appeasement towards Ireland, disarming, with considerable skill, his opponents within the government. His first comprehensive cabinet paper in May 1936, marked a turning-point in Anglo-Irish relations, demonstrating an astute analysis of the impasse already reached, his own preference for a conciliatory policy, and an acceptance on his part of de Valera's claims that he had to bear his republican critics constantly in mind: 'these advanced Republicans might become formidable if he lightly made them a present of the Republican cause.'[20]

[18] Deirdre MacMahon, 'Malcolm MacDonald and Anglo-Irish Relations: 1935-38', MA thesis, UCD, 1975, p. 11. Malcolm MacDonald (1901-81), Parliamentary Under-Secretary for Dominion Affairs, 1931-5; Dominions Secretary, Nov. 1935-Jan. 1939 (excepting May-Oct. 1938); enjoyed a unique rapport with de Valera among British politicans, Chamberlain not excepted; largely responsible for success of Anglo-Irish Agreement, 1938, for which Churchill never forgave him — regarding him as 'rat poison'; as Minister of Health visited Dublin on three occasions in June 1940 to discuss Irish neutrality with de Valera.

[19] Malcolm MacDonald, *Titans and others* (London: 1972), p. 65.

[20] MacDonald, cabinet memorandum 'Relations with the Irish Free State', May 1936, PRO CAB 64/34 CP 124(36).

To those in Whitehall whose duty it was to monitor developments in the Free State, there was now increasing evidence that de Valera was a gradualist, adopting as one writer to the Dominions Office put it, 'Fabian tactics' on Partition.[21] Another correspondent, after an interview with the Irish leader, assured London that de Valera himself claimed he was 'disarming the gunman by a peaceful process.'[22] But de Valera's gradualism was more apparent to the Dominions Office than to Baldwin's cabinet, who, content that their retaliatory levies on imports from Ireland compensated for the unpaid land annuities, had settled for a policy of drift: they seemed, if anything, bored with de Valera. Indeed Irish policy was scarcely under active consideration when MacDonald became Dominions Secretary — the Irish Situation Committee, for instance, not having met for the previous ten months.

That de Valera was now electorally secure was becoming widely accepted in London;[23] and MacDonald, for one, actually saw some advantages in this. A settlement concluded with him would prevent the Free State slipping into even more republican hands: and the other alternative, for which London had been hoping — and working, where possible — since 1932, the return of a Cosgrave government,[24] would hardly bring political quiet. It would leave an unappeased Fianna Fail in the wings, awaiting their turn, and doubtless becoming even more republican in opposition. MacDonald, the first British Minister to recognize that the 1921 Treaty was outdated, argued in just this sense to his colleagues. Because of de Valera's 'unique position and influence in Irish politics', he wrote, any settlement with him had 'much more prospect of being permanent than one concluded with any other possible southern Irish leader.'[25]

[21] Charles Spring Rice to Batterbee, 11 Aug. 1936, PRO DO 35/399/11111A/229.

[22] Major-General Sir George McK. Franks, memo of interview with de Valera, 12 Mar. 1936, forwarded to Dominions Office, PRO DO 35/399/11111A/213.

[23] In the summer of 1936 Dulanty told MacDonald that there was 'now no chance' of Cosgrave returning to power adding that McGilligan agreed with this view, MacDonald, note of conversation with Dulanty, 26 Aug. 1936, PRO CAB 27/527 CAB 27/527 ISC(32)117; Cosgrave to Bodkin, 1 Sept. 1936, Bodkin papers, MS 7003/60.

[24] Thomas, memorandum 21 June 1932, PRO CAB 27/525 ISC(32)36.

[25] As note 20 above.

Once awakened by MacDonald's initiatives to the importance of Irish policy, British ministers came to appreciate that
de Valera's goal remained the essentials of Document No. 2:
external association for a united, independent Ireland with
local autonomy for Ulster.[26] For the British government, this
policy had some limited appeal; after all, de Valera's espousal
of external association, justified by him only as a concession
to the north, might curb Fianna Fail's republican separatist
instincts. For de Valera too, Fianna Fail's need to make some
concessions to Ulster opinion could be invoked to justify a
closer relationship with Britain than the party would otherwise
have supported. Convinced as he was about the injustice and
the intractability of Partition, a policy of propaganda, economic coercion,[27] and secret diplomacy seemed best, with an appreciation that if the context changed any opportunity to
weaken Partition should be exploited. What seems certain is
that given the nature of Fianna Fail's political support, de
Valera could scarcely have formulated a more conciliatory
northern policy: Document No. 2's concessions to Ulster
were already anathema to many republicans.[28] It was incum-
bent on Fianna Fail, at minimum, to champion the *aspiration*
to Irish unity.

Although MacDonald's tenure of the Dominions Office
brought a more sympathetic approach to Dublin, there was
little change on Partition. The British were still extremely
reluctant to become embroiled in the issue and were confident
that it could be safely kept in the background. Anthony Eden
in October 1935 — a month before MacDonald was appointed
— informed his cabinet colleagues that Walshe had informed
him at Geneva that de Valera 'fully appreciated' that a united
Ireland 'could not come about all at once. The most therefore
that could probably be hoped for at this stage would be some
declaration by both Governments in Ireland expressing a
hope that at some future date when both parties desired it a
united Ireland might come about.'[29]

[26] Ibid., see also Sir Warren Fisher's views in PRO CAB 27/527 ISC(32)118,
7 Nov. 1936.
[27] See Lucien Memminger (US consul Belfast) to SS, 26 May and 26 Oct.
1932, NA, R.G. 84, American Legation Dublin papers, 1932, vol. 5.
[28] MacBride, speech, *Sligo Champion*, 18 Apr. 1936.
[29] Anthony Eden, 'Note of meeting with J. P. Walshe', 15 Oct. 1935, PRO
CAB 64/34 CP 124(36), appendix III.

Whereas the British believed that office had mellowed de Valera,[30] they still considered that on fundamentals, including Partition, he was contrary and probably immovable.[31] One significant element in the British cabinet, led by Hailsham, thought it obvious that de Valera was pursuing his 'obsession'[32] of an all-Ireland republic and that it would be 'a pity to revive a dormant issue' by encouraging any renewal of even exploratory talks.[33] Inskip supported this line believing that de Valera 'would not listen to arguments of any kind.'[34] But MacDonald's enthusiasm for 'a careful effort to reconcile differences'[35] prevailed against such scepticism and Baldwin's indifference,[36] and he eventually won cabinet approval for a continuation of his bilateral talks with de Valera, begun in the spring of 1936.

The best evidence for de Valera's views at this juncture comes from MacDonald's detailed memorandum of a lengthy conversation which he had with the Irish leader in London on 7 July. MacDonald found de Valera in a 'practical mood', this being indicated by the fact that in four hours talk he had 'never mentioned Oliver Cromwell or any character or event which troubled Ireland prior to 1921.' MacDonald informed his colleagues that de Valera's

personal preference was for an independent Republic, but above all else he wished for a united Ireland, and therefore in 1921 he had given careful thought to the possibility of finding some compromise which would ultimately bring the majority and the minority in Ireland together. He had considered what was the furthest that he and those who agreed with him could go to meet the feelings of the Northern majority and those who agreed with them.

This was the provenance of his theory of external association; it was the furthest he could possibly go in the direction of

[30] PRO CAB 27/523 ISC(32) 23rd meeting, 12 May 1936. Ibid., ISC(32) 24th meeting, 25 May 1936.
[31] PRO CAB 27/523 ISC(32) 23rd meeting, 12 May 1936.
[32] PRO CAB 27/523 ISC(32) 25th meeting, 17 June 1936.
[33] PRO CAB 27/523 ISC(32) 23rd meeting, 12 May 1936. For Hailsham's confidential views of de Valera's 'bigoted' outlook on Anglo-Irish relations, see Hailsham to Granard, 5 Mar. 1934, in R. F. V. Heuston, *Lives of the Lord Chancellors: 1885–1940* (Oxford: 1964), p. 478.
[34] PRO CAB 27/523 ISC(32) 25th meeting, 17 June 1936.
[35] As note 20 above.
[36] Interview, Malcolm MacDonald.

compromise. Were he to go further, 'he himself would be overthrown by his followers.' Despite the 'intense' dislike of the Crown in the Irish Free State he thought he could successfully advocate its retention for external functions; but that was the limit to which he could go. 'Even if he were willing to advocate more than that, and if he were to carry the day immediately, the success would be temporary. What he wished was for some settlement which would have some prospect of being permanent.'

The aim which 'lies closest to his heart', MacDonald noted, is that of a united Ireland; he had insisted that if only Britain had the will, she 'could persuade the North to join in a United Ireland'. MacDonald attempted to disabuse him on this point but de Valera insisted that at least if Britain used her influence with the north, she 'could do much to make them favour a United Ireland'. The issue, in de Valera's view, was of 'supreme importance' since good relations between Ireland and Britain depended on a solution. He laid great emphasis, as was customary in all his talks with British officials, on the difficulties of curbing republican extremists: 'He was opposed to those in the South who asked him to use force to bring in the North. He would not use force; but he would employ reason, and was willing to wait for reason to prevail.'[37]

It was de Valera's belief that Irish negotiators in London should exploit British fears of an even more intransigent government emerging in Dublin[38] and the need to assuage republican opinion was a persistent theme in his diplomatic communications with London.[39] On this occasion, for instance, he suggested that

the *tendency* in the Irish Free State *was for the voters to move to the Left.*[40] He was having great trouble with the extreme Republicans, and was doing everything he could to break their influence. But the

[37] MacDonald, memorandum, including a note of conversation with de Valera, 7 July 1936, PRO CAB 27/527 ISC(32)108.

[38] MacSwiney to de Valera, 30 June 1936, MacSwiney papers, P48/C/20.

[39] MacDonald, cabinet memorandum 'Relations with the Irish Free State', 15 June 1936, PRO CAB 64/34.

[40] The British described in left-right terms what was, in fact, a continuum in Irish politics ranging from those who espoused a republican-separatist position to those who favoured an independent state within the Commonwealth.

movement of opinion seemed to be in their direction, and he himself
was being spoken of now as belonging to the Right![41]

(v) DE VALERA, THE RATCHET EFFECT, AND IRISH NATIONALISM

This is an appropriate point at which to consider whether
Irish nationalist politics was not a demonstration of a ratchet
effect at work — a ratchet effect being where policy is amenable to change in one direction only.[42] In the case here considered — Ireland's relationship with Britain — was it not the
case that changes tolerable to Irish nationalist opinion had to
be towards the separatist end of a unionist-separatist continuum? The course of Irish nationalism in the twentieth
century seems to show such a ratchet effect: agitation for
Home Rule gave away to a Dominion settlement, itself only
justified because it could be used as a 'stepping-stone' to
greater independence; later, under de Valera's leadership, the
'restless Dominion' which he inherited was incrementally
nudged towards a relationship of external association with
the Commonwealth; and once his External Relations Act was
repealed in 1948, it was thereafter inadmissible for the twenty-
six-county Republic of Ireland to contemplate rejoining the
Commonwealth, even to facilitate a pan-Irish *rapprochement*
in the interests of re-unification. This syndrome, even if not
identified and labelled, was felt to be at work by all political
factions in the south.[43] The key to both London's and
Belfast's understanding of Irish nationalist politics,[44] it was

[41] MacDonald, ISC memorandum, containing a note of his conversation with
de Valera, July 1936, PRO CAB 27/527, ISC(32)108. Italics added.

[42] The ratchet metaphor is derived from: 'ratchet: set of teeth on edge of bar
or wheel in which a pawl engages to ensure motion in one direction only' (*Concise
Oxford Dictionary of Current English* (London: 1964, 5th edn.).

[43] De Valera, speech on 1916 Rising, *Irish Press*, 22 Apr. 1935; also, DE: 55:
2270-86, *passim*, 10 Apr. 1935; Senator Joseph Connolly expected Fianna Fail's
'ultimate successors in government' to come from 'the extreme Republican viewpoint', *Fianna Fail Bulletin*, Apr. 1936. MacSwiney to de Valera, 11 May 1936,
MacSwiney papers P48/C/20. J. P. Walshe to Frank MacDermot, 24 Nov. 1941,
MacDermot papers, 1065/14/8.

[44] 'Irishmen got more extreme as time went on', Sir John Simon, 3 Mar. 1938,
PRO CAB 27/642 INC(38)3; Craigavon, interview, *Sunday Dispatch*, 23 Oct.
1938. American diplomats in Dublin also recognized this syndrome, Denby to SS,
22 Mar. 1935, NA, R.G. 59, 841D.00/1081; Owsley to SS, 23 Jan. 1936, ibid.,
841D.00/1095.

particularly evident once Fianna Fail was in power, since their programme was based on moving gradually towards external association, which was in the direction of separatism. Against this background, it is interesting to consider some of de Valera's ideas as he revealed them in his private talks with the Dominions Secretary.

MacDonald elucidated the nuances of de Valera's position for circulation to his colleagues, sometimes finding it prudent to cast the Irish leader in as moderate a light as possible consistent with the opinions exchanged by both men at their meetings. This was to shelter MacDonald's essentially conciliatory policy from its formidable opponents in the British government.[45] Making some allowances for this factor, MacDonald's accounts offer remarkable evidence on the evolution of de Valera's thinking on Anglo-Irish relations. The de Valera–MacDonald talks were often exploratory in character, both men 'thinking aloud' in order to exchange views frankly and without committing their respective governments. Nothing in the picture of the pragmatic, almost Anglophile, de Valera portrayed by MacDonald, contradicts the picture of the cautious, pacific, gradualist already suggested here. It should be remembered, too, that de Valera was a secretive politician, leading an Anglophobic party, and had every reason not to trumpet his personal appreciation of the considerable strategic and economic interdependence between Ireland and Britain.[46]

On the controversial question of the Crown, which had split Irish politics since the Treaty, MacDonald reported de Valera's views in considerable detail after two long conversations in January 1937. As these immediately followed the Abdication crisis, which de Valera had met by rushed legislation to limit the Crown to external functions, MacDonald was, manifestly on this occasion, obliged to record de Valera's views with some precision. It would seem from these conversations that de Valera was hoping to keep the ratchet locked

---

[45] MacDonald describes his own role as 'a sort of diplomatic liaison officer' between de Valera and 'the group of very pro-Ulster, anti-de Valera, right-wing Conservative ministers', in the National government. Letter to author, 15 May 1979.

[46] Interview, Malcolm MacDonald.

at external association. Commenting on his recent External Relations Act, he emphasized not his exclusion of the Crown from internal affairs but, rather, the 'big thing' which Fianna Fail had done in voluntarily recognizing the King's role in external relations. Emphasizing the fact that Irish public opinion was unaware of the Crown's limited functions, de Valera argued that, slowly, 'Irishmen would become reconciled to the King. But if he forced the pace now, that process would be checked and destroyed.' MacDonald put it to de Valera that it seemed to him that for reasons which the British 'perfectly understood' de Valera was

reluctant . . . to use in his actual legislative documents precise language to describe the facts as they were. The facts, as he described them, regarding Irish Free State Membership of the Commonwealth and the recognition of the King were one thing, the language in the Acts seemed a somewhat different thing. To put it plainly, he dared not in the document 'call a spade a spade'.

MacDonald informed his cabinet colleagues that de Valera had admitted 'that this really was so,' claiming that his 'domestic political difficulties were very real.' MacDonald recorded that he had assured de Valera that the British government 'would be ready to recognise his difficulties',[47] a point scarcely appreciated by British ministers many of whom were, by now, exasperated by de Valera. Ramsay MacDonald felt trapped in a 'metaphysical discussion' over external association,[48] a concept which Simon characterized as the 'shadow of a shade'.[49] Presently, Malcolm MacDonald sent a further paper to the cabinet outlining London's options. Without denying the unsatisfactory nature of Dublin's initiative, he stressed as always the positive dimensions; he argued that 'it must be a very serious blow' to the republicans in the Free State

that their unrivalled leader has recognised the position of the Crown and actually passed legislation to maintain it in some form. It is true that Mr de Valera himself still hankers after a united Irish Republic

[47] MacDonald, cabinet memorandum 'Relations with the Irish Free State', 16 Jan. 1937, PRO CAB 64/34 CP 14 (37).

[48] PRO CAB 27/524 ISC(32) 30th meeting, 15 Dec. 1936.

[49] Ibid., ISC(32) 29th meeting, 17 Nov. 1936.

within the Commonwealth. He told me so frankly, but at the same time he kept saying that in five or ten years time the Irish, who could only accept the King reluctantly now, may have learned to accept him more readily.[50]

Against this evidence suggesting that de Valera expected Irish nationalism's ratchet to lock at external association must be placed a number of Irish speeches in which he implied that the ratchet would inevitably turn to the position espoused by the party: an independent united republic.[51] However it was MacDonald's belief that de Valera's External Relations Act 'really represents the beginning of Mr de Valera's own permanent acceptance of the King as King of Ireland and head of the Commonwealth.' MacDonald did not preclude the possibility that 'this theory . . . is wrong' and that de Valera's recent moves represent 'only one step in the direction of abolishing the King altogether'. His own impression, however, was that he had correctly assessed de Valera's motives: 'Mr de Valera wants a united Ireland, and he also wants to remain a member of the Commonwealth of Nations, and I believe he is at least convinced that he cannot attain either of these objects unless he is ready to accept the King.'[52]

There is one other possible explanation of the difference in emphasis between what de Valera told MacDonald and what he said to the party. It is possible that he was only too confident of the ratchet effect and was relying on it, in time, to pull Fianna Fail towards the Republic while, in the interim, he kept his 'bridge' open to Ulster and could honourably defend those Irish interests in trade, finance, and defence which derived from Dominion status.

Although de Valera persistently reminded the British during these years of his fundamental objections to Partition, they remained merely listeners to his grievances, successfully resisting any attempts to make the question one for negotiation rather than debate. This had distinct advantages for de Valera.

---

[50] MacDonald, cabinet memorandum 'Relations with the Irish Free State', 18 Jan. 1937, PRO CAB 64/34 CP 15(37).

[51] See de Valera's statements to successive Fianna Fail conferences, 1933-5, *Irish Press*, 9 Nov. 1933, 14 Nov. 1934, 4 Dec. 1935.

[52] As note 50 above.

More aware than his supporters of the intractability of Partition, he was — as successive American ministers in Dublin had noted — content to pursue a policy of gradualism: he did not believe in 'hastening too rapidly towards the Republican goal'.[53] Yet there were some fundamental dimensions of his republican programme which were essential to maintain Fianna Fail's support and some members of the party believed these should be expedited in advance of any movement on Partition. MacEntee, for instance, stressed in July 1936, the need to work 'towards the national objectives so that when we have a republican constitution, if these people want to come in with us they will have to accept the Republic as well as every other thing.'[54]

Just as the British reminded him that he ought to heed Ulster's views, thereby hoping to curb his republican instincts, so he, in turn, informed them that as no progress had been made on abolishing Partition, he felt free to proceed with his new Constitution.[55] The publication of this, in draft form, in May 1937 with its formal expression of the south's irredentist claim on the north, brought the Partition question to the forefront in Anglo-Irish relations. The period which followed, including as it did the comprehensive intergovernmental negotiations of January–April 1938, is critical in any consideration of de Valera's record on Partition. Not since 1921, when he had controversially left the detailed negotiations to others, was London so seriously engaged in a review of the Anglo-Irish relationship.

---

[53] Owsley to SS, 23 Jan. 1936, NA, R.G. 59, 841D.00/1095; Sterling to SS, 4 Feb. 1932, NA, R.G. 84, American Legation Dublin papers, 1932, vol. 4; Denby, biographical sketch of de Valera, 25 Mar. 1936, NA, R.G. 59, 841D.001/3.

[54] *Irish Press*, 27 July 1936.

[55] Longford and O'Neill (1970: 307).

5. *'Hibernia Irredenta'*: 1937–1939

(i) THE 1937 CONSTITUTION: 'AS FEW FICTIONS AS POSSIBLE'[1]

'I can truthfully say that I am more confident now that I have a good chance of seeing the attainment of our objectives than I was when we started twenty years ago.' (De Valera to Ard Fheis, 1937.)[2]

The new Constitution, long promised by de Valera, marked the culmination of a fifteen-year campaign against the Treaty. Its purpose was to destroy that settlement, justify de Valera's constitutional opposition to it, and positively to vest the state's sovereignty in the people through a written constitution. Its republican core was fundamental to Fianna Fail's political programme. If it offended politicians in Belfast or London, this was a price de Valera was prepared to pay; it had not been drafted to satisfy them but rather, if possible, Irish republicans. In fact it won several rebukes from all three of these parties and from the opposition in the Dail, but it was accepted, if narrowly, by the electorate and, in time, won the broad support of Irish nationalists. De Valera was disappointed with its initial reception; in vain, he had sought all-party support for it in the referendum campaign,[3] claiming that its rejection by the electorate would prove a 'national disaster'.[4] But despite persistent appeals, the proposed Constitution was not recommended to the voters by opposition parties.

---

[1] De Valera told the Dail in 1948 that 'our Constitution was intended to be as explicit as it possibly could be, with as few fictions as possible'. DE: 113: 421, 24 Nov. 1948.

[2] *Irish Press*, 13 Oct. 1937.

[3] Longford and O'Neill (1970: 299); see also Aiken, DE: 67: 336-7, 13 May 1937.

[4] *Irish Press*, 18 June 1937.

Although some of its Dail critics considered the Constitution paradoxical on Irish unity,[5] the opposition based their rejection of it on grounds other than its particular expression of anti-Partitionism — Articles 2 and 3.

Article 2 claimed for the nation, jurisdiction over the entire island; Article 3 accepted that *de facto* the laws of the state could only be exercised in the twenty-six counties 'pending the reintegration of the national territory'.[6] A matter for concern in Belfast and London, as will be seen, and broadly dismissed as naïve and counter-productive in the press,[7] Articles 2 and 3 provoked scepticism rather than opposition from Fine Gael. They were strenuously opposed, when in draft form, by the Secretary of the Department of Finance, J. J. McElligott.[8] Offering the Department's commentary in a critical spirit, McElligott objected to the irredentist claim on the north, whose validity in international law he doubted. Articles 2 and 3 seemed 'rather to vitiate the Constitution, by stating at the outset what will be described, and with some justice, as a fiction'; further, he argued, they would 'not contribute anything to effecting the unity of Ireland, but rather the reverse.'[9] In a later comment, McElligott repeated his view that the claim to territory 'which does not belong to Saorstat Eireann' gave a

permanent place in the Constitution to a claim to 'Hibernia Irredenta'. The parallel with Italy's historical attitude to the Adriatic seaboard beyond its recognised territory is striking and in that case it is likely to have lasting ill-effects on our political relations with our nearest neighbours.[10]

McElligott's broadsides proved futile, no trace of their thinking being incorporated in the Constitution when published.

---

[5] See exchanges between de Valera and McGilligan, DE: 67: 448, 13 May 1937.

[6] Article 2, *Bunreacht na hEireann*. Throughout this book the document is referred to by its more popular title, 'the 1937 Constitution'. For Articles 2 and 3, see Appendix 2, pp. 339-40.

[7] *Irish Times*, 1, 3, and 10 May; *Irish Independent*, 21 June 1937.

[8] J. J. McElligott (1893-1974), participant in 1916 Rising; joined Department of Finance, 1923; Secretary of Department and head of civil service, 1927-53.

[9] McElligott's memo is dated 22 Mar. 1937, quoted in J. R. Fanning, *The Irish Department of Finance: 1922-1958* (Dublin, 1978), p. 267.

[10] Department of Finance submission on 'Second Revise' of draft Constitution, early April 1937, by J. J. McElligott, quoted, Keogh (1979).

A more likely source of influence, whose lobbying seems to have been taken into account was the interventionist faction within Fianna Fail which had suggested that an all-Ireland republic should be unilaterally declared in the new Constitution.[11] The unilateral initiative, it must be remembered, had successful precedents. Indeed the induction of most Fianna Fail TDs into political activity dated from the 1919-23 period during which their classic pose was based on a unilateral assumption of authority by their group, whether as Sinn Fein abstentionist MPs setting up Dail Eireann, as IRA volunteers, or as workers in the Sinn Fein courts or in the 'underground' government departments before the Treaty.[12] Later a similar strategy was attempted in opposition to the Free State, republicans unilaterally maintaining a rival 'Dail', 'cabinet', and 'army'. Moreover, since 1932, de Valera's successes in Anglo-Irish relations had largely been a result of unilateral initiatives.

Given this background, it is scarcely surprising that one faction in the party believed that through the formal declaration of a united country in the Constitution, de Valera could precipitate a crisis and, perhaps, open up the Partition question.[13] Certainly Article 2, *without* Article 3's *de facto* acceptance of interim Partition, and *with* seats in the Dail for northern MPs, was the most radical initiative available to the Fianna Fail government, and was probably what the interventionists had in mind when they called for the abolition of Partition through the new Constitution. But having failed to persuade the 1936 Ard Fheis to demand that the new Constitution provide Dail seats for Northern MPs, Donnelly's group had to settle for an assurance 'that there would be no words in the new Constitution that could possibly place bounds to the march of a nation.'[14] Undeterred, Donnelly called a meeting of the National Executive of Fianna Fail to discuss his resolution that 'an all-Ireland convention be called before the Constitution is introduced and that steps be taken to approach again the question of the re-unification of Ireland on the basis as adumbrated in President de Valera's letter of the 19th

[11] *Irish Press*, 4 Nov. 1936; agenda 1936 Ard Fheis.

[12] De Valera told the 1936 Ard Fheis that 'unilateral action is not going to end Partition.' *Irish Press*, 4 Nov. 1936.

[13] Ibid., for reports of 1936 Ard Fheis; also *Fianna Fail Bulletin*, Nov. 1936.

[14] *Irish Press*, 4 Nov. 1936.

July 1923.'[15] This referred to a specific version of de Valera's federal solution which was less conciliatory towards the Ulster unionists than de Valera's position in the late 1930s. In 1923 de Valera had proposed a six-county plebiscite with the expectation that 'Derry City and the greater parts of the Counties Tyrone and Fermanagh as well as South Armagh and South Down would be represented directly in the National Parliament.' 'On no plea', he had then argued, 'could the "Ulster" minority demand anything more.'[16] But by 1937 he clearly preferred a different emphasis. Unfortunately the minutes of the National Executive meeting merely record that 'after a long discussion the motion by Mr Donnelly was put and defeated by 21 votes to 4.'[17] De Valera — an infrequent attender at such meetings in these busy years — took the chair on this occasion.

Such pressure by Donnelly gives some indication of the expectations of de Valera's republican wing. This lobbying and de Valera's hopes — to some extent fulfilled — that his Constitution would wean some IRA members into constitutional politics, rendered it necessary to include as a minimum, his irredentist claims in the Constitution.[18]

Article 3 which accepted *de facto* Partition, 'pending the reintegration of the national territory', was considered by many to render nugatory Article 2's claim that the entire island comprised the 'national territory'. To a wide spectrum of political opinion, these Articles, taken together, seemed to be paradoxical and contradictory — 'make-believe' was the verdict of both Cosgrave[19] and of the most stubbornly orthodox of all republicans, the '2nd Dail'.[20] Ulster unionists agreed: Craigavon thought the Articles made 'not a pin of difference'.[21] There was nothing in this remarkable unanimity to contradict McElligott's original verdict that the Articles were 'a fiction'. For their part, Fianna Fail speakers, while emphasizing the

[15] Minutes, Fianna Fail National Executive, 1 Feb. 1937.
[16] Quoted by Donnelly, DE: 67: 110, 11 May 1937.
[17] *Irish Press*, 4 Nov. 1936.
[18] Interviews, Sean MacBride, Michael O Morain.
[19] *Irish Times*, 3 May 1937.
[20] Statement by '2nd Dail', *Irish Freedom*, June 1937; see also ibid., July 1937.
[21] *Irish News*, 6 May 1937; see also editorials, *Belfast Newsletter*, 1 and 7 May 1937.

desirability, necessity, and inevitability of unity,[22] argued that the Constitution would form 'a secure basis' for national unity.[23] Nor would it need to be changed in any detail in a future united Ireland.[24]

When the Dail came to consider the document, two of de Valera's most persistent critics on Ulster, MacDermot and Donnelly, tabled the first two resolutions; both men were preoccupied by Partition, both wanted to involve the north in the shaping of any Constitution but their attacks came from diametrically opposed positions. Donnelly, in order to give the people of Ulster 'a voice and a vote' in the Constitution, called on the Dail to defer a second reading, at least until 1938, to enable 'a special Governmental Department' to be set up which would concentrate on the Partition question: its role would be the 'uniting and co-ordinating' of all the anti-Partitionist forces throughout Ireland, organizing the Irish lobby abroad,

focussing through the home and foreign Press world opinion on this grave national issue, and pressing the English government to reopen negotiations on the reunification of Ireland, so that, if and when a solution of the problem is found, *Bunreacht na hEireann* can be submitted to the whole people of Ireland for ratification or otherwise.

Partition, he insisted, was 'the predominant national issue. Nothing else counts; nothing else matters . . . We cannot call this a nation until we get back that territory.'[25] Without winning any support, Donnelly's proposal was dismissed by MacEntee: it had not 'the slightest chance' of proving of practical value.[26]

MacDermot, a strong advocate of a pluralist, united Ireland moved a resolution calling on the Dail to decline to give a second reading to the Constitution 'since, while purporting to establish a Constitution for the whole of Ireland, it offers no basis for union with the North and contains various provisions tending to prolong partition.' Although the concept was not

---

[22] Aiken, *Irish Press*, 10 May; O'Kelly, ibid., 23 June; de Valera at Dundalk, ibid., 28 June; and at Trim, ibid., 1 July 1937.
[23] *Irish Independent*, 26 June 1937.
[24] See Derrig, DE: 68: 392, 14 June 1937.
[25] DE: 67: 104–118, 11 May 1937.
[26] Ibid., cols. 205–10.

then current, MacDermot's essential objection is on the grounds that the Constitution was an expression of the political culture of a republican, Gaelic, Catholic Ireland; it was, 'at heart', partitionist. The south, argued MacDermot, should offer the north 'an Ireland in which a place can be found for their traditions and aspirations as well as for ours.'[27] Having failed with his original resolution, MacDermot scrutinized the rest of the Constitution, clause by clause, and was the author of several amendments, most of them inspired by his desire that the north should not be alienated. To this end he recommended that the preamble should include some acknowledgement of the sentiments of Ulster unionists and of the need to conciliate 'our various traditions and aspirations so as to fuse them into one national consciousness'. But, peremptorily dismissed by de Valera, and finding no support in the house, this amendment was negatived.[28]

MacDermot also attacked Article 44's reference to the 'special position' of the Catholic Church. Whereas he believed that it 'really means nothing', he was certain it would be misunderstood in Ulster.[29] De Valera refused MacDermot's call for its deletion claiming that all the religious articles were 'the result of serious deliberation and careful thought'[30] — the entire Constitution had, in secret, been shown to the Pope.[31] As for the specific criticism that the 'special position' clause would hinder Irish unity, de Valera merely remarked: 'we can only take these things as they come.'[32] Moreover in the course of the exchanges with MacDermot on this amendment, he gave further evidence that in terms of political culture, he preferred a society based on majority — in this case, Catholic — norms: 'If we are going to have a democratic State, if we are going to be ruled by the representatives of the people, it is clear their whole philosophy of life is going to affect that, and that has to be borne in mind and the recognition of it is important in that sense.'[33]

---

[27] Ibid., cols. 76–84, 11 May 1937.
[28] Ibid., cols. 1923–5, 4 June 1937.
[29] Ibid., cols. 1888–95, 4 June 1937.
[30] Ibid., cols. 1890–4.
[31] Tomas O Neill and Padraig O Fiannachta, *De Valera*, vol. 2 (Dublin: 1970), p. 337.
[32] DE: 67: 1892, 4 June 1937.   [33] Ibid., col. 1890.

The Minister for Education, Tomas Derrig, spoke even more explicitly on this theme. Insisting that 'every endeavour' had been made by the framers of the Constitution 'to see that it would suit and be appropriate to any development that might take place towards a united Ireland', Derrig defended the government against the criticism that the document made little appeal to Ulster. If the alternative, he admitted, was to wait until 'we are appreciably nearer to a united Ireland, we will have to wait a very long time.' Claiming that the government had 'given a great deal of attention to the matter', Derrig continued,

we have been listening for a number of years to this thing — that in everything from the Irish language generally to the provisions about divorce, we are holding up the ultimate reunion of this country. Are we then to assume, or can it be claimed to be the logical outcome of these arguments, that we are simply to refuse to put our own ideas into law and refuse to put before the Irish people the instrument which we, as responsible for the government of the country, regard as being suitable to the country's requirements?[34]

Although Fine Gael critics, notably FitzGerald, McGilligan, and Dillon, supported MacDermot's claim that the Constitution would hinder unity, this seems to have been a minority view.[35] The Constitution's provisions on Partition were as often criticized — inside and outside the Dail — on the grounds that they were not sufficiently republican.[36] Only a minority alluded to the pervasive antipathy to such a Constitution on the part of Ulster unionists. Indeed one independent deputy

[34] DE: 68: 392-3, 14 June 1937. Tomas Derrig (1897-1956), TD, 1927-65; Minister for Education, 1932-9, 1940-8.

[35] DE: 67: 249, 373, 413, 12-13 May 1937. Desmond FitzGerald (1888-1947), TD, 1918-37, Minister for External Affairs, 1922-7, Minister for Defence, 1927-32; with McGilligan, influential Irish contributor to Imperial Conferences, 1923-30; father of Garret FitzGerald, leader Fine Gael, 1977-, Taoiseach, 1981-2. Patrick McGilligan (1889-1979) native, co. Derry, TD 1923-65; Minister for External Affairs, 1927-32, Minister for Finance, 1948-51, Attorney General, 1954-7; moderate on Partition; Professor of International and Constitutional Law, UCD. James Dillon (1902-), TD, 1932-69; son of John Dillon; began his career as an independent, later helped to form Fine Gael, from which he resigned in 1941 as the only member of Dail who advocated abandonment of Irish neutrality in favour of support for Allies; member Coalition governments, 1948-51, 1954-7; leader Fine Gael, 1959-65.

[36] Sinn Fein statement, *Irish Press*, 16 June; Brian O'Higgins, letter, ibid., 30 June; Tom Barry at Bodenstown, *Irish Independent*, 21 June 1937.

claimed that the guarantee of religious freedom should appeal 'to these objectionable religious bigots' in Ulster who were 'the barrier to unity'.[37]

The Constitution's debt to the social teaching of the papal encyclicals was widely commented upon. Approval came from the *Catholic Standard*, the *Irish Catholic*,[38] and from the Archbishop of Tuam, Dr Gilmartin.[39] Further, the outgoing Moderator of the Presbyterian Church of Ireland, Dr F. W. O'Neill, who had been consulted by de Valera on the religious clauses, broadly approved of the document. He was 'impressed by the unbiassed fairness' with which the small Protestant minority in the south had been treated and he welcomed the Christian tone of the document.[40] Coming as it did from the leader of Presbyterians throughout the thirty-two counties, this was a valuable endorsement. It was 'a joy', said MacEntee, 'to read the utterance' as it disposed of the Rome Rule myth. In the same speech MacEntee argued that it was to the credit of Fianna Fail that they had the 'moral courage almost unique in the world today to adopt as part of the Constitution the fundamental teachings of the Holy Father in regard to the Family.'[41] His colleague, O'Kelly, in one speech made two claims for the Constitution, that it was 'worthy of a Catholic country', and brought nearer 'the promised land' of a united Irish republic.[42]

During the election and referendum campaign, a considerable diversity of viewpoints was expressed on *how* unity might come. Two weeks before polling day, a prominent Fianna Fail backbencher, the 1916 veteran Richard Walsh, claimed at an election meeting in Mayo that 'Fianna Fail had no objection to the use of force to achieve Irish independence provided peaceful methods failed.'[43] Although Walsh's speech was not specifically disowned by de Valera, he immediately

---

[37] Kent, DE: 67: 237, 12 May 1937.
[38] Both quoted in *Irish Press*, 7 May 1937.   [39] Ibid., 10 May 1937.
[40] Ibid., 8 June 1937.   [41] Ibid., 18 June 1937.
[42] Ibid., 24 June 1937. S. T. O'Kelly (1882-1966), opposed 1921 Treaty and continued his work of seeking international recognition for the 'Irish Republic'; founder member, Fianna Fail and appointed to all de Valera cabinets until his election as second President of Ireland, 1945-59.
[43] Ibid., 15 June 1937.

rejected the use of force, arguing throughout the rest of the campaign that force was 'impracticable':

Some have mentioned force. There has been no question of force in regard to the Six Counties. We recognise it would be a distasteful task, and one which probably would not succeed, and which ultimately if it did would not make for the kind of re-union we want.[44]

De Valera, in contrast to the more hawkish speeches by party colleagues, emphasized the need to achieve such economic progress south of the border that the north would be attracted into a united country. He repeatedly exhorted election meetings to work for the abolition of Partition by exploiting the fact that the twenty-six counties was 'wonderfully situated to make our state one of the most prosperous in the world.'[45] He even expressed optimism: increasingly, he claimed, the Ulster unionists saw their fears of unfair treatment in a united Ireland as 'hallucinations';[46] however, unity must be based on a common pride in Irish citizenship,[47] and in making a 'stirring appeal for the Irish language', he argued that 'there was no use in being an imitation country.'[48]

De Valera, who remained confident that throughout Ireland, three votes in four and 'probably higher' would vote for 'unity and one state',[49] revealed his attitude most clearly when responding to a heckler at a meeting in Monaghan:

Somebody has asked me about the Six Counties, continued Mr de Valera, 'My reply is get a copy of the new Constitution. There is in it an assertion that the national territory is the whole of Ireland, not part of it.'

Asserting that the Constitution was 'the only basis' that he could see for unity, de Valera claimed that one third of the six-county population was already anxious to join the south

and if you can get another one sixth of the whole population of the six counties to support the idea of unity of Ireland, then you will have a majority for the unity of Ireland. When we have got that majority the problem of the unity of the country will be solved.[50]

---

[44] At Carrickmacross, ibid., 28 June 1937.
[45] At Sligo, ibid., 18 June 1937.   [46] At Kilkenny, ibid., 23 June 1937.
[47] Ibid., 28 June 1937.   [48] At Kilkenny, ibid., 23 June 1937.
[49] At Bray, *Sunday Independent*, 27 June 1937.
[50] At Monaghan, *Irish Press*, 28 June 1937.

Those voters whose support for de Valera was based on their belief that only he could solve 'the national question',[51] might have noticed the range of opinion within Fianna Fail, not only on how Partition might end, but also on when. Two weeks before polling day, de Valera admitted that unity might not come within 'a short time',[52] a prediction which may have caused misgivings in the party because during the rest of the campaign, he gradually changed his emphasis. He first predicted unity 'long before twenty years',[53] then 'before a very short time',[54] then within a 'relatively short time',[55] and, finally, on polling day, 'soon'.[56] Moreover, he promised that an incoming Fianna Fail government would give precedence to the Partition issue with the new Constitution forming 'the basis of the re-union'.[57] The document's 'big concessions' to Ulster, were, he said, the best offer he could make to appease unionist opinion. Emphasizing this to the Dail, he then devalued these 'concessions' by implicitly acknowledging the ratchet effect when talking of the greater hopes and expectations of the younger generation: perhaps 'we are reaching the old fogey stage by now', adding, to reassure his republican wing, that 'this is not the last.'[58]

London had no inkling that de Valera intended to be so provocative on Partition in his Constitution. MacDonald's attention had been focused on the clause which would cover the south's relationship with the Commonwealth and repeatedly, but unsuccessfully, had pressed Dulanty for a preview. In fact, MacDonald first saw the draft Constitution on the day of its press publication; it was a considerable disappointment to him. He had been hoping that the ratchet was locked at the point to which de Valera had brought it with his External Relations Act. Indeed, with the threat of a European war rendering good, certainly better, Anglo-Irish relations a primary British interest, MacDonald, early in April, made one of

---

[51] Margaret Pearse, ibid., 17 June; T. J. Keane, ibid., 18 June; and resolution of Buncrana UDC, ibid., 13 June 1937.
[52] At Sligo, ibid., 18 June 1937.   [53] At Gort, ibid., 21 June 1937.
[54] At Kilkenny, ibid., 23 June 1937.   [55] Ibid., 30 June 1937.
[56] At Ballybofey, ibid., 1 July 1937.   [57] Ibid., 17 June 1937.
[58] DE: 68: 430-1, 14 June 1937.

Britain's rare appeals to the Northern Ireland government for some gesture on Partition.[59] Unaware that Articles 2 and 3 were already at the printers in Dublin, MacDonald sounded Craigavon on the possibility of some co-operation with the south in order to get the Free State 'more firmly' in the Empire. He emphasized to the Ulster leader that de Valera's External Relations Act although unsatisfactory, had, at least, recognized the King. Moreover, de Valera's motive had been to appease Ulster, hoping that 'he had left the door open to a possible united Ireland'. If, however, de Valera were to find 'that Northern Ireland would take no step whatever in that direction . . . then he might well, in a fit of impatience, or as a result of Republican political pressure, abolish the King altogether so far as Southern Ireland was concerned.'

MacDonald, while assuring Craigavon that no coercion would be applied, wondered whether the Ulster leader could make a response, 'however slight', to de Valera. Craigavon declined: Ulster Unionists had 'no confidence whatever' in any 'assurances and guarantees of fair treatment'. If Ireland were to be united, 'the situation would soon become similar to the present situation in Spain.' MacDonald hastened to reassure Craigavon that his proposition was merely an advisory council interesting itself perhaps in postal or wireless services. Craigavon remained obdurate: 'fundamental distrust' was how MacDonald summarized Craigavon's view of the south. This was before the publication of de Valera's constitution.[60]

Once published, MacDonald noted Craigavon's view that whereas Articles 2 and 3 were 'very objectionable, it would be a mistake to take too much notice of them',[61] a response similar to that of the British cabinet. Halifax reflected the impotence and exasperation of his colleagues when he noted that it was 'hopeless and a waste of time to attempt to discuss these constitutional niceties' with de Valera, much of whose behaviour was 'really play-acting' which it would be a great

[59] See MacDonald's note of talks with Dulanty in April and May 1937, PRO DO 35/890/X.1/56, *passim*; also Dulanty to MacDonald, 1 May 1937, ibid., —/57.
[60] MacDonald, note of talk with Craigavon, 7 Apr. 1937, PRO DO 35/890/X.1/54.
[61] Holograph draft by MacDonald, PRO DO 35/892/X.1/111.

mistake to treat . . . too seriously.'[62] The British Attorney-General's view on the Articles was that they were without 'legal result',[63] a verdict with which Northern Ireland's legal adviser Professor A. L. Queckett concurred, adding, however, that they were 'framed in words which may well create an impression that the position of Northern Ireland is something different from that for which provision has been made by the enactments of the Imperial Parliament.'[64]

It was also feared that there would be confusion over Article 4, which provided for a change of title from the 'Irish Free State' to 'Eire, or in the English language, Ireland'. Mac-Donald noted that to accept the new title without comment would be open to the 'gravest objection' and would be 'violently' opposed by Northern Ireland as it would be 'tantamount to a recognition of the claim . . . to the whole of the island.'[65] Having agonized over this article for many months — the Stormont cabinet even discussed the possibility of changing their own title by substituting 'Ulster' for 'Northern Ireland'[66] — the British government decided on a formal statement explaining their position.[67] In time, they established — much to Dublin's annoyance — 'Eire' as a synonym for the twenty-six-county state.

Initially, London delayed any official communication to Dublin concerning the Constitution. Busy with the Imperial Conference, then being held in London — with de Valera, incidentally, a prominent absentee[68] — they were anxious to sound Dominion leaders on the document. MacDonald asked Dulanty to inform de Valera that silence did not mean they

---

[62] PRO CAB 27/524 ISC(32) 34th meeting, 9 June, 1937.

[63] Somervell to MacDonald, 8 July 1937, PRO DO 35/891/X.1/98.

[64] Professor A. L. Queckett (Parliamentary Counsel, Northern Ireland), note on Articles 2 and 3 of Irish Constitution, 18 May 1937, PRO DO 35/891/X.1/77.

[65] MacDonald and others, rough draft of note on new Irish Constitution (July 1937), PRO DO 35/891/X.1/98.

[66] Craigavon told his cabinet that MacDonald was 'very much perturbed' by Articles 2 and 3; whether Northern Ireland should change its name to 'Ulster' as a 'counter-stroke' was discussed on 7 Dec. 1937, PRONI CAB 4/389/2.

[67] MacDonald, revise of draft note on new Irish Constitution (July 1937), PRO DO 35/892/X.1/111.

[68] MacDonald's first intimation that de Valera would not attend,was gleaned from *The Times* report of de Valera's statement to the Dail; MacDonald, note of talk with Dulanty 20 May 1937, PRO DO 35/891/X.1/67.

were 'indifferent or had decided to be acquiescent'.[69] At a comprehensive, informal discussion on Ireland, the Dominion Prime Ministers were agreed on the intractability of Partition, which MacDonald feared might 'prove the Achilles heel' in Anglo-Irish relations. MacDonald alluded to de Valera's consistency since 1921 when he had first espoused external association.

Having said this for so many years I think that he will continue to say it all his days. My own view is that he hopes that North and South will come together in the end on this basis. He knows that it would be impossible for the North to come in if the King's position were to be further reduced.[70]

Rather than use his Dail majority to enact the new Constitution, de Valera insisted on putting it to a referendum. This was essential if it was to have optimum credibility with those who had opposed what de Valera now described as the 'disgraceful' and 'battered' Treaty.[71] To finally eclipse the Treaty, republicans were now invited to vote for de Valera's new Constitution. In these circumstances, it was scarcely surprising that his appeals for all-party support won no favour with Fine Gael. Fianna Fail's efforts to win endorsements from northern nationalists proved more fruitful and helped to offset the criticism that it was illogical to presume that a southern electorate could endorse a Constitution including a claim to the thirty-two counties.[72] Explicitly de Valera had claimed that 'the majority of the people' would be acting 'on behalf of the whole'.[73]

Held on the same date as a general election, the Constitution won a comfortable majority, being supported by 685,105 votes to 526,945. It is clear that some opposition voters supported the Constitution whilst others of them may well have abstained rather than vote against. This would be the most likely explanation for the fact that with a 74.7 per cent turnout for

[69] Ibid.

[70] Relations with the Irish Free State were discussed at an informal meeting of principal delegates to the Imperial Conference, 14 June 1937, PRO DO 35/891/X.1/82.

[71] *Irish Press*, 23 June 1937.

[72] DE: 67: 1913, 4 June 1937. [73] Ibid., cols. 1912-13.

the election, only 68.4 per cent marked their referendum papers and that whereas 727,409 first preference votes were cast for candidates opposed to Fianna Fail, some two hundred thousand fewer votes were registered against de Valera's proposed Constitution.[74]

(ii) THE ANGLO-IRISH AGREEMENT, 1938

De Valera confided to a British intermediary that since he had 'delivered the goods' to his own supporters, the way was now 'clear for a closer *rapprochement*' both with Britain and Northern Ireland. Pleading innocence to the charge that his politics had alienated the north, he allowed that some 'wooing and winning' of Ulster would be helpful and he expressed an intention to examine the possibility of functional co-operation with the north.[75] He discussed his strategy and Britain's policy on Partition at two lengthy meetings with MacDonald at Geneva in September. De Valera insisted that his remaining 'great objective' was the ending of Partition, which he would like to see realized 'in his lifetime'. Apart from sentiment, the security of both countries necessitated a settlement: 'if partition were still in being when the next war came', MacDonald informed his colleagues, de Valera 'was afraid that it would be a powerful element influencing people in Southern Ireland to oppose us. He feared that there would be serious trouble on the border, which would be extremely embarrassing to him and an additional centre of trouble for us.' MacDonald was pessimistic: de Valera's recent Constitution would make northern hostility 'even stiffer, if that were possible'. In Mac-Donald's view 'there was no possibility whatever of any alteration in the present situation in the near or even the more distant future.' Reluctantly, de Valera acquiesced: he was, MacDonald noted, 'very sorry . . . but he must accept the fact.'[76] De Valera's note of this conversation places consider-

[74] M. Manning, 'Ireland', in D. Butler and A. Ranney (eds.), *Referendums: a comparative study of practice and theory* (Washington DC: 1978), pp. 198–201.
[75] Batterbee, memo to MacDonald of talk with Edith Ellis, reporting her interview with de Valera, 28 May 1937, PRO DO 35/891/X.1/75. Ellis was a family friend of the MacDonald family.
[76] MacDonald, memo of conversation with de Valera 6 Oct. 1937, PRO CAB 24/271, CP 228(37).

able emphasis on Partition. Before MacDonald left, 'he had quite definitely my views' on a number of matters among them that 'the ending of partition was absolutely necessary for the good relations we both desired.' But this was scarcely news to MacDonald; it had prefaced every discussion between de Valera and London since 1932. The significant point here is that de Valera, who then lists the preconditions for an Anglo-Irish agreement on defence, finance, and trade, and who was presently to conclude just such an agreement, excludes any preconditions on Partition, and explicitly acquiesces in its postponement. De Valera wrote that settlement on the other matters 'would help to make the solution of partition itself easier'; later, he notes that MacDonald's 'steadfast view was that the partition solution would have to wait. I said we would therefore have to consider a campaign to inform British and world opinion as to the iniquity of the whole position.'[77]

This evidence shows that de Valera, unlike so many of his followers, appreciated that no solution of Partition was possible at the intergovernmental negotiations which, to London's surprise, he soon suggested. Indeed it was only when prompted by detailed press questioning, that de Valera claimed that Partition would be included in the discussions,[78] a comment which precipitated the Northern Ireland election which Craigavon decided on, in bed, the following morning, when he read the accounts of de Valera's press conference.[79] Some British ministers, too, were surprised: de Valera had made no mention of Partition in his letter suggesting talks;[80] the British had ignored the issue in their exhaustive preparatory documentation;[81] and when, only some hours before the negotiations opened, MacDonald told his colleagues to expect a lengthy elaboration by de Valera of his case against Partition, the Prime Minister, Neville Chamberlain records the view that

[77] De Valera, memo 17 Sept. 1937, quoted, Longford and O'Neill (1970: 309-10).

[78] Note the tone of de Valera's replies to press questions when announcing the talks, *Irish Press*, 13 Jan. 1938.

[79] Lady Craigavon, diary 12 Jan. 1938 (presumably an error for 13 Jan.).

[80] De Valera to MacDonald, 24 Nov. 1937, PRO CAB 27/527 ISC(32)126, appendix A.

[81] Cabinet memorandum, 'Report on the general constitutional position and the prospects of a settlement of outstanding questions with the Irish Free State', 15 Dec. 1937, PRO CAB 64/34, CP (300)37.

he had 'never contemplated . . . any lengthy discussion' on Partition.[82]

At a private preliminary meeting MacDonald had found de Valera's general attitude to be 'stiffer' than it had been some months before. MacDonald told him that 'no settlement' of Partition was possible at the London talks. De Valera had mooted the possibility of meetings between Belfast and Dublin ministers and had even referred to the possibility of the setting-up of a Council of Ireland. MacDonald had emphasized the impracticability of these suggestions 'at present or in the near future'. However MacDonald did suggest to his colleagues that in order to disabuse de Valera of his belief that Britain positively desired a partitioned Ireland, a statement, 'at a later stage', confirming that Britain would accept a voluntary union between north and south might be possible. Stanley Morrison believed that any such statement would require to be 'most carefully drafted' in order to avoid the suggestion that the British government 'were putting Northern Ireland in the dock, and placing upon them the sole responsibility' for Partition. Chamberlain agreed; his own belief was that a united Ireland was inevitable 'but this aim would have to be realised by a very different road to that by which Mr de Valera and his colleagues were approaching it.'

There followed some discussion of de Valera's style as a negotiator: MacDonald thought him friendly, and frank, but obstinate: Chamberlain feared that de Valera's 'mentality was in some ways like Herr Hitler's. It was no use employing with them the arguments which appealed to the ordinary reasonable man.' This judgement was offered in the context of a general agreement by the British ministers that Fianna Fail's tariff policy since it discriminated particularly against Northern Ireland was 'bad politics' as far as re-unification was concerned. Adjustment of this policy to take heed of Northern Ireland's

[82] Minutes, Irish Negotiating Committee, 17 Jan. 1938, PRO CAB 27/642, INC(38) 1st meeting. Also, H. V. Johnson (US Embassy, London) to SS, 17 Jan. 1938, NA, R.G. 59, 741.41D/49. Neville Chamberlain (1869-1940), Prime Minister, 1937-40; member Irish Situation Committee, 1932-8; mellowed towards de Valera in 1936 and became an early supporter of Malcolm MacDonald's Irish initiatives; as Prime Minister, Chamberlain included Ireland in his policy of appeasing Britain's adversaries; only British Prime Minister to enjoy rapport with de Valera; managed Curtis proposal, June 1940.

interest was seriously debated on the British side in their preparation for the talks.[83] Under considerable pressure from the Northern Ireland government, and with Samuel Hoare the Home Secretary lobbying within the cabinet for some concessions by Dublin on this front, this — and not Partition — formed the 'Ulster dimension' to the negotiations in the months ahead.

Invited by Chamberlain to open the discussions at the first meeting, de Valera talked about Partition. He repeatedly couched his argument in the context of the common defence interests of both countries. In the event of a European war, his government would be in 'great difficulties' if Partition were still unsolved; he might find himself in a situation similar to John Redmond's during the Great War when he was 'faced with difficulties which proved beyond his control'; 'agitation and grave unrest' would be inevitable; 'incidents might occur which would be misunderstood by the Government and people of the United Kingdom.' Later, the British record of the conference notes de Valera's warning that 'he and his colleagues would hold themselves completely free to take such action, in support of their point of view, as they might think fit to do.'

At almost every opportunity, even after the discussion had moved on to the question of defence, de Valera brought the argument back to the Partition theme; he warned that a 'mistake' made by the Irish negotiators on this question might throw the country 'into turmoil', adding that he hoped that British ministers realized that 'there were many people of the Left Wing in Eire who welcomed the adage that "England's difficulty is Ireland's opportunity" and who would be only too ready to prepare accordingly.' Rejecting Chamberlain's attempt to disclaim any British responsibility, de Valera emphasized London's duty to redress the grievances of northern nationalists. Further, to encourage Irish unity, he suggested that Chamberlain should bring 'pressure . . . of a moral character' to bear on Northern Ireland. When challenged by Hoare that if the 'ultimate solution' of Irish unity were to

[83] Minutes, INC, 17 Jan. 1938, PRO CAB 27/642, INC(38) 1st meeting.

be reached, it would be necessary to persuade rather than coerce Ulster, de Valera replied that while he believed that 'the coercion of Northern Ireland would, in all the circumstances, be justifiable', he would not himself favour such a policy as it 'would merely create greater difficulties than it would solve.' Later, he emphatically rejected any advocacy of coercive force being used against Ulster going so far as to say that 'he himself would be disposed to join with Northern Ireland if the United Kingdom attempted to coerce her by force.'[84]

The Partition issue having dominated the opening skirmishes, it was now hoped by Britain that it would be nursed into the background whilst the bargainable issues of defence, finance, and trade were tackled. For his part, de Valera clearly appreciated that there was no prospect, on this occasion, of serious negotiations on the abolition of Partition:[85] what was imperative was to ensure that he did not leave his government, vulnerable to republican critics both outside and within Fianna Fail. His strategy was to emphasize in principle his fundamental objection to Partition and to seek some amelioration of it in practice. As the negotiators, in effect, agreed to disagree on Partition, de Valera expressed his regret that 'one very important part of the mission of himself and his colleagues to London must be left undone. Some patching in regard to other questions might be possible but it must be realised that the conference had failed to get down to bedrock.'[86] Such exchanges can scarcely be regarded as political negotiations on Partition: this was merely the reiteration of what were, by now, the very well-known views of each side.

The debate on Partition had not been entirely barren: gains included the greater mutual understanding of the difficulties which the issue presented to both Dublin and London; the clarification — welcome to Chamberlain, although Hoare remained sceptical[87] — that Dublin did not intend their tariff policy as a punitive measure against Northern Ireland; and

[84] Conference between representatives of UK and Eire, 17 Jan. 1938, PRO CAB 27/642, IN(38)1.

[85] He admitted as much to 'an English politician' while in London, Johnson to SS, 25 Jan. 1938, NA, R.G. 59, 741.41D/52.

[86] As note 84 above.

[87] Minutes, INC, 18 Jan. 1938, PRO CAB 27/642, INC(38) 2nd meeting.

the formal, if *private*, confirmation by British ministers that their government would support a united Ireland if based on voluntary agreement between north and south.

Indeed London came close to publicly disclaiming any interest in Partition during the course of these negotiations. From the record of his personal interventions, it would seem that MacDonald may have favoured such a concession on the British side. If he did, he seems to have been anxious not to appear too eager to win his colleagues' approval. In discussing the press communiqué which would follow the first day's talks, MacDonald advocated a statement that the British government 'had once again made it clear that the issue was primarily one for discussion between Eire and Northern Ireland.' MacDonald added that it might be difficult to win de Valera's approval for such a statement as it 'would indicate that he had been "turned down flat".' This remark, however, may have been made to mask MacDonald's personal hope that his colleagues might approve a public declaration that Partition was indeed a problem to be solved within Ireland and that Britain would not veto any settlement which had Ulster's approval. Earlier, at this same meeting, he had suggested such an initiative, but without any support.[88] Yet, within twenty-four hours, he again suggested such a public statement which he disingenuously characterized as 'entirely innocuous'.[89]

That de Valera was pressing MacDonald on the point, is clear from a note of their last conversation before de Valera returned to Dublin. MacDonald informed his colleagues of an appeal made by the Irish leader: 'I gathered that what he had in mind was a declaration that if the North wished to join the South we would not oppose union, and that indeed we thought a united Ireland was ultimately desirable.' He reassured his colleagues that he had told de Valera that he 'did not hold out any hope' that any such statement could be made; but, as an aside, he added that such a declaration was 'the one really good card' still in Britain's hand and that perhaps it would be 'worth considering whether we should play it later on. For instance if the Irish Ministers prove very difficult about

[88] As note 83 above.   [89] As note 87 above.

making some concession to the North regarding customs duties, we might try to do a deal on this.'[90]

MacDonald went so far as to formulate a draft declaration which was shown to de Valera: emphasizing that Northern Ireland's consent was a necessary precondition, the statement added that if 'closer relations' between north and south or a united Ireland were acceptable, in the future, to Northern Ireland, the British government 'far from raising any difficulties, would, on the contrary, be ready to take any practicable steps to facilitate any arrangement desired by the two parties.'[91] Whether Ulster's friends in the British cabinet could have vetoed such a declaration was never to be tested as it was deemed unsatisfactory by the Fianna Fail cabinet and was never made public.[92]

At the conclusion of the first round of talks the British were content that the customary, ritual exchanges on Partition had been completed and that the negotiators could proceed to other issues. Chamberalin confided to his sister his optimism that agreement was possible on all questions except Partition. Even that, in time, might be settled, but not, he thought, before Ulster had confidence in the southern government 'and that cannot be attained except slowly, and step by step. But if Dev [*sic*] will heed the good advice I gave him[,] I should not despair of ultimate agreement on unity.'[93]

De Valera seems to have been encouraged by Chamberlain's advice that he should concentrate on persuading Ulster – and indeed, British – opinion to his viewpoint.[94] He also intended, as will be seen presently, testing American support for his policy. But given his appreciation of the intractability of the issue and of British intransigence, he also took pains to prepare his supporters for his possible acquiescence in its postponement. The note struck by Chamberlain conveys this impression as do three private memoranda cabled from the

[90] MacDonald, note of talk with de Valera 19 Jan. 1938, PRO CAB 27/642, INC(38)1.

[91] 'Draft declaration by the prime minister of the United Kingdom as communicated to Mr de Valera' (Jan. 1938), PRO DO 35/893/X.11/287, reproduced in Appendix 3, pp. 340.

[92] Longford and O'Neill (1970: 322-3).

[93] Neville to Ida Chamberlain, 16 Jan. 1938, Chamberlain papers, NC18/1/1035.

[94] Sean MacEntee, interview *Irish Times*, 25 July 1974.

London talks by Paddy Quinn, the political correspondent of the *Irish Independent*. Quinn, after a briefing from de Valera, cabled his editor that de Valera's 'attitude clearly shows he is accepting settlement with Partition shelved.' Dulanty and Walshe gave Quinn the same impression, Walshe characterizing de Valera's desideratum as wanting the British 'to do something to show t[ha]t unity o[f] Ireland was something wh[ich] Brit[ish] sh[oul]d assist bringing about.' Quinn concluded: 'I cannot quote him but it looks like shelving Partition in favour settlem[e]nt other issues.'[95]

Nor did MacDonald contradict this conclusion in a private letter to the Canadian Prime Minister, Mackenzie King. There was, wrote the Dominions Secretary, a 'reasonable chance' of an agreement on other issues but on Partition 'nothing can be done — at present, at any rate.'[96] Meanwhile Washington was being informed from its London Embassy of de Valera's 'very frank' views at the end of the first round of negotiations 'both about the difficulties of his own position in Ireland and those confronting the British Government.' De Valera had confided in an 'English politician' who had gained the impression, as had the British negotiators,

that Mr de Valera is now by no means 'the inexperienced political fire-brand of the immediate post-war era', but has been chastened by the burden of office and made amenable by the responsibility of dealing with practical political matters, to the extent that he is most anxious for a full agreement, if any progress, however little, can be made on the partition problem.

The 'little' progress, according to this source, was expected to be some 'amelioration' of the conditions of nationalists within Northern Ireland.[97]

De Valera's biographers claim that MacDonald now 'worked without success on Lord Craigavon in the direction of Irish unity', and that whereas the Ulster leader's public attitude 'remained unaltered', Craigavon was 'privately impressed' by MacDonald's arguments.[98] But they adduce no evidence for

[95] Quinn to Geary, telegram 18 Jan. 1938, Quinn papers.
[96] MacDonald to Mackenzie King, 23 Jan. 1938, Mackenzie King papers, M.G. 26, J.1, vol. 253, f. 215766-8.
[97] H. Johnson to SS, 25 Jan. 1938, NA, R.G. 59, 741.41D/52.
[98] Longford and O'Neill (1970: 317-8).

this inherently implausible claim and there is ample evidence to refute it.[99] They also suggest that at the end of the first round of talks de Valera was 'still hoping for substantial progress towards the ending of partition.' It may be that this claim rests on de Valera's decision at this point to test the efficacy of lobbying the United States government for support. Although his biographers claim that this initiative yielded important support from President Roosevelt, the evidence they quote scarcely justifies the claim.[1]

A detailed study of United States archives does reveal considerable pressure by de Valera on the Partition issue at this juncture: his Minister in Washington made representations to the State Department;[2] he sent his press secretary, Gallagher, to America to appeal to Roosevelt to help with this 'wonderful chance' to end Partition;[3] he himself seems to have made the greatest impression on Cudahy, the American Minister in Dublin, to whom, in an 'obdurate, uncompromising spirit', he had insisted before the talks had opened in London that the 'supreme issue' was Partition: 'The British were responsible for this anomalous, intolerable situation; they had done it, now let them undo it.'[4]

After the first round of talks, Cudahy sent a personal letter to Roosevelt appealing to him to intervene on the Partition issue. Suggesting that de Valera spoke 'reasonably enough' and was 'perfectly content' to tolerate a northern parliament if its powers were devolved from Dublin rather than London, Cudahy urged Roosevelt to call in the British ambassador at Washington.

I believe if you saw Sir Ronald Lindsay at the White House and told him you were interested in the settlement of Anglo-Irish differences, and hoped the present negotiations might succeed, the effect would be conclusive for success. You are the only one who can do this, and if you do not do so I think the opportunity for cooperation between these

---

[99] Interview, Malcolm MacDonald.

[1] Longford and O'Neill (1970: 318–9).

[2] Cordell Hull, 'Memo of conversation with MacWhite', 27 Jan. 1938, Hull papers, box 59, file 226.

[3] Gallagher papers, MS 18,375; de Valera to Roosevelt, 25 Jan. 1938, Roosevelt papers, PSF 56.

[4] Cudahy to SS, 14 Jan. 1938, NA, R.G. 59, 741.41D/48.

two neighbouring islands which means so much for the peace of the world, will be lost for a generation, at least.

Cudahy anticipated the likely response from the British Ambassador in Washington advising Roosevelt that he

will tell you he can do nothing, that the question of Ulster and Irish unity must be decided by Ulster that London can have nothing to do with it. But if Mr Chamberlain sends for Lord Craigavon, ... and appeals to him as a patriot, tells him that the defense of England is at stake, the result will be surprising.

Moreover, in Cudahy's view, Chamberlain could withdraw troops and financial aid to Northern Ireland, all in the interest of an Anglo-Irish *rapprochement* to be justified on strategic grounds. Cudahy was willing to return to Washington for talks if Roosevelt so wished.[5]

It is difficult to evaluate the significance of this initiative; it made little impact within the State Department and Roosevelt's reply was perfunctory.[6] Nevertheless Gallagher credits Roosevelt with being responsible for 'a resumption of negotiations when they had broken down'[7] and Roosevelt himself boasted to his intimates in government that he had been 'largely responsible' for the eventual Anglo-Irish agreement. His Secretary of the Interior, Harold Ickes, noted the President's claim that 'probably history would never know what part he had played, because the letters that he had written both to de Valera and Chamberlain were written in longhand and transmitted confidentially.' It was clear to Ickes that Roosevelt considered himself 'a determining factor' in bringing about the eventual agreement.[8] Such a claim must be attributed to ignorance or conceit. Nothing in the detailed official archives nor in the published extracts of Roosevelt's letter to de Valera, contradicts MacDonald's retrospective verdict that Roosevelt's intervention was of little consequence.[9] On Partition, Roosevelt confined himself to the harmless reassurance, always forthcoming from third parties, that any Irish

---

[5] Cudahy to Roosevelt, 22 Jan. 1938, Roosevelt papers, PSF 56.
[6] Roosevelt to Cudahy, 9 Feb. 1938, ibid.
[7] Gallagher papers, MS 18,375.
[8] Ickes, diary 3 July 1938, Ickes papers, reel 2/12, p. 2830.
[9] Interview Malcolm MacDonald; Longford and O'Neill (1970: 318-9).

rapprochement would be welcome.[10] Nor is de Valera's playing of the American card inconsistent with the suggestion that he approached these negotiations with modest expectations on Partition. A rebuff from Roosevelt could scarcely do harm; it would, anyway, be couched in diplomatic language while his approach to Washington would be evidence of earnestness on the issue.

The Irish cabinet minutes perfunctorily record that on 21 January, 'The Taoiseach gave a general report on the matters discussed at the Conference with the representatives of the British Government.'[11] Again, the researcher must rely on the indirect evidence of British and American official papers for some gleanings of what was said in Dublin.[12] That de Valera's report of his first round of talks disappointed some of his colleagues seems clear. Presently MacDonald was being told by Dulanty that it was de Valera's fear that some Fianna Fail TDs might lose their seats or that there might be a split in the party if no progress were to be made on Partition.[13] Dulanty sought 'something positive' on Partition, instancing the possible formation of an all-Ireland body to discuss 'railway questions': MacDonald ruled it out as 'quite impracticable'.[14] Chamberlain agreed, informing the cabinet on 26 January that if de Valera were to hinge a resumption of negotiations on condition that a cross-border Joint Council be established, then 'the negotiations would break down.' Although willing to shelter de Valera from his extremists as far as was possible,[15] the British now believed that on Partition, de Valera must 'get out of his head any idea that anything could be done at present.'[16]

---

[10] Longford and O'Neill (1970: 318-9).

[11] Cabinet minutes 21 Jan. 1938, SPO CAB 2/1.

[12] Not only are the available Irish records meagre (see, for instance, files S 10631, S 10634 in the SPO Dublin) but even Longford and O'Neill with access to de Valera's papers, and Fanning with access to Department of Finance files rely, in the main, on British records for this period, Longford and O'Neill (1970: 313-26), Fanning (1978: 297-307).

[13] MacDonald, note of talk with de Valera 19 Jan. 1938, PRO CAB 27/642 INC(38)1.

[14] MacDonald, note of talk with Dulanty 24 Jan. 1938, ibid., INC(38)3.

[15] See, for instance, MacDonald's care in handling a parliamentary question, file, PRO DO 35/890/X.1/PQ10.

[16] Cabinet minutes 26 Jan. 1938, PRO CAB 23/92 2(38)4.

Further disappointments followed for de Valera. There was increased support for Ulster Unionists in the Northern Ireland election held between the first and second rounds of the London negotiations.[17] MacDonald reported de Valera as 'somewhat embarrassed' by the calling of this election.[18] The available evidence on the Irish side suggests that de Valera, discomfited by Craigavon's initiative, favoured a boycott of the election by anti-Partitionists. One indication of this was that he himself did not defend his seat in South Down; also the *Irish Press* called for a boycott, which northern nationalists found confusing, particularly when Fianna Fail headquarters declined to say whether this reflected party policy. Privately, northern nationalists expressed indignation or disappointment at de Valera's attitude. This evidence, however, is only suggestive.[19] Motive may also be considered. Here, de Valera had many reasons to prefer a boycott: it would excuse his own controversial decision not to contest South Down; it would distort the voting figures, thereby robbing Craigavon of the inevitable propaganda coup which would follow a hard-fought 'border poll' election; above all, de Valera may have feared the strategy which his own interventionist faction might adopt in liaison with successful nationalist MPs. Some of the latter, after all, thought the major election issue was 'a vote for implementing the Constitution of Eire and against Partition'. Implementation of the Constitution must have sounded to de Valera ominously like yet another request from northern MPs for admission to the Dail.[20]

Some indication of how Fianna Fail's interventionists were thinking can be gleaned from Donnelly's motion to the incoming National Executive elected by the 1937 Ard Fheis. Emphasizing that a new departure would be appropriate once the new Constitution became law in December, Donnelly called for nothing less than that Fianna Fail should be

[17] The US consul in Belfast believed the election result represented a 'definitive answer' to de Valera on Partition, E. L. Ives to SS, 10 Feb. 1938, NA, R.G. 59, 841E.00/5.   [18] As note 83 above.
[19] Cahir Healy to secretary, Fianna Fail, 17 Jan., Healy papers, D2991/A/62B; Healy to *Irish Press*, 14 Jan., ibid., −/62A; Senator T. McLaughlin (convenor of nationalist convention, South Down) to Healy, 21 Jan., ibid., −/63A; Maguire to Healy, 15 Jan. 1938, ibid., −/B/14/1B.
[20] Maguire to Healy, 15 Jan., ibid., −/B/14/1B; Joseph Stewart MP to Healy, 13 Feb. 1938, ibid., −/A/68.

remodelled and made applicable to all Ireland under its present title, or if necessary under another name, with a view to recommending:

(a) contesting all parliamentary seats in Northern Ireland at coming General Election
(b) holding a General Election in Southern Ireland [*sic*] on same date,
(c) the formation of an all-Ireland national Party under the leadership of Mr de Valera with headquarters in Dublin.[21]

First tabled before de Valera suggested talks in London, it is possible that Donnelly's subsequent agreement to defer the resolution was at de Valera's request. Donnelly, having asked for a postponement was then absent through illness for a number of meetings and the resolution, being overtaken by events, was never considered by the National Executive.[22]

Meanwhile, Craigavon achieved a propaganda coup through his party's success in the Stormont election. Having called the election as a plebiscitary protest against the London talks, he did not hesitate in forwarding to Hoare his 'brief appreciation' of the voting figures. His central concern was to emphasize the substantial endorsement of the British link: 'there cannot now be any possible doubt in de Valera's mind on that issue.' What Craigavon thought 'most significant' were the internal divisions between nationalist and republican factions; his claim was that 'the elements in Ulster which are tugging Southward are only a small body of the Republican-Communist type and that the Nationalists as a whole are quite content with, and indeed happy in their association with Great Britain.' De Valera, he thought, had 'lost caste among thinking Nationalists'. Exhorting Hoare to work for a 'satisfactory trade agreement', he concluded on a typical note: 'See, however, that it is fair; compromise can be stood over, not surrender!'.[23] Hoare reassured Craigavon that he would do his best 'to see that Ulster's strong views are not ignored.'[24]

Indeed, assiduously, from their earliest preparations for the talks, the British had been seeking some trade concessions for Northern Ireland, not only to meet pressure from Belfast,

---

[21] Minutes, Fianna Fail National Executive, 8 Nov. 1937.
[22] Ibid., 22 Nov., 6, 20 Dec. 1937.
[23] Craigavon to Hoare, 15 Feb. 1938, Templewood papers, X/3.
[24] Hoare to Craigavon, 17 Feb. 1938, ibid.

but also because the British Treasury, as their chief negotiator on this occasion, S. D. Waley, put it, had 'a very lively interest in the prosperity of Northern Ireland — which comes to us when bankrupt.'[25] The Permanent Secretary to the Treasury, Warren Fisher, added his own revealing comment that the Treasury would 'gain greatly from the termination of the present wholly uneconomic partition.'[26] If Ulster was without friends in the Treasury, she had her supporters in the Irish Situation Committee. On 17 February, Hoare, Morrison, and Hailsham all expressed dissatisfaction at what they considered was appeasement of the south: Hailsham feared that an unsatisfactory trade agreement would present de Valera 'with a lever . . . to force the termination of Partition. Ulster manufacturers might in fact get into such desperate straits they would either vote for inclusion in Eire or move their factories into Eire.' MacDonald, as usual, attempted to calm his colleagues: they should remember that they were dealing with a 'strange people who were more influenced by sentimental than by logical and economic considerations.'[27]

With, in the meantime, a briefing from Andrews, Ulster's supporters on this committee were even more sceptical of the draft trade agreement at their next meeting held on the eve of the resumption of talks with the Irish ministers. Hoare believed that the Northern Ireland government would come out 'root and branch' against such an agreement. All were agreed that de Valera should be told that 'he would never win Northern Ireland over to his point of view if he persisted in inflicting this injury on its trade.' MacDonald warned his colleagues that they 'would again have to listen' to de Valera's line on Partition and he also repeated his suggestion of a possible British declaration that they reserved no veto on Irish unity in the event of Northern Ireland's consent. Morrison stated that he was 'by no means' satisfied with the draft declaration suggested by MacDonald: 'If it meant something Ulster would be upset, and if it meant nothing it would serve no useful purpose. He objected to the declaration because in effect it placed Ulster in the dock.' If published it would 'cause great astonishment and deep resentment'. MacDonald

[25] Waley, minute 14 Jan. 1938, PRO T 160/747/F14026/04.
[26] Fisher, minute ibid.
[27] Minutes, ISC, 17 Feb. 1938, PRO CAB 27/524 ISC(32) 36th meeting.

rejoined that it would not now be used since de Valera on some vital defence matters was only prepared to give a unilateral statement in the Dail rather than incorporate them in the proposed agreement.[28]

De Valera, who insisted on the second round of negotiations being prefaced by a private meeting between himself and Chamberlain, again raised the Partition issue. No defence agreement would be tolerable to his own extremists, he told Chamberlain, without 'some arrangement for the termination of Partition.'[29] Quinn cabled to his editor: 'Deadlock on Partition . . . Dev [sic] has just seen us but we cannot quote him. He told Chamberlain unity o[f] Ireland was fundamental.'[30] Later, at the formal negotiations, de Valera doggedly insisted that the Partition and defence issues should be linked. Claiming an impasse, Chamberlain asked de Valera if he had any other suggestions. De Valera then proposed that the negotiations be confined to finance and trade and that without any defence agreement, the British should surrender the Treaty ports to his government. If, subsequently, the Partition question was satisfactorily settled, then 'he would be able to go a long way' towards the defence agreement then being contemplated.

If, however, it was not found possible to solve the partition difficulty, he would have to say that in the unhappy event of Eire being involved in some conflict she would naturally have to see where, in her own interests, she could best obtain assistance.[31]

Explicitly, de Valera told the British negotiators that one section of his public opinion, which he could not afford to ignore, would urge that defence 'should be made a lever' in order to bring effective pressure on Britain over Partition. Chamberlain exhorted de Valera to make some 'gesture of good-will' towards Northern Ireland, instancing some concession in the proposed trade agreement. De Valera believed it was impossible to make concessions to the north which would not, in effect, also be enjoyed by Britain: 'He was

[28] Minutes, ISC, 22 Feb. 1938, PRO CAB 27/524 ISC(32) 37th meeting.
[29] Minutes, ISC, 24 Feb. 1938, PRO CAB 27/524 ISC(32) 38th meeting.
[30] Quinn to Geary, telegram 22 Feb. 1938, Quinn Papers.
[31] Conference between representatives of UK and Eire, 23 Feb. 1938, PRO CAB 27/642 IN(38)6.

certainly animated by no ill-will against Northern Ireland; he wished it every prosperity, if only for the reason that one day, sooner or later, it would be part of a reunited Ireland.' Pressed by Chamberlain, on this point, Irish ministers promised to consider making 'some concessions on the particular duties which bore hardly on Northern Ireland.' De Valera also expressed his intention of using a successful Anglo-Irish agreement 'as a jumping-off ground for entering into better relations with Northern Ireland.' First, though, 'he would have to do something to steady and to educate his own people.'

By this stage Dulanty could foresee a settlement on all questions except Ulster.[32] If disappointment and intransigence had been the response within Fianna Fail to the lack of progress on Partition, alarm was the reaction among northern nationalists, some of whom refused to believe that Partition would not be solved at these talks.[33] Complicating de Valera's problems, a delegation of northern nationalist MPs arrived in London, uninvited and unannounced. On 23 February, Quinn cabled his editor: 'De Valera asks as personal favour that movements Nationalist MPs be published without linking up Irish delegation with them for he has not asked them to come and knows nothing of their plans.'[34] Their plans evidently included talks with de Valera and — reluctant, or not — he spent 'practically [the] entire day' with them on 24 February.[35] After the meeting Healy suggested that northern nationalists 'would regard it as a betrayal of all our interests' if de Valera 'ignored the problem of partition by getting Trade and Defence Agreements only.'[36]

However it was to be the Unionists rather than the Nationalists of Ulster whose demands were to influence the remaining weeks of the negotiations and trade policy between north and south was the principal issue.[37] At the resumed negotiations on 3 March, de Valera flatly rejected the proposal that the

[32] Quinn to Geary, telegram 23 Feb. 1938, Quinn papers.
[33] Maguire to Healy, 20 Jan. 1938, Healy papers, D2991/B/4/1C.
[34] As note 32 above.
[35] Quinn to Geary, telegram 24 Feb. 1938.
[36] Longford and O'Neill (1970: 321); *Belfast Newsletter*, 22-8 Feb. 1938, *passim*.
[37] Minutes, ISC, 25 Feb. 1938, PRO CAB 27/524 ISC(32) 39th meeting.

south should allow free entry for manufactures of Northern Ireland origin. Irish public opinion 'would be very strongly opposed' to any such concession as it would be seen as 'an important step towards stabilizing' Partition and allowing the north 'the best of both worlds'. Whereas the south appreciated that in a united Ireland, the 'industrial supremacy of Northern Ireland would have to be faced and acquiesed in', if Partition were to remain, any 'open door' policy would not be tolerable as it would be 'highly prejudicial, and in some cases, disastrous to Eire's industries.' MacDonald, however, thought that if the proposal were rejected, then the British government could do little to help de Valera with his goal of removing that 'cloud of ill-will and suspicion which went to the very root' of Partition. De Valera was adamant: his public opinion would not tolerate concessions; moreover, Northern Ireland 'would laugh' at what they would see as 'an act of almost incredible stupidity and weakness'. He was prepared, however, to consider 'some plan for an exchange of preferences'. Chamberlain was 'bitterly disappointed', more particularly, because, — as he now felt obliged to disclose to the Irish negotiators — Belfast had been informed of the proposal following what the British considered to be de Valera's 'not altogether unfavourable' response when the idea had first been mooted. Although it had seemed possible to British ministers that the Ulster Unionists might consider it 'the thin end of the wedge so far as partition was concerned', they had, in fact welcomed the proposal. Now, if it were to be rejected by Dublin, the position would be 'very much worse than if the proposal had never been formulated at all.'[38] De Valera remained unmoved. The political gulf between north and south proved to be too great and economic interests too divergent for much success to attend this attempt by the British to create what would clearly have been a greater measure of economic unity throughout Ireland. No further progress was made at what was to be the last formal session of the negotiations on the following day. British ministers, determined not to abandon Ulster's interests, said 'how very disappointed' they were at the Irish attitude. In further

[38] Conference between representatives of UK and Eire, 3 Mar. 1938, PRO CAB 27/642 IN(38)7.

discussion, the probable effects of free entry for Northern Irish goods into the south were detailed by Lemass who suggested that the autarkical policies of the south would have to be abandoned if the proposal was put into effect.[39] The north had dismissed the original draft trade agreement as inequitable and indefensible; now the south was returning an identical verdict on the free trade proposal. There was a distinct possibility that the entire negotiations would founder.

Meanwhile the Stormont government was becoming more intransigent as they came to appreciate that London needed at least their acquiescence for any Irish settlement. At a meeting with Hoare on 5 March, Andrews, who had been handling the discussions for the Northern Ireland government, warned Hoare that the proposed agreement was so unsatisfactory that he and Craigavon would have no alternative but 'to launch an attack' on the British government 'for their surrender of Northern Ireland's vital interests' or both resign from the government. Hoare believed the position of Northern Ireland, already intransigent, 'had considerably hardened.'[40]

British ministers now feared a breakdown in the negotiations which would have 'Northern Ireland and Eire scowling at one another across the border.'[41] While de Valera had suggested that free trade might have 'most devastating' effects on the south's economy, Andrews had pleaded that without it, the north's industries would 'face disaster and collapse'. The British did not accept these arguments at face value because Northern Irish civil servants had admitted to the Board of Trade that their government's objections were 'really political and not economic'; and British ministers, from talking to civil servants from Dublin, had come to the conclusion that de Valera, too, was hindered by political rather than economic impediments.[42]

Against this background, the British prepared a 'final offer' which Chamberlain put privately to de Valera. On 8 March,

[39] Ibid., 4 Mar. 1938, ibid., IN(38)8.

[40] Minutes, ISC, 8 Mar. 1938, PRO CAB 27/524 ISC(32) 41st meeting.

[41] Simon's comment, minutes, ISC, 10 Mar. 1938, PRO CAB 27/524 ISC(32) 42nd meeting.

[42] Waley to Fisher, 29 Feb. 1938, PRO T 160/747/F14026/04; also, minutes, ISC, 8 Mar. 1938, PRO CAB 27/524 ISC(32) 41st meeting.

Chamberlain suggested that with some agreed exceptions, the south should permit free entry to the north's exports but that the abolition of tariffs should be gradual over a period of five years; at the end of this period, the trading relationship between north and south would, suggested Chamberlain, be 'exactly the same as it would have been almost at once had the negotiations resulted in the immediate termination of Partition.' Moreover Chamberlain impressed on de Valera 'the very powerful appeal' which he could make to his public opinion along these lines.[43]

This meeting seems not to have been a success. Quinn cabled to his editor in Dublin, that he believed the Irish leader had made 'no progress' with Chamberlain.[44] On the following day, de Valera told Quinn that 'nothing has b[ee]n settled yet and t[ha]t it is all in t[he] lap o[f] t[he] gods';[45] and on 10 March Lemass's list of proposed tariffs did not satisfy the British, 'They want v[er]y much more.'[46] Chamberlain believed the negotiations had reached a 'deadlock' but on the following day he interested de Valera in 'a new and final offer'. De Valera was 'surprised and anxious to accept' although his colleagues, on hearing the details, thought the offer '"appalling"'. Chamberlain confided to his sister that he now believed that a settlement was in sight if the cabinet in Dublin approved the terms. If the agreement went through he expected the extreme right in Britain to suggest that he had 'weakly given way when Eire was in the hollow of my hand'; in fact, he believed he had only conceded 'small things' and, among the gains, he listed the prospect of better north–south relations in Ireland.[47]

At this meeting, Chamberlain had brought forward the card which MacDonald had been mooting since the previous December: the possibility of a public declaration by Britain that she would not veto a united Ireland which had the consent of the north. In Dublin, de Valera's cabinet was still unimpressed: the draft declaration on Partition, 'containing

    [43] As note 40 above.
    [44] Quinn to Geary, telegram 8 Mar. 1938, Quinn papers.
    [45] Ibid., 9 Mar. 1938.   [46] Ibid., 10 Mar. 1938.
    [47] Neville to Hilda Chamberlain, 13 Mar. 1938, Chamberlain papers, NC18/1/1041.

as it did nothing of a positive character', was 'altogether inadequate'. As for concessions to Northern Ireland, in present circumstances, Dulanty reported to MacDonald, these were 'a sheer impossibility'.[48] De Valera confided to Cudahy that there were 'sharp differences' within his cabinet.[49] Mac-Donald believed that de Valera and at least two of his negotiating team, although they 'intensely disliked' the concessions to Northern Ireland' had reluctantly, and without success, recommended the agreement to their colleagues. However, with some modifications, the Irish ministers were prepared to accept the whole of the agreement except for the provisions which gave 'concessions to Northern Ireland by name'. Some of their concessions on imports would, in effect, be of benefit solely to Northern Ireland since this was the only part of the United Kingdom with an interest in exporting the goods in question to the twenty-six counties.

MacDonald's appreciation of the position was forwarded to Chamberlain to brief him for the talks he had now proposed with Craigavon. 'Unless we can make a beginning', he advised Chamberlain, the Partition issue 'is going to upset all our efforts to settle the old quarrel at any time in the reasonably near future. We have got to try to break through the suspicions and distrust which at present exist.' MacDonald was convinced that de Valera could not yield any further concessions to the north: 'The issue then is — this agreement or nothing.'[50]

Chamberlain wrote to Craigavon emphasizing those aspects of the proposed agreement which would benefit the north; some of de Valera's concessions although they 'would not appear to be made directly to Northern Ireland' would, in effect, be that.[51] As in his private meetings with de Valera, Chamberlain succeeded in persuading Craigavon to agree terms more moderate than those preferred by his colleagues. Indeed, two of the latter, Andrews and Brooke — the two men who would, in due course, succeed to the leadership of Ulster

---

[48] Dulanty to Walshe, 14 Mar. 1938, Longford and O'Neill (1970: 323).

[49] Cudahy to SS, 19 Mar. 1938, NA, R.G. 59, 741.41D/65.

[50] MacDonald, memo for Chamberlain, 'Rough notes on points which might be made to Lord Craigavon'; also, 'Note on latest position regarding negotiations with Eire', both 16 Mar. 1938, PRO DO 35/893/X.11/139.

[51] Chamberlain to Craigavon, 17 Mar. 1938, ibid.

Unionism — had been prepared to resign rather than accept the draft agreement which had been forwarded to Belfast. Craigavon, having left the detailed negotiations to them through ill health, had now resumed control, ignored their misgivings and settled privately with Chamberlain. Worse, he failed to inform them of the line he intended to take leaving them under the impression that he supported their view. Then, having excluded his civil service experts, he astounded Andrews and Brooke by capitulating to Chamberlain's terms at a formal negotiating session![52] Some Ulster Unionists by this stage believed that Craigavon was 'ga-ga'.[53] Chamberlain, for his part, believed both north and south 'so unreasonable'[54] and was far from content with the measure of acquiescence in British policy forthcoming from Craigavon.

Further concessions, or, as Chamberlain put it, 'sufficient sops to keep Northern Ireland quiet',[55] were necessary, Fisher advising that, if yielding to Craigavon would facilitate an enduring settlement with the south, then 'I advocate our being blackmailed.'[56] Chamberlain wrote once again to Craig-- avon: not for the first — or, indeed, the last time — the Ulster Unionists were invited to support what they perceived as the appeasement of the south; and again, London's appeal was being made in the name of wider British interests. In his letter, Chamberlain exphasized the importance of demonstrating 'that the policy of peace by negotiation can be successful.' He was hoping for success with both Anglo-Italian and Anglo-Irish agreements because it was 'very necessary that an impression of solidarity here should be made, and not least in Berlin.'[57] Craigavon again crossed to London, and again insisted on leaving his civil servants out of the formal session with British ministers. The business was dispatched, London agreeing 'to

---

[52] Spender, holograph notes, prefacing diary, vol. 10, Spender papers, D715/10. Sir Basil Brooke (1888-1974), MP NIHC, 1929-68, Minister, 1933-43, Prime Minister, 1943-63; defended discrimination against Catholics since they were not 'King's men'; later, Lord Brookeborough; criticized at his funeral service as an obscurantist.

[53] Lady Londonderry to Hoare, 3 May 1938, Templewood papers, X/4.

[54] Neville to Ida Chamberlain, 20 Mar. 1938, Chamberlain papers, NC18/1/ 1042.

[55] Neville to Hilda Chamberlain, 9 Apr. 1938, ibid., —/1046.

[56] Fisher, minute 26 Mar. 1938, PRO T 160/747/F14026/04/2.

[57] Quoted, Buckland (1979: 115).

pay most, but not all, of the price demanded for Northern Ireland's acquiescence.'[58] Included in the further concessions to the north was the withdrawal of any British statement concerning her future approval of a united Ireland if this had Ulster's support.[59]

An Anglo-Irish agreement was signed in London on 25 April. Retrospectively, de Valera thought it his greatest political achievement.[60] This was because of its importance in the context of neutrality. His biographers suggest that he was 'heartily disappointed' that no progress had been made on Partition.[61] Quinn believed that there was 'nothing doing re Partition — there never was and de Valera knew there never could be.'[62] What is manifest is that de Valera's primary concern was not Partition, which he believed intractable in the short term, but the return of the Treaty ports, thus facilitating southern neutrality in a European war which he believed imminent.

In the Dail debate on the Agreement, de Valera theorized about the economic consequences of the re-unification of the country. It would entail 'big and heavy problems', not least the absorption of the north's 100,000 unemployed. Presuming that the south would not 'grumble' at taking on such a 'burden', de Valera, in an aside, tilted at one faction in the south which had, by now, a vested interest in Partition: 'I understand', he said, 'that a number of industrialists down here would be shivering if we had the whole country in now.'[63] That the Irish negotiating position had been inhibited by what Quinn called 'that section of racketeers wh[ich] is making money on tariffs'[64] seems to have caused some misgivings in the Irish cabinet.[65]

In general, de Valera was pleased at the degree of consensus being shown in the Dail; he emphasized the merits of isolating

[58] Buckland (1979: 115).   [59] As note 48 above.
[60] In reply to question from historian, T. D. Williams. I am grateful to Professor Williams for this information.
[61] Longford and O'Neill (1970: 325).
[62] Quinn, memo to Geary 14 Mar. 1938, Quinn papers.
[63] DE: 71: 424; 29 Apr. 1938; L. E. Woods to Cudahy, 14 Jan. 1938, NA, R.G. 84, American Legation Dublin papers, 1938, 59A 543.
[64] As note 62 above.
[65] De Valera, DE: 71: 450; 29 Apr. 1938; also, MacEntee, ibid., col. 389; Spender, note of conversation with Maffey, 11 Dec. 1940, Spender papers, D715/15.

the Partition issue and reminded deputies that all parties in the south were now 'consecrated to try to end that wrong'.[66] While admitting that the British might 'have to proceed slowly' about convincing the Ulster Unionists of the need for Irish unity, he hoped that he had 'gone some distance' in persuading London to his viewpoint.[67] There was some criticism that he had failed to win a guarantee from London that they would prevent the Stormont 'puppet Parliament' from discriminating against the northern minority.[68] This was unfair; in fact, de Valera had persuaded the Dominions Office to insist that the Home Office inquire into various allegations of discrimination by the Ulster Unionists. The document listing the nationalists' grievances which had been provided by de Valera[69] included a lengthy list of statements from Unionists, including Northern Ireland's first three Prime Ministers, advocating discrimination against Catholics in public and private employment, and detailed the widespread gerrymandering of constituencies to favour local Unionist minorities. Although the Home Office staunchly defended Northern Ireland from these charges,[70] the Dominions Office seems to have been impressed, Harding minuting that although he did not believe in pressing the Home Office further on the matter, it was his impression that they were 'beginning to wake up to the fact that the situation wants careful watching!'.[71] MacDonald, too, was converted, minuting: 'I am convinced that as soon as the present Irish talks are over we must go quietly and carefully into the position of the minority in the north.'[72]

(iii) '. . . ALL THE SADLY FAMILIAR ARGUMENTS'

Aware of the comparative popularity of the Agreement and his need to increase his party's strength in the Dail, de Valera

---

[66] DE: 71: 431; 29 Apr. 1938.   [67] Ibid., col. 433.

[68] Ibid., col. 340-1, 29 Apr. 1938.

[69] Cahir Healy documented some of the grievances, Healy to L. J. Walsh, 18 Mar. 1938, Healy papers, D2991/A/78; the document is in PRO DO 35/893/X.11/123.

[70] See PRO DO 35/893/X.11/251, *passim*.

[71] Harding to Hartington, 9 Mar. 1938, ibid., —/892/X.11/123.

[72] MacDonald, minute 5 Mar. 1938, ibid., —/118.

called a general election for June. During the campaign, considerable emphasis was placed on the fact that Partition had now been isolated as the sole remaining grievance in Anglo-Irish relations.[73] A strong Fianna Fail government would be the obvious choice, the electorate was assured,[74] to work towards 'the final realization of the dream of seven centuries'.[75] Ministers did not conceal that ending Partition would be 'most difficult',[76] but it would be achieved 'before this generation is all in its grave':[77] the obvious man to accomplish the task was de Valera,[78] leading what O'Kelly described as 'a national government'.[79] There were, too, some valuable endorsements from northern nationalists.[80] De Valera, in his message to the electorate also drew on historical parallels, renewing, on behalf of Fianna Fail, the resolve of the provisional government of the Irish Republic in 1916:

To pursue the happiness and prosperity of the whole nation and of all its parts, cherishing all the children of the nation equally and oblivious of the differences carefully fostered by an alien government, which have divided a minority from the majority in the past.

However idealistic the sentiments of the 1916 Proclamation, they were unlikely to rally the Ulster unionists. Yet, de Valera here invoked them for just this purpose.

There is the clearest evidence that within a few years we shall have in this part of Ireland a homogeneous people, . . . all animated by the single purpose of enhancing the glory and advancing the prestige of our nation. That spirit will reach across the border, dispelling ancient prejudices, until the whole of the land of Patrick responds to it and the dream of the dead generations is completely realised.[81]

O'Kelly added a characteristic flourish with his famous 'whip John Bull' remark. In the Agreement, Fianna Fail had 'whipped him right, left and centre. And with God's help we'll do the same again when the opportunity arises.'[82]

---

[73] *Irish Press*, 1 June 1938.   [74] Ibid., 28 May 1938.
[75] Election message, ibid., 30 May 1938.
[76] James Ryan, ibid., 11 June 1938.
[77] Frank Aiken, ibid., 31 May 1938.
[78] Lemass, Aiken, O'Kelly, ibid., 6 June; Neal Blaney, ibid., 9 June 1938.
[79] O'Kelly, ibid., 11 June 1938.
[80] Ibid., 30 May, 1 June 1938.
[81] De Valera, message to electors, ibid., 14 June 1938.
[82] Ibid., 9 June 1938.

None of this helped to nurture the frail plant of north-south co-operation which had been sown during the London talks. Spender, Secretary of Finance at Stormont Castle and a leading interpreter of the Stormont mind to Whitehall, added a caustic postscript to yet another letter of complaint to the Treasury about the unfairness of the Anglo-Irish Agreement: 'The speeches made during the Eire election hardly indicate the arrival at that millennium which the Chancellor apparently envisages.'[83]

Nor did republican diehards believe that the millennium had arrived: the 1938 Agreement was 'national apostasy'.[84] Critics included de Valera's Minister to France, Art O'Brien, who was now privately complaining of 'too much unnecessary compromise'.[85]

Manifestly, there were bruised feelings within the Northern Ireland cabinet concerning the Anglo-Irish Agreement. Nor can relations have been improved by the south's accusations of discrimination and gerrymandering — and the fact that Whitehall had now begun to ask for explanations. In short, a climate of ill will prevailed between north and south and whereas there were some politicians and civil servants in Dublin, Belfast, and London who seem to have been anxious to expedite north-south co-operation where mutual benefits would accrue,[86] there were others who seemed distinctly less sympathetic. Stormont's Home Affairs Department's handling of two episodes — an invitation to de Valera to unveil a statue of Saint Patrick in Northern Ireland and the arrest and imprisonment of Eamonn Donnelly in July for agitating against Partition[87] — demonstrated no anxiety to establish better cross-border relations. The Dominions Office, while believing Donnelly may have been 'unnecessarily provocative', concluded that in Northern Ireland to suggest that 'partition should be ended is a crime!'[88]

[83] Spender to Waley, 11 June 1938, PRO T 160/747/F14026/04/2.
[84] MacSwiney, *Cork Examiner*, 28 Feb. 1939.
[85] Art O'Brien to MacSwiney, 7 July 1938, MacSwiney papers, P48/C/24.
[86] Leydon's views, reported by Jenkins, 1 July 1938, PRO DO 35/893/X.11/227.
[87] PRO DO 35/893/X.11/217 and —/236, *passim*.
[88] Stephenson, minute 29 Sept. 1938, PRO DO 35/893/X.11/243.

On his release, Donnelly remained in the north to further defy the Exclusion Order[89] and to orchestrate the lobbying of Fianna Fail by various factions in the north. As Healy saw it, Donnelly's role was nothing less than the nationalists' 'representative' on Fianna Fail's National Executive.[90] As the minutes of their meetings reveal, the Partition issue had become increasingly salient throughout 1938. The Executive's approach seemed, generally, cautious. This certainly was Donnelly's criticism. On 5 October he described to Healy his attempts to force an all-Ireland anti-Partition convention on the Executive; he exhorted northern MPs to 'force the pace' on the basis of their recent '"evacuation by the British" resolution'. When this had been passed a week earlier, Donnelly had approved: 'Let them get out of Ulster and we'll settle the matter quite nicely.'[91]

Opinion in Ireland tended to see the return of the Treaty ports as an Irish gain from Chamberlain's overall policy of appeasement, and this encouraged the hope that the remaining grievance of Partition might also be settled on Dublin's terms. Such expectations quickened during what Donnelly termed the 'three psychological weeks'[92] in September when Hitler's irredentist claims in the Sudetenland were, with British acquiescence, appeased. Britain's Defence Minister, Sir Thomas Inskip, after a meeting with de Valera on 8 September noted de Valera's claim that he had his 'own Sudeten in Northern Ireland and he had even thought sometimes of the possibility of going over the boundary and pegging out the territory which was occupied by a population predominantly in sympathy with Eire and leaving Northern Ireland to deal with the situation.'[93] De Valera was an enthusiast for Chamberlain's appeasement policy and among the keenest supporters of the

---

[89] Dulanty made representations on 10 Sept. that Donnelly was being harassed by the RUC, Machtig note of 17 Sept. 1938, PRO DO 35/893/X.11/236.

[90] Healy to Donnelly, 6 Oct. 1935, Healy papers, D2991/A/95B.

[91] Donnelly to Healy, 29 Sept. and 5 Oct. 1938, ibid., −/88, −/94.

[92] *Irish Press*, 23 Nov. 1938.

[93] Inskip, note of talk with de Valera, 8 Sept. 1938, Halifax papers, FO 800/310. T. W. Inskip (1876–1947), first Viscount Caldecotte, Minister for the Co-ordination of Defence, 1936-Jan. 1939; Dominions Secretary, Jan.–Sept. 1939, May-Oct. 1940.

Munich agreement with Hitler — 'the greatest thing that has ever been done'.[94] Along with his personal regard for Chamberlain and his anxiety that war should be avoided, de Valera believed that the Irish case for unity was more convincing than was the German claim to the Sudeten territories.[95]

Passing through London on 4 October, de Valera had separate meetings with Devonshire, MacDonald, and Chamberlain. Well used to his lectures on Partition, they now found him 'in a state of considerable excitement' on the issue.[96] He suggested to Chamberlain that 'if a crisis arose such as might have arisen over recent European troubles', then the northern minority problem might 'become a positive danger.'[97] To Devonshire, he made the point that the Poles and the Hungarians, 'were getting their just rights' and asked: 'what about his minority'? He said that 'there was a time when if he felt strong enough he would have moved his troops up to the line to which he thought he was justly entitled, just as Hitler was doing.' But he would not now adopt that solution because it would not solve the problem. Pleading British inability to improve north-south relations, Devonshire exhorted de Valera to establish closer relations with the north 'over such matters as railway management, control of animal diseases, possibly even defence', but de Valera insisted that this would not be enough, 'That in the course of time his party would be superseded by something to the left of them who would not be as patient and law-abiding as he had been.'[98]

On 17 October in an interview in the *Evening Standard*, de Valera detailed proposals for a federal solution which henceforth was to form the basis of his policy on the north. He appealed to the Northern Ireland government to accept the same devolved powers from Dublin as they were then accepting from London. De Valera excluded a plebiscite or

---

[94] Diana Cooper noted de Valera's comment at 'a British Empire dinner' in Geneva, 14 Sept. 1938 when the proposed summit was announced, quoted Duff Cooper, *Old men forget* (London: 1953), p. 229.

[95] Cudahy to SS, 20 Oct. 1938, NA, R.G. 59, 841D.00/1144.

[96] Devonshire, note of talk with de Valera 4 Oct. 1938, PRO DO 35/893/X.11/247.

[97] Chamberlain, note of talk with de Valera 4 Oct. 1938, ibid.

[98] As note 96 above.

boundary commission which although it 'would give us territory', would only perpetuate Partition. Speaking with care
and emphasis, he added that although the Stormont government was not *entitled* to local autonomy over the entire six
counties, *'we make the concession'* provided minority rights
were safeguarded. He wanted to make it 'as easy as possible'
for the north to 'join us' because it was his 'fixed belief' that
once they were working together on such a basis, the border
would eventually disappear.[99]

Although heralded in the south as a major initiative, this
interview contained little that was new. An almost identical
offer had been mooted in an interview in the *New York
Times* the previous January and had been widely publicized
in the Irish newspapers, including the unionist press in Belfast.[1]
There were, however, some—probably deliberate—differences
of emphasis. In January de Valera had said that a local parliament in the north-east 'could not justify any claim to its
present boundaries', but added that with guarantees of fair
treatment for the nationalists, the boundary *'might* be tolerated under an All-Ireland Parliament.'

In the *Evening Standard* interview he had used the phrase,
'we make the concession' of tolerating the existing boundary.
Given de Valera's habit of using press interviews in a deliberate
manner to test support for a particular line of policy,[2] and
knowing the strict terms under which many interviews were
agreed, often including de Valera's right to correct attributed
quotations before publication,[3] it seems possible that what

[99] De Valera, interview *Evening Standard*, 17 Oct. 1938, reprinted De Valera:
speeches: 1980: 358–62.

[1] De Valera, interview *New York Times*, reported *Belfast Newsletter*, 27 Jan.
1938.

[2] There are many examples of this: parts of the original draft defence agreement mooted by the British in the 1938 negotiations were not acceptable to de
Valera as part of a signed agreement whilst he was willing to arrange a press interview in which he would incorporate them in his policy. See MacDonald at ISC
meeting, 22 Feb. 1938, PRO CAB 27/524 ISC(32) 37th meeting. In September
1922, de Valera asked for some 'leading questions' in order to promulgate a particular line during the Civil War, 'Correspondence of Mr Eamon de Valera and
others', Dublin, 1922.

[3] 'He is very particular about newspaper interviews', John Gunther, 'The truth
about de Valera', *Strand Magazine*, July 1936; cuttings dated 17 and 21 Aug. 1923
in Mulcahy papers, P7/B/364; see also 6 pp typescript interview with de Valera by
Joseph F. O'Connell Jr, corrected in de Valera's hand, Gallagher papers, MS
18,375 (11).

had been flown as a kite in January was now the basis of what was to be his final policy on Partition.

Longford and O'Neill, noting that he was no longer appealing 'for a rectification of the boundaries', justify the change on the grounds that such a re-partition 'would still be no more than a half measure or palliative.'[4] This, however, ignores the significant change from his 1921-3 policy which had been willing to grant local autonomy only to those areas of the north-east with a unionist majority; in fact, as has been noted above, Donnelly had tried, unsuccessfully, to hold de Valera to this in the Dail debate on the Constitution.

Craigavon ridiculed de Valera's offer: 'If the imagination could picture anything as fantastic happening' then, in a short time, Northern Ireland's representatives 'would be completely swamped . . . and thus reduced to complete impotence in resisting the establishment of a republic — Mr de Valera's aim.' Dismissing de Valera's 'dishonest propaganda' as an 'insult' and emphasizing his belief that public opinion in Britain 'would rise in indignation' if any British government showed 'the slightest signs' of its intention to betray Ulster, Craigavon concluded his broadside with a message which was clearly intended for London as well as Dublin: 'Therefore, as someone must make a decision, we are here now to say that, in no circumstances whatever, will we listen to the rattling of the sabre or, for that matter, the cooing of the dove, where the integrity of Ulster is concerned.'[5]

Batterbee sent on the clipping of this interview to Devonshire with a note regretting Craigavon's stated lack of trust in de Valera's word.[6] Devonshire shared this regret, but thought that, read in its context, Craigavon's interview was 'no more than a bare statement of fact'; nor was he sure that it was 'altogether a bad thing that Mr de Valera should be, brought sharply up against the realities of the situation', because he was 'certainly not aware of them when I saw him last.'[7]

By now the Dominions Office was impatient with Dublin's handling of the Partition issue. MacDonald believed that since

[4] Longford and O'Neill (1970: 341).
[5] Craigavon interview *Sunday Dispatch*, 23 Oct.1938.
[6] Batterbee to Devonshire, 25 Oct. 1938, PRO DO 35/893/X.11/250.
[7] Devonshire, minute 25 Oct. 1938, ibid.

the April Agreement, de Valera had 'taken no steps . . . to woo the North', but rather, had 'done the very opposite'. Devonshire agreed and resented, in particular, de Valera's expectation that London would be his 'catspaw' in coercing the north.[8] British frustration with de Valera's public speeches was not lessened by their amazement at the *naivete* of what he was suggesting in private. The abolition of the oath of allegiance *in Northern Ireland* was one idea he favoured, and the unfortunate Dulanty had had to argue at the Dominions Office that Dublin would consider it 'an excellent gesture' if republican prisoners were released in the north to mark the inauguration of de Valera's new Constitution![9] MacDonald did not hide his frustration: Britain was willing to help 'our friends in Eire', he minuted, 'but it is up to them to assist occasionally; the two barriers to a united Ireland at the moment are Eire and Northern Ireland; the United Kingdom is no bar.'[10]

It was now common knowledge in republican circles that a resort to force was being prepared by the IRA. This was invariably de Valera's cue for an anti-Partition propaganda offensive. To defend his approach to the Partition issue was difficult, more particularly as he was wont to admit that he had no policy likely to succeed. His certainties were two: that no other nationalist grouping had an effective strategy and that any resort to force would be calamitous. However, circumstances now demanded a hawkish line from him on Partition.[11] Moreover, he was deeply pessimistic about the dangers of a European war, believing that the opportunist instinct in Irish nationalism would come to the fore in any situation which could be construed as 'England's difficulty'.[12] Also, given the barren nature of his earlier relationships with British politicians, he now sensed the importance of pressing

---

[8] MacDonald's and Devonshire's comments, both dated 21 Aug. 1938, PRO DO 35/893/X.11/234.
[9] Harding to Batterbee, 1 June 1938, PRO DO 35/893/X.11/210.
[10] MacDonald, minute 21 Aug. 1938, ibid., –/234.
[11] Donnelly to Healy, 5 Oct. 1938, Healy papers, D2991/A/94; Healy circular invitation letter to nationalist conference, 20 Feb. 1939, ibid., –/117B.
[12] Cudahy to SS, 13 Feb. 1939, NA, R.G. 59, 841D.00/1151.

Chamberlain and MacDonald for some concessions on Partition since they were, comparatively, sympathetic.

That the Fianna Fail party was agitated on the issue is clear from the party's *Bulletin*, from the proceedings of the National Executive and from the resolutions arriving at headquarters for the Ard Fheis to be held in late November. Replying to a lengthy debate on Partition, de Valera again played what might be termed his '1921 card'. Before the Treaty had been signed, he reminded delegates, his united republican cabinet had ruled out force against Ulster and had been willing to settle for external association. He now threatened to resign rather than 'shift an inch' from this policy which had been designed to encourage Ulster unionists 'to form part of the Nation'. Perhaps patience would be needed, but it would be far better 'to wait a long time to get them that way than to get them any other way.'[13]

That 'other' methods had some supporters at the Ard Fheis was clear from some suggestions made during the debate on how unity might be achieved. One speaker thought compulsory military service should be introduced in the south; another regretted that force had been excluded as an option, since this 'tied their hands'. Some delegates complained, unsuccessfully, that the presence of the press 'shackled' those who might want to have a 'heart to heart' talk; those with 'hard things to say' did not want to be 'fettered and muzzled'.[14] Once again, it was de Valera who calmed the extremists. However, his own speeches during this period including one that the state was not a dominion and declaring his preference for a republic exasperated those with responsibility for Irish affairs in the Dominions Office to whom it was manifest that whatever slim chance there was of making progress on the Partition issue was being damaged by such assertions. Their chagrin was all the greater because of their own support for some of his charges that the northern nationalists were

---

[13] *Fianna Fail Bulletin*, Dec. 1938; *Irish Press*, 23 Nov. 1938; agenda, 1938 Ard Fheis.

[14] H. McDevitt, a Donegal delegate, who had favoured an 'in camera' session to discuss Partition, suggested in public session that force should not be excluded. *Irish Press*, 23 Nov. 1938.

suffering from widespread discrimination by Ulster Unionists.[15] Pressure from the Dominions Office had rendered it
necessary for the Home Office to defend Northern Ireland's
record in considerable detail.[16]

Just before Christmas, Dulanty, on a visit to Dublin, again
reported to de Valera, MacDonald's 'strong view' that the
anti-Partition campaign would 'do no good to his cause', as it
would only alienate Ulster. Dulanty reported that de Valera
'understood this point of view, but said that no man sitting in
his chair could stand out of the partition campaign.' Unless
he kept 'some sort of control over it' by entering into it, 'it
would get into unconstitutional channels'. MacEntee agreed
with de Valera's assessment; 'the extremists would have got
control' of the campaign had de Valera not intervened. The
'rank and file in the party were feeling extremely bitter about
partition' and it was MacEntee's opinion that de Valera
'could not help himself'.[17]

Chamberlain, for one, should not have been too surprised
by these developments. At one of their private meetings
during the 1938 talks, he had told de Valera that without a
shift in British public opinion, concessions on Partition could
not be made to Dublin's viewpoint. He had also assured the
Irish leader that he would raise no objections if de Valera
were to organize an anti-Partition movement within Britain.
MacEntee later recalled that Chamberlain was 'tacitly accepting' Irish involvement 'in the evangelising of the great British
public'.[18] The Fianna Fail National Executive was the agency
chosen by de Valera to pursue this goal and throughout 1938
they discussed the sending of money, speakers, and advisers
to British cities to liaise with local Irish groups.[19] In October
the executive established a sub-committee 'to consider the

[15] Frustration with de Valera's public speeches is manifest in the Dominions
Office at this juncture, PRO DO 35/893/X.11/257.
[16] See the Home Office files in defence of Northern Ireland in PRO DO
35/893/X.11/251.
[17] MacDonald, note of talk with Dulanty 23 Dec. 1938, PRO DO 35/893/
X.11/265. De Valera spoke in a similar sense to the American Ambassador in
Paris, Bullitt to SS, 9 Mar. 1939, NA, R.G. 59, 841D.01/166.
[18] *Irish Times*, 25 July 1974.
[19] Minutes, Fianna Fail National Executive, 1938, *passim*.

most effective means to organize public opinion in England
on the subject of Partition.'[20]

An invitation from Roosevelt to de Valera to attend the
New York World's Fair provided an opportunity of awakening
American interest in the Partition issue, de Valera announcing
his intention of touring the major Irish-American centres.
MacDonald, informed of these plans, supposed that de Valera
'would make some frightful speeches'. Dulanty attempted to
reassure him by emphasizing that de Valera's adviser in
America — presumably Sean Nunan — had warned him that
he could not 'raise the fiery cross' as he had on his tour of
1919–20.[21] By now, de Valera must have realized that support
for his approach was waning among Irish-Americans. Indeed
an apathetic and implicitly partitionist attitude towards Ulster
was reported to Gallagher by Charles E. Russell, president of
the organization which had remained loyal to de Valera since
he had founded it in 1920 — the American Association for
the Recognition of the Irish Republic. Russell had written of
his concern in the wake of the Anglo-Irish Agreement that,
among members, the 'general feeling' was that the south 'had
won all she wanted . . . and why bother about Ulster, anyway?
If Ulster wished to deprive herself of these advantages, let her
go her way and find out her blunder.'[22] Some months later
Russell's views had hardened: Ireland 'without Ulster' was, he
wrote, 'not the Ireland of our hopes and dreams'.[23]
   De Valera's supporters expected him to use his American
tour for anti-Partition propaganda,[24] a possibility which the
State Department feared and which they did all they could to
discourage.[25] Cudahy elicited a promise of 'tact and discrimination' from de Valera whose approach was typically more
moderate and pragmatic than his diehard supporters desired.[26]

[20] Ibid., 10 Oct. 1938.
[21] MacDonald note of talk with Dulanty 23 Dec. 1938, PRO DO 35/893/
X.11/265. Sean Nunan, de Valera's secretary on US visit, 1919–20; later Irish
career diplomat.
[22] C. E. Russell to Gallagher, 17 May 1938, Gallagher papers, MS 18,351.
[23] Russell to F. P. Walsh, 15 Oct. 1938, F. P. Walsh papers, box 113.
[24] See F. P. Walsh correspondence with Irish-American activists, Jan.–Apr. 1939,
ibid., passim.
[25] Hull to Cudahy, 1 Apr. 1939, NA, R.G. 59, 841D.00/1152.
[26] Cudahy to Roosevelt, 6 Apr. 1939, Roosevelt papers, PSF 56.

Meanwhile the McGarrity faction in the United States had long since tired of de Valera's coaxings and cajolements to rely on constitutional agitation for the republic and was, to de Valera's knowledge, plotting with the IRA leadership to finance a campaign of force.[27] Sean Russell, chief of staff of the IRA, 'believed that even if de Valera would not or could not openly support the campaign, he would at least tolerate the IRA's activities in order to reap the benefits — the end of partition.'[28] This view was shared by many extremists and attempts had been made in November under the auspices of the Old IRA to persuade Fianna Fail to participate in a conference with other national organizations 'with a view to considering plans to deal with the Partition problem.' The National Executive refused the bait; referring the invitation to de Valera, they recommended sending not a delegation but 'a suitable reply'.[29] There was a clear attempt by the IRA to establish a national front organization within their own control[30] and republican criticism of de Valera's policy was, by now, strident.[31] Desmond Ryan, historian, journalist, and an early biographer of de Valera charged his republican critics with 'racial hatred, pietism, near-Fascism, corpse-worship and personal spite'.[32]

On 12 January, Britain's Foreign Secretary, Lord Halifax received an ultimatum from the IRA demanding a British withdrawal from the north within four days, failing which the IRA would declare war on the United Kingdom. Four days later a series of bomb explosions caused material damage but no loss of life in major British cities. The attacks caused alarm in government circles in London, Belfast, and Dublin;

---

[27] Gallagher to McGarrity, 25 June 1938, McGarrity papers, MS 17,544(1); see also, T. P. Coogan, *The IRA* (1970: 118-130).

[28] Bell (1971: 147-8).

[29] Minutes, Fianna Fail National Executive 14 Nov. 1938.

[30] Patrick Maxwell to Healy, 23 Feb. 1939, Healy papers, D2991/A/120.

[31] MacSwiney to 'The Editor' (Oct. 1938), MacSwiney papers, P48/C/22(1); 'Wolfe Tone and the President of the Executive Council for Three-Quarters of Ireland: a dialogue', *Irish Freedom*, July 1937; Cudahy to SS, 20 Oct. 1938, NA, R.G. 59, 841D.00/1144.

[32] Typescript, 'History's warning to Irish terrorists', n.d. (1939), Ryan papers, LA10/D/277. Desmond Ryan, active in anti-Partition campaign in London, 1938-9; his biography of de Valera, *Unique Dictator*, published 1936.

in Berlin, they were noted with satisfaction.[33] The IRA leadership may have believed that they had sufficient recruits 'to Blow or Burn England from her Moorings',[34] but, in reality, the strategy had no possibility of success. Dulanty believed the IRA to be 'madmen' anxious to prevent any permanent reconciliation between Ireland and Britain. He told the Dominions Office that he himself doubted the wisdom of some of de Valera's recent anti-Partition speeches but that de Valera felt the need 'to convince his countrymen that he really was getting a move on upon constitutional lines.' Devonshire appreciated that this was de Valera's motive but thought that the public in Britain and America 'would find it difficult to dissociate Mr de Valera's remarks and the still more inflamatory utterances of some of his followers, from the acts of violence which have followed them.' Further, Devonshire hoped that de Valera appreciated that his recent interventions and the IRA violence 'made any prospect of ultimate re-union . . . infinitely more remote.' According to Devonshire's minute, Dulanty

emphasised the fact that Mr de Valera would be horrified by these acts of lawless violence and that his speeches had been mainly directed towards preventing these and I replied that the man who shouted 'Don't nail his ears to the pump' might have claimed the same motive, but with equally little success.[35]

There is some evidence to suggest that, at this juncture, de Valera had to heed the IRA 'fellow-travellers' in his party. The Dominions Office had suggested to Dulanty that de Valera should dissociate his government from the outrages. Dulanty said he had thought of this himself and 'had been in touch with certain people in Dublin by telephone' but that he gathered that 'in view of the "political position in Eire", it would be difficult for Mr de Valera to do this at the moment'.[36] Cudahy recorded de Valera's assessment of

[33] Longford and O'Neill (1970: 341-2); T. D. Williams, 'Neutrality!', *Irish Press*, 6 July 1953; Lord Templewood (Samuel Hoare), *Nine troubled years* (London: 1954), pp. 243-4.

[34] Hayes to Russell, 10 June 1939, quoted, Sean Cronin, *The McGarrity papers* (Tralee: 1972), p. 171.

[35] Devonshire, minute 18 Jan. 1939, PRO DO 35/893/X.11/271.

[36] Machtig, minute of telephone conversation with Dulanty, 19 Jan. [1939], ibid.

the IRA threat at just this point: the 'great danger' with the IRA

and their illegitimate methods was that the cause of their violence was legitimate, and while at the present time the number of terrorist-extremists was limited they might well serve as a nucleus around which thousands would rally and thus present a real menace to the stability of law and order. Mr de Valera said he thought the British were mad in not realizing the jeopardy to the North if war should come, for in his opinion it would be next to impossible to attempt to restrain sentiment in Ireland which would insist upon marching across the northern border and taking by force what had been denied by law.

Moreover, de Valera believed that illegal guns dumped since the Troubles of 1919–23 might 'come forth like magic if some concerted attack were made on the North at a time when the hands of England were tied.'[37] Some weeks later de Valera told Cudahy that he had informed British ministers

just as emphatically as he could that if he had at his disposal the force of Hitler he would move on to the North and settle Partition conclusively. The only other method was by discussion and conference and repeatedly he had held his hand out for a conference but there was no response from the North.[38]

Further indications of the difficult context in which de Valera was now working can be gleaned from the recommendations of the anti-Partition sub-committee of the Fianna Fail National Executive on 13 February. Emphasising the 'urgent need' for 'a firm direction in the present crisis' and, 'in order that our supporters in newspapers and on platforms shall speak with one voice', the committee asked the National Executive 'to obtain a reiteration of our claim to the whole of Ireland from the Government and an official demand for the evacuation of the North'. Moreover, the Committee believed *the state* should take over the anti-Partition movement 'as the only way to avert disaster'. A lengthy discussion but no decisions followed the tabling of this resolution.[39] But all of this anti-Partition propaganda was now merely of use as a 'safety-valve' among nationalists; whatever success it had

[37] Cudahy to SS, 23 Jan. 1939, NA, R.G. 59, 841D.00/1149.
[38] Cudahy to SS, 13 Feb. 1939, NA, R.G. 59, 841D.00/1151.
[39] Minutes, Fianna Fail National Executive, 13 Feb. 1939; National Anti-Partition Council to de Valera, 27 Apr. 1939, SPO S 12432.

enjoyed in winning converts in Britain had been nullified by the IRA bombing campaign, a factor clear to Irish lobbyists in London who complained of the 'easy optimism' in Dublin concerning the anti-Partition campaign.[40]

In a Senate debate on Fianna Fail's northern policy, de Valera insisted that his was not a pacifist position: 'If we had behind us the strength of some of the continental Powers — I can say publicly what I have said privately — I would feel perfectly justified in using force to prevent the coercion' of the Border nationalists. But implicit in de Valera's argument — and the probable purpose of his speech — was the lesson that such a use of force could *shift* the border, not abolish it.[41] The Ulster Unionists characterized de Valera as 'justifying the use of force if there were any chance of force succeeding.' He would also, the Unionists claimed, impose the Irish language on a united Ireland and declare an independent, neutral republic if the north ever accepted any of his offers of unity under the 1937 Constitution.[42]

Privately the Stormont government attempted to press home their advantage. On the outbreak of the IRA campaign in Britain, Andrews informed Chamberlain that he could 'not help feeling that many of the statements and claims which Mr de Valera and his colleagues have recently made have encouraged the members of the IRA to believe that now that they have got rid of Britain in Eire all they have to do is fight on and they will get Ulster.'[43] If Andrews was hinting here at collusion between de Valera and the IRA, Whitehall did not agree. Chamberlain was advised to take the line in reply that the violence was 'all very unpleasant, but that it is not thought that it should be regarded as an attack by Mr de Valera'.[44] The Northern Ireland government pressed for a specific commitment from London. They believed that in the new circumstances it would be 'most helpful', if the British government publicly reaffirmed Northern Ireland's constitutional right to

[40] Desmond Ryan to Paddy Little, incomplete copy, letter 5 Mar. 1939, Ryan papers, LA10/Q/1/10.
[41] SE: 22: 980–1, 7 Feb. 1939.
[42] *The Times*, 10 Feb. 1939.
[43] Andrews to Chamberlain, 18 Jan. 1939, PRO DO 35/893/X.11/273.
[44] W. C. Hankinson to J. E. Stephenson, 24 Jan. 1939, ibid.

remain within the United Kingdom and that any 'necessary assistance' would be forthcoming should the need arise.[45] Even the Home Office, usually sympathetic, advised against attempting to satisfy the Unionists who would want a declaration which would preclude 'any change in the present position'. Whitehall had no intention of going that far, Chamberlain replying to Andrews that to suggest 'that Great Britain should say that, if the people of Northern Ireland desire to join the south, that they are not to do so for imperial reasons, is to put the British government in a position to which they have never aspired and do not aspire.'[46] Lord Londonderry thought such 'anaemic statements' were 'really amazing' and complained to Hoare of the government's 'pusillanimous' Irish policy; nor had he any long-term faith in future British governments resisting Dublin's pressure over Partition. 'The British Government can always put on a squeeze, as you know, without appearing to coerce, and a Socialist Government would certainly do this.' Londonderry wrote that 'the British Government should state quite categorically that they have no idea of Ulster joining up with the Free State.' Hoare, in reply, sided with Chamberlain: any possible united Ireland to which Ulster would be attracted 'would be in such conditions as to make it perfectly safe' for Britain and in present conditions unity was 'inconceivable' so rendering the whole question 'academic'.[47] Hoare also reassured Londonderry that 'the very suggestion that these despicable terrorist attempts should in any way deflect British opinion is so ridiculous that it is not worthy even of a repudiation'; further, Hoare denied that the cabinet displayed 'antagonism . . . towards Ulster'.[48] Londonderry's son, Robin, himself a Conservative backbencher, thought MacDonald's 'pitiful cringe to de Valera' merely encouraged 'a creature like Goring [*sic*] to ask for more.'[49] Craigavon, in mid-cruise when the IRA campaign

---

[45] As note 43 above.

[46] Draft letter prepared for Chamberlain, PRO DO 35/893/X.11/278; also, extract from Chamberlain to Londonderry, 31 Jan. appended to Londonderry to Hoare, 6 Mar. 1939, Templewood papers, X/4.

[47] Londonderry to Hoare, 6 Mar. and reply 11 Mar. 1939, Templewood papers X/4.

[48] Hoare to Londonderry, 1 Mar. 1939, Templewood papers, X/3.

[49] Quoted in Martin Gilbert, *Winston Churchill: v: 1922–1939* (London: 1976), p. 1027.

was launched, stated in Ceylon that Ulster was 'prepared to
fight to the end rather than yield. There can never be a compromise.'[50]

The continuing IRA campaign in Britain posed a challenge
to de Valera's cabinet. Repressive legislation was one possible
response if it proved tolerable to the Fianna Fail parliamentary
party; even then, given the prevailing political climate, it
might have been counter-productive. De Valera insisted on
the merits of his own political approach. The government, he
argued, was 'always alert and active and never misses an
opportunity of trying to end Partition.'[51] MacDermot, now a
de Valera appointee in the Senate but as acerbic as before in
his denunciations of Fianna Fail's approach to Partition,
sensed, after six months of the IRA campaign, 'a widespread
suspicion' that Fianna Fail 'if they do not actually approve
what is going on, at any rate regard it with a considerable
degree of complacency.'[52]

The files of the Department of Justice give some indication
of the concern of the civil servants at what they saw as an
alarming and deteriorating situation: the absence of extradition for terrorist offences created a 'hiatus' in Irish law;
arguments against its inclusion were 'mainly of a political
character'; amending the law might always be 'misunderstood'
as being done only at the behest of Britain.[53] Arguments were
put forward for 'strong police powers' as a preventative
measure; if illegal republican activities 'appear not to be
regarded seriously by the Government', argued one departmental paper, 'this facilitates recruitment to the IRA particularly by the young in search of adventure'.[54] That public
opinion was ambivalent about suppression of the IRA is clear
from the civil servants' comments and from the government's
approach.[55] De Valera, an implacable opponent of the IRA,
as has been shown, clearly lacked confidence that coercive

[50] Craigavon, interview *Sunday Express*, 22 Jan. 1939.
[51] Notes on Treason Bill, 16 Feb. 1939, Gallagher papers, MS 18,375(11).
[52] SE: 23: 956, 26 July 1939.
[53] Secret memo re Offences Against the State Bill, 6 Apr. 1939, SPO S 10454D.
[54] General observations on the Draft Bills, Office of the Minister for Justice,
SPO S 10454B.
[55] S. A. Roche to Minister for Justice, 8 Mar. 1939, ibid.

legislation would be effective. He believed 'it was hopeless to gauge by any test of logic' the implacable extremist element. 'There was something in the Irish nature which revelled in heroic suffering and sacrifice and this sentiment, which had prevailed throughout the generations, could not disappear overnight.' He confided to Cudahy that whereas he would not hesitate to maintain order, his government was 'treading on dangerous ground'. Given the widespread Anglophobia in the country, 'the feeling would be that the existing Irish Government was acting as a policeman for England.'[56]

Meanwhile throughout these months of deteriorating north-south relations, officials from London, Belfast, and Dublin were struggling to implement the new trade relationship between north and south. T. G. Jenkins, Assistant Secretary at the Board of Trade in London, thought Dublin generally unhelpful in the early months. Moreover, noting the 'uneasiness and ill-feeling' in Unionist circles following de Valera's *Evening Standard* interview, he believed civil servants could do nothing more than 'shed a silent tear about it.'[57] At a meeting with de Valera in February, he took his opportunity of putting his complaint directly. De Valera was 'cordial and friendly' — and unapologetic: 'sentiment in Eire compelled him to speak'. While assuring de Valera that the matter was all 'outside my province altogether', Jenkins ventured to suggest that if de Valera's goal was to unite the thirty-two counties, then surely he had to convince the unionists that 'they would be at least as well off politically and economically under a Dublin Government as they were at present.' To achieve this, Jenkins recommended 'a generous gesture' in some 'small matters' which he had been trying to persuade Lemass was 'at any rate worth a trial'. De Valera declined to make promises: whereas Jenkins had found Lemass 'genuinely anxious' to improve north-south relations, in de Valera's case he had 'no doubt that whenever it comes to a choice between politics and common sense, politics will win.'[58] Whitehall believed that here were 'all the sadly familiar arguments'.[59]

[56] Cudahy to SS, 13 Feb. 1939, NA R.G. 59, 841D. 00/1151.
[57] T. G. Jenkins to John Leydon, 22 Nov. 1938, PRO DO 35/893/X.11/258.
[58] Jenkins note of talk with de Valera, 1 Feb. 1939, PRO DO 35/893/X.11/276.
[59] Inskip, minute 23 Feb. 1939, ibid.

They were to become even more familiar in the weeks which followed. Inskip spent almost four hours with de Valera on 24 March and his detailed note of their conversation, gives some indication of de Valera's scenario on how Irish unity might be brought about. Ruling out force as impractical, de Valera reckoned that the four counties which were 'predominantly with him' would, in a plebiscite, vote themselves out of Northern Ireland.

So far as the 'Ascendancy Party', mainly in Down and Antrim, were concerned, they would do what the Unionists had done in Southern Ireland, namely, make a way of living in peace and harmony with their neighbours, notwithstanding differences of political outlook. This process would be hastened if we withdrew our army from Northern Ireland. The Ascendancy Party, as he called them, would be faced with the possibility of a 'revolt' and they would, before long, reconcile themselves to the position and make terms.

Inskip suggested to de Valera that such an outline, sounded to him 'very like the use of force'; that presumably when de Valera spoke of 'a revolt . . . he meant not a political revolt but something like a military or forcible revolution.' Inskip could not accept that Ulster 'would not fight'. De Valera 'agreed that this was a possibility, but he still thought that the maintenance of British forces in Northern Ireland perpetuated an unnatural state of affairs.'[60]

Chamberlain listened to some of these same arguments when de Valera visited him at Chequers the following morning. In particular de Valera complained about the coercion of the predominantly nationalist border areas 'and added that England was being blamed because she stood in the way and covered Northern Ireland with her protection, without which Eire would make short work of her.' De Valera then tried to coax some concessions from Chamberlain, arguing that unless some change was forthcoming on Partition, his speeches on his American tour might have to be provocative. Chamberlain was not perturbed by this prospect; instead, he chided de Valera for neglecting the 'great opportunity' during the 1938 negotiations of making some tariff concessions to Northern Ireland. Had he done this, 'he would at least have had a

---

[60] Inskip, note of talk with de Valera 24 Mar. 1939, PRO DO 35/893/X.11/296.

nucleus there who might have moderated the more extreme views of the majority'; instead, during the intervening twelve months, he had 'embittered feeling in Northern Ireland' where he now 'had not got a single friend'. Chamberlain concluded this lecture by asking whether de Valera could not now offer some tariff concession to the north, to which de Valera 'offered a somewhat lengthy explanation' of why he found this difficult. Asked whether he could reassure Ulster on the question of a republic, Chamberlain records de Valera as being satisfied with the then Commonwealth link, although if 'some move' could be made on Partition, it would be a position 'much easier to maintain'. Asked to confide 'honestly whether he thought the majority of people in Ireland wanted her to cut loose from the Empire', de Valera accepted that they did, because, in his view, 'mistakenly, they believed they would never have complete independence unless they were a separate Republic.' Chamberlain's rebuttal of this argument — with which de Valera is recorded as having 'entirely agreed' — was that a republic outside the Empire because of its strategic vulnerability, would have to submit to 'much closer restrictions' than would be necessary within the Commonwealth.

Thus, yet again, Chamberlain and de Valera found themselves discussing Partition in the context of what both men appreciated was a common external threat to the peace of both countries. Indeed Chamberlain believed that it was only by approaching the Ulster Unionists on the basis of 'national safety' that he could possibly induce them to 'make some contribution to [Irish] unity'.[61] De Valera gratefully accepted Chamberlain's promise to make some such approach and thus closed what was to be the last meeting between de Valera and the only British Prime Minister whom he admired, trusted, and whose outlook on the Partition issue, he believed was broadly sympathetic.[62]

While the principals were thus engaged, J. P. Walshe, the Secretary of the Department of External Affairs, put a

[61] Chamberlain, note of talk with de Valera 25 Mar. 1939, PRO FO 800/310.
[62] De Valera told a press conference in London in 1951 that he had once convinced a British Prime Minister that Partition was an 'anachronism and an anomaly', *Irish Press*, 17 Mar. 1951. He made no secret of his admiration for Chamberlain, interviews with Sean MacEntee, Frank MacDermot, James Dillon.

proposition to Devonshire which the latter circulated to his colleagues. Walshe asserted that 'substantial advantages' would follow from a 'frank conversation' between de Valera and a Northern Ireland minister. Walshe claimed that, to de Valera, the Ulster unionist viewpoint was 'wholly incomprehensible', it meant 'nothing at all to him'; further, that 'his Chief was becoming more and more obsessed' about Partition and showed 'angry resentment' at Britain's failure to make progress towards ending it. Devonshire, for his part, was against any such meeting. Because Northern Ireland viewed the idea of closer association with the south 'with the utmost repugnance . . . there was no chance of a deal anyhow'; Northern Ireland's terms would be 'far higher than Eire could possibly agree to'. Walshe's argument was that 'it did not matter how high' Northern Ireland pitched its claims 'or how little result was achieved'; his goal in pressing for the meeting was to 'disabuse Mr de Valera of his present fixed conviction' that Britain was solely responsible for Partition.[63]

The Dominions Office communicated all of this information to Hoare at the Home Office and to Chamberlain, but at Harding's suggestion they omitted a concluding paragraph from Devonshire:

It should not be forgotten that Mr Walshe is a Jesuit and that his object in pressing for this conversation to take place may be quite different from what he told me: but what he said seems to me to make sense and I think that no harm and possibly considerable good, might come from such a conversation.

Inskip minuted that he was 'a little suspicious' of the proposal coming from Dublin for a de Valera–Craigavon meeting; he justified this by pointing out to his colleagues that de Valera 'wants to put partition 'right in front of the window' and a meeting with Craigavon would be 'the very thing from his point of view'. But this suspicion seems to have been only tentatively held since Inskip added that he also appreciated 'the force of Mr Walshe's point' and in a letter to Chamberlain on the same day he cites Walshe's argument at face value. In this letter, Inskip bemoans de Valera's recent reference to the Crown and to neutrality which had, 'to put it mildly, not

[63] Devonshire, note of talk with Walshe 13 Apr. 1939, PRO DO 35/893/X.11/303.

improved the atmosphere'. Inskip, who had recently been warned by Dulanty that de Valera was in danger of suffering Cosgrave's fate unless the British got 'something begun concerning partition', now warned Chamberlain that he felt de Valera vulnerable to being 'displaced by people more extreme than himself'. This was 'not a new experience for Irish leaders' but the syndrome whereby Irish negotiators had to be appeased to defend them against such extreme domestic opponents, was, argued Inskip, familiar to Ulster which would consider 'as both futile and mischievous' any approaches by London to 'meet or to help Mr de Valera'. However, Inskip still favoured some approach to Craigavon, although Hoare's 'very strong opinion' was that to invite the Ulster leader 'to discuss better relations with Eire at this juncture' would be 'useless'.[64]

Whether this was a personal initiative on Walshe's part or whether it was mooted with de Valera's support, and, if the latter, whether de Valera knew the grounds on which Walshe sought the meeting, remains obscure. That Craigavon would have declined any such invitation must have been clear to Dublin: some months earlier an American journalist had told de Valera that Craigavon would 'not consider' any tripartite meeting;[65] and another journalist after a public rebuff by Craigavon had noted that he had 'never heard one man tell another so politely and charmingly to go to blazes and mind his own business.'[66]

No matter how, why, or by whom, the Partition question was raised during this period, one factor seemed constant: each episode demonstrated the gulf between the two Irish governments. Their respective positions on whether the London government's conscription bill should be applied to Northern Ireland illustrates the cleavage. To have the north excluded from the Bill, would clearly be a boost to de Valera's flagging reputation with northern nationalists; he also believed it would be immoral and foolhardy in the extreme to attempt

[64] PRO DO 35/893/X.11/303, *passim.*

[65] Sam Brewer of the *Chicago Tribune* had so informed de Valera in November 1938, Cudahy to SS, 4 Nov. 1938, NA, R.G. 59, 841D.01/161.

[66] Lady Craigavon, diary 9 May 1939.

to conscript northern nationalists into the British army. So serious was the issue to de Valera that he postponed his American tour to handle the crisis.

Donnelly, for his part, was anticipating political gains if the British attempted to impose the measure on the north. 'Conscription! Damn the bit of harm a fight over this will do', he wrote, confiding to Healy his enthusiasm about de Valera's 'bold' decision to cancel his American tour. 'But what a fight! That awful "dud" party of his would be better worth £10 a week to keep them at their homes. Let us hope that this is the first step in the final drive forward.'[67] Craig-avon travelled to London 'hoping, expecting and believing' that there would be no differentiation between the mainland and Northern Ireland. Lady Craigavon's diary records that the Ulster leader used 'all his powers of pressing and persuasion but to no purpose' because the British government 'were frightened of the issue being complicated by de Valera kicking up a dust.' Chamberlain spoke bluntly: '"If you really want to help[,] don't press for conscription[:] it will only be an embarrassment." What else could J[ames] do than say very well I wont'?[68]

Lady Londonderry felt 'very very strongly' that the British government was guilty of yet another foolish appeasement. 'It is the old old story. If you want the British government to do anything — you must make yourself a real nuisance — in fact like de Valera.' She found particularly galling that it was now 'openly being said' in the north that the British government 'would never dare' to introduce conscription there. Frustrated at the poor representations made to London of Ulster's real interests, she expressed little faith in the British government's future policy on Partition: with sarcasm, she argued to Hoare that 'the same arguments will hold just as good when the six counties are demanded — i.e. that de Valera will make trouble — and that the Americans are behind him.' Hoare in a restrained reply insisted that the conscription question was 'extremely difficult' and that the decision taken was in the Empire's best interests.[69]

[67] Donnelly to Healy, 28 Apr. 1939, Healy papers, D2991/A/135B.
[68] Lady Craigavon, diary 2 May 1939.
[69] Lady Londonderry to Hoare, 3 May and reply, 4 May 1939, Templewood papers, X/4.

Whereas Robert Brennan, the Irish Minister in Washington, believed that 'the time had definitely passed' when it was worth while 'to talk anti-British stuff in America',[70] and despite pressure from American diplomats in Dublin,[71] de Valera insisted that it was 'probable' that he would make anti-Partition speeches on his American tour.[72] Later, under further pressure, he promised to move 'very carefully' and to use 'tact and discrimination'.[73] The British however, believed him to be well past arguing with: apprehensive that he was 'getting more and more worked up about partition', Inskip believed that 'by the time he reaches the USA, he will be thinking of little else.'[74]

Meanwhile, the pressures from within his own party, were, if anything, increasing. On 28 August, the National Executive of Fianna Fail decided that speakers from the Executive and from the Dail should participate in a series of anti-Partition rallies in the north, 'all speakers to be prepared for arrest and imprisonment in the event of active opposition to such meetings by the Northern Government.'[75] Donnelly had also been active on another front: he wrote to Healy of his proposal to press for the elimination of Article 3 from the Constitution, which limited the Constitution's jurisdiction to twenty-six counties pending the 'reintegration of the national territory'. Such a change would, in effect, be a unilateral declaration of a united Ireland and, by implication, an invitation to the nationalist citizens, elected representatives, and local authorities to switch their allegiance to Dublin. The deletion of Article 3 had its advocates among the interventionists: what Donnelly called the 'best types' in Dublin were 'all delighted' with the proposal. Northern nationalists 'should demand the application of [the] constitution to us and keep at it. Now is the time. Only Dev [*sic*] can battle with any

---

[70] Sir Robert Lindsay to Sir Alexander Hardinge, after Lindsay's talk with Brennan, 1 Mar. 1939, PRO DO 35/899/X.161/4.

[71] Cudahy to Roosevelt, 6 Apr. 1939, Roosevelt papers, PSF 56.

[72] Cudahy to SS, 13 Feb. 1939, NA, R.G. 59, 841D.00/1151; see also papers prepared by de Valera's press secretary, Gallagher, for the tour, Gallagher papers, MS 18,375(11).

[73] MacVeagh to SS, 3 Apr. 1939, NA, R.G. 59, 841D.00/1153; Cudahy to Roosevelt, 6 Apr. 1939, Roosevelt papers, PSF 56.

[74] Inskip, minute 4 Apr. 1939, PRO DO 35/899/X.161/4.

[75] Minutes, Fianna Fail National Executive, 28 Aug. 1939.

hope of victory or negotiate with any hope of success, and we must make him do it.'[76]

The outbreak of the Second World war changed the context in which these initiatives were considered. Nevertheless, the interventionists in the party seem, if anything, to have escalated their demands for anti-Partitionist pressure as war became more and more inevitable. For de Valera, however, Partition was to take second place to securing a policy of neutrality for the twenty-six counties, not only because it was the only policy which could win widespread support, but because it represented the final proof of the south's sovereignty which, in his view, was vested not in the Treaty of 1921-2, but in Fianna Fail's programme, including the 1937 Constitution. After eight years in power, de Valera could claim to have achieved much of his party's original programme. But every gain had further alienated the Ulster unionists. And as the north became a belligerent in the War and the south faced 'The Emergency', the line on the map became something more than a customs frontier and an international border: it separated the south which valued neutrality, independence, and 'frugal comfort'[77] from the north which had self-consciously joined what Unionist leaders emphasized was one of the most fateful struggles in history, a fight for freedom, Christianity, democracy, and civilization itself.

---

[76] Donnelly to Healy, 28 Apr. 1939, Healy papers, D2991/A/135B.
[77] See de Valera, 'The Ireland that we dreamed of', 17 Mar. 1943, De Valera: speeches: 1980: 466-9.

6. 'The Emergency' and After
1939–1948

(i) THE PHONEY EMERGENCY?

In November 1940, the novelist Elizabeth Bowen suggested to the Ministry of Information in London that although Irish neutrality must appear 'an affair of blindness, egotism, escapism or sheer funk', it ought to be understood as a positive '*free* self-assertion' of her independence.[1] De Valera, for his part, insisted that neutrality was based on prudence, not cowardice; he did fear that Ireland might become a 'cockpit',[2] or a 'side-show'[3] to a German invasion of Britain. He also feared that if the British returned either by invitation or invasion they might not withdraw at the conclusion of the war.[4] De Valera knew well that no policy other than neutrality was politically possible: politicians,[5] diplomats,[6] the press,[7] the churches,[8] ex-unionists,[9] Irish writers[10] — and the voters, when consulted[11] — all approved. What began as 'a gambler's

[1] Elizabeth Cameron, 'Notes on Eire', 9 Nov. 1940, Halifax papers, FO 800/310. Cameron was the married name of the novelist Elizabeth Bowen (1900-73); b. Dublin; Anglo-Irish; occasionally reported to British Ministry of Information her impressions of Irish politics during the War; CBE, 1948.

[2] *The Times*, 4 Feb. 1942.

[3] Mulcahy, recording de Valera's view, 'The X summary', 5 July 1940, Mulcahy papers, P7a/210.

[4] Mulcahy, 'Notes for Defence Conference', 29 May 1941, ibid., P7a/214.

[5] Interview, James Dillon; exchange of letters between Cosgrave and de Valera, July 1940, quoted Longford and O'Neill (1970: 371).

[6] Cudahy to R. W. Moore, 29 Nov. 1939, forwarded to Roosevelt, Roosevelt papers, PSF 56; John H. Kelly to Mackenzie King, 4 Oct. 1940, PAC R.G. 25, vol. 1949, file 822-39c. Kelly was Canadian High Commissioner in Dublin 1940-1.

[7] See summary of editorials, Gallagher papers, MS 18,334.

[8] Ibid., for *Church of Ireland Gazette*; see also T. D. Williams, 'Neutrality!', *Irish Press*, 1 July 1953.

[9] Percy Lorraine, confidential report Dec. 1940, Halifax papers, FO 800/310.

[10] See Gallagher papers, MS 18,341.

[11] O'Leary (1979: 34-7); Longford and O'Neill (1970: 401-2, 409-10).

throw', in time, hardened into a 'habit of mind'.[12] It was
supported by factions as far apart as republican extremists
and those southern Irishmen who were in the war as volunteers
in the British armed services![13]

De Valera believed it would have been 'suicide' to abandon
neutrality;[14] his Minister in Washington thought 'revolution'
might have followed;[15] and Britain's representative in Dublin
thought the consequences 'beyond computation'.[16] Although
scarcely popular in London or Washington, there were some
who appreciated that Irish neutrality might even be the best
possible policy from the Allied viewpoint; the south was
virtually defenceless and her involvement in the war would
have entailed spreading even more thinly the Allies' already
overstretched defensive capacity.[17] What was clear was that
given Ireland's recent history and the continuing grievance of
Partition, military support for the Allies was not politically
possible.

The outbreak of war heightened expectations in some
quarters of the Fianna Fail party that Partition could be
abolished. Although party headquarters attempted to channel
this pressure into propaganda efforts,[18] the approval for an
opportunist resort to force won some support at the Ard
Fheis in December. Donnelly argued that if they did not re-
unite the country while the war was on, 'they could whistle
for it afterwards.'[19] Opposition politicians even suspected —

[12] *The Times*, 28 Apr. 1942, 19 Oct. 1944.
[13] The left-wing republican leader, Frank Ryan, then in Berlin, was anxious to
return to Ireland to help in unifying his 'friends' behind de Valera's 'foreign
policy', Ryan to Leopold Kerney (Irish Minister in Madrid) 14 Jan. 1942. I am
grateful to Brian Lenihan, the Irish Foreign Minister (1979–81) for permission to
consult a series of letters from Ryan to Kerney, June 1940-Aug. 1942, in the
archives of the Department of Foreign Affairs, Dublin. For Irishmen in British
army supporting Irish neutrality, *The Times*, 28 Apr. 1942. See also Hubert Gough
to Bodkin, 23 May 1943, Bodkin papers, 6935/400.
[14] Longford and O'Neill (1970: 395).
[15] Welles memo, 9 Nov. 1940, *FRUS*, 1940, p. 167.
[16] Maffey to Eden, 26 Oct. 1939, PRO CAB 66/2 WP(39)97.
[17] Sean Lemass, interview with Michael Mills, *Irish Press*, 25 Jan. 1969; W. L.
Langer and S. E. Gleason, *The world crisis: American foreign policy: vol. 1: the
challenge to isolation, 1937-1940* (London: 1952), p. 717.
[18] Minutes, Fianna Fail National Executive, 18 and 25 Sept., 20 Nov. 1939,
8 Jan., and 1 Apr. 1940.
[19] *Belfast Newsletter*, 13 Dec. 1940.

although this was denied within Fianna Fail — that de Valera had demoted his Defence Minister because Aiken believed "that the Army should be ready to march into Ulster at any time.'"[20] What was manifest was that one faction in Fianna Fail approved of the hallowed republican maxim that 'England's difficulty was Ireland's opportunity'.[21] The first wartime Ard Fheis heard delegates advocate the use of force against Northern Ireland. De Valera gave his usual reply. He was not a pacifist in principle; if force 'promised success' he would not 'shirk the sacrifice of energy, wealth, or even life that would be entailed.' But Fianna Fail's aim was not merely 'to get these people momentarily or temporarily united to us' but rather to arrive at a situation where unity could be stabilized.[22] On the second day of the Ard Fheis de Valera mooted the idea that a transfer of populations between Irish emigrants in Britain and those in Northern Ireland who refused to consider themselves Irish might provide a solution to the Partition question.[23]

To defend his Partition strategy against extreme party opinion, de Valera had yet again offered offence to the Ulster unionists. In contrast, he was much more sensitive when it came to defending his ascendancy as nationalist leader from any erosion on his republican flank. This is manifest in the early reports of Sir John Maffey as Britain's first diplomatic representative in Ireland. He records de Valera as complaining that his every action was 'studied by men bitterly opposed to any sort of *rapprochement* with the United Kingdom'; it was, he said, 'beyond belief' how easily suspicions could be aroused.[24] In particular he was concerned at the erosion of

[20] Mulcahy, memo of conversation with 'R', 20 or 26(?) Oct. 1939, Mulcahy papers, P7a/219. Internal evidence suggests that 'R' was a member of the Fianna Fail government, probably James Ryan who was Mulcahy's brother-in-law and whom he met socially during these years. 'R', speaking 'in lodge', claimed that Aiken had been assigned to other duties not because he favoured force against Northern Ireland but because he was 'obstinate and ignorant . . . intolerant and dictatorial'.

[21] It would be difficult to exaggerate the pervasiveness of this outlook among Irish republicans; MacSwiney to de Valera n.d. (June 1940) MacSwiney papers, P48/C/20. MacSwiney to Cardinal MacRory, 27 June 1940, ibid., P48/C/32.

[22] *Belfast Newsletter*, 13 Dec. 1940.

[23] *Irish Times*, 14 Dec. 1939.

[24] Maffey's reports of his talks with de Valera, 14, 20, and 22 Sept. 1939, PRO DO 35/1107/W.X.1/5. Sir John Maffey (1877–1969), British career civil

support among northern nationalists for his pacific approach to the Partition issue. At the height of the conscription crisis in the north in April 1939 it had twice been suggested to him that he should launch an all-Ireland 'scheme for Irish National Service'.[25] A month later, one of the proposers complained to Healy that he had been 'agitating for a considerable time to have young men from the North enrolled as volunteers in the Twenty-Six Counties; but so far without success.' Aiken, when refusing one request, had said that 'we would have to make local arrangements ourselves.'[26]

To de Valera, all of this evidence justified his prewar forebodings that the British would 'rue the day' they had imposed Partition;[27] its existence now left him and them with an unstable and unpredictable security problem. 'The Nation is on the March' intoned the IRA propaganda machine,[28] exhorting the people to 'rise now' and help in 'the destruction of the British Empire'.[29] Although poorly led and with negligible support in the south, the IRA remained potentially exploitable by the Germans and clearly posed serious security problems for the government;[30] as de Valera admitted to the American Minister in Dublin, David Gray, they 'appealed to something very deep in the Irish heart.'[31]

Along with their fears of irregular activity by the IRA, Dail politicians also feared the possibility of reprisals south of the border by a 'Wilson-minded group' from the north.[32] What in

servant; came out of retirement to become UK representative to Eire, 1939–49; de Valera found him tactful; created Lord Rugby, 1947.

[25] Patrick Maxwell to de Valera, 28 Apr. 1939; also Sean Dowling and Roger McCorley, National Anti-Partition Council, to de Valera, 27 Apr. 1939, SPO S 12432.

[26] Maxwell to Healy, 24 June 1939, Healy papers, D2991/A/142A; ibid., 30 June 1939, −/152B.

[27] Raoul Dandurand quoting a prewar conversation he had had with de Valera at the League of Nations at Geneva, Dandurand to Mackenzie King, 1 Jan. 1941, Mackenzie King papers, M.G. 26, J4, vol. 384, file 8.

[28] IRA circular, NLI MS 21,155(4).

[29] 'Irishmen, stop and think', duplicated typescript, NLI MS 18,945.

[30] This is manifest from the reports and memoranda in the US State Department files, Dec. 1939-May 1940, NA, R.G. 59, 841D.00/1230, −/1237-8, −/1243, −/1252, −/1254, −/1257-9.

[31] Gray to Roosevelt, 15 Apr. 1940, Roosevelt papers, PSF 56.

[32] Mulcahy, memo of meeting with de Valera and O'Kelly, 13 Sept. 1939, McGilligan papers, P35/C/182. Field-Marshal Sir Henry Wilson, sometime Chief of

particular terrified de Valera was the prospect of a German invasion of nationalist areas north of the border. If he were in charge of German strategy, he told Gray, he would land in these areas and proclaim himself 'a liberator. If they should do that[,] what I could do I do not know.'[33] This contingency was also feared by Richard Mulcahy[34] and was formally raised by another Fine Gael member at the all-party advisory Defence Conference. T. F. O'Higgins[35] asked whether southern troops should be willing to help the north to fight the Germans if they landed there: few other questions would have elicited such revealing answers from the Dail parties. Labour thought any such aid would amount to collaboration with the British in their '"occupation and exploitation of the Six Counties"'; Fine Gael, on the contrary, believed that not to assist 'would be disgraceful and absurd'; while Fianna Fail ministers, Aiken and Boland, were non-committal, believing that if the contingency were to arise, any decision would have to be referred to the Dail. This demonstrated that parties agreed on neutrality could be deeply divided on any deviation from that policy.[36]

The IRA, in fact, tried to interest Berlin in a plan for the joint invasion of Northern Ireland — 'Plan Kathleen'. It was 'so amateurish' that some Germans suspected a British plot. Hermann Goertz, the only German agent to enjoy any success in Ireland, believed the proposed plan to be 'childish' and 'completely useless'.[37] Six months before the war had started, the German High Command had expressed an interest in

the Imperial General Staff, had been a rabid critic of Sinn Fein twenty years before. When he became military adviser to the Northern Ireland government in 1922, it was widely believed in Dublin that he might approve a reconquest of the south if that proved opportune.

[33] Gray to Roosevelt, 6 June 1940. Roosevelt papers, PSF 56.

[34] Mulcahy memo, 22 May 1940, Mulcahy papers, P7a/211. Richard Mulcahy (1886-1971), chief of staff, IRA, during War of Independence; GOC, Free State army in Civil War; TD, 1918-37, 1938-43, 1944-61; leader Fine Gael, 1944-59; member of advisory all-party Defence Conference during Second World war; supported Irish neutrality while strongly sympathetic to Allies; brother-in-law of two of de Valera's senior ministers, S. T. O'Kelly and James Ryan.

[35] T. F. O'Higgins, member of Fine Gael shadow cabinet, future Minister for Defence (1948-51); brother of Kevin O'Higgins.

[36] Mulcahy's notes of Defence Conference meeting, 25 July 1940, 'German attack on six counties', Mulcahy papers, P7a/212.

[37] Enno Stephan, *Spies in Ireland* (London: 1963 edn.), pp. 96, 163.

Goertz 'kindling some sort of rebellion in Ulster'.[38] Once war started, those in Berlin interested in fomenting trouble for Britain in Ireland appreciated the strategic vulnerability of the border and hoped for an IRA concentration on the six counties. Goertz urged on the IRA leadership — by which he was very unimpressed — the need to avoid all friction with the southern government. Later he wrote that if the IRA had confined its activities to the north and had fought 'arms in hand, bleeding heavily', in pursuance of its goal of Irish unity 'undoubtedly, there would have been a large measure of support from most of the people in Eire.'[39] Naïvely, it was German policy to attempt 'to effect an alliance between the IRA, the Irish Army and subsequently the government.'[40] The Germans were ill-informed about the nuances of Irish politics and believed that, as the IRA shared with Fianna Fail the goal of uniting Ireland that Goertz could assist in establishing some *modus operandi* between them. This demonstrated a naïve view of both parties.[41]

Although Irish sympathies were largely pro-Ally, there were, as de Valera told Maffey as early as September 1939, 'a good many waverers' who had been impressed with Germany's early successes: 'That was the way of the world.'[42] In considering German–Irish relations during this first year of the war, a distinction must be made between Irish *sympathies* and Irish *interests*. Whereas majority sympathy, from the beginning of hostilities, was overwhelmingly pro-British, it seemed prudent to ensure that in the event of a German victory, Irish interests would not be neglected. Among these interests was control over the nationalist campaign against Partition. Even though the Fianna Fail government was deeply apprehensive about a German victory, they could not afford to ignore the danger that their own leadership of Irish nationalism could be usurped if they allowed others to make progress in undoing Partition. Moreover, in the first year of

[38] Ibid., p. 82.
[39] Hermann Goertz, 'Mission to Ireland', *Irish Times*, 25 Aug. 1947.
[40] T. D. Williams, 'Neutrality!', *Irish Press*, 10 July 1953.
[41] Ryan to Kerney, 14 Jan. 1942, Ryan letters, see note 13 above.
[42] Maffey, report 24 Sept. 1939, PRO DO 35/1107/W.X.1/5.

the war, Germany seemed, to many observers, to be invincible: American diplomats and journalists, even members of the British war cabinet were deeply pessimistic about Britain's prospects.[43] Dublin's policy seems to have been based on the expectation that the United States would not enter the war[44] and that 'a speedy conclusion of peace' on terms which would be 'reasonably tolerable' to Britain was the most likely outcome.[45] It is against this background that Irish diplomatic relations with Berlin must be judged.

As the official Berlin archives make clear, from the very eve of the war — late August 1939 — Irish foreign policy was vigilant in protecting Irish interests in the event of a German war victory. Walshe was reported by the German Minister, Eduard Hempel, as suggesting on 26 August that Berlin should make a 'formal declaration . . . that Germany has no aggressive aims in Ireland, but on the contrary has sympathy for Ireland and Irish national aims. — mentioning, if necessary Northern Ireland.'[46] Ribbentrop thought it would be a mistake to expressly mention Northern Ireland but suggested to Hempel that he should reassure the Irish government of 'the wide sympathy felt in Germany for . . . the national aspirations of the Irish people.'[47] By November, Hempel was advising Berlin against precipitate interference which might destroy 'the possibility of a future utilization of the Irish cause for our interests'. He foresaw circumstances where the Partition grievance might become a factor in Germany's favour: if Britain were to invade the south, or, if she were to become considerably weakened, then there might be some attempt to regain the north. 'Then we might expect the rise of an active nationalist movement on a broad basis, perhaps, inclusive of

[43] Hempel reported that the Department of External Affairs in Dublin believed that Chamberlain, Halifax, Simon, and Hoare were interested in a negotiated peace, Hempel to Foreign Ministry, 22 July 1940, *DGFP*:D:10:doc.201. See also Gray to Roosevelt, 21 Oct. 1941, Roosevelt papers, PSF 56.

[44] Gray to Roosevelt, 6 June 1940, Roosevelt papers, PSF 56.

[45] Hempel to Foreign Ministry, 22 July 1940, *DGFP*:D:10:doc. 201.

[46] Hempel to Foreign Ministry, 26 Aug. 1939, *DGFP*:D:7:doc. 303. Eduard Hempel, German career diplomat, never joined Nazi party; appointed Minister to Ireland, July 1937, remained in Dublin post until end of war; de Valera found his conduct irreproachable; in penury in 1945, de Valera granted him political asylum; later returned to Germany.

[47] Ribbentrop to Hempel, 29 Aug. 1939, ibid., —/doc. 428.

the Government.' Hempel reported that he had 'occasionally heard the hope expressed' that Germany, at an opportune moment, might 'promise Ireland our support for the return of Northern Ireland, to be made good at the conclusion of peace.' Hempel added that 'the proper moment' had not yet arrived for such an announcement. He believed such a hope of German aid in ending Partition, was 'probably entertained . . . in some Government circles, although hardly by de Valera so far.'[48]

Although willing to regard Irish grievances as potentially exploitable in Germany's interest, the political élite in Berlin was ill-informed and prejudiced about Ireland[49] considering the country to be largely within Britain's sphere of influence.[50] The British, being especially preoccupied by their strategic vulnerability, scarcely believed this.[51] Maffey from his earliest talks with de Valera, consistently emphasized the strategic interdependence of the two islands. De Valera for his part, concentrated on the Irish map, the subject of Partition recurring 'again and again'. Maffey reported to London that

we always performed a circle, the President saying that Eire could not consider any policy today except in the light of the crime of partition, while I said that the prospects of readjusting partition must be affected by the policy of Eire to-day.[52]

This 'circle' was to remain the basis of Anglo-Irish relations throughout the war underlining the interdependence of neutrality and Partition, the latter invariably cited by the Irish to counteract criticism of neutrality. Indeed when a new trade agreement was being discussed in May 1940, British ministers were 'willing to give Eire a good mark' for not having once mentioned 'Northern Ireland[,] Partition or the Boundary'

---

[48] Hempel to Foreign Ministry, 14 Nov. 1939, ibid., —/doc. 355.

[49] Ribbentrop's views, quoted Stephan (1963: 147); interview, David Kahn, author of *Hitler's spies: German military intelligence in World War II* (London: 1978), *Irish Press*, 15 Sept. 1978.

[50] Norman Rich, *Hitler's war aims: the establishment of the New Order: vol. 2* (London: 1974), p. 397.

[51] H. Duncan Hall, 'Fighting Ulster and neutral Eire', in W. Y. Elliott and H. D. Hall, *The British Commonwealth at war* (Harvard: 1943), p. 478.

[52] Maffey, 'Memorandum' 14 Sept. 1939, PRO DO 35/1107/W.X.1/5.

during the course of the negotiations.[53] Neutrality now took precedence over anti-Partitionism in Irish politics.

That the continuance of Partition prevented any deviation from neutrality was clear. What was not was whether some move towards a united Ireland might be traded for concessions on neutrality. And if Ireland were to be united, would she join Britain at war? De Valera had invited conjecture on this topic by his constant pre-war emphasis on the limitations which Partition placed on possible defence co-operation with Britain. The American Minister, Gray,[54] was anxious to explore this issue in Belfast and Dublin. His motivation was clear — to shelter Roosevelt from the pressures of those whom Gray characterized as 'the professional anti-Lion boys' among Irish-Americans. He did not underestimate the difficulties of attempting to interest Craigavon and de Valera in some compromise settlement: it was like 'walking on the sulphur crust over a crater full of melted lava'; it was 'a hundred to one chance but it ought to be taken.'[55] Others, too, were sceptical: Skelton, Canada's Foreign Minister thought it 'very doubtful' that Gray would meet with any success.[56] Before offering his services as honest broker, Gray had spoken to Ireland's diplomatic representatives in London, Paris, Rome, and the Vatican, also to the Pope and to many of the political élite in Britain. He was not, he insisted, 'conducting a negotiation or proposing a mediation'. While not discouraging his efforts, the Irish diplomats were scarcely optimistic. Dulanty, Gray wrote,

was very doubtful of any success with Ulster. His idea is that it will take years, that the most that can be hoped for in a reasonable future is a joint commission on roads or a joint art exhibition or even an all-Irish football team. But he said: 'For heaven's sake explore away and if you turn up any chance tell us.'

[53] Extract, Robertson to Gransden, 6 May 1940, copy for Craigavon, PRONI CAB 9R/60/5.

[54] David Gray (1868-1962), journalist, diplomat; US Minister to Ireland, 1940-7; a friend of Roosevelt and related to him by marriage, his official reports to the State Department were paralleled by confidential letters to the President; poor relationship with de Valera, mutual dislike at least from 1941.

[55] Gray to Roosevelt, 8 Apr. 1940, Roosevelt papers, PSF 56.

[56] O. D. Skelton, memo (May 1940), Mackenzie King papers, M.G. 26, J4, vol. 359, file 3844.

In London Gray also 'talked Ireland' with a number of influential politicians and with the American Ambassador, Joseph Kennedy. All were agreed that Ulster could not be coerced, as was an irascible Churchill, who 'roared for a time' about the Irish. Informally, and 'off the record' Churchill was prepared to arrange that Gray meet Craigavon to sound him on concessions on Partition if the south reconsidered its policy of neutrality; but Churchill insisted that it was 'all up to Ulster'.[57] Gray's understanding of Churchill's position was that he would 'under no circumstances . . . tolerate any coercion of Ulster[,] direct or indirect'; but that any settlement agreeable to Belfast and Dublin, provided it was 'not inimical to the vital interests' of the British, would have his approval.[58] In his early meetings with de Valera, Gray was lectured on Partition and given the 'map treatment'; de Valera, he reported to Roosevelt, 'keeps coming back to the Ulster question insisting that the British are making a terrible mistake in not settling it.' Gray suggested to him that 'he might be making a bad mistake' not to take advantage of the current crisis by making a 'bold and original' defence concession to the north; it was 'obviously the time to convince Ulster of the South[']s friendliness.' It was Gray's opinion that de Valera appreciated that such a course would win concessions but that it was 'a hard pill to swallow in his present state of mind'.[59]

Asked if he intended 'to prepare [the] public mind for the realities' de Valera had replied to Gray 'yes[,] but slowly.'[60] The realities in Gray's and Maffey's book were that Ireland, south or north, or both — could be the object of the Nazi's next expeditionary force. The British failure to prevent the fall of Norway in April, caused alarm in Dublin, as did its direct sequel in British politics, the fall of the Chamberlain government. His successor, Winston Churchill, had been a persistent critic of de Valera's politics since the latter's opposition to the Treaty in 1921. As a backbencher, he had stood out against the return of the Treaty ports in the 1938

---

[57] Gray to Roosevelt, 8 Apr. 1940, Roosevelt papers, PSF 56.
[58] Transcript of *aide-memoire*, Gray to Churchill, shown to de Valera, ibid.
[59] Gray to Roosevelt, 15 Apr. 1940, Roosevelt papers, PSF 56.
[60] Gray to Hull, 18 May 1940, *FRUS*: 1940: 3: p. 160.

Agreement, calling the decision 'incredible' and 'feckless'.[61] His recall to his old desk at the Admiralty on the outbreak of the war had offered Churchill every opportunity to criticize Irish neutrality; he recommended to the cabinet that they 'take stock of the weapons of coercion';[62] he complained of the 'odious' approach by Dublin to Anglo-Irish relations;[63] he was 'sick' of the Irish;[64] he queried whether their neutrality had any validity: 'Nothing had been defined. Legally I believe they are "At war but skulking".'[65] To de Valera, this change of leadership was drastic — the most sympathetic leader with whom he had ever dealt was being replaced by one of Ulster unionism's stoutest defenders.[66] Craigavon, for his part, was 'very delighted' that his 'old friend' was now Britain's war leader.[67]

On the very day, 10 May, on which Churchill was moving into Downing Street, Belgium and Holland fell to the Germans. Without waiting for instructions, Maffey called on de Valera to question once again what he clearly saw as de Valera's complacency in the face of the 'maniacal force let loose in the world'. In what was an uncomfortable encounter, Maffey failed to budge de Valera from his set course; Maffey concluded that he was 'not a strong man' and had a 'tendency to surrender always to the extremist view'.[68] Gray was also critical; he thought de Valera 'frightened' by the new situation 'but not prepared to cope with it . . . he is not the man for a war.'[69] Indeed, having spoken with James Dillon of Fine Gael, Gray thought it 'not impossible' that a national government might be formed.[70] That the idea was at least under active

[61] W. S. Churchill, *The second World War: i: the gathering storm* (London: 1949 edn.), pp. 247-9.

[62] Cabinet minutes, 24 Oct. 1939, PRO CAB 65/1 WM 58(39)8.

[63] Nicholas Bethel, *The war Hitler won* (London: 1972), p. 243.

[64] Gray to Roosevelt, 8 Apr. 1940, Roosevelt papers, PSF 56.

[65] Churchill to Eden, 20 Oct. 1939, Halifax papers, FO 800/310.

[66] Longford and O'Neill (1970: 361) describe it as 'a drastic change'; interview Malcolm MacDonald; Terry de Valera, letter, *Irish Times*, 7 Nov. 1979; see also Garner (1978: 233-4).

[67] Lady Craigavon, diary 13 May 1940; see also W. B. Spender, diary 13-18 May 1940, Spender papers, D715/14.

[68] Maffey, 'Memorandum' 10 May 1940, PRO CAB 67/6 WP(G) (40)128.

[69] Gray to Roosevelt, 16 May 1940, Roosevelt papers, PSF 56.

[70] Ibid., 31 May 1940.

consideration is clear from Mulcahy's notebooks for the third week in May. Some 'very alarmed' Fianna Fail ministers thought of approaching Fine Gael to discuss the possibility; Mulcahy, however, believed it 'nonsense' to consider the formation of a national government until 'something very serious arises'. By 20 May, Mulcahy believed the 'physical collapse' of de Valera could be ruled out, as could action by him which 'would suggest alternative leadership to his own, graciously and with his full co-operation.' Full Fianna Fail support would be necessary for the success of any national government, and if one were to be formed without de Valera's approval, Mulcahy feared that Fianna Fail would fragment and an 'irresponsible opposition' would result.[71]

That de Valera survived as the country's leader throughout the war and as party leader until the end of the fifties has probably obscured the fact that to some of his contemporaries his leadership seemed vulnerable during these months. The previous February, Maffey had mooted the demise of de Valera's 'unpopular and incompetent' administration — 'his eyesight is fading fast' — and advised London that there was 'no reason to despair of other and more helpful trends gradually gathering force.'[72]

(ii) JUNE 1940: PARTITION — NEGOTIABLE BY LONDON?

That Germany could not be defeated was now a fairly common belief throughout Western Europe. It was now imperative, at least, to prepare for the contingency of a German invasion of Ireland. What agitated the British was that, due to Partition, responsibility for the defence of the island of Ireland was shared by three separate authorities, the governments in Dublin, Belfast, and London. Partition had another disadvantage. As a highly emotive issue within Ireland, it remained a critical factor in shaping Irish attitudes towards the war: to solve it might win Irish co-operation; to leave it unsolved, might result in it being exploited by the Germans. For the first time since its enactment twenty years before, Partition

---

[71] Mulcahy, note 15 May 1940, Mulcahy papers, P7a/210.
[72] Maffey to DO, telegram 8 Feb. 1940, Hankey papers, CAB 63/147; see also interview with Dulanty, 26 July 1940, in Crozier (1973: 179-80).

was seriously questioned by London. Was it, any longer, the least deadly alternative of Britain's policy options towards Ireland? Could de Valera, who had always pointed to just these dangers, now take advantage of London's willingness to reconsider her support for Partition?

De Valera, too, had his idea of a least deadly alternative: that the north should join a united Ireland, whose neutrality would be guaranteed by all sides, including the Germans.[73] Some opinion in Fianna Fail believed that the prospect of thus escaping the war's excesses would prove attractive to the Ulster unionists.[74] To Britain, however, the abandonment of the Northern Irish ports was strategically impractical, a consideration, which Gray noted, had not occurred to de Valera when the American Minister discussed Dublin's choices with him. Gray favoured 'concerted action' with the north: 'a compromise now might produce results that would otherwise be impossible for years to come[,] assuming the allies won. If they did not win[,] Irish freedom was a vanished dream. He agreed in principle but could devise no line of compromise.'[75]

That some Anglo-Irish bargain on Partition in return for defence co-operation was now a possibility was appreciated by Hempel. On 23 May, he cabled Berlin that any such agreement between Dublin and London 'could strongly, and perhaps decisively, influence conditions in England's favour and probably bring England political advantage in the USA, which perhaps has a hand in the game.' He added his own assessment of de Valera's policy: that whereas he would invite British aid if Germany invaded Ireland, his democratic principles would preclude him 'seeking German aid in the event of a British attack'. He would instead 'offer resistance by a call for national unity' and 'attempt to localise the conflict and set all wheels in motion in the USA'. Even in these circumstances, Hempel did not expect de Valera to be vulnerable to the danger of internal disturbances fomented by the IRA.

[73] Explained to MacDonald in June 1940, Chamberlain, memo 'Eire: negotiations with Mr de Valera', 25 June 1940, PRO CAB 66/9 WP (40) 223.

[74] *Irish Press*, 13 Dec. 1939.

[75] Gray to Roosevelt, 16-21 May 1940, Roosevelt papers, PSF 56. Frank MacDermot lobbied de Valera along similar lines, MacDermot to de Valera, 5 June 1940, MacDermot papers, PROI 1065/14/7.

However, any German assistance, 'especially a simultaneous proclamation of the liberation of Northern Ireland as a German war aim', would probably give the IRA movement 'a powerful impetus'. Hempel added that, in his view, the liberation of Northern Ireland was a matter in which there was no German interest.[76]

At their meeting on 10 May, Maffey apparently in the belief that the question was 'academic', had asked de Valera bluntly: "'If the Partition question were solved today would you automatically be our active Ally?'" He recorded de Valera as replying: "'I feel convinced that that would probably be the consequence.'"[77] This reply may have been in the nature of 'bait' from de Valera; it was not a flat promise and all other evidence suggests that any abandonment of neutrality was unlikely;[78] the reply's significance lies in the fact that Maffey communicated it to London on 16 May where the question was, by then, not at all academic.[79]

Adding to Dublin's alarm at Germany's success was the discovery of evidence that German Intelligence was attempting to land spies in Ireland.[80] De Valera emphasized the menace of an IRA–German link. A small group was clearly 'meditating treason'; it was, he said, 'no time for nonsense'.[81] De Valera now sanctioned top-level staff talks between the Irish and British armies — Walshe also attended — to prepare plans for British help in the event of a German invasion. The British believed the staff talks useful, but very much 'second best' to an abandonment of neutrality and the adoption of a common defence policy for the two islands.[82] To encourage de Valera to make neutrality negotiable, some British ministers were now prepared to question London's support for Partition. Negotiations were proposed, the political aspect being entrusted to Chamberlain.

[76] Hempel to Foreign Ministry, 23 May 1940, *DGFP*: D: 9: doc. 310.
[77] As note 68 above.
[78] Gray to Roosevelt, 19 June 1940, Roosevelt papers, PSF 56.
[79] See reports by chiefs of staff, 27 May 1940, PRO CAB 65/7 WM 141(40)9.
[80] Stephan (1965: 115).
[81] *Irish Press*, 27 May 1940.
[82] Minutes of meeting between representatives of the government of Eire and representatives of the DO and service departments of the UK, 23 and 24 May 1940, PRO PREM 3/130.

The mutual ignorance and lack of rapport between Dublin and Belfast could be blamed on both sides. In March 1940 de Valera had publicly called on the Ulster unionists to become 'a proud part' of 'their own nation': in joining up with the south, they would be realizing 'the dream of centuries'.[83] Unionists could not be wooed on this basis; nor were they interested, at the end of April, in a kite which they believed was being flown with de Valera's approval 'to ascertain whether the North would join the South if certain concessions were made.'[84] Instead, the Unionists were anxious to extract all propaganda value from the south's neutrality which Craigavon constantly reminded London was 'in every way . . . a menace to the British flank.'[85] London did not need Craigavon to point out this danger: what they needed were concessions from him to avert it. And he was presently subjected to a campaign of cajolement, persuasion, and political pressure. Baldwin begged him 'to be helpful . . . at this time of national danger. If it is a question of meeting de V. [sic] well I know the difficulties in ordinary times. But the times are not ordinary.'[86]

Endemically suspicious that a British government might betray them to the south, some members of the Ulster Unionist élite were now 'very uneasy' about possible developments. Even if de Valera were to get 'some eye-wash concession', Spender was 'very doubtful' if the south would join the war. As for the north's duty, Spender thought that the European situation was 'so serious that there is no knowing what sacrifices' it would be right for Northern Ireland to make.[87]

Nor had Spender much confidence in Craigavon as the best man to defend Ulster's interests, particularly in negotiations with Chamberlain. As Spender's diary reveals, the memory of Craigavon's *volte face* of March 1938 still rankled.[88] Against a background of 'great scares' and 'panic',[89] Craigavon met

[83] *Irish Press*, 20 Mar. 1940.
[84] W. B. Spender diary, 15 Apr.-4 May 1940.
[85] Lady Craigavon, diary 17 Apr. 1940.
[86] Baldwin to Craigavon, c. 23 May 1940, quoted in Lady Craigavon's diary, 24 May 1940.
[87] Spender, diary 20-5 May 1940.
[88] Ibid., 16 Nov. 1940, 20 May 1943.
[89] Lady Craigavon, diary 4 June 1940; Spender, diary 8 June 1940.

Chamberlain on 5 June. On his return to Belfast he reassured
the press that British ministers regarded Ulster 'as a rock of
Gibraltar'.[90] Maffey's emphasis was different when briefing
Gray who was due to meet Craigavon two days later: Downing
Street had given the Ulster leader 'merry hell[,] all but ordering
him to make up with de Valera and end Partition on the best
terms he could.' Maffey said that they had found Craigavon
'very tough' and — like de Valera — keen to blame the other
side for poor north-south relations: 'They told him to forget
it[;] that Ireland had to defend itself as a unit and he must
take his medicine.' The British had communicated none of
this to de Valera, 'as he will be stubborn enough without
knowledge of this advantage.'

Thus briefed by Maffey, Gray was expecting to make some
progress with 'a crushed statesman' although he had been
warned by Craigavon's colleagues, Andrews and Brooke, that
even if a settlement were agreeable to the Prime Minister,
they were 'not interested'. But Gray found Craigavon's orthodoxy unimpaired by his London talks; the Ulster people, he
insisted, 'were not interested in southern Ireland'. When Gray
sounded him on the contingency which most frightened de
Valera — a German invasion of the north posing as liberators
— he replied: 'Oh[,] we'll take care of them.' He thought co-
operation with the south on defence questions would be fine
but was a matter for London and he 'absolutely refused to
take any step that would recognize the South in any way that
differentiated Ulster from Britain.'[91] Gray thought him 'so
nice and so dumb'; he 'intended to do nothing or learn nothing.
He was the perfect Bourbon.'[92]

There were now some in Britain who believed that London's
support for Partition should be questioned in the interest
of agreeing defence co-operation with Dublin. The trade
union leader, Ernest Bevin[93] — soon to be in parliament and in

[90] Lady Craigavon, diary 4-6 June 1940.
[91] Gray to Roosevelt, 6 June 1940, Roosevelt papers, PSF 56.
[92] 'So nice and so dumb', was Gray's verdict on Craigavon and Abercorn, Gray
to Welles, 23 June; the 'perfect Bourbon' verdict, he reserved for Craigavon alone,
Gray to Roosevelt, 19 June 1940, Roosevelt papers, PSF 56.
[93] Ernest Bevin, among earliest British opponents of Nazism; critic of Chamberlain; empathy for Churchill as war leader; Minister of Labour and National Service,
1940-5; Attlee's Foreign Secretary, 1945-50.

Churchill's War cabinet — sought expert advice from Lionel Curtis[94] who had been a central figure in the Treaty settlement of 1921. Curtis, now in All Souls, Oxford, met Bevin on 11 June and then consulted five academics, including the historian, Arnold Toynbee,[95] and a former Irish Minister in Berlin, Daniel Binchy,[96] all of whom were 'to be trusted absolutely'. Bevin also spoke to the American Ambassador, Joseph Kennedy, who informed the State Department on 18 June that Bevin believed it imperative that something be done for Ireland 'within 48 hours'.[97] The initiative, presently to be undertaken, had already been hatched in All Souls; on 12 June, Curtis advised Bevin that the group whom he had consulted were all agreed that to start what he termed 'this initiative' with a draft of a permanent, federal constitution for Ireland 'would court disaster from the outset'. Curtis had therefore 'drafted a proposal for a provisional arrangement which might lead on to an agreed federal solution after the war.'[98]

Curtis's idea was that a private appeal should be made by Churchill to Craigavon

to invite Mr de Valera to form a joint executive authority for the defence of Ireland for the duration of the war, consisting of members of the Cabinets of Southern and Northern Ireland with de Valera as Chairman. This joint executive authority should be charged with the duty of organising an Irish army solely for the defence of all Ireland, but not for service beyond its shores.

This joint cabinet would be responsible to a legislature formed by merging the Dail and Stormont, the new arrangement having responsibility exclusively for defence and supplies; north and south, in all other respects, would be governed as before.[99] Although two of his advisers preferred a less

---

[94] Lionel Curtis (1872-1955), co-founder *Round Table*; adviser to and secretary of British delegates at Anglo-Irish Treaty negotiations, 1921; adviser to Colonial Office on Irish affairs, 1922-4; appointed research fellow, All Souls, Oxford, 1921.

[95] Arnold Toynbee ((1889-1975), historian; director of studies, Royal Institute of International Affairs, 1925-56 and director of its foreign research and press service, 1939-43.

[96] Daniel Binchy, diplomat, scholar; Irish Minister to Berlin under Cumann na nGaedheal government.

[97] Joseph Kennedy to SS, 18 June 1940, NA, R.G. 59, 841D.01/181 1/2.

[98] Curtis to Ernest Bevin, 12 June 1940, enclosing 'Memorandum on Ireland', Curtis papers, MS 90.

[99] Curtis, 'Memorandum on Ireland', Curtis papers, MS 90.

ambitious all-Ireland body 'analogous to the Supreme Allied Council', Curtis believed that this would 'get nowhere, if it had to pass all its measures through two legislatures.'

Curtis hoped that if Craigavon had 'the imagination to take this bold initiative', then American influence would be brought to bear on de Valera to point out

that this provisional arrangement for the duration of the war would accustom leaders for All Ireland to work together for their common security. Ere long it might be found possible to appoint Commissioners with expert advisers to work out a permanent scheme for the unification on federal principles, leaving the six counties their present provincial powers.

H.M.G. should also inform de Valera that it would do all in its power to encourage and bring about a movement to end partition after the war.

Should Craigavon decline to co-operate, Curtis suggested that London could make the proposal public and offer to legislate as necessary at Westminster. In that eventuality, Curtis believed it 'quite possible' that unionist opinion would accept the scheme because Craigavon's position is 'much weaker than it *was* before the war'.[1]

It would seem probable that Churchill was initially unaware of the Curtis memorandum. A week after receiving it, Bevin — in his own name — forwarded to the Prime Minister a much-simplified version of this proposal for his 'immediate consideration'.[2] Churchill, while noting that he could 'never be a party to the coercion of Ulster', had no objection to Ulster being persuaded: 'The key to this is de Valera showing some loyalty to Crown and Empire.'[3]

France fell to the Germans in the second week in June. Hitler now told his generals that Britain's situation was 'hopeless',[4] a verdict reflected in the abject pessimism of Chamberlain's diary.[5] That Ireland was in a state of 'hopeless unpreparedness' was Labour leader, William Norton's

[1] Curtis to Bevin, 12 June 1940, ibid.
[2] Bevin to Churchill, 18 June 1940, PRO PREM 4/53/2.
[3] Churchill, margin note 18 June 1940, ibid.
[4] Hitler, directive no. 16, 16 July 1940, H. R. Trevor-Roper (ed.), *Hitler's war directives: 1939-1945* (London: 1966 edn.), p. 74.
[5] Chamberlain, diary 30 May, 17 June 1940, Chamberlain papers, NC2/24A.

estimate: the government's response to the crisis, he complained
to de Valera, had been 'weak, vacillating, uninspiring'.[6] Gray
noted 'a before the battle atmosphere' in Dublin. Invasion, he
reported to Roosevelt, was thought to be probable and imminent.[7]

The crisis did result in an all-party recruiting drive for the
Irish army. The campaign's success resulted in an army with
more soldiers than guns, a situation not entirely unsatisfactory
since there were some, at least, of the new recruits whom de
Valera did not wish to arm. They were, apparently, safer in
uniform than not, but safer still without weapons — a point
which well indicates the peculiar subtleties of de Valera's
dilemma at this critical time.[8] It remained true that a severe
shortage of arms was a major problem for the Irish government. Gray appealed to Washington for some arms for de
Valera who was 'frantic because he had practically nothing.'[9]
Gray was anxious to put de Valera 'under all the obligation
possible[,] immediately' because, as he told Roosevelt, 'the
time may come soon when the most useful thing I can do for
you is strongly to urge compromise with Ulster on Mr de
Valera'; this was to prevent him from 'insisting on too much
and muffing the situation completely' as was feared by 'the
Opposition and some members of his own government'.[10]

On 16 June Chamberlain informed the War cabinet of
his lack of progress with the proposed discussions on Ireland.[11]

[6] Norton to de Valera, 11 June 1940, SPO S 11896A. William Norton (1900–
63), TD, 1926-7, 1932-63; leader Irish Labour Party, 1932-63; Tanaiste (deputy
Prime Minister) 1948-51, 1954-7; member all-party, advisory Defence Conference,
1940-5.

[7] Gray to Roosevelt, 19 June 1940, Roosevelt papers, PSF 56. Sterling (US
Minister at Stockholm) to SS, 22 June 1940, NA, R.G. 59, 740.0011/European
War, 1939/4086.

[8] Gray reported de Valera as telling him that he 'dares not arm volunteer force'.
Gray to Hull, 18 May 1940, FRUS: 1940: 3: p. 160. It was Frank Ryan's view
that his former IRA colleagues should have joined the Irish army during the war,
Ryan to Kerney, 14 Jan. 1942, Ryan letters; the chief of staff of the IRA, Stephen
Hayes, recalled that the 'recruiting grounds of the ordinary young fellows growing
up in the country was closed to us because of the Local Defence Forces organized
by the Government which took all the manpower', quoted, T. P. Coogan, The
IRA (London: 1970), p. 159. This evidence refers not to the professional soldiers,
but to the new recruits in the LDF.

[9] Gray to Welles, 23 June 1940, Roosevelt papers.

[10] Gray to Roosevelt, 19 June 1940, Roosevelt papers, PSF 56.

[11] War cabinet, minutes 16 June 1940, PRO CAB 65/7 WM 168(40)5.

At his meeting with Craigavon eleven days earlier, he had agreed that the Stormont cabinet would 'endeavour to put forward some proposal which might be helpful' in winning the south's co-operation:[12] in the interim, with each day bringing more alarming news from the continent, Craigavon had shown no flexibility. Chamberlain reproached him for this, emphasized the worsening international situation, and invited him to join de Valera and himself for tripartite talks in London.[13]

De Valera however 'was not to be caught in a trap of this kind' in London;[14] a visit there would only raise expectations on Partition and nothing but its 'complete disappearance' would satisfy Irish opinion. He did consent to talks in Dublin, the British deciding to appoint Malcolm MacDonald as their negotiator. MacDonald, it was agreed by the cabinet, would emphasize to de Valera that 'it would be too late to do anything after the invasion had started'; the 'whole thing might be over in a matter of hours' with de Valera himself 'probably shot'. Anticipating that de Valera would raise Partition, Mac-Donald would then suggest 'that a Council for the defence of all Ireland should be set up, which would consider not only matters of defence, but would form a bridge for eventual discussions on partition.' If de Valera accepted this proposition, MacDonald would meet Craigavon and persuade him to accept it also.[15]

London prepared the ground as best they could for Mac-Donald's visit. The south was 'crawling . . . with ex-colonels' and others, all warning of the consequences of a German invasion;[16] both de Valera and Craigavon heard the Canadian government's view that north–south co-operation was necessary to stop 'the totalitarian hordes' who were 'now crushing

[12] Chamberlain to Craigavon, 12 June 1940, PRO PREM 3/131/2.
[13] As note 11 above.
[14] Garner (1978: 240).
[15] War cabinet, minutes 16 June 1940, PRO CAB 65/7 WM 168(40)5.
[16] Mulcahy memo, 29 June 1940, Mulcahy papers, P7a/220; J. F. L. Bray, 'Memo to the prime minister on the dangers of Ireland's disunity and neutrality', 10 June 1940, PRO DO 35/1107/W.X.1/88; minutes, meeting of Dominion High Commissioners, London, 14 June 1940, PRO DO 121/8; C. H. Rolph, *Kingsley, the life, letters and diaries of Kingsley Martin* (London: 1973), pp. 230-1.

every people who stand in their path'.[17] MacDonald spent over three hours with de Valera on 17 June impressing on him that whereas a German invasion of Ireland would 'embarrass' the British, it would be 'disastrous' for Ireland. The 'wisest course' would be abandonment of neutrality and 'complete co-operation' with Britain to which de Valera gave 'an emphatic negative'. MacDonald then mooted the possibility that in defence of Irish neutrality, de Valera might invite British assistance; again, de Valera declined, adding that the 'position might have been different if there had been a United Ireland.' MacDonald then suggested that as a step towards this goal, de Valera should agree to 'a joint council for the defence of the whole island', but whereas MacDonald envisaged this as a 'step . . . towards' a united Ireland, de Valera rejected it as 'a blow to the national unity of Eire'.[18] De Valera struck MacDonald as 'tired and frightened and without much grasp of the situation.'[19]

Having heard MacDonald's account on 20 June, the British War cabinet approved Chamberlain's proposal for a second visit. Chamberlain reminded his colleagues that in the view of the chiefs of staff, access to Eire for the British army, air force, and navy was essential; he suggested that in return for such access and the internment of potential fifth columnists, de Valera 'would be content to accept a declaration' stating that the British government 'were, in principle, in favour of the establishment of a United Ireland.' Later, Craigavon 'would have to be told that the interests of Northern Ireland could not be allowed to stand against the vital interests of the British Empire. Anticipating Craigavon's question as to 'whether the United Ireland would form part of the British Empire', Chamberlain suggested that the answer to this 'was clearly in the affirmative, though of course full Dominion status carried with it the right to secede from the Commonwealth.' Further, Chamberlain argued that if de Valera rejected this offer,

[17] Mackenzie King to de Valera, 16 June 1940, Mackenzie King papers, M.G. 26, J4, vol. 384, file 8. A similar telegram was sent to Craigavon.
[18] War cabinet, minutes 20 June 1940, PRO CAB 65/7 WM 173(40)9.
[19] Chamberlain diary note of talk with MacDonald after his return from Dublin, Chamberlain papers, NC2/24A.

MacDonald 'should insist' that the proposal be put to the Fianna Fail cabinet, some members of which, he understood, 'were likely to take a less rigid view.' As MacDonald's return to Dublin was approved, there was little optimism around the cabinet table. Churchill thought that Britain must avoid putting undue pressure on 'the loyal province of Ulster', a viewpoint which found support from Attlee, Halifax, and Anderson, the latter arguing that 'any substantial advance' towards Irish unity was unlikely as it was impossible to coerce either the north or the south.[20] Even Chamberlain, the initiator and 'manager' of the initiative, was less than optimistic. He wrote privately of de Valera's 'unshakeable obstinacy': 'I am still at him, but fear he won't be moved till the Germans are in Dublin.'[21]

At the second meeting, three proposals were discussed. MacDonald suggested:

That there should be a declaration of a united Ireland in principle, the constitutional and other practical details of the Union to be worked out in due course; Ulster to remain a belligerent, Eire to remain neutral, at any rate for the time being; if both parties desired it, a joint Defence Council to be set up at once; at the same time, British naval ships to be allowed into Eire ports, British troops and aeroplanes to be stationed at certain agreed points in the territory, the British Government to provide additional equipment for Eire's forces, and the Eire Government to take effective action against the Fifth Column.

De Valera emphatically rejected this as it would break the 'national unity' which had been established in response to the German threat. Instead, de Valera mooted:

That Eire and Ulster should be merged in a United Ireland, which would at once become neutral; its neutrality to be guaranteed by Great Britain and the United States of America; since Britain was a belligerent its military and naval forces should not take any active part in guaranteeing that neutrality, but American ships could come into the Irish ports, and perhaps American troops into Ireland, to effect this guarantee.

This, in turn, was 'rejected firmly' by MacDonald, for, as Chamberlain told the War cabinet, 'a number of reasons which are obvious'. Then MacDonald suggested another possibility:

---

[20] As note 18 above. John Anderson, Home Secretary, 1939–40.
[21] Neville to Ida Chamberlain, 21 June 1940, Chamberlain papers, NC18/1/1162.

'That there should be a declaration of a United Ireland in principle, the constitutional and practical details of the Union to be worked out in due course; this United Ireland to become at once a belligerent on the side of the Allies.' De Valera expressed some interest in this third suggestion; if there were not only a declaration in principle but also agreement on the constitution of a united Ireland, then, the south *'might* agree to enter the war at once. He could not be certain about this. Perhaps the existing Government would not agree to it, and would be replaced by another Government which did.'

MacDonald believed it impossible to agree a new Constitution 'in the short time which might be at our disposal before invasion took place'; neither could the British government approach Ulster on the basis that the south *might* enter the war. De Valera replied that 'he could not go further than "might", with a big question mark after that "might".'[22]

Given what seemed an unbridgeable gap between Mac-Donald and de Valera, it would scarcely have been surprising if the talks had been broken off at this juncture. Instead, the British made concessions to de Valera's position in what were the first written proposals of the negotiations. The memorandum was drafted by Chamberlain on 25 June: 'Showed the memo to Winston who approved it and brought it to Cabinet at 6 when it was unanimously approved. Malcolm to go tomorrow.'[23]

The document which MacDonald handed to de Valera on 26 June envisaged (i) a British declaration accepting the principle of a united Ireland; (ii) the immediate establishment of a joint north–south body 'to work out the constitutional and other practical details of the Union of Ireland'; (iii) the immediate establishment of a north–south Defence Council; (iv) the south to join the Allies 'forthwith' and to invite British military, naval, and air support to help defend the south against invasion; (v) the south to intern all German and Italian aliens and to suppress the IRA; (vi) the British to provide immediate arms supplies to the south. In an introductory

[22] Chamberlain, memo 'Eire: negotiations with Mr de Valera', 25 June 1940, PRO CAB 66/9 WP(40)223.
[23] Chamberlain diary, 25 June 1940, Chamberlain papers, NC2/24A.

preface, the memorandum sought Dublin's opinion on such a plan; it was not described as a specific *offer*, but if acceptable to Dublin, then the British government would 'at once seek to obtain the assent thereto of the Government of Northern Ireland.'[24] On the British side, there was considerable speculation on whether de Valera spoke for all of his cabinet in these talks. He had promised to put this written proposal to his colleagues and, having done so, Lemass, Aiken and himself had what MacDonald described as a 'most unsatisfactory' discussion on 27 June.

MacDonald found Aiken, who did 'most of the talking' on the Irish side, to be even more persistent than de Valera in insisting on a united and neutral Ireland; in contrast, Lemass 'seemed to be prepared to discuss our plan in a more reasonable way, but his contributions to discussion were usually cut short by fresh uncompromising interventions from one or other of his colleagues.' MacDonald got the impression that de Valera 'had not passed on to his colleagues the assurance I gave him yesterday that declaration of a United Ireland should settle the issue once and for all, and that there would be no going back on that', for he said that one of the principal reasons why the cabinet 'regard the plan as unacceptable is that they believe that [a] United Ireland will not materialise from it.' MacDonald repeated his assurance 'categorically' to Lemass, Aiken, and de Valera, telling them 'that if they rejected [the] plan on this ground[,] it was a false point. I think Lemass, and even Aiken, was impressed.' MacDonald suggested further amendments to the document to underline Britain's commitment to Irish unity. A revise would be sent to Dublin which de Valera proposed to discuss with his colleagues before sending a final answer. MacDonald remained 'definitely of opinion' that the Irish would reject the plan.[25] On receipt of his telegram, Chamberlain wrote in his diary: 'MacDonald's report of his visit is discouraging — the de Valera people are afraid we are going to lose, and don't want to be involved with us.'[26]

[24] Proposals taken by MacDonald to Dublin, 26 June 1940, PRO CAB 66/9 WP(40)233, annex I.
[25] MacDonald's report to cabinet (via Maffey), 27 June 1940, ibid., annex II.
[26] Chamberlain diary, 28 June 1940, Chamberlain papers, NC2/24A.

At this stage, the British invited American support for their proposal.[27] Having been briefed by Maffey, Gray's understanding of the plan was that 'It guaranteed the whole[,] lock[,] stock and barrel, prov[id]ing for the immediate setting up of a commission to draft a new all Ireland Constitution but insisting on a declaration of War by Eire.'[28] Moreover, this estimation of the offer predates the improved final revise which Maffey delivered to de Valera on 29 June. In addition to pledging British support for a united Ireland, London was now willing to add that the 'declaration would take the form of a solemn undertaking that the Union is to become at an early date an accomplished fact from which there shall be no turning back'; and to the clause detailing the setting-up of the joint north-south body to work out the constitutional details of unity, London was now prepared to state that their purpose in giving assistance to this body would be 'to establish at as early a date as possible the whole machinery of government of the Union.' All of this was subject to the north's approval but in a further concession to de Valera's objections, London deleted the requirement that the south enter the war. Britain would now be content with an invitation to British army, navy, and air forces 'to co-operate with Eire Forces and to be stationed in such positions in Eire as may be agreed between the two Governments, for the purpose of increasing the security of Eire against the fate which has overcome neutral Norway, Holland, Belgium, Denmark and Luxemburg.'[29]

Three days before de Valera received this final revise, Chamberlain had sent on to Craigavon a copy of the first written proposals of 26 June. In reply he received a 'short but violent telegram':[30]

Am profoundly shocked and disgusted by your letter making suggestions so far reaching behind my back, and without any preconsultation. To such treachery to loyal Ulster I will never be a party.[31]

[27] War cabinet, minutes 27 June 1940, PRO CAB 65/7 WM 184(40)11.
[28] Gray to Roosevelt, 28 June 1940, Roosevelt papers, PSF 56.
[29] 'Text of communication handed to Mr de Valera on Saturday, 29 June 1940', PRO CAB 66/9 WP(40)233, annex III.
[30] Chamberlain, diary 27 June 1940, Chamberlain papers, NC2/24A.
[31] Craigavon to Chamberlain, 27 June 1940, PRO PREM 3/131/2.

Nor was Craigavon alone among Unionists in sensing treachery in the MacDonald–de Valera talks. Spender believed the political situation was 'drifing to a very delicate and dangerous condition . . . It is assumed that if Ulster makes some spectacular sacrifice, Eire would declare war on Germany but there is no clear evidence that de Valera would do so.' Spender thought it 'just possible' that de Valera had promised to abandon neutrality in return for 'getting all he wants', but, 'as in the past', the south, having struck their bargain, would subsequently 'regret their inability to carry out their undertaking.'[32] In assessing their duties and interests, Ulster Unionist ranks were now divided. One senior minister, Brooke, admitted privately that if the south were to join the war on Britain's side in return for postwar Irish unification, Craigavon's cabinet would be split with his own vote favouring a new relationship with the south.[33] Moreover, it was Gray's estimate that Craigavon did not realize what the British were 'intending behind his back'.[34] And was not Craigavon's 'furious'[35] response to news of the Dublin talks, an indication that he, at least, suspected London's willingness to review Partition without Ulster's consent? Despite London's reassurances, there was clearly considerable suspicion among Unionists that in these new circumstances Britain would be willing, as Spender put it, 'to "sell the pass"'.[36] It was, after all, a moment in history when Churchill believed that a British defeat would have allowed the 'whole world' to 'sink into the abyss of a new dark age'.[37] Unlike the circumstances of the Curragh mutiny, whose lesson was thought to be that Ulster could not be militarily coerced, the context was now entirely changed. The form which 'coercion' of Ulster would now have taken would have been a public appeal to their loyalism to approve a new relationship with the south in the interests of the Empire, democracy and civilization.

[32] Spender, diary 4 July 1940.
[33] Interview, Frank MacDermot; J. Carroll, *Ireland in the war years, 1939–1945* (Newton Abbot: 1975), p. 59. See also Brooke's comments on this period in a debate in the Northern Ireland House of Commons at the conclusion of the war, NIHC: 29: 80, 24 July 1945.
[34] Gray to Roosevelt, 28 June 1940, Roosevelt papers, PSF 56.
[35] Lady Craigavon, diary 27 June 1940.
[36] Spender, diary 1–6 July 1940.
[37] HC: 362: 60, 18 June 1940.

Nor can Craigavon's somewhat dilatory approach to the crisis have strengthened the north's position in London. On 29 June, the Saturday on which de Valera received the final British revise, Craigavon made a public speech insisting that he would be 'no party' to any change in the constitutional position of Northern Ireland. He was prepared to enter into the 'closest co-operation' with de Valera on defence questions provided he supported the British war effort, expelled the Axis diplomats and 'undertakes not to raise any issue of a constitutional nature.'[38]

The last two weeks in June were also an active period for German–Irish relations. On 17 June Hempel reported to Berlin Walshe's hope that Hitler's recent statement that he had no 'intention to destroy the British Empire, did not mean the abandonment of Ireland.' Hempel found Walshe especially interested in what Hempel told him 'about the importance of the outcome of the war for the final realization of Irish national demands.'[39] Four days later, Hempel reported 'a growing realization, at any rate on the part of Walshe and Boland, of the great and decisive importance even to Ireland of the changed situation in world affairs and of the obvious weakness of the democracies.' He added that F. H. Boland had told him 'in strict confidence' of British pressure for a bargain on neutrality and Partition which de Valera had rejected '"most vehemently"'.[40] On 1 July — while de Valera's cabinet was still debating the final British offer — Hempel cabled Berlin that de Valera was under 'increasingly powerful pressure' from the British, 'to bring about the end of Irish neutrality through a dangerous playing on the question of Northern Ireland.' Hempel requested permission to reassure him that Germany would not collaborate with the IRA or use Ireland as a base from which to attack Britain. Such an unambiguous assurance, he believed, was necessary to strengthen de Valera's resolve to resist British pressure.[41] Nothing in

[38] Craigavon, speech 30 June 1940, *Keesings contemporary archives*, 1–8 July 1940, p. 4127.

[39] Hempel to Foreign Ministry, 17 June 1940, *DGFP*: D: 9: doc. 473;

[40] Ibid., 26 June 1940, doc. 506. F. H. Boland (1904–), diplomat; assistant secretary, Department of External Affairs, 1938–46, secretary, 1946–50; Ambassador to UK, 1950-6.   [41] Ibid., 1 July 1940, 10: doc. 79.

Hempel's dispatches to Berlin during this period would be inconsistent with a policy on Dublin's part to attempt to 'play off' London against Berlin. If neutrality was sacrosanct and Dublin had no interest in anything less than a united, neutral Ireland, then it is possible that those responsible for Irish policy during these days believed that the best exploitation of the British offer was to use it as a lever to exact promises from Berlin. Irish ministers may have expected — even though they did not desire — a German victory. In recent talks with O'Kelly, MacEntee, Walshe, and de Valera, Gray had stressed that 'if Germany crushes Britain and permits her resurgence as a third-class power' Germany would keep Ireland as a Gibraltar to watch Britain.[42] Gray reported that this scenario had not been disputed by the Irish: 'They naturally feel very timid these days and wishfully think that by not . . . plumping with England they are going to make their lot easier in the event of a German crushing victory.'[43]

Dublin's policy was based on the assumption that America did not intend to abandon her neutrality.[44] If she had entered the war, de Valera told Gray, 'it would alter our situation over-night.'[45] Gray believed that if the United States became a belligerent, the Irish government 'could take the chance they dare not now take.'[46] Gray feared that 'if Ulster doesn't offer to throw in with the south at once it will be too late. It may be too late anyway. These people unarmed can't make resistance and how rally them for a losing cause?' Gray's 'own belief' was 'that if Ulster would consent to the ending of partition under suitable guarantees' de Valera 'could capitalize it politically' and join Britain at war. 'But de Valera won't say he will do it. He told me a month ago when I was exploring the possibility[:] "The neutrality of Ireland is not for sale" and with some heat.'[47]

Thus policies and attitudes in Washington, Berlin, and Belfast had a bearing on the deliberations of the Irish cabinet

[42] Gray to Roosevelt, 19 June 1940, Roosevelt papers, PSF 56.
[43] Ibid., 28 June 1940. Kirk (US Embassy, Berlin) to SS, 12 July 1940, NA, R.G. 59, 740.0011/European War, 1939/4599.
[44] Gray to Roosevelt, 6-12, 19, and 28 June 1940, Roosevelt papers, PSF 56.
[45] Ibid., 19 June 1940.　　　　[46] Ibid., 6-12 June 1940.
[47] Gray to Welles, 23 June 1940, Roosevelt papers.

as they considered the final British document. Delivered to
them on Saturday 29 June, the British government was expecting an early decision that same weekend. As the records
already quoted reveal, the final British plan bore little resem-
blance to MacDonald's first suggestion of just ten days before.
Having railed against Partition since its enactment twenty
years earlier, Fianna Fail ministers were now invited to consider what was — whatever its limitations — the first substantial
proposal from London to question that policy. But there
were strong arguments against acceptance. Any abandonment
of neutrality in advance of a German invasion, would create a
rift in the Fianna Fail party and cabinet; even if invited into
the south to help defend Ireland against a German invasion, it
seemed likely to the cabinet that some British troops would
be attacked by republican extremists; in the event of a German
invasion, a government which had invited prior British aid,
would be open to the charge that it was the British presence
which had precipitated the attack; further, there was a suspicion in de Valera's mind, at least, that if the British ever
returned to the Treaty ports — even by invitation — they
might never leave; moreover, Germany, at this hour in the
war, seemed invincible; and, lastly, there was Ulster.[48] Was
this not a repeat of the Home Rule controversy during the
Great War? Was de Valera not being cast in the role of
Redmond? Were not Fianna Fail being invited to repeat the
mistakes of the Irish Party by accepting London's pledge of
Irish unity in return for participation in 'a British war'? To a
cabinet dominated by men who had helped to eclipse the
Irish Party for just such a mistake, the parallel must have
seemed ominously uncomfortable. Adding strength to these
suspicions was the overt insistence in both the written documents submitted to Dublin that Ulster's approval would be
necessary. For instance, the final revise, which solemnly
undertook that Irish unity would 'become at an early date an
accomplished fact from which there will be no turning back'

[48] Mulcahy, memos 15 May, 4 and 5 July 1940, Mulcahy papers, P7a/210, and
29 May 1941, ibid., —/214; Gray to Roosevelt, 19 June, 7 Aug. 1940, Roosevelt
papers, PSF 56; Gray to SS, 23 July 1940, NA, R.G. 59, 841D.00/1275; Longford
and O'Neill (1970: 364-8); interview Sean MacEntee; de Valera, Dail debate, fifteen
years later, DE: 152: 551, 12 July 1955.

also included an introduction which stated that 'the whole plan depends upon our obtaining the assent of Northern Ireland.' Chamberlain promised that Britain 'should do our best' to secure this, but he could not, 'of course, give a guarantee that Northern Ireland will assent.'[49] Was this not London's traditional insistence that Ulster had a veto on Irish unity? If the British document seemed somewhat contradictory in tone — if it seemed to speak with 'two voices' — was this not because it had, effectively, been drafted by both Chamberlain and Churchill?[50]

On 4 July de Valera wrote to Chamberlain informing him of his cabinet's rejection of the 'purely tentative' plan. This rejection was on the grounds that whilst it envisaged 'the immediate abandonment' of neutrality, it gave 'no guarantee' of unity. Craigavon and his colleagues 'could at any stage render the whole project nugatory.'[51] De Valera's biographers report that the British proposals 'had a certain allure, but, from the moment he studied them de Valera was not impressed.' He thought the offer

largely illusory. Speaking of it years later he mentioned that when he was a child it was customary for two boys swopping treasures to insist on "equal holds" — that each should have a firm grip on what he was to receive before he loosened his grip on that with which he was parting. The offer . . . did not give "equal holds".[52]

Such concentration on the 'Ulster clauses' to justify rejection was not surprising. As they had done in the Treaty negotiations in 1921, Irish nationalists still appreciated the propaganda benefits of 'breaking on Ulster': to reject a partitioned Ireland would always seem more tolerable to international opinion, than to refuse Dominion status in 1921 or refuse participating in the fight against Germany in 1940. But it does not fully explain Irish motivations. Lack of public support was also mentioned by de Valera in his letter to Chamberlain: 'Our people would be quite unprepared for it,

[49] Chamberlain, diary 27 June 1940, NC2/24A.
[50] Garner (1978: 240-3); Winant to SS, 11 Mar. 1941, NA, R.G. 59, 740.0011/European War,1939/8944.
[51] De Valera to Chamberlain, 4 July 1940, PRO CAB 66/9 WP(40)251.
[52] Longford and O'Neill (1970: 366).

and Dail Eireann would certainly reject it.'[53] Aiken's retrospective verdict is that the offer was 'insulting':[54] Mulcahy's
contemporary assessment was that any proposal by de Valera
to join the Allies would have been opposed by 'perhaps more
than half of his own party, one third of Fine Gael and perhaps
the whole of Labour.' Moreover those dissenting would have
'the greatest possible capacity for nuisance and damage.'[55]
One critical factor for Irish policy-makers was not mentioned
then, or since: in late June 1940, the Irish political élite was
convinced that Britain was unlikely to win the war. At best
she could hope for a negotiated peace.[56] Consequently, Irish
thoughts turned to defending Irish interests in anticipation of
a peace dictated from Berlin.

The conclusion seems inescapable that no British offer,
other than the establishment of a guaranteed, united, neutral
Ireland would have had any serious appeal to the Fianna Fail
cabinet. When MacDermot, back from Belfast, tried to interest
de Valera and Aiken in what he thought were the promising
results of a talk with Brooke, he was cursorily dismissed:
Aiken's words were: "'Get this into your head MacDermot,
there are *no* conditions under which we would abandon
neutrality".'[57] At least one Ulster Unionist emissary met de
Valera in Dublin at this time. Mulcahy noted that de Valera
had told a Unionist Senator that if the south went into 'the
war in return for Unity', the country would be 'split from
top to bottom'.[58] This Unionist industrialist, Senator Herdman,[59] may also have been Craigavon's 'friend' who met de
Valera 'quite unofficially' in Dublin for an hour on 25 June.
Craigavon informed Chamberlain: 'My friend suggested that
if he would declare himself as willing to come in with Britain
I would be glad to meet him anywhere at any time over
mutual civil defence provided no "constitutional" questions

[53] De Valera to Chamberlain, 4 July 1940, PRO CAB 66/9 WP(40)251.
[54] Interview, Frank Aiken.
[55] Mulcahy, memo 5 July 1940, Mulcahy papers, P7a/210.
[56] Gray to Roosevelt, 25 Aug. 1940, Roosevelt papers, PSF 56; Gray to Hull,
17 Nov. 1943, Gray papers, box 4; Gray's reports to SS, 29-31 May 1940, NA,
R.G. 59, 841D.00/1260-2.
[57] Interview, Frank MacDermot.
[58] Mulcahy, memos 4 and 5 July 1940, Mulcahy papers, P7a/210.
[59] Sir Emerson C. Herdman; Ulster linen merchant; served for twenty-five
years as a Unionist Senator in the Northern Ireland parliament.

were touched upon. Mr de Valera's answer was[:] "quite impossible".'[60]

Neither de Valera nor Craigavon deviated from their entrenched positions during this crisis. Craigavon's primary instinct was to offer de Valera unacceptable terms thus showing London where their true interests lay; de Valera appreciated that the factors encouraging caution concerning the British offer were overwhelming. In addition to those already mentioned, the expectations of extreme republicans,[61] northern nationalists,[62] and the evidence in mid-June of an embryonic, marginal pro-Nazi party[63] must all have encouraged rejection. Sharing as they did what was in June 1940 the widely held view that Germany would win the war, or, at least, dictate the peace, the Irish political élite must have believed that it would have been reckless to risk Irish interests by joining what was thought to be the losing side.

Another factor weighed with de Valera: his particular suspicion of Churchill's *bona fides* towards Ireland. Chamberlain, he knew to be sympathetic towards Irish unity, but Churchill's antipathy to the south was well known. In any cabinet disagreement on the coercion of Ulster, whose will would prevail? As the British records reveal, such suspicion was well founded.[64] Not only had Chamberlain and Churchill very different outlooks on Ireland, they were also diametrically opposed in temperament; Chamberlain was morose, defeatist, and extremely concerned about a German invasion

[60] Craigavon to Chamberlain, 26 June 1940, PRO PREM 3/131/2.

[61] MacSwiney to de Valera, n.d. (June 1940), MacSwiney papers, P48/C/32. Stephan (1965: 69).

[62] Cahir Healy to Churchill, 3 July 1940, PRO DO 35/1107/W.X.1/92. Coinciding with the de Valera-MacDonald talks, there was a bitter public controversy between Tommy Mullins of Fianna Fail headquarters and Healy, *Irish News*, 26 June 1940.

[63] See affidavits from unnamed informant in Mulcahy papers, P7a/220, *passim*, but especially 31 May 1940.

[64] Churchill noted in the margin of his copy of MacDonald's telegram from Dublin on 27 June: 'But all contingent upon Ulster agreeing, and S. Ireland coming into the war.' PRO PREM 3/131/2. On 7 July Churchill reassured the Revd. James Little, Ulster Unionist MP, that 'There is not however and never has been any question' of coming to an agreement with the south 'without the knowledge and consent' of Northern Ireland, PRO PREM 4/53/6. In July 1940 Churchill may have considered sending troops from Northern Ireland across the border to occupy Lough Swilly, see Stephan Roskill, *Churchill and the admirals* (London: 1977), pp. 122-3.

of Ireland.[65] Churchill, on the other hand was enjoying the war[66] and strategically even foresaw some advantages to Britain if a 'civil war' broke out in Ireland in the wake of a German invasion: "we sh[oul]d have split the Sinn Feiners effectively and sh[oul]d have the greater part of the pop[ulatio]n on our side for the first time in history.'[67]

Chamberlain did not believe that Ulster was the main ground on which de Valera had declined the initiative. On 7 July, he wrote to his sister:

the real basic fact is that it is not Partition which stands in the way at this moment but the fear of Dev [*sic*] and his friends that we shall be beaten. They don't want to be on the losing side and if that is unheroic[,] one can only say that it is very much the attitude of the world from the USA to Roumania and from Japan to Ireland.[68]

On 6 July Chamberlain told the cabinet that de Valera's reply was 'a flat refusal. He proposed to inform Lord Craigavon that the negotiations had come to an end.'[69]

Meanwhile Craigavon, doubtless aware of how inoperable his scheme was, suggested in a memorandum on 6 July, a Military Governor for 'all Ireland, for the period of the war, without any consideration of the political border.' He had a 'very satisfactory chat' with Churchill in London on 7 July, reported the details to his cabinet on the 10th, by which time he had publicized an unacceptable offer to de Valera who had duly rejected it.[70] Lady Craigavon noted her husband's words in her diary for 11 July: 'It is finished, it will not be raised by me again . . . We are closing the gates again as our ancestors did at Derry.'[71]

[65] Neville to Hilda Chamberlain, 15 June, and to Ida Chamberlain, 7 July 1940, Chamberlain papers, NC18/1/1161-2. Also Chamberlain, diary 13 May, 17 June, 1 July 1940, ibid., NC2/24A.

[66] Interview Malcolm MacDonald.

[67] Churchill to Ismay, 31 May 1940, PRO PREM 3/129/1; see also Churchill's notes for speech to secret session of House of Commons, in W. S. Churchill (ed. C. Eade), *Secret session speeches* (London: 1946), p. 16.

[68] Neville to Ida Chamberlain, 7 July 1940, Chamberlain papers NC18/1/1162.

[69] War cabinet, minutes 6 July 1940, PRO CAB 65/8 WM 195(40)11.

[70] Craigavon, memo 'All Ireland Defence Force', 6 July 1940, PRO PREM 3/131/2; Lady Craigavon, diary 7 July 1940; NI cabinet minutes, 10 July 1940, PRONI CAB 4/447/6; *Northern Whig*, 9 July 1940.

[71] Lady Craigavon, diary 1 July 1940.

(iii) REALPOLITIK

In 1956 David Gray suggested that the 'accumulating evidence' suggested that even before the fall of France, de Valera had 'believed that Hitler would win the war, and that in payment for keeping the Allies out of the Eire ports he would obtain Northern Ireland on his own terms.'[72] De Valera cursorily replied that Gray's claims were 'unfounded and foolish'.[73] A more telling rebuttal can be found in Gray's contemporary assessment. In November 1940 he had been disinclined to blame a 'very defeatist if not pro-German' Walshe for considering 'as a possibility if not a probability' an Irish regime based on a German control of Europe.[74] That a German victory was then expected in Dublin is clear from a variety of sources.[75] That same month Hempel reported to Berlin that Irish political circles believed that Britain lacked confidence about the war's outcome and hoped in any negotiated peace to have 'possession of Ireland when the future new order is established'; moreover Dublin feared that Britain would 'attempt to make sure of that before the war ends.'[76] After the war, it was not in the south's interest to admit that for most of 1940 and 1941 at least, a German victory was considered probable in Dublin. But to base policy on the expectation of a German victory was, unfairly, in some quarters, confused with *sympathizing* or *aiding* such an outcome. The Irish were not alone in expecting a German victory. In December 1940, Maffey presumed to advise the Ulster Unionists to prepare for such a contingency, surprising and annoying Spender with the suggestion that 'if the British Empire were defeated' that 'it would be very greatly to the advantage of Northern Ireland to join up with Eire and that the British government would advise Ulster to do so.'[77]

[72] David Gray, 'Introduction' to W. A. Carson, *Ulster and the Irish Republic* (Belfast: n.d. [1956]), pp. iv–v.

[73] *Irish Times* clipping, c. May 1957, NLI MS 16,221.

[74] Gray to Hull, 18 Nov. 1940, *FRUS*: 1940: 3: pp. 170–1; also, Gray to Roosevelt, 13 Feb. 1943, and Gray, memo of talk with Cosgrave, 19 Oct. 1942, Roosevelt papers, PSF 56.

[75] Gray to Hull, 24 Nov. 1940, *FRUS*: 1940: 3: pp. 172–3; also Gray to Roosevelt, 5 Apr. 1943, Roosevelt papers, PSF 56.

[76] Hempel to Foreign Ministry, 29 Nov. 1940, *DGFP*: D: 11: doc. 419.

[77] Spender, note of conversation with Maffey 11 Dec. 1940, Spender papers, D715/15.

Although Hitler himself claimed in December 1940 that 'possession of Ireland could have the effect of ending the war', he accepted the counsel of his military advisers that, strategically, German 'occupation of the island of Ireland' was 'impossible', if Ireland were not at war with Britain.[78] The following year when Rudolph Hess[79] was being questioned after his flight to Britain, his interrogator 'dropped a fly at him on Ireland' and received the reply that Hitler had 'no intention *vis-a-vis* that country. It had done nothing for Germany, and why should Germany do anything for her?'[80]

While Irish army intelligence stymied the clumsy[81] attempts by the German secret service to establish effective links with the IRA, Hempel attempted to introduce the anti-Partition card into German-Irish diplomacy. In so far as Irish policy can be inferred from Hempel's dispatches, the note struck is one of reticence and prudence. In December 1940 Hempel reported that neither de Valera nor any official of External Affairs had 'ever mentioned to me the possibility of recovering Northern Ireland with German help.'[82]

However Berlin recorded Leopold Kerney, the Irish Minister in Madrid, as believing that de Valera

saw in a German victory the only possible chance of ending partition, but was unable to take any anti-British step in view of the defencelessness of Southern Ireland. If Germany could only provide Ireland with arms and organise successful assistance, Ireland might no longer, at a critical moment of the war, remain neutral.[83]

Subsequently, de Valera rejected this interpretation.[84] There is no doubt that his sympathies were pro-British throughout

[78] War diary of Wehrmacht operations Staff for 3 Dec. 1940, *DGFP*: D: 11: doc. 416: note 2; Report of the C. in C., Navy to the Führer, 3 Dec. 1940, reprinted in *Brassey's Naval Annual, 1948* (London: 1948), pp. 156-8.

[79] Rudolph Hess (b. 1896), Hitler's deputy; in spring 1941 flew to Scotland seeking peace terms with Britain; imprisoned until 1946 when sentenced for war crimes at Nuremburg.

[80] Ryan to Kerney, 6 Nov. 1941, Ryan letters.

[81] H[ermann Goertz] to James O'Donovan, 30 Sept. (1940), James O'Donovon papers, MS 21,155(2); Ryan to Kerney, 14 Jan. 1942, Ryan letters.

[82] Hempel to Foreign Ministry, 7 Dec. 1940, *DGFP*: D: 11: doc. 466.

[83] Quoted, S. Cronin, 'Germany and Ireland in World War Two', *Irish Times*, 6 July 1978.

[84] Confidential source. See also, T. D. Williams, 'Neutrality!', *Irish Press*, 10 July 1953.

the war but his outlook was even more emphatically pro-Irish and his interpretation of Irish interests prudently included anticipating the possibility of a German victory. By autumn 1941 Hempel believed that the Irish 'preferred having friends on both sides in case of negotiated peace'.[85]

The possibility of a German invasion of the north, ostensibly to unite Ireland, was still de Valera's worst fear. That such a development would have caused confusion within Fianna Fail's ranks is clear; only Fine Gael seem to have been confident that the correct response would be aid to the Unionists and British. Cosgrave wrote to Mulcahy: 'If we could help the north and don't, we are plumping for German occupation of a part of our country. Dermot [?MacMurrough] over again in a new shape.'[86] In general, Mulcahy was critical of de Valera's policy: he disliked the 'prevarications, contradictory statements and the extraordinary equating of the British with the Germans.'[87] O'Higgins agreed. His paper, for a front-bench meeting in March 1941, suggested that 'the most serious aspect' of Irish neutrality as practised was the 'indifference as to which side may become our enemy and therefore which side may become our ally'; if Britain in desperation seized the ports we must make war on Britain and 'make a Nazi victory a certainty'. O'Higgins believed the most probable outcome of the war was a negotiated peace, in which case Ireland would learn that because of neutrality she had 'made an enemy of Britain for many years to come, and . . . Partition as permanent as British power can make it. Any future Commonwealth Conference will see our representatives begging for the scraps.' In the event of a German victory, O'Higgins believed that Ireland would become a German base. He suggested that policy should be reviewed in the light of these probabilities and considered exclusively in terms of Ireland's rights, which

[85] C. J. Carter's paraphrase of translation of Hempel to Foreign Ministry, Oct.-Nov. 1941, in C. J. Carter, *The shamrock and the Swastika: German espionage in Ireland in World War Two* (Palo Alto: 1977), p. 164.

[86] Cosgrave to Mulcahy, c. 25 July 1940, Mulcahy papers, P7a/212. Diarmuid MacMurrough (1110-1171), King of Leinster, execrated in Irish historical memory for inviting Henry II to Ireland; according to the Book of Leinster, 'Thenceforward is the miserable reign of the Saxons, amen, amen.'

[87] Mulcahy, memo 27 Dec. 1940, ibid., —/210.

could be 'summed up in one sentence, Ireland's territorial unity — the restoration of Ulster to Ireland.' O'Higgins's preferred solution to this dilemma was to lend or lease ports to the Allies on the strength of an American guarantee of their evactuation at the end of the war.[88]

Throughout 1941, before the Japanese attack on Pearl Harbor precipitated their entry into the war, the Americans were thought of as possible guarantors of Irish neutrality and the vital Atlantic trade.[89] Ulster Unionists, too, appreciated that it was now vital for Britain to keep the Americans 'sweet'. Spender disapproved of a British MP's suggestion that 'we should go to America cap in hand to ask for their help in settling the Irish Question.' Such an approach would give to de Valera 'just that handle which he requires to go on pressing impossible demands', foremost amongst them being the north's inclusion in a united neutral Ireland to be declared a republic at the war's conclusion. To give any encouragement to such an impossible aspiration was 'merely to reopen in America a question which is very nearly dead and which certainly is much better left quiescent until peace comes.'[90] One course which was mooted during the winter of 1940-1 was the possibility of inviting the United States — still a non-belligerent — to lease the Treaty ports, thereby guaranteeing Atlantic shipping and strengthening Irish neutrality. In Washington, no less than in London or Berlin, it was appreciated that some move towards Irish unity remained the obvious 'currency' for any negotiation with de Valera on neutrality.[91] Walshe thought that if Ireland were to be united and her independence guaranteed, de Valera might abandon neutrality under

[88] T. F. O'Higgins, copy of memo to be discussed at forthcoming Fine Gael front bench meeting, 3 Mar. 1941, ibid., —/215.

[89] Joint Intelligence Staff, 'The invasion of Eire — a pocket appreciation', n.d. (June 1941), PRO PREM 3/130.

[90] Spender to Ian Hannah MP, 17 Dec. 1940, Spender papers, D715/15.

[91] Gray to Hull, 10 Nov. 1940, *FRUS: 1940: 3*: pp. 168-9; Hull, memo of conversation with Brennan and Aiken 11 Apr. 1941, Hull papers, box 59, file 226; Felix Frankfurter, memo for Roosevelt June 1941, reprinted M. Freedman, *Roosevelt and Frankfurter: their correspondence: 1928-1945* (London: 1967), pp. 608-9; Robertson to King, 29 Nov. 1941, Mackenzie King papers, M.G. 26, J4, vol. 283, file 2954.

'very strong pressure' from the Allies.[92] Again, de Valera's deputy Prime Minister, O'Kelly, was reported as confiding to Gray that he 'would consider a deal with recognition of the two islands as a unit for defense as the price for ending Partition', but, Gray added, in his report to Roosevelt, 'Mr D. V. lays his ears back and tells me that though he can see the force of treating the two islands as a unit for defense he has a *right* to have Partition ended without paying any price. So there you are.'[93] It was already clear to Washington, as it was to London and Ottawa, that neutrality now took precedence in de Valera's timetable over any moves towards unity.[94] The Canadian war cabinet, when discussing the possibility of Canada leasing the Irish ports, appreciated that any such request would represent a 'serious embarrassment' to de Valera.[95]

With support from the Stormont and British cabinets, the extension of conscription to Northern Ireland again became an issue in May 1941.[96] It was 'emphatically' welcomed by the Stormont cabinet which was even prepared 'as a last resort' to approve of the setting up of 'concentration camps for thousands of resisters'.[97] Unionists hoped that nationalist representatives would endorse their appeal.[98] But conscription was anathema to anti-Partitionists.[99] Fine Gael believed it would represent 'a major[,] irretrievable and probably fatal political blunder'; it would amount to a 'scoop' for de Valera who would turn it to his political advantage.[1] Gray predicted that de Valera would 'raise anti-British feeling and call a Holy War'. Maffey shared these apprehensions.[2]

[92] Kelly to Mackenzie King, 3 Feb. 1941, Mackenzie King papers, M.G. 26, J4, vol. 384, file 8.

[93] Gray to Roosevelt, 22 June 1941, Roosevelt papers, PSF 56.

[94] Joseph Kennedy to Joseph Scott, copy forwarded to J. C. Walsh, 17 July 1940, J. C. Walsh papers, box 3.

[95] Canadian cabinet war committee, 19 Nov. 1940, PAC, R.G. 2, 7C, vol. 3.

[96] See Bevin, cabinet memorandum 'Application of conscription to Northern Ireland', 21 May 1941, PRO CAB 66/16, WP (41) 107.

[97] Herbert Morrison, cabinet memorandum 'Application of conscription to Northern Ireland', 22 May 1941, PRO CAB 66/16, WP (41) 108.

[98] Healy papers, D2991/A/152-3, 155, *passim.*

[99] *Irish Press* clipping, 23 May 1941, SPO S 12432.

[1] Gray to Hull, 22 May 1941, *FRUS*: 1941: 3: pp. 234-5.

[2] Maffey to DO, 25 May 1941, PRO CAB 66/16, WP (41) 113.

De Valera however was again as moderate as the circumstances premitted. He appealed to extreme republicans to
cancel a Dublin protest meeting;[3] he lobbied Gray for American support, initially arguing that an 'escape clause for
Catholics' on grounds of conscience would make the measure
tolerable; however, he later contacted Gray to say that on
reconsideration he must oppose the measure in principle.[4]
Maffey was impressed by the moderation of the specially
convened Dail debate in which all parties agreed that conscription would be 'exceedingly dangerous'.[5] Donnelly, however,
was not satisfied with de Valera's response; he did not know
why there should be 'any "shilly-shallying"'.[6] Ottawa and
Washington both advised against conscription, as did Maffey
who agreed the case was in principle 'unanswerable', but
believed the 'expediency of the measure' was 'most doubtful'.[7] Churchill realized his mistake. With the Ulster cabinet
weakening,[8] he informed the Commons on 27 May that after
'a number of enquiries in various directions', the government
had concluded that 'it would be more trouble than it is worth
to enforce such a policy'.[9] De Valera, fearing a misreading
that an Anglo-Irish defence understanding had been Britain's
price for acquiescence, did not seek the credit for the change
in British policy.[10] He was given it by some, including his
own apologists and the Ulster Unionists, Spender complaining
to Churchill that the cheering which had greeted the change
in policy in the House of Commons, proved that a large body

[3] Maurice Moynihan, holograph note 28 May 1941, SPO S 12432.
[4] Gray notes, 27 May 1941, Gray papers, box 10.
[5] Cosgrave's view, other party leaders agreeing, DE: 83: 969–78, 26 May 1941.
[6] *Irish Press*, 27 May 1941.
[7] Maffey to DO, 25 May 1941, PRO CAB 66/16 WP (41) 113; de Valera to
Mackenzie King, 23 May 1941, Mackenzie King papers, M.G. 26 J4, vol. 384,
file 8; DO file, 'Northern Ireland conscription: Canadian and American attitude',
May 1941, *passim*, PRO DO 35/1109/W.X.37/7; de Valera to Churchill (via
Dulanty), 26 May 1941, PRO DO 35/1109/W.X.37/9; J. W. Pickersgill, *The Mackenzie King record: vol. 1: 1939–1944* (Toronto: 1960), p. 218.
[8] Winant to Hull, 26 May 1941, *FRUS*: 1941: 3: p. 239.
[9] HC: 371: 66, 27 May 1941.
[10] (Mulcahy), note on conversation with de Valera 23 May 1941, McGilligan
papers, P35C/182.

of its members were prepared to 'play up to any demands made by de Valera'.[11]

Whatever Unionist interest there might have been twelve months before for some bargain on Partition and defence, Unionist antipathy for Fianna Fail was now more intense than ever. In October 1941, the Canadian High Commissioner in Dublin, John D. Kearney was received at Stormont Castle, presumed to be flying a kite for de Valera. He argued that the 'moment was now favourable' to tackle Partition, 'to heal this wound', but, pressed by Spender, he could give no assurances that the resulting united Ireland would support the Allies. Spender took care to write to Lord Hankey in London, hoping that British ministers would not 'get entangled in further political discussions'; exerience had shown him that 'one cannot disregard proposals put forward by the Eire Government, no matter how wild they may appear at first sight.'[12] The British thought Spender had 'read rather more' into Kearney's remark than the Canadian High Commissioner had intended.[13] Kearney, however, persisted in the belief that some deal on Partition and neutrality was possible. The following month he asked de Valera directly if the ports would be available if the Americans were to enter the war and could guarantee an end to Partition. Kearney learned that 'even a promise of unity of Ireland would not alter his attitude.'[14]

The Japanese attack on Pearl Harbor precipitated America's declaration of war on 7 December; at 2 *a.m.* on the following morning, Maffey delivered what he himself considered a 'Churchillian' telegram to de Valera. The message was brief:

Following from Mr Churchill for Mr de Valera. Personal. Private and Secret. Begins. Now is your chance. Now or never. A Nation once again. Am very ready to meet you at any time. Ends.

[11] Spender, diary 26-31 May 1941; Edmund Warnock, NIHC: 24: 2610, 20 Jan. 1942.

[12] Spender to Hankey, 21 Oct. 1941, Hankey papers, CAB 63/147. Kearney represented Canada in Dublin, 1941-5. Lord Hankey, formerly secretary to the cabinet, was now a member of it.

[13] Cranborne to Hankey, 29 Oct. 1941, ibid.

[14] Kearney to Robertson, 20 Feb. 1942, PAC, R.G. 25, vol. 1949, file 822-39C.

De Valera believed that this was Churchill's 'way of intimating "now is the chance for taking action which would ultimately lead to the unification of the country".'[15] De Valera's own note of the conversation concludes: 'I indicated to Sir John Maffey that I did not see the thing in that light. I saw no opportunity at the moment of securing unity, that our people were determined on their attitude of neutrality, etc.'[16]

Maffey shared de Valera's impression that Churchill was mooting another deal on Partition and neutrality. His report summarized de Valera's position as being that 'neither he nor anybody else would have a mandate for entering the war on a deal over partition.'[17] Lord Cranborne, Dominions Secretary, was alarmed at this misinterpretation of Churchill's phrase, 'A nation once again.' Cranborne had taken this to mean that 'by coming into the war, Ireland would regain her soul.' He warned Churchill that de Valera's cabinet 'on consideration, might accept your invitation on this basis, and then feel that we had led them up the garden path'; and he sought permission from the Prime Minister to inform Maffey 'of the true interpretation of the phrase.' Churchill minuted on this letter: 'I certainly contemplated no deal over partition. That could only come by consent arising out of war comradeship between North and South.'[18] Maffey, briefed by Cranborne, took the opportunity at a further meeting with de Valera to make it clear that Churchill was suggesting no 'deal over partition'.[19]

At de Valera's suggestion Cranborne visited Dublin where he had a 'long, friendly, but fruitless talk' on 17 December. De Valera accepted that some postponement of the solution of Partition might be inevitable although he did not 'rule out the possibility' that, after the war, his federal proposals might be acceptable if linked with a 'joint strategic plan for the defence of the British Isles'. Cranborne emphasized that to be discussing post-war contingencies was 'entirely academic'. The only chance of ending Partition was through the community of interest which would follow Eire's participation in the war

[15] Churchill to de Valera, 8 Dec. 1941, PRO PREM 3/131/6.
[16] Longford and O'Neill (1970: 393).
[17] Maffey to DO, received 8 Dec. 1941, PRO PREM 3/131/6.
[18] Cranborne to Churchill, 8 Dec. 1941, ibid. Lord Cranborne was Dominions Secretary, 1940–2, 1943–5.
[19] Maffey to DO, 10 Dec. 1941, ibid.

alongside Britain. 'For Eire to link her entry into the war with a solution of the Partition question, which was necessarily a long-term problem, was to ignore the urgency of the present position.' De Valera insisted that 'in existing circumstances, with the Partition problem as an open sore, any attempt to bring a United Ireland into the war at our side would be doomed to failure. From this position, I could not budge him.'[20]

Strategically, Northern Ireland was providing the Allies with what Craigavon had described as their 'pied a terre in Ireland',[21] their 'buffer against Hitler'.[22] Indeed since the summer of 1941,.American technicians had been helping to 'make a fortress of Ulster', much to de Valera's annoyance. When American troops followed in January 1942, chagrin and resentment was de Valera's response. Their arrival in Northern Ireland 'embarrassed him', reported Maffey, 'and he believed he would be expected to say something publicly.'[23] Denying the right of foreign troops to be based in Ireland, de Valera reiterated the 'unabated' claim to Irish sovereignty over the entire island.[24] Although he clearly thought this as moderate as possible,[25] it offended American opinion.[26] Pressed, the Americans denied that the move implied support for Partition; further, Roosevelt assured de Valera that there was no danger of an American invasion of the south.[27] Thereafter, Roosevelt gave de Valera the 'absent treatment'.[28] Churchill did likewise. He discouraged visits by senior politicians to Dublin and persistently declined to reassure de Valera that Britain would respect Irish neutrality.[29] Churchill's

[20] Cranborne, Cabinet memorandum 'Discussions in Dublin', 19 Dec. 1941, PRO CAB 67/9 WP(G)(41) 158.
[21] Lady Craigavon, diary, 7 Nov. 1940.
[22] *Daily Express* interview, quoted ibid., 13 Nov. 1940.
[23] *FRUS*: 1942: 1: pp. 751-5, *passim.*   [24] *The Times*, 28 Jan. 1942.
[25] Longford and O'Neill (1970: 397-8).
[26] B. Cockram, 'Note about Ireland', 14 Apr. 1945, PRO DO 35/1228/W.X.101/1/69; Mulcahy memo, 4 Feb. 1942, Mulcahy papers, P7a/214.
[27] Welles, memo 6 Feb. 1942, *FRUS*: 1942: 1: p. 755; Cordell Hull, *The memoirs of Cordell Hull, vol. 2* (New York: 1948), p. 1355.
[28] Roosevelt to Gray, 16 Sept. 1942, Roosevelt papers, PSF 56; Ickes diary, 6 Feb. 1942, Ickes papers, reel 5, p. 6328.
[29] Churchill to Cranborne, 19 Feb. 1941, PRO PREM 3/131/4; Menzies (1967: 37).

support for Ulster persisted: he told Averell Harriman, '"No good making enemies of friends in order to try to make friends of enemies."'[30] What reads like a concerted campaign in the American press, to undermine Ireland's 'irresponsible neutrality' gathered momentum in 1942. Ireland, it was suggested — and some former de Valera supporters joined the chorus[31] — could either help the democracies or 'play Hitler's game'.[32]

Although anxious to ignore Ireland if at all possible, it was still appreciated in London and Washington that Partition resulted in a continuing complication in strategic planning for the defence of the North Atlantic. Roosevelt believed it 'a pity that Ireland has lived in a dream world under the rule of a dreamer.' In December 1942, he confided to Gray: 'If and when we clean up Germany, I think that Churchill and I can do much for Ireland and its future — and I think that he and I can agree on the method with due consideration of firmness and justice.'[33]

Gray believed that de Valera had 'damned little time to go into reverse and get on the band wagon.' Unless he conciliated British and Northern Irish sentiment, 'he was assuming the responsibility of blocking a settlement for a generation.'[34] Had Ireland joined the Allies and won Ulster's support for Irish unity, British politicians maintained that they would have supported it:[35] but with the nationalist and unionist ortho-doxies remaining sacrosanct in Dublin and Belfast, London's support was never to be put to the test and the status quo was maintained throughout the rest of the war. Various schemes were mooted to effect some bargain over Partition and neutrality: Dillon put forward such a plan involving the

---

[30] Averell Harriman, personal notes Dec. 1941, in W. Averell Harriman and Elie Abel, *Special envoy to Churchill and Stalin, 1941-46* (London: 1976), p. 115.

[31] W. J. Maloney, 'De Valera's neutrality', *The Nation* (New York), 31 Jan. 1942, pp. 141-5.

[32] See the Irish supplement, ibid.

[33] Roosevelt to Gray, 18 Dec. 1942, Roosevelt papers, PSF 56.

[34] Gray to Roosevelt, 9 Jan. 1943, ibid.

[35] Col. Donovan to Secretary of the Navy, 11 Mar. 1941, Roosevelt papers, box 4, safe file, Ireland; Gray, memo, 28 Nov. 1942, 'Discussion of Anglo-Irish problems at Ambassador Winant's dinner', NA, R.G. 59, 123 Gray, David/62.

Americans but it came to nothing;[36] another plan whereby the Stormont parliament would be 'superceded' by 'a joint American and British Commission' which would 'take over the running of Northern Ireland' also failed despite the efforts of two British MPs who argued in Dublin that 'faced with losing the War', the Americans were 'bloody-minded' and 'nothing would stop them'.[37] Another scheme which failed was that mooted by northern nationalists for a neutral, federal Ireland, to come into effect when 'a strong Irish army' could replace 'the present American-British army in occupation in Northern Ireland' — the new Irish army was to have been recruited from within the north and from the Irish living in Britain or already enlisted in the British army.[38]

A definite casualty of the war was American goodwill towards the ending of Partition. Whatever sporadic interest may have remained was rooted in strategic self-interest; empathy for Dublin's case faded as the war progressed. Gray who had been so enthusiastic in 1940 to remove Partition, and who, even after the failure of the MacDonald talks, thought that 'this thing ought to be ended for everybody's sake',[39] subsequently lost interest. By 1942, he was advising Dublin that the issue should be 'suppressed';[40] by 1943, he believed de Valera had 'lost his chance' to end it.[41] The State Department by then had not 'the slightest desire' to become involved.[42] More significantly, there was a distinct loss of sympathy for the south's viewpoint among British politicians.[43] Massey, the Canadian Representative in London, reported to Ottawa that before the war there had been many in Britain who would have been glad to see Ireland 'united, independent and forgotten'; but now the strategic importance of Northern Ireland was manifest.[44] Gray noted among

[36] Gray to Hull, 27 Jan. 1942, *FRUS*: 1942: 1: p. 752.
[37] Mulcahy, note 17 Aug. 1942, Mulcahy papers, P7a/217.
[38] Explained by Harry Diamond MP, NIHC: 30: 1951-2, 8 Oct. 1946.
[39] Gray to Roosevelt, 25 Sept. 1940, Roosevelt papers, PSF 56.
[40] Gray to Hull, 21 Mar. 1942, *FRUS*: 1942: 1: pp. 759-60.
[41] Gray, memo 14 May 1943, *FRUS*: 1943: 3: pp. 132-42.
[42] Hull to Winant, 13 Nov. 1943, ibid., pp. 161-2.
[43] Interview Malcolm MacDonald; Bernard Donoghue and G. W. Jones, *Herbert Morrison: portrait of a politician* (London: 1973), pp. 307-8.
[44] Massey to SSEA, 23 May 1945, DEA Ottawa, R.G. 25, vol. 1949, file 822-39C. Vincent Massey, Canadian High Commissioner, London, 1935-46.

British cabinet ministers 'a definite weariness if not disgust with the subject of Ireland.'[45]

Gray with his belief in de Valera's capacity for 'skillful and mischievous intrigue',[46] believed that the Irish leader was intent 'to fish in the troubled waters of postwar American politics'. This was not only the most promising, but, in Gray's view, the only anti-Partitionist strategy open to the Irish government if the Allies won the war.[47] Despite F. H. Boland's assurances that de Valera wanted 'to let sleeping dogs lie',[48] it was widely believed in Washington that de Valera, with his 'illusions' of the efficacy of an appeal to American opinion,[49] intended to 'stir up trouble'[50] and, moreover, hoped to win a seat at the peace table at the war's conclusion.[51] To avoid 'ceaseless agitation, disorder and growing bitterness', Gray was intent on damaging de Valera's credibility in the United States.[52] His stratagem was to prepare for Roosevelt a document insisting on the Allies' need for the Irish ports in advance of the Normandy landings. This was to be presented as an ultimatum to de Valera, on the assumption that he would refuse. There were however — especially in London — some misgivings that de Valera might somehow use a demand for the ports as an opportunity to revive the, by now, quiescent Partition issue, a course which the British would have found 'extremely embarrassing'.[53] For this reason, the demand for the ports was dropped and a request for the removal of Axis diplomats from Dublin substituted. De Valera rejected the

[45] Gray reporting the consensus among Attlee, Morrison, Cranborne, and Maffey, memo 28 Nov. 1942, 'Discussions of Anglo-Irish problems at Ambassador Winant's dinner', NA, R.G. 59, 123 Gray, David/62.

[46] Gray, memo 14 May 1943, *FRUS*: 1943: 3: pp. 132-42.

[47] Gray 'Memorandum of the Irish situation' 16 Aug. 1943, NA, R.G. 59, 841D.00/8-1843.

[48] Gray, memo of conversation with F. H. Boland, 8 July 1943, NA, R.G. 59, 841D. 00/1406.

[49] H. H. Wrong, Under-SSEA, Canada, to L. B. Pearson, Canadian Legation, Washington 28 July 1943, PAC, R.G. 25, vol. 1949, file 822-39C.

[50] E. Reid to SSEA, 11 Mar. 1944, ibid., vol. 781, file 398; Gray to Stettinius, 22 Oct. 1943, NA, R.G. 59, 841D.24/152.

[51] Ickes, diary 20 Mar. 1943, Ickes papers, reel 5, p. 7572.

[52] Gray to Hull, 28 Sept. 1943, *FRUS*: 1943: 3: pp. 153-4.

[53] Hull to Winant, 13 Nov. 1943, ibid., pp. 161-2; British wariness of Gray's stratagems is manifest in Eden's files, Avon papers, FO 954/6/8-104 *passim*.

demand outright, suspected the motives of the Allies, was aware of the dangers of publication and sought — unsuccessfully — to have the Note withdrawn.[54]

As American press coverage showed, the Note served its purpose. An opinion poll showed that 38 per cent of Americans approved trade sanctions against Ireland while a further 35 per cent thought a degree of force should be used against de Valera's government to ensure compliance with American wishes.[55] British diplomats in the United States could now report that Irish diplomats there believed 'the wisest policy' was 'like Brer Rabbit, to lie low and say nothing until the general atmosphere improves in the detente of the post-war years.' There was, however, no room for complacency on the British side: 'instincts' were 'more long-lived than memories' and a mistake by Britain could always 'justify the American-Irish to themselves in beating their drums once more.'[56] Gray, feigning innocence in Dublin concerning his own motives,[57] was pleased with the outcome of his stratagem. On 15 March he wrote to Hull: 'The general condemnation of de Valera by our press will have its effect without our taking further official measures.'[58] Three days later he reported Irish disquiet at the treatment of the issue in the American newspapers 'as they never believed they would lose American sympathy.'[59]

As can be seen from de Valera's handling of his wartime policy, he was, essentially, as moderate as circumstances allowed him to be. Because neutrality represented a conclusive expression of the sovereignty of the twenty-six counties, his consistent refusal to trade it for a possible ending of Partition was defensible, given Fianna Fail's basic strategy. Throughout every crisis and in all his political and diplomatic activity, he

[54] Cranborne, Cabinet memorandum 'Ireland', 7 Mar. 1944, PRO CAB 66/48 WP (44) 151. Gray to Hull, 24 Feb. 1944, *FRUS*: 1944: 3: pp. 224-6; *The Times*, 18 Mar. 1944.

[55] Dwyer (1977: 190-3).

[56] B. Cockram, 'Note about Ireland' 14 Apr. 1945, PRO DO 35/1228/W.X.101/ 1/69.

[57] Gray to de Valera, 2 Mar. 1944, PRO CAB 66/48 WP(44)151, annex III; memo of Gray's reply to telephone query from ?*Irish Press* journalist, Gallagher papers, MS 18,334.

[58] Gray to Hull, 15 Mar. 1944, *FRUS*: 1944: 3: pp. 240-1.

[59] Gray to Hull, 18 Mar. 1944, ibid., p. 242.

remained cautious in handling Partition. Within Fianna Fail, he deflected Donnelly's agitation to convene special conferences 'to discuss and take immediate steps' to secure its 'complete abolition' — this, in the summer of 1940![60] Not only were such special conferences not approved, but the opportunist faction — some of whom advocated force at the first wartime Ard Fheis in 1939 — did not have another conference platform until 1943, when de Valera advised against a prolonged debate on Partition. In the event, he had to rely on press censorship to delete references advocating 'terrorist methods'.[61]

Along with containing the extremists within his party, de Valera also advised Cardinal MacRory to stop 'making cracks at the Ulster Government'[62] and he took every opportunity to tell Maffey, Hempel, and Gray of the dangers inherent in any use of force to attempt to undo Partition. Canadian diplomats in Dublin consistently reported de Valera's lack of interest in making Partition and neutrality matters for joint negotiation.[63] Maffey concluded by April 1943 that the Fianna Fail government 'did not wish for a solution on any grounds that were possible.'[64] Two years earlier, the former — and future — Prime Minister of Australia, Robert Menzies, accurately summarized de Valera's pragmatism; he recorded de Valera as recognizing

that Great Britain could not possibly throw Ulster into Eire if that meant that Ulster was also to become neutral and that Great Britain was to be deprived of even those bases which she then had. In effect, the campaign for union could not usefully or sensibly be pursued during the war, assuming the neutrality of Eire.[65]

[60] Minutes, Fianna Fail National Executive, May–June 1940, *passim*.

[61] *Belfast Newsletter*, 13 Dec. 1939; *Irish Press*, 29 Sept. 1943; Gray to Hull 1 Oct. 1943, *FRUS*: 1943: 3: pp. 154-5.

[62] Gray to Roosevelt, 25 Sept. 1940, Roosevelt papers, PSF 56. Joseph Cardinal MacRory; as archbishop of Armagh, leader of Irish Catholics, 1928-46; as a rabid anti-Partitionist, unsympathetic to Allied cause in Second World War.

[63] Kelly to Mackenzie King, 4 Oct. 1940, PAC, R.G. 25, vol. 1949, file 822-39C; Mackenzie King to Kelly, 28 Nov. 1940 (not sent), ibid.; Kearney to Robertson, 17 Oct. 1941, 20 Feb. 1942, Mackenzie King papers, M.G. 26, J4, vol. 283, file 2954; memo on discussion with Kearney *et al.*, 24 Nov. 1943, ibid.

[64] Maffey, memo of conversation with de Valera 17 Apr., copy in Gray to SS, 21 Apr. 1943, NA, R.G. 59, 841D.00/1387.

[65] Menzies (1967: 41).

Such caution was consistent with de Valera's policy throughout the twenties and thirties of insisting that each stage of 'the national advance' must be secure before risking any step, particularly one concerning the north which might upset the consensus already reached in the south. Neutrality, it must also be said, was a very *popular* policy: 'To let in the stranger is easy; to get him out again may mean centuries of blood and sacrifice. The Irish people want neither an old master nor a new one.'[66] Consistently de Valera's regime in the thirties had seen itself as the custodian of the nation which it had a duty to 'restore'; now it was claimed that 'Ireland's survival as a nation and the safety of the remnant of her long persecuted people depends on the maintenance of her neutrality.'[67]

(iv) THE IRISH QUESTION REVIEWED: 1945-8

At the conclusion of the war, Bernard Shaw wrote that de Valera had been 'triumphantly saved . . . by the folly of the Fuhrer in making for Moscow instead of for Galway', and by the fact that 'the abhorred Partition . . . gave the Allies a foothold in Ireland'.[68] This latter point found support from sources as diverse as Spender, Eisenhower, and *The Economist*.[69] For the Allies an abiding lesson of the war was that Ireland remained strategically vital and that only by relying on Northern Ireland's loyalty to Britain could the Atlantic be secure against a future enemy. Were it not for Ulster's loyalty, claimed Churchill, 'slavery and death' would have been Britain's fate.[70] As Dublin had feared,[71] Britain's wartime indebtedness to Ulster gave to the Unionists a security which they had not known since Partition had first been enacted. Some measure of the shift in sympathies can be gleaned from the attitude of the British Treasury; parsimonious and sarcastic about Northern Ireland's claims in 1938, Treasury officials,

[66] *Irish Press*, 6 Oct. 1941.
[67] Irish Legation to the State Department, 15 May 1941, *FRUS*: 1941: 3: p. 232.
[68] *The Times*, 18 May 1945.
[69] Spender, diary 18 May 1945; Eisenhower, quoted Gray, 'Introduction', W. A. Carson, *Ulster and the Irish Republic* (Belfast, n.d. (1956)); *The Economist*, 18 July 1942.
[70] Churchill to Andrews, *The Times*, 10 May 1943.
[71] Gray to Roosevelt, 11 July 1941, Roosevelt papers, PSF 56.

by 1942, were concerned that Northern Ireland had 'considerable leeway' to make up.[72] Such parity, compounded by the extension to the north of the British welfare state, further deepened the gulf between north and south.

The gulf was also psychological: neutrality had been 'a narcotic';[73] the south's 'almost total isolation from the rest of mankind' resulted in her missing 'the shared experience, the comradeship in suffering, the new thinking about the future'.[74] O'Faolain believed that Ireland had been 'snoring gently behind the Green Curtain that we have been rigging up for the last thirty years —Thought-proof, World-proof, Life-proof.'[75] De Valera's critics maintained that he had a tendency to chase rainbows',[76] he was living in a 'Celtic twilight',[77] seeking 'a Gaelic sanctuary'.[78] Unionists joined in the chorus. Spender believed de Valera's hope was to keep the south 'as remote from the world's affairs as Mars'.[79]

With the news of Hitler's death on 30 April 1945 de Valera insisted — ignoring his closest advisers[80] — on expressing his sympathy to Hempel. He believed Hempel's conduct throughout the war to have been 'irreproachable' and he believed it would have been 'an act of unpardonable discourtesy' not to have called.[81] He was aware of the inevitable propaganda, telling Hempel: 'No matter. I do what I think is right.'[82] Maffey,

---

[72] See, for instance, Treasury file on Anglo-Irish negotiations, 1938, PRO T 160/747/F14026/04/2, *passim*; R. J. Lawrence, *The government of Northern Ireland* (Oxford: 1965), p. 70.

[73] Alexis FitzGerald, 'Irish democracy', *University Review*, vol. 2, no. 2, 1958, p. 44.

[74] Lyons (1971: 549-51).

[75] Sean O'Faolain, 'Autoantiamericanism', *The Bell*, Mar. 1951, p. 18.

[76] R. M. Smyllie, 'Unneutral, neutral Eire', *Foreign Affairs*, vol. 24, p. 236.

[77] Constance Howard, 'Eire', in Arnold and Veronica Toynbee (eds.), *The War and the neutrals* (London, 1956), p. 256.

[78] Maffey, 'The Irish Question in 1945', 21 Aug. 1945, PRO CAB 129/2 CP (45) 152, annex I.

[79] Spender to Powell, 18 Jan. 1941, Spender papers, D715/15.

[80] Confidential source; Kearney found the Department of External Affairs 'profoundly depressed' in the aftermath of the visit, Maffey to DO, 21 May 1945, PRO DO 35/1229/W.X. 110/3.

[81] De Valera to Brennan, Whit Monday 1945, quoted Longford and O'Neill (1970: 411).

[82] Quoted in C. J. Carter, 'Ireland: America's neutral Ally: 1939-1941', *Eire-Ireland*, vol. 12, no. 2, p. 12.

who believed 'the "absent treatment"' had resulted in an
'eclipse which had closed down on him and the Irish Question', believed that de Valera's condolences to Hempel, particularly as they had been followed by the revelations of
Buchenwald, 'gradually took on a smear of turpitude'. Maffey
was upset some days later when Churchill, in his victory
broadcast at the conclusion of the war, focussed attention on
de Valera with a bitter attack on Irish neutrality. De Valera
made a politically brilliant reply. According to Maffey, he
'saw his advantage, found the authentic anti-British note and
did not put a foot wrong.'[83] Maffey sympathized 'very deeply'
with the Dominions Office at what he presumed was their
chagrin at Churchill's mistake: Ireland needed 'quiet treatment and a patient, consistent policy. But how are you to
control Ministerial incursions into your china shop? Phrases
make history here.'[84] Canada's representative, Kearney, shared
Maffey's disappointment: '"We had him on a plate. We had
him where we wanted him. But look at the papers this
morning!"'[85]

Maffey summarized Britain's interest in a position paper
which he appropriately entitled, 'The Irish Question in 1945'.
He recommended that Britain should act with forbearance,
'not talking too much and leaving others to judge the moral
issue'; in that case the south 'will come badly out of all this
in the eyes of the world' and her powers for anti-British 'mis-
chief' would be greatly reduced. There was no assumption in
Maffey's paper that Partition would provide a long-term
solution to the Irish Question; he believed the Catholic birth-
rate would eventually create a nationalist majority and he
predicted a resort to force: 'It will cause guns to go off in
Ireland once again. The Catholics of the North will call out to
the Catholics of the South, saying: "We are only doing what
you did in 1916. Are you going to leave us in the lurch?"'

Nor did he believe that Britain's strategic interests, which
he believed paramount, would be protected by a united Ireland
solution: 'The idea that Northerners forced into the South
would leaven the South with British loyalties is childish. Mr de

[83] Maffey to DO, 21 May 1945, PRO DO 35/1229/W.X.110/3.
[84] Maffey to Machtig, 21 May 1945, ibid.
[85] Maffey to DO, 21 May 1945, Ibid.

Valera has thrown that fly over me in vain.'[86] Maffey was
vigilant in monitoring United Kingdom policy to ensure that
de Valera was not given a 'dangerous handle' with which to
exploit the Partition issue. Consequently it was with some
alarm that he reported to the Dominions Office in October
1945 a meeting with de Valera who was 'greatly agitated'
about a Stormont threat to expel southern workers who had
migrated to the north to work during the war. The issue,
wrote Maffey, was 'full of politics' and was then 'the sole
preoccupation' of de Valera's government.[87]

Despite de Valera's anger and apprehension, at the prospect
of any legislation which would limit 'the free movement of
Irishmen in Ireland', his initial response was again moderate
and pragmatic. He told Maffey that he had envisaged 'an
orderly and measured process of return' to the south of those
who had emigrated to Britain for wartime work and wondered
why the southern workers in the north could not also 'be
handled in that spirit?'[88] With de Valera's help, and despite
blatantly insensitive speeches by the Unionists, the issue was
by the following spring, 'quite quiet'.[89]

Although no juncture in European history could have been
less propitious to seek sympathy for Irish grievances on Partition, Donnelly believed that the end of the war would be
'the psychological moment' at which 'to make partition the
burning question it used to be years ago before it became
submerged in matters not so important.' In making these
points to what was to be the last wartime Ard Fheis of Fianna
Fail, Donnelly announced that he had 'come with a message'
from the northern representatives who were asking all southern
parties to join with them in forming an anti-Partition body to
prepare a political and propaganda campaign against Partition.
Donnelly deprecated all the 'empty talk' about the abolition

[86] Maffey, 'The Irish Question in 1945', 21 Aug. 1945, PRO CAB 129/2 CP
(45) 152 annex I.

[87] Maffey to DO, 16 Oct. 1945, PRO DO 35/1229/W.X.123/5; Spender had
been sceptical of Unionist ministers handling of this issue during the war, Spender
diary, 23-8 Mar. 1942; P. Bew, P. Gibbon, H. Patterson, *The state in Northern
Ireland: 1921-1972* (Manchester: 1979), pp. 110-14.

[88] Maffey, report of talk with de Valera 16 Oct. 1945, PRO DO 35/1229/
W.X.123/5.

[89] R. Price, note 20 May 1946, PRO DO 35/1228/W.X.101/146.

of Partition and insisted that progress could only be made
through a new nation-wide organization embracing nationalists
north and south.[90] Although Gray remained diligent in
warning Washington of de Valera's hope of using America as
a debating forum for the Partition controversy,[91] Donnelly
was better placed to appreciate the extent of de Valera's
interest. Reporting progress to Healy, he wrote that Labour
and Fine Gael had shown more support than had Fianna Fail.
Donnelly doubted if de Valera

will come as far as either. You must keep harping on unity in the South
as well as the North, and insist on making and keeping partition a
national issue instead of a party slogan. Always remember de Valera has
no team, and whatever he says, the party will agree.[92]

Twelve months later — optimistic because of the victory of
the Labour party in the British election — two northern
nationalists, McAteer and Conlon, invited all 'nationally
minded' groups and public representatives to a conference in
Dungannon where the Irish Anti-Partition League was inaugurated.[93] This development can scarcely have met with de
Valera's approval; it was, after all, partly the fruit of Donnelly's
interventionist tactics,[94] was an implied criticism of de Valera's
own anti-Partition strategy and challenged his leadership on
the issue. Disillusionment with Fianna Fail was now widespread among northern nationalist leaders[95] and this new
development clearly rendered more difficult any attempt by
de Valera to follow MacEntee's advice to remain silent on the
north as 'the only way' to make progress.[96]
Meanwhile a 'Friends of Ireland' group of Labour back-
benchers at Westminster interested themselves in Partition and

[90] *Irish Press*, 11 Oct. 1944.
[91] Gray to SS, 20 Nov. 1944, enclosing memo of conversation between Frank
Gallagher, F. H. Boland, Erskine Childers, George Backer (director of London
office of the US Office of War Information) *et al.*, NA, R.G. 59, 841D.00/11-2044;
Gray to Hickerson, 3 Jan. 1946, ibid., 841D.00/1-346.
[92] Donnelly to Healy, 24 Nov. 1944, Healy papers, D2991/A/164B.
[93] Phoenix (1978: ch. 3, pp. 13-14). Malachy Conlon, nationalist MP and anti-
Partition activist. Edward McAteer, nationalist MP, 1945-69; leader Nationalist
Party, 1964-9.
[94] Donnelly to Healy, 24 Nov. 1944, Healy papers, D2991/A/164B.
[95] *Irish News*, 26 June 1940; differences between Healy and MacEntee, Apr.
1944, Healy papers, D2991/A/160A.
[96] Interview Sean MacEntee, *Irish Times*, 13 Dec. 1979.

to Maffey's discomfort sought guidance from de Valera. One MP had told Maffey he had been 'tremendously impressed' with what de Valera had told him. Maffey asked what that was.

He told me that Mr de Valera had said that every concession, every chance, had been offered by him to the North and that his offers had been rejected. Now he could do no more. If the unity and independence of all Ireland were established he would give new consideration to his own policy towards England.

Maffey informed the Dominions Office that the MP had 'found this very impressive': his colleague had 'more ballast', but was also 'under the spell'.[97]

Of more concern to London and Washington was the potential exploitation of the Irish ethnic vote in the United States. Although Maffey believed that Irish influence there had been 'greatly reduced' and might be 'permanently reduced if we play our hand patiently', he warned London to remember that 'for the outside world Dark Rosaleen has a sex appeal, whereas Britannia is regarded as a maiden aunt.'[98] Maffey expected that Irish propaganda in the United States was likely to be employed 'with vigour, ruthlessness and often covert rather than open methods.'[99] Gray was even more apprehensive: in September 1945, he passed on information to the State Department that de Valera had recalled all Irish ambassadors for a week-long conference to discuss the possibility of 'starting on an anti-Partition propaganda campaign in the United States and British Dominions when the first favorable opportunity arises.' When Gray advised his source — 'a friend and admirer of Mr de Valera's' — that America's debt to Northern Ireland for wartime bases would stymie Dublin's plans, his informant replied '"we have plenty of means of putting political pressure on you in America and we are going to do it."' Gray noted the presence at the Dublin talks of 'the Irish "Dr Geobbels"',[1]

[97] Maffey to Machtig, 16 Jan. 1946, PRO DO 35/1228/101/1/95; the two MPs were V. La T. McEntee, Labour MP 1922-4, 1929-50, and Fred Longden, Labour MP 1929-31, 1945-50.

[98] Maffey, 'The Irish Question in 1945', 21 Aug. 1945, PRO CAB 129/2 CP (45) 152, annex I.

[99] Maffey to DO (May 1945), quoted in 'Propaganda on Eire's role in the War', PRO DO 35/1230/W.X.132/1/140.

[1] Gray to Hickerson, 26 Sept. 1945, NA, R.G. 59, 711.41D27/9-2645. J.P. Goebbels, German Minister of Propaganda, 1939-45.

Frank Gallagher, who was running de Valera's 'propaganda machine . . . the most effective in the world now that Goebbels is dead.'[2] Already on the State Department's files was Gallagher's understanding of the government's anti-Partition strategy: 'The de Valera solution . . . would be an appeal to the outside world for recognition of Eire's moral right', which Gallagher had 'no doubt would eventually result in "justice" being done.'[3] Gray, summarizing de Valera's record on the issue, approved his 1930s policy of disavowing force and relying on conciliating and attracting the north. Now he detected a change, de Valera insisting 'that as a matter of *right* he is entitled to Northern Ireland and that the British government should force it into union with Eire.' Privately de Valera admitted that it was unlikely that Irish unity could be achieved voluntarily, and so he suggested an exchange of populations between Ulster unionists and Irish emigrants in Britain. Gray was not impressed: to propose expelling the unionists was 'about as practicable as expelling the New Englanders from Massachusetts.'[4]

Gray must have been in danger of boring the State Department with his forebodings about de Valera's American intentions. He admitted to being 'an alarmist' on the subject,[5] but so obsessive was he that his zeal occasionally embarrassed Washington.[6] Routinely, the State Department insisted to all lobbyists that — as Alger Hiss, then Director of the Office of Special Political Affairs, put it — Partition was not an issue in which the United States 'might properly intervene'.[7]

Meanwhile, under pressure from their Dublin Embassy, the Foreign Office prepared a list of the probable Irish arguments in the expected propaganda campaign and the British rebuttals commended to British Embassy staffs abroad. The British

[2] Gray, 'The United States and Irish Partition' (Jan. 1946), NA, R.G. 59, 841D.00/2-1446.

[3] A. S. Brown, memo 7 Nov. 1944, ibid., 841D.00/11-2044.

[4] As note 2 above.

[5] Gray to Hull, 31 Aug. 1944, NA, R.G. 59, 841D.01/8-3144.

[6] J. C. Pool to Wailes, Hickerson, 16 Jan. and Hickerson to Gray, 11 Feb. 1946, ibid., 841D.00/1-346.

[7] Hiss to J. J. Reilly (National President, American Association for the Recognition of the Irish Republic), 18 Sept. 1945, ibid., 841D.00/8-745. Alger Hiss was convicted of spying for the Soviet Union in 1950.

believed that the Irish could be expected to make the claim
that Partition was

A crime against the Irish people and against nature. Maintained (i) externally by subsidies and force from Britain, which thereby demonstrates the hypocrisy of her war aims and of her pretended solicitude
for the rights of small nations, and (ii) internally by a Northern Ireland
Government employing brutal methods, religious intolerance and
political gerrymandering to keep in subjection a large and increasing
Roman Catholic minority which desires union with Eire.

The British reply should be that there was 'no argument' in
favour of the south's independence that was not also an
argument for Partition because 'the great majority of the predominantly Anglo-Scottish, Protestant and industrial community of Northern Ireland' had no wish to be incorporated
in the Irish, Roman Catholic, and largely agricultural south.
Partition, in fact, enabled both parts of Ireland 'to choose
their own form of government in accordance with the terms
of the Atlantic Charter and of President Truman's Twelve
Fundamentals of American Foreign Policy.'[8]

During the war, Ulster Unionists had been vigilant in denying de Valera any opportunity 'to reopen in America a question
which is very nearly dead'; now the Stormont Prime Minister,
Brooke, was contemplating a visit to put Ulster's case in
North America. The Home Office expressed approval, only to
be rebuked by the Foreign Office who strongly advised against.
British representatives in the United States believed the move
would be 'disastrous'; the Irish issue had 'mercifully' been
absent from the headlines for the previous twenty-five years:
'Emphasis on Ulster particularism would therefore awaken
sleeping dogs, which we had every reason to hope were not
merely somnolent but lethargic.'[9]

One advantageous result of the war was the establishment
of a British Embassy in Dublin which allowed de Valera to
make direct representations of his viewpoint to London without depending on Dulanty. In May 1946 he requested a meeting

[8] R. R. Sedgwick, revise of N. E. Archer's 'Note on principal Eire propaganda
claims with answers thereto' (Nov. 1945), PRO DO 35/1228/W.X.101/1/69.

[9] DO file, 'Northern Ireland's projection in the United States', June 1946-Jan.
1947, *passim*, PRO DO 35/1231/W.X.168/4.

with Maffey to impress on him the "'tragic difficulty'" facing the government in dealing with those willing to use force against Partition. De Valera added that 'if he were today a young man in Northern Ireland, he felt that he would be giving his life to fight the existing order of things.'[10] In general however, de Valera was recorded by the summer of 1946 as adopting 'a more tolerant and reasonable attitude'.[11] Norman Archer — on the British Embassy staff in Dublin — reported a conversation in which de Valera 'clearly intended to create the impression of a reasonably balanced approach to the partition question. As a tactician, he has perhaps decided that this is more likely to be effective that an obvious fanaticism.' Archer paraphrased de Valera's arguments:

One had to estimate the respective weights and positions of the two extreme views in the island and then to choose some middle course between them. If, from time to time, either extreme altered, one could move one's own course a little one way or the other. If one pursued this policy with care, the extremists on both sides might in time gradually become more tractable.[12]

In September, de Valera tried to interest the visiting Labour minister, Herbert Morrison, in his federal proposals but Morrison thought it would be a mistake 'to rush the issue'.[13] Morrison was, by now, a convert to Ulster's case and defended her interests within the Labour Party and cabinet.[14] He admitted to de Valera that if, in time, there was a change of view in Northern Ireland, 'that would be another matter, but to expect us to coerce Ulster was expecting too much, especially in view of the troubled world in which we all lived.'

[10] Maffey, note of conversation with de Valera 18 May 1946, PRO CAB 129/10 CP(46)212.

[11] Hickerson, memo 8 Aug. 1946, NA, R.G. 59,841D.00/7-2646.

[12] Archer, note of talk with de Valera, 5 July 1946, PRO DO 35/1228/W.X.101/154. Norman Archer, principal secretary, office of UK Representative to Eire, 1941, 1944-8.

[13] Morrison, Cabinet memorandum 'Eire and Northern Ireland', 16 Oct. 1946, PRO CAB 129/13 CP (46) 381. Herbert Morrison (1888-1965), Labour politician; his responsibility for home security in Churchill's War cabinet converted him to support of Ulster unionism; sympathized with Ulster's case in post-war Labour government.

[14] After the war, according to his biographers, 'Morrison's Irish preferences were . . . firmly changed', and he 'continued to keep a protective eye on Ulster's interests in the Labour Cabinet.' Donoghue and Jones (1973: 307-8, also p. 435).

De Valera, Morrison informed his colleagues, was 'not cross' with this line of argument. 'He rather shrugged his shoulders and indicated that in that case the difficulties in our relationships would have to continue.'[15] Both the Irish and British governments appreciated that the strategic dimension of the Partition issue was the most salient. This had also emerged in Archer's conversation when de Valera had agreed with Archer's suggestion that those interested in Partition 'would benefit from a drive round the Antrim coast road whence the narrowness of the north-western channel is so strikingly evident.' De Valera had 'dangled the usual "carrot" as to the defence problem being solved by early agreement once Ireland's unity had been achieved.' Queried on his definition of 'early', de Valera 'felt convinced that the period between one Irish General Election and the next would be sufficient.' He was however 'less confident in replying to the old question whether this proposed defence agreement would necessarily "involve Ireland in all England's wars".'[16]

Archer's note of this July talk seems to have created initial interest on the part of Labour's Commonwealth Relations Secretary, Viscount Addison,[17] who asked whether there was 'any useful action' which the British government could take with a view to 'furthering closer association between Eire and Northern Ireland'.[18] His civil servants seem to have thought this naïve and gently reminded their minister of the strategic lessons to be learned from de Valera's wartime neutrality; it was 'unthinkable' to consider any policy which might result in the loss of *all* Irish ports.[19] By the time Addison brought the issue to the cabinet in October, he was insisting that it must 'never be forgotten' that all de Valera could contemplate in June 1940 was 'a united Ireland on the basis of the whole being neutral in the war.' Britain's policy should be one of silence on Partition: 'any suggestion that we are prepared to give the matter consideration, is, in view of the strong feelings

---

[15] As note 13 above.   [16] As note 12 above.
[17] Viscount Addison, a friend and colleague of Attlee from 1929, he was the elder statesman of Attlee's postwar cabinet; Dominions Secretary, 1945-7.
[18] Addison minute, 23 July, Stephenson to Machtig 24 July 1946, PRO DO 35/1228/W.X.101/154.
[19] Stephenson to Machtig, 24 July 1946, Ibid.

existing on both sides, certain to lead to serious trouble. We must be careful not to find ourselves on a slippery slope.'[20]

Meanwhile in domestic politics, de Valera's failure to make progress on Partition rendered him vulnerable to his republican critics. Foremost among these was Sean MacBride, a lawyer and former chief of staff of the IRA, who, although he had in March 1944 addressed de Valera as 'Dear Chief' and put himself 'at your disposal' — an offer which was declined[21] — now launched a rival constitutional republican party, Clann na Poblachta, dedicated 'to stem the decadence of our political life'.[22] Espousing a more agitational approach to Partition, and a more radical left-wing stance on economic matters, the new party also recruited dissident members of Fianna Fail and with two by-election successes in 1947 posed a formidable challenge to Fianna Fail as the mainstream nationalist-republican movement. De Valera responded to the challenge by opting for an early general election called for January 1948.[23]

One plank in Clann na Poblachta's platform was to emulate the First Dail by admitting Northern Irish MPs to the Dublin parliament and 'when they come, we would say to the world, are you going to permit a foreign power to occupy the territory from which these men come?'[24] Fianna Fail's criticism of this plan as 'completely foolish'[25] was dismissed as spoiling tactics by de Blacam — himself among the leading deserters from Fianna Fail to the new party. He believed that Fianna Fail — now, in his view, with 'no plan to end Partition' — were guilty of 'a terrible desertion from the principles of 1932'.[26] MacEntee insisted that the proposal was 'absurd'; if northern MPs had full voting rights in the Dail, 'it would follow that the government should undertake extending its authority over all Ireland, even by arms.'[27] MacBride claimed that these

[20] Addison, Cabinet memorandum 'Eire and Northern Ireland', 18 Oct. 1946, PRO CAB 129/13, CP (46) 391.
[21] MacBride to de Valera, 20 Mar. 1944, SPO S 13450A.
[22] MacBride and J. J. Killean to W. G. Fallon (duplicated, fund-raising letter), 14 Sept. 1946, Fallon papers, MS 22,585.
[23] M. Manning, *Irish political parties* (Dublin: 1972), pp. 101-6; interview Sean MacBride.
[24] *Irish Press*, 19 Jan. 1948.   [25] Boland speech, ibid., 28 Jan. 1948.
[26] Ibid., 19 Jan. 1948.   [27] Ibid., 29 Jan. 1948.

attacks were based on a misreading of his party's policy which foresaw the nomination of northern MPs to the Senate and their being granted a mere 'right of audience' in the Dail.[28] What was significant here was that Clann na Poblachta's more radical approach to Paritition discomfited Fianna Fail and had greater electoral appeal even if it promised to be counter-productive.

This election was also marked by the most overt intervention by northern nationalists in any southern election when the Anti-Partition League sent a questionnaire to all parties and asked voters 'to support no party which does not pledge itself to give active and open support as a government to the work of the Anti-Partition League . . . including the giving of reasonable financial support and publicity.'[29] The League also sent circulars calling for a meeting between the incoming government and the League executive 'to discuss what approach' should be made to the British government on Partition.[30] De Valera, in his reply, agreed to consider the League's advice, but insisted — as any vigilant democrat ought to have done — that the making of policy must remain the sole responsibility of the elected government.[31] MacBride's reply was less explicit; he promised greater co-operation with the League especially on 'publicity and propaganda'.[32]

Fianna Fail's persistent claim throughout the election was that their party was best placed to secure a thirty-two-county, Gaelic-speaking republic: it should be left to de Valera to complete the struggle of the centuries.[33] Indeed, those attending the party's final rally were told that they had a patriotic duty to vote for Fianna Fail although 'they could, if they wished, be renegade Irishmen and knife Eamon de Valera in the back.'[34] Although no coalition strategy had been agreed before polling day, the combined opposition parties won sufficient seats to end Fianna Fail's sixteen-year tenure of office:

---

[28] Ibid., 21 Jan. 1948.   [29] Ibid., 14 Jan. 1948.
[30] Ibid., 21 Jan. 1948.   [31] Ibid., 2 Feb. 1948.
[32] Statement, P. J. Scott-Maunsell, of the Anti-Partition League, ibid., 2 Feb. 1948.
[33] De Valera, speeches at Kilmihil, 2 Jan., Milltown Malbay, 3 Jan., Dublin 4 Feb., Lemass, Carrick-on-Suir, 2 Feb.1948, ibid.
[34] Matt Feehan at Fianna Fail final rally, Dublin, ibid., 4 Feb. 1948.

an unlikely coalition, their fundamental point of agreement was a belief in ousting de Valera from power.[35]

De Valera's years in power had achieved much of his programme in the years since 1932. But all his gains had one inevitable side-effect, the further alienation of the Ulster unionists. On Partition, Fianna Fail reckoned that Articles 2 and 3 in the 1937 Constitution were a considerable advance, but again, these had served only to estrange the unionists. Moreover, the latter's political weight in London had been considerably enhanced by their war record, just as Dublin's had been weakened. There were lessons in all of this for anti-Partitionists — and, perhaps, some had learned them. But among the incoming Coalition government were some individuals keen to outbid Fianna Fail in opposing Partition. Clann na Poblachta's approach was reminiscent of the interventionism which Donnelly had, in vain, advocated. The Coalition years were to provide further lessons on Partition to the south's politicians.

[35] O'Leary (1979: 38–41).

7. 'Hoping for a Miracle': 1948–1959

The Taoiseach [de Valera]: 'If I am asked: "Have you a solution for it?" in the sense: "Is there a line of policy which you propose to pursue, which you think can, within a reasonable time, be effective?" I have to say that I have not and neither has anybody else. All I can do is choose the methods which seem most likely to produce the best results.'
Mr McQuillan: 'Hoping for a miracle.'[1]

(i) OPPOSITION

The incoming Coalition government was prepared to give the Ulster Unionists 'any reasonable constitutional guarantees' if they were willing to accept a unitary or federal Ireland.[2] Brooke, who had heard these arguments before, thought the tone of the Coalition's anti-Partitionist speeches 'less aggressive and more ingratiating' than de Valera's, but, of course, no offer was of any interest: 'They may bid as high as they please, but our answer remains the same — "Ulster is not for sale."'[3] Despite constant rebuffs Dublin's enthusiasm never waned, the change of government in the south rekindling public interest in the Partition question. There were many reasons for this: first, the Coalition — with Clann na Poblachta to the fore — seemed determined to open up the issue, believing naïvely that the Labour government in London would be more sympathetic to Dublin's claims;[4] second, Fianna Fail, without

[1] DE: 126: 2024, 19 July 1951.
[2] Typescript of MacBride interview with *Manchester Guardian*, 21 Sept. 1948, McGilligan papers, P35/218.
[3] Brooke, statement 30 July 1948, *Keesing's Contemporary Archives*, 31 July–7 Aug. 1948, p. 9426.
[4] In August 1948, Gray, by now in retirement, learnt privately from Rugby that Attlee was 'quite sound on the Partition question', Maffey to Gray, 3 Aug. 1948, Gray papers, box 4.

the constraints of office, and with their leadership of the anti-
Partition cause in question, responded with a less cautious
approach; third, and most importantly, the Coalition's decision
to repeal the External Relations Act precipitated a crisis in
Anglo-Irish relations which had profound consequences for
the Partition question.

The tenuous link with the Commonwealth which the Act
embodied had always been justified by de Valera as necessary
bait for the Ulster Unionists. In this respect it had proved a
conspicuous failure; treated with contempt by them,[5] it left
de Valera vulnerable to republican sneering,[6] British be-
musement,[7] and constant harassment across the floor of the
Dail that the formula which the Act embodied was a 'disgust-
ing, fraudulent, dishonest attempt to blind our people'.[8] Moreover, an element within Fianna Fail regularly called for its
repeal,[9] a course which de Valera had contemplated while in
power.[10] Once the Coalition mooted the idea, he promised no
opposition from the Fianna Fail benches.[11]

Controversially announced by the Taoiseach, John A. Costello[12] in Canada, the declaration of intent to repeal the Act
provided a six-month drama in Anglo-Irish relations. The
verdict of Maffey — now Lord Rugby — was that Costello
had been 'slapdash and amateur' — the fact was that Fine Gael

[5] See debate, NIHC: 32: 3641-81, 30 Nov., and 3684-3753, 1 Dec. 1948.

[6] MacSwiney, 'The New Agreement', copy letter to 'The Editor', 7 May 1938,
MacSwiney papers, P48/C/22.

[7] Churchill, *The Times*, 15 March 1944 for comment that he was 'not prepared
to attempt exact definitions which might be difficult even for eminent jurists'; a
Special Correspondent in *The Times*, 20 Oct. 1944 wrote that the relationship
between Eire and Britain was 'an exception to all rules'. *The Economist* believed
it had been reduced by de Valera to 'a solemn farce', 23 Oct. 1948.

[8] Dillon in the Dail, DE: 101: 2179-2183, 19 June 1946; also interview James
Dillon; also see McGilligan, DE: 106: 2306, 20 June 1947.

[9] Agenda, 1944 Ard Fheis; also see debate and de Valera's defence of his
formula against its critics within the party at the 1945 Ard Fheis, *Irish Press*, 7 Nov.
1945.

[10] *Irish Press*, 15 June 1949; Longford and O'Neill (1970: 430).

[11] DE: 112: 2441, 6 Aug. 1948. Mackenzie King recorded Costello's private
view that 'no other political party would for a moment support any continued
link with the Crown.' Mackenzie King, diary 9 Sept. 1948, Mackenzie King papers,
M.G. 26, J13.

[12] John A. Costello (1891-1976), lawyer, politician; Attorney-General, 1926-32;
first elected to Dail, 1933; although an expert critic of some Fianna Fail policies,
concentrated on his legal career until 1948, when, although not Fine Gael leader,
became Taoiseach of first Coalition government; Taoiseach again, 1954-7.

'had a sudden brainwave that they would steal the "Long Man's" clothes'.[13] That Costello was 'playing into de Valera's hands' was the report received by the Department of External Affairs in Ottawa,[14] while the State Department in Washington was briefed from their man in Dublin that there was confusion in Fianna Fail ranks.[15] McCartan believed that Fianna Fail disliked being outflanked on their republican wing — 'the last straw'.[16] It was Rugby's view that repeal of the Act had destroyed 'the best chance of a friendly solution' and he predicted a stimulation of national sentiment on both sides of the border. Although 'all the best Irish opinion' deprecated violence, Irish politicians were 'not free agents and they know it'; their oratory was, in Rugby's view, 'a summons to battle' which had the effect of 'poisoning young minds': 'Inexorably, inevitably, the Irish Republic now created will be pushed from behind to work out the destiny so long and so passionately preached. "Ireland shall be free from the centre to the sea." The Government need not move, will not move.'

Rugby had no doubt about the 'significant consideration' for the United Kingdom: this was that 'each party must now outdo its rivals in a passionate crusade for Irish unity.' Whilst the firebrands in the Dail who advocated force were not representative, it was 'regrettably true that, in the atmosphere of a national drive against Partition, words like these may provoke irresponsible elements to act, and that once the spark of violence has been kindled it will not be possible for any Eire Government to put it out.' Rugby believed that the 'Republican bandwagon' had come 'triumphantly home with practically every politician, on board' — yet again, the ratchet effect at work.

No leading politician dare to appear reluctant to join the anti-Partition bandwagon or to seem doubtful about the wisdom of giving it a shove. And yet it should be evident that there is a stiff ditch in front of them, dug deep by Eire's neutrality in the war, and now deeper still by the formal declaration of a Republic — a move away from Crown and

[13] Rugby to DO, 15 Oct. 1948, PRO CAB 21/1835; Lyons (1971: 556–60); Costello interview, 24 June 1969, transmitted '7 Days', *RTE*, 6 Jan. 1976.

[14] Robertson to Pearson (Turgeon for Mackenzie King) 20 Sept. 1948, DEA Ottawa, Privy Council Office, vol. 107, W-10–11, I-11.

[15] Garrett to SS, 7 Dec. 1948, NA, R.G. 59, 841D.00/12-748.

[16] McCartan to Maloney, 6 Feb. 1949, Maloney papers, box 21.

Commonwealth which has still further outraged the feelings of the loyalists of the North.[17]

Although not surprised by the repeal of the External Relations Act — they had predicted its demise since its enactment — Ulster Unionists expressed concern to London about the implications for them of the south's policy. They sensed both danger and opportunity. They detailed for London's attention their reluctance to acquiesce in the south's new title of 'Republic of Ireland' which might, they feared, be construed internationally as an admission that Partition was temporary, if not as an acceptance of the south's territorial claim. They lobbied vigorously for British reassurances that they would be protected from the south's attacks, whether diplomatic or military. Brooke also played the 'Ulster in danger' card; he believed that if the Ulster people felt threatened, they would, like their forefathers, be prepared to fight in defence of their way of life.[18] He also reported to London that there was in republican circles,

a good deal of talk . . . about the creation of a 'Sudeten' situation. The policy advocated is to foment disturbances in Northern Ireland, and to bring pressure on the Eire government to send troops into Northern Ireland to 'protect the nationally-minded people'.

The Unionists, however, believed that the Dublin government was 'not likely . . . to yield to such pressure' in which case the 'irregulars propose to undertake this task themselves.' In detailing these fears to London, Brooke sought — and obtained — Attlee's reassurances that Britain would defend Northern Ireland if attacked.[19]

Of greater interest to London was the wider security question of defending the North Atlantic, a dimension which, Sir Norman Brook, Secretary to the cabinet, argued was 'self-evident'. He suggested to Attlee that because of these considerations, the Ulster Unionists should be given 'a rather more sympathetic hearing than they might be thought to deserve on their strict merits.' Bearing in mind the lessons of

[17] Rugby, memo 'Repeal of the Eire External Relations Act', 3 Dec. 1948, PRO CAB 21/1837.
[18] *The Times*, 23 Oct. 1948; also ibid., 26 Nov. 1948.
[19] Minutes of meeting between representatives of governments of UK and of NI, 18 Jan. 1949, PRO CAB 21/1842.

the war, he believed that it would, henceforth, be impossible
for any British party to retain a 'detached attitude' on Partition: they would be 'compelled to take a positive line' in
support of Northern Ireland.[20] This advice was closely followed
by Attlee's government. Although London had always justified its veto on Irish unity by citing Ulster unionist intransigence, they were now strengthening the veto by effectively
passing it into the custody of the Ulster Unionists themselves.
The relevant clause in the Ireland Act gave a solemn guarantee
that 'in no event will Northern Ireland or any part thereof
cease to be a part of His Majesty's dominions and of the
United Kingdom without the consent of the parliament of
Northern Ireland.'[21]

De Valera was visiting London when he first heard of this
development. He telephoned Rugby — a few weeks into his
retirement — to seek a meeting. Rugby declined: it was
'neither convenient, expedient or congenial'.[22] Publicly de
Valera claimed:

If this thing is done to our country, I say for myself that then feelings
will be back to what they were in 1919 to 1921. If these people are to
tell us that our country can only be united by setting us an impossible
task, we hope another way will be found that will not be impossible.
We had hoped for something different than that.[23]

In no speeches since the Sudeten crisis of ten years before
had de Valera been so agitated about the Partition question.
During these days he variously described the new British
guarantee to Stormont as calamitous, fantastic, outrageous,
almost incredible, stupid, and mad: 'it makes one desperate'
to see the border nationalists being obliged to 'lie under the
heel of the Ascendancy in the neighbourhood of Belfast'.[24]
Clearly, de Valera believed the Ireland Act would entrench
Partition. He told the Dail that he had tried to secure from a
British Prime Minister a declaration that the British desired

[20] Brook to Attlee, 5 Jan. 1949, PRO CAB 21/1838.
[21] Ireland Act, 1949, Chs. 12, 13, Geo. VI, no. 41. Attlee noted that Costello
had 'tightened the ligature' around 'the body of Ireland.' Attlee, note, [May
1949], Attlee papers, MS 83/76–80.
[22] Rugby to Liesching, 2 May 1949, PRO DO 130/99/277/49.
[23] *Irish Press*, 2 May 1949.
[24] Ibid., 9 May 1949; also ibid., 4, 7, and 14 May; DE; 115: 810, 10 May 1949.

and would use their influence to secure Irish unity. If the
British 'were sincere a declaration of that sort would not be
too much to expect. We have never got that. Instead we have
got the contrary assertion now.'[25] Although he must have
been, by now, apprehensive, if not alarmed, at the results of
the government's 'interventionist' policy on Partition, de
Valera refrained from public criticism. The note he struck,
while bellicose, was relatively moderate. Others, including at
least one future front-bench spokesman for Fianna Fail,
advocated force in the wake of the Ireland Bill.[26] Lemass,
who now suggested that the ending of Partition would prove
to be the most difficult of Fianna Fail's national aims, predicted that history might well record that what had been lacking
during recent months was the 'wise leadership' of de Valera.[27]
This assessment was probably fair. It seems improbable that
de Valera — if he would have broken with the Commonwealth
at all — would have mishandled the announcement of his
decision in the manner in which Costello did, thereby excusing
the subsequent lack of consultation with Dublin when the
Partition clause in the Ireland Act was being drafted.

It certainly seems probable that if the British threatened a
guarantee to Stormont such as that which they later passed in
1949, that de Valera would have opted to retain his tenuous
link with the Commonwealth. It is true that de Valera mooted
the repeal of the Act to Rugby in 1947[28] and that the latter
believed that he would have proceeded with it if he had been
returned at the 1948 election.[29] Moreover, the public record
and his biography emphasize his indifference if not support
for repeal, once the Coalition's decision had been taken,[30]
but it should not be assumed from this that the decision met
with his approval. There is some evidence which suggests a
contrary interpretation to that in the official biography: de
Valera was personally shaken when he first heard the news of

[25] DE: 115: 813, 10 May 1949.
[26] Joseph Dowling (Fianna Fail spokesman on Labour, 1973-7), speaking as a
delegate to the Ard Fheis, *Irish Press*, 7 Nov. 1951; see also, Henry Harrison,
leaflet, 'The Ireland Bill: one amendment obviously indispensable', Henry Harrison
papers, MS 8,755(2).   [27] *Irish Press*, 7 May 1949.
[28] Longford and O'Neill (1970: 430).
[29] Rugby to CRO, 15 Oct. 1948, PRO CAB 21/1835.
[30] Longford and O'Neill (1970: 431-5).

the decision to repeal the Act, and his own suggestion, in 1947, that he might consider repeal, may merely have been a kite to test London's interest in a Council of Ireland.[31]

Most tellingly, in contrast to Longford and O'Neill's version, the unpublished draft of an earlier attempt at an 'official' biography by Frank Gallagher — also written with de Valera's cooperation — suggests that the repeal of the Act was the 'height of political folly': it 'troubled' de Valera, 'for he believed harm would come to the cause of unity from the bridge to the North East being destroyed. The decision was taken and announced without consulting him and at that stage he would only weaken Ireland's position vis-a-vis Britain by opposing.'[32]

While this drama in Anglo-Irish relations was still being enacted, the government, in January 1949, persuaded Fianna Fail to join an all-party anti-Partition group to be known as the Mansion House Committee. Given de Valera's lack of enthusiasm for involvement in any anti-Partition strategy which he was not controlling and MacEntee's advice against participation,[33] it seems probable that Costello's private view was fair — that de Valera's support for the Committee's work was 'grudging and unproductive'.[34] The first initiative of the Committee was to organize a campaign fund to be collected outside all church gates on the Sunday prior to the Northern Ireland election of February 1949. That the funds thus collected went to finance anti-Partitionist candidates in the election, drew the wrath of the unionists, although the net result of the intervention was very much to their advantage since it ensured yet another plebiscitary election.[35] The note struck by the Mansion House Committee was, anyway, unlikely to win converts from traditional unionist voters since it described them as the 'Quisling Irish'.[36] As early as the 1950

---

[31] Ibid., p. 430; DE: 113: 413–4, 24 Nov. 1948; interview Liam MacGabhann, political reporter *Irish Press.*

[32] Gallagher papers, MS 18,375(6).

[33] Sean MacEntee, interview *Irish Times,* 13 Dec. 1979.

[34] Chapin to SS, 29 Jan. 1949, NA, R.G. 59, 841D.00/1–2849.

[35] *Keesing's Contemporary Archives,* 19–26 Feb. 1949, pp. 9813–4; Cornelius O'Leary, 'Northern Ireland: 1945–1972', in J. J. Lee, *Ireland: 1945–1970* (Dublin: 1979), pp. 156–7.

[36] *Keesing's Contemporary Archives,* 19–26 Feb. 1949, p. 9814.

Ard Fheis, three future members of the Fianna Fail parliamentary party voiced doubts about participation in the Committee and de Valera himself considered standing down in favour of another party nominee.[37] Discomfited by the Coalition's zeal as anti-Partitionists, de Valera's response was to ensure that his role would not be confined to the chorus line but that he would also perform in his preferred role as soloist. Always a believer in the power of international opinion, he was now clearly willing to ignore any disadvantages in a policy of total propaganda: 'The phrase "Partition must go" must henceforth be on every Irishman's lips, to be used on every appropriate or inappropriate occasion, that is, in season and out of season, until the continuing crime against our country shall have ceased.'[38] He toured Australia, New Zealand, the United States, and Britain.[39] The State Department, still apprehensive about his possible effect in America,[40] were reassured from Dublin that in Irish political circles, there was an attitude of 'chuckling criticism' concerning de Valera's efforts:[41] moreover, his rhetoric was mainly for home consumption in Ireland. De Valera was a politician, and Irish nationalist propaganda abroad was merely 'the best way to practise his trade' at this time.[42]

Nor was he, in any significant way, appealing to international opinion. His audiences were largely composed of the converted.[43] Labour MP, Hugh Delarghy,[44] then chairman of the Anti-Partition of Ireland League in Britain, shared platforms with de Valera at his major meetings in British cities. 'Enormous and enthusiastic meetings they were, in the biggest halls', recalled Delarghy, but, in retrospect, he believed they

[37] J. J. Callanan, Michael Yeats, and Joseph Brennan, *Irish Press*, 1 Nov. 1950.
[38] De Valera: speeches: 1980: 522-6.
[39] See *Irish Press* supplement, *With de Valera in America and Australia: world appeal against Partition* (Dublin: 1948).
[40] Garrett to Armour, 1 July 1948, NA, R.G. 59, 711. 41D1/7-148.
[41] Edward McLaughlin (Dublin) to SS, 2 June 1948, ibid., 841D.00/6-248.
[42] W. S. Anderson (London) to SS, 19 Oct. 1948, ibid., 841D.00/10-1948; also Garrett to SS, 30 July, and V. Chapin (Dublin) to SS, 14 Oct. 1948, ibid., 841D.00/7-3048 and —/10-1448.
[43] Interview, Liam MacGabhann who reported de Valera's tours for *Irish Press*; Bodkin to Costello, 22 Feb. 1949, Bodkin papers, 7003/134.
[44] Hugh Delarghy (1980-76), journalist, politician; Labour MP 1945-76; member Friends of Ireland group within Labour Party; sometime columnist, *Irish Press*.

'were all flops. They were not political meetings at all. They were tribal rallies: tribesmen met to greet the Old Chieftain. The melodies of 1916 were played. A few IRA veterans, with their Black and Tan medals, formed guards of honour. Sympathetic Englishmen who attended went away bewildered.'[45]

Some commentators have suggested that it was de Valera's emphasis on the issue which encouraged the Coalition government to join the propaganda crusade.[46] But given his earlier caution on the subject and his fear — privately acknowledged before he lost office — that Clann na Poblachta 'would try to steal his Republican vestments',[47] it seems more likely that de Valera was encouraged in his resort to propaganda by the belief that this was necessary if he was to retain his leadership of mainstream Irish nationalism. Rugby's initial impression was that de Valera was making the running on Partition[48] but as early as August 1948 the British cabinet had anticipated — correctly, as has been seen — 'six or eight difficult months' in Anglo-Irish relations.[49] Perhaps competitiveness on the Partition issue was inevitable given the particular party political alignments at this juncture. Whatever the motives of the parties, this period of Coalition government from 1948 to 1951 marked a distinct phase in the history of Partition. Propaganda was tried and failed. There was one gain: C. Northcote Parkinson when he learned of the anti-Partition campaign formulated another of his laws: 'Propaganda begins and ends at home.'[50]

The abject failure by all southern parties during this period to weaken, still less to end Partition, was scarcely surprising.

[45] Hugh Delarghy, 'The man who outlived his memory', New Statesman, 5 Sept. 1975.
[46] Conor Cruise O'Brien, 'Ireland in international affairs', in Owen Dudley Edwards (ed.), Conor Cruise O'Brien introduces Ireland (London: 1969), pp. 123-7. Some northern nationalists complained that the Fianna Fail government 'had promised to consider the possibility of providing a Fianna Fail official to act as (Anti-Partition) League Organizer in Britain, but nothing came of this.' 'Note of discussion with delegation from the Irish Anti-Partition League received by the Taoiseach (J. A. Costello) on 24 April 1948', McGilligan papers, P35/B/145; Maguire to Healy, 3 Nov. and reply, 5 Nov. 1950, Healy papers, D2991/B/4/11A-B.
[47] Lord Longford and Anne McHardy, Ulster (London: 1981) p. 96.
[48] Rugby to Machtig, 5 and 30 Mar. 1948, PRO DO 130/91/277/48.
[49] Noel-Baker to Attlee, 10 Aug. 1948, Attlee papers, MS 73/12-16.
[50] Interview, Conor Cruise O'Brien.

Such was the nature of Partition that frontal pressure tended only to reinforce it. Also, the passing years, the very different experience of the war and the extension of the British welfare state to the north had similar effects; and, as has been noted elsewhere, disputed boundaries, once thought to be temporary, have a tendency to strengthen existing differences once they become operable.[51] During thirty years of independence all Dail politicians were staunch anti-Partitionists with an ability to neglect, if not indeed to insult, the susceptibilities of northern unionists. Catholic norms were espoused, apparently without any embarrassment at their illogicality in the context of the anti-Partition campaign. Some did see the incongruity: two of the key figures of the 1920s, Ernest Blythe and Tom Johnson, both with first-hand experience of Ulster and, neither of them, Roman Catholics, acknowledged a deterioration in the south's approach to unity. In 1949 Blythe's criticism of the anti-Partition drive was shared by Johnson who privately argued that the 'revival of militant Catholicism' now lent credence to the 'Rome Rule' doubts of the Unionists. 'At any time up to 15 or 20 years ago', Johnson would have refuted this charge, but now he was embarrassed by the pronouncements of his successors in the Labour movement. He wondered what the Northern Protestant Labour voters could think when, in the south, 'a Labour leader states that the "Labour Party's policy is based on the papal encyclicals and they proudly acknowledge the authority of the Catholic Church on all matters which related to public policy and public welfare."' This was 'the essence of the Partition problem' and Johnson could see no solution at that time; if anything, he believed that, in the immediate future, there would be an intensification of 'the militant movement of the Catholic Church'.[52]

Corroborative testimony comes from a disinterested outsider, the historian J. D. Clarkson: 'It is the Church that rules Ireland today, and no politician, however anxious to differ-

---

[51] A point noted by Rose (1976: 65) and by political geographers, Cohen (1964: 190), Mitchel (1971: 58), Orme (1970: 249-50).

[52] Johnson to Blythe, holograph draft, n.d. (1949) re Blythe's memo on Partition, Thomas Johnson papers, MS 17,231. Thomas Johnson (1872-1963); an Englishman, he learned his politics as a trade union activist in Belfast before the First World war; TD, 1922-7; first parliamentary leader of the Irish Labour Party; before the acceptance of the Dail by Fianna Fail, leader of the Opposition; Senator, 1928-36.

entiate himself from his followers would dream of challenging that basic fact.'[53] The interest of these assessments is that they both pre-date the major Church–State clash in post-independence Ireland, the 'Mother and Child' crisis, which was to have a 'disastrous effect' on Partition, as it was 'resolved, apparently, by the abject capitulation of the secular to the spiritual power.'[54]

In the second controversy of the Coalition's tenure of office, decisions were again taken by the government which proved inimical to Irish unity. Again, it seems probable — it was certainly believed by Fianna Fail — that under de Valera's leadership such problems would have been avoided.[55] The controversy concerned the provisions of proposed health legislation to which the Catholic hierarchy took exception and in which the Coalition government was seen to accede to their pressure.[56] That nationalist opinion largely ignored the central issues raised by this crisis, was, in itself, an indication of how partitionist the south had become. The Ulster Unionists concluded that 'in any matter' where the Church decided to intervene 'the Eire Government must accept the Church's policy and decision irrespective of all other considerations.'[57]

No party, such as Fianna Fail which proclaimed itself to be in the Wolfe Tone tradition, dedicated to uniting 'Protestant, Catholic and Dissenter in the common name of Irishman' should have remained aloof from this controversy. Here was an issue which was ripe for misunderstanding in the north and which was predictably and brilliantly exploited by the Ulster Unionists.[58] If it was the Fianna Fail view that the

[53] J. D. Clarkson, '"Big Jim" Larkin: a footnote to nationalism', in E. M. Earle (ed.), *Nationalism and internationalism* (New York: 1950), p. 55.

[54] Lyons (1971: 569); Paul Blanchard, *The Irish and Catholic power* (Boston: 1953), pp. 55–71; John H. Whyte, *Church and state in modern Ireland: 1922–1970* (Dublin: 1971), chs. 7–8.

[55] T. P. O'Neill in a brief résumé of de Valera's career, published on his death, suggested that 'Perhaps his principal contribution' in the 1950s lay 'in his quiet and tactful withstanding of pressures of Church on State', 'Eamon de Valera: 1882–1975', *Ireland Today*, no. 872, 26 Sept. 1975, Bulletin of the Department of Foreign Affairs, Dublin.

[56] Our concern here is with how the controversy was perceived by the Ulster unionists. For a detailed account of a very complex issue see Whyte (1971: ch. 8, *passim*). [57] Ibid., p. 233.

[58] Ibid., pp. 231–2; W. A. Carson to G. C. Duggan, 16 June 1957, NLI MS 16,221; NIHC: 35: 894, 9 May 1951.

bishops had interfered improperly, there was an onus on them to say so: if, on the other hand, they believed that this did not amount to 'Rome Rule' they had an equal obligation to speak publicly in this sense. In fact, de Valera maintained an 'astute aloofness'[59] which may have maintained party unity and been electorally prudent but which compounded the considerable damage which the whole episode caused to the prospects for Irish unity.

The cursory two paragraphs which his biographers devote to the episode underlines how marginal was Fianna Fail's response; they reveal that de Valera 'kept a tight reign' on his Dail colleagues, many of whom would have 'willingly stirred up further trouble in the broken ranks of the Government parties.' De Valera himself 'took no part in the Dail debate apart from a disdainful comment: "I think we have heard enough". Tactically it was the shrewdest way.'[60]

De Valera himself believed it had been an error to publish the exchanges of correspondence with the bishops.[61] His own instinct was for private soundings with the hierarchy before deciding on his party's policy.[62] Himself a devout Catholic, he was complacent about how inimical to Protestants was the south's political culture. Privately challenged a decade earlier that the north feared clerical domination by the 'priest-ridden' south, de Valera had replied that the north was 'gradually finding out that what used to be' was 'no more'.[63]

Although not precipitating an immediate election, the withdrawal of the proposed Mother and Child legislation and the resignation of the responsible minister, Noel Browne, caused such dissension within the Clann na Poblachta party, that it can be presumed that it was largely responsible for the calling of a general election some weeks later. In this election campaign so little mention was made of the issue by Fianna Fail speakers that one can presume that the Dail directive for silence was extended to cover the campaign. Only two oblique

[59] John A. Murphy, 'Eamon de Valera: the politician', *Ireland Today*, no. 872, pp. 7-9.
[60] Longford and O'Neill (1970: 436-7).
[61] Whyte (1971: 288-9).
[62] Ibid., chs. 7-9; *passim*, Noel Browne, letter *Irish Times*, 29 Nov. 1979.
[63] Dandurand to Mackenzie King, 1 Jan. 1941, Mackenzie King papers, M.G. 26, J4, vol. 384, file 8.

comments are to be found in the *Irish Press* reports of the Fianna Fail election speeches; the outgoing government, it was suggested, had 'forged many weapons' for the Ulster Unionists[64] who could not be expected to join a parliament 'where ministers could rankle for hours to the disgrace and shame of the nation.'[65]

In contrast, considerable attention was paid to the *volte face* of Fine Gael on the Commonwealth link: the repeal of the External Relations Act was 'unfair,unsporting and indecent'.[66] In general, the note struck was that the 'national advance' had been halted by Fianna Fail's loss of power in 1948.[67] MacEntee told the final election rally:

The one man who had been making real headway towards the ending of Partition was Mr de Valera. The people of the north looked upon him as a great Irishman, a world figure, a statesman who in the sphere of international politics was regarded as a man whose word was his bond. And if the Northerner was going to discuss the re-unity of our country, he would be more prepared to sit down and discuss it with Mr de Valera than with any other man.[68]

While de Valera's pre-eminence as the leader most likely to achieve Irish unity was stressed,[69] there was also considerable emphasis, especially in de Valera's own speeches, on how unlikely was unity in the forseeable future.[70] The Coalition ministers were berated for their unfulfilled promises: 'anyone who told the people that Partition could be solved in three months or six months, in five years or ten years, was speaking in a manner unworthy of a child'.[71]

[64] P. McGrath, TD, *Irish Press*, 7 May 1951.
[65] Erskine Childers, TD, ibid., 5 May 1951. Noel Browne (1915–), politician, psychiatrist; belonged to socialist wing of Clann na Poblachta; alienated medical profession, government colleagues, and Catholic hierarchy with his Mother and Child scheme; vetoed by bishops, it was dropped, whereupon Browne made correspondence public, whereupon Ulster Unionist Party republished all, including Dail debate, as evidence that 'Home Rule was Rome Rule'; Browne later joined Fianna Fail, Labour Party, and other minor parties; retired from Dail, 1982; outspoken critic of south's failure to woo north by espousing secular politics.
[66] *Irish Press*, 5 May 1951.
[67] De Valera, Nenagh, ibid., 22 May 1951.
[68] MacEntee, final rally, GPO, Dublin, ibid., 30 May 1951.
[69] Briscoe and Ryan, ibid., 29 May;de Valera and MacEntee, ibid., 30 May 1951.
[70] See 'points from speeches', ibid., 24 May and de Valera, final rally, GPO, Dublin, ibid., 30 May 1951.
[71] Ibid., 24 May 1951.

Another theme of Fianna Fail's campaign which had a bearing on Partition was their insistence that they had a better record on security than the outgoing administration.[72] Fianna Fail had the will, the experience, and the republican credentials, effectively to curb the IRA.[73] That Clann na Poblachta's claim to assume the republican mantle in constitutional politics had been demonstrated to be bogus was Fianna Fail's essential message to the electorate:[74] Fianna Fail was 'a strong single column'[75] whose 'policy and mission' was to save the country.[76] De Valera himself claimed that Fianna Fail was 'striving to try and re-establish the nation that was held in subjection for seven and a half centuries. We are trying to restore that nation to what the men who died to restore it wanted it to be — not something less than that.'[77] He well knew that his prospects of restoring the 'historic Irish nation' were still remote, and — he believed — had been rendered more so by the Coalitition's term in power. Their concentration on Partition had resulted in strengthening the Unionists, both in their constitutional position and in terms of British opinion. Paradoxically, this was accompanied by a quickening of expectations and resentments among Irish nationalists, some of whom believed that the abject failure of such an intensive anti-Partition campaign by government and opposition, demonstrated the inadequacy of constitutional methods. De Valera as he resumed office was warned by one of his northern supporters that the whole position was 'breeding dangerous apathy' and that force might again be resorted to unless a successful policy was forthcoming: 'None of us wants another bloody Easter Day, but it may have to come ... it depends on you and Fianna Fail.'[78]

Perceptions in Dublin differed: Fianna Fail, on their return to power, followed a policy on Partition of 'silence and discretion'.[79] Obligatory, ritual gestures were forthcoming on

---

[72] Boland, ibid., 16 May; Fianna Fail advertisement, ibid., 17 May 1951.

[73] Childers, ibid., 17 May; MacEntee, ibid., 18, and 23 May; Moylan, ibid., 27 May; O'Daly, ibid., 28 May; Aiken, ibid., 30 May 1951.

[74] See de Valera's speeches on this theme, ibid., 7, 14, 15, and 17 May 1951.

[75] De Valera, ibid., 7 May 1951.

[76] Vivion de Valera, ibid., 7 May 1951.   [77] Ibid., 21 May 1951.

[78] Maguire to de Valera, 27 May 1951, Healy papers, D2991/B/4/14G.

[79] Cruise O'Brien (1969: 123-7).

suitable occasions; they appeased the faithful and further alienated — if that were possible — the northern unionists. Other gestures — unnecessary and certainly unsuited to a party dedicated to Irish unification — went to prove that the Coalition parties had no monopoly of Partitionist behaviour while zealously espousing an anti-Partitionist stance. Some months after his election victory, de Valera joined McQuaid, the Catholic Archbishop of Dublin, at a ceremony at which 'Our Lady, Queen of the Most Holy Rosary' was named as Patroness of the Irish army. McQuaid sent a telegram to the Pope promising him the 'filial homage' of the state's defence forces,[80] just as Costello had promised his government's 'filial loyalty' to the Pope three years before.[81] 'Respectful homage' was all de Valera had offered in 1932.[82]

(ii) 'HANDING ON THE INHERITANCE: 1951-59'[83]

The 1950s marked an inauspicious period in de Valera's career; indeed he may then have lost hope of making progress on the Partition question. His biographer, O'Neill, in an obituary note, excused de Valera's lack of success during this period on the grounds that Partition was, by now, 'outside the field of practical politics';[84] moreover, de Valera himself, in 1973, in his last public speech, admitted to one period when he had despaired of Irish unity.[85] That this was probably in the 1950s is suggested both by O'Neill's comment and by de Valera's persistent pessimism concerning the prospects for unity during these years.[86] With the resort to propaganda a failure and his 'bridge' of external association destroyed, his options on Partition, as he resumed power in 1951, were severely limited. The then Irish Ambassador in London, F. H. Boland, recalls that, diplomatically, the issue was by then 'not active at all'.[87]

---

[80] *Irish Press*, 8 Oct. 1951.   [81] Whyte (1971: 158).
[82] Ibid., p. 48.
[83] This title is borrowed from the Longford and O'Neill biography in which it is the title of chapter 34, which covers, in less than eleven pages, de Valera's career from 1951 to 1959. Longford and O'Neill (1970: 439-49).
[84] O'Neill (1975: 6).
[85] De Valera, last public speech, Dublin, *Irish Times*, 25 June 1973.
[86] *Irish Press*, 9 Mar., 20 Nov. 1957; DE: 170: 1072, 17 July 1958.
[87] Interview, F. H. Boland.

There was dissent, cynicism, and disillusionment among those who had been in the forefront of the anti-Partition agitation in the previous two years.

Moreover de Valera may have believed that the recent emphasis on anti-Partition propaganda had had the effect of encouraging extremism[88] and once he resumed office, he allowed the Mansion House Committee to become virtually defunct, but without formally disestablishing it. MacBride's lament to Healy, in February 1953, was that after two years of Fianna Fail in power, the Partition issue was 'in the doldrums: neither Aiken nor de Valera even mentioned [it] in introducing their estimates', the usual occasion for reviewing policy; moreover, there had been only one meeting of the Mansion House Committee in the previous twelve months and it was de Valera's intention to 'wind it up soon'.[89]

The lobbying of Fianna Fail by northern nationalists continued. Maguire was sceptical of all federal solutions whether proposed by de Valera or MacBride; nor was he reassured by Healy's suggestion that it was possible that neither leader believed a federal offer would be taken up and so could safely offer it to demonstrate their opponents' intransigence. Maguire replied: 'do you solemnly make that statement that "neither MacBride nor Dev [sic] believe that Federation would be accepted"? That means both are dishonest! We are well represented — aren't we? . . . I want . . . to "kick out" this proposal.'[90] Maguire was equally direct in his communications with de Valera: 'You and . . . MacBride have done definite harm by your Swiss Federation idea. It is partition, and no political subtlety will disguise it.'[91]

De Valera invariably seemed more willing than other nationalists to admit the intractability of the Partition problem: it was 'extremely difficult . . . tantalising . . . exasperating'.[92] His own conviction by now was that nothing better

---

[88] MacEntee, *Irish Times*, 13 Dec. 1979; Lynch, *Sunday Press*, 21 Feb. 1971; memo on Ireland Bill, 12 May 1949, NA, R.G. 59, 841E.00/5-1249; Maurice Moynihan, note, in De Valera: speeches: 1980: 588, n.4.

[89] MacBride to Healy, 26 Feb. 1953, Healy papers, D2991/A/270.

[90] Maguire to Healy, Healy papers, D2991/B/4/14F. Canon Thomas Maguire, northern priest active in anti-Partition politics; delegate to Fianna Fail conferences in 1930s.   [91] Maguire to de Valera, 27 May 1951, ibid., D2991/B/4/14G.

[92] DE: 147: 196, 28 Oct. 1954.

than a policy of patience and opportunism was possible.[93] But such an approach could not still the impatience of northern nationalist activists who continued to establish branches of the Anti-Partition League 'all over unoccupied Ireland' in order to oblige the Fianna Fail government 'to put Partition in the very forefront of its programme' at the next general election.[94]

One initiative advocated by the northern nationalists was a particular embarrassment to de Valera: this was the claim that MPs elected in Northern Ireland should have the right to take seats in the Dublin parliament. When it had first been mooted, de Valera had admitted that he had 'for a moment . . . played around with the idea' but found it impractical.[95] Subsequently, he had considered it 'time out of mind' but saw no merit in it.[96] In fact de Valera had more than 'played around with' such a policy: he had initially championed it as a precondition for the Dail's acceptability to republicans.[97] But from the founding of Fianna Fail in 1926 de Valera had refused to be tied to support such a stragegy.[98] Such caution — indeed, heresy — was difficult to defend against republican critics who could insist that this was an illogical attitude for a party with Fianna Fail's roots and aspirations, and which, indeed, in 1937, had initiated a territorial claim on Northern Ireland in the state's Constitution. His republican critics, within and outside Fianna Fail, liked to remind de Valera that he had once insisted that the right of northern elected representatives to enter the Dail 'was the symbol of the unity of the country'.[99] To add to his difficulties, considerable

[93] Irish Press, 13 Oct. 1954; DE: 126: 2022, 19 July 1951.
[94] Healy to Fr E. L. Curran, 21 Nov. 1952, Healy papers, D2991/A/256.
[95] DE: 147: 201, 28 Oct. 1954.
[96] DE: 126: 2278-90, 19 July 1951.
[97] Minutes, 'Committee of Ten', 19 May 1922, Mulcahy papers, P7/A/145; Comhairle na dTeachtai, 7 Aug. 1924, MacSwiney papers, P48/C/8; Irish Press, 4 Nov. 1936; minutes, Fianna Fail National Executive, 1 Feb. 1937; DE: 67: 110, 11 May 1937.
[98] MacSwiney to O'Kelly, 8 June 1926, MacSwiney papers, P48/D/25; copy MacSwiney to ?, 15 June 1926, ibid., P48/D/13.
[99] De Valera's claim, minutes Comhairle na dTeachtai, 7 Aug. 1924; MacSwiney kept the minutes and was vigilant in reminding republicans of de Valera's inconsistencies on this policy, MacSwiney papers, P48/C/8; see also Art O'Connor to MacSwiney, 4 Apr. 1927, ibid., P48/C/21.

pressure was applied by northern nationalists throughout the 1950s for admission to the Dublin parliament. They claimed they 'would form a direct, personal, official link between the Irish government and its foreign-occupied territory'; moreover, they could, 'at the discretion of the Irish Government, be used abroad'.[1] McAteer wrote that he was concerned 'only with the symbolism of the thing', but his request was for '*my* seat in the Dail'.[2] That such claims were 'natural and proper' was allowed by the Coalition's Attorney-General in a cabinet paper in 1949, but he concluded that it was impossible 'without amendment of the Constitution'.[3]

Nor did the fact that the other parties in Dail Eireann were open minded on the issue, make Fianna Fail's stance any easier to maintain. Healy, who must have discussed the question with him on many occasions, summarized de Valera's objections. The northern MPs would, on the Partition question, be 'talking to the converted' in the Dail, their participation in other business would amount to representation without taxation for the northern electorate, and, there would be the possibility that northern MPs would take sides between the Dail parties which would not be in the national interest.[4]

While other anti-Partitionists tended to approve any policy which created movement on the issue, de Valera was more circumspect, looking ahead to the probable consequence of any initiative. He must have foreseen that the admission of northern representatives to the Dail would have increased support for the faction within Fianna Fail which advocated the extension of the Dail's sovereignty to include nationalist strongholds north of the border, and who, indeed, argued that the Dail should seek the allegiance of nationalist-controlled local authorities in such areas.[5] There was also the possibility that the irredentist claim in his own Constitution would be invoked to embarrass him into adopting policies whose possible

---

[1] Memo, Healy to Costello, Nov. 1954, Healy papers, D2991/A/408.
[2] McAteer to MacBride, 5 Mar.1949, McGilligan papers, P35B/146.
[3] Cecil Lavery, Attorney-General, 'Memorandum for the Government: Six County Parliamentary Representatives: Question of attending Dail and Seanad', 10 Mar. 1949, ibid.
[4] Healy to Frieda Le Pla, 20 June 1953, Healy papers, D2991/A/286E; also de Valera, *Irish Press*, 15 June 1949.
[5] J. J. Callanan, 1951 Ard Fheis, *Irish Press*, 7 Nov. 1951.

consequences alarmed him. Clearly discomfited by the persistence of the proposals to admit northerners to the Dail, Fianna Fail remained the only southern party consistently opposed to the idea, a stance which was easily construed as partitionist; in his last term as Taoiseach, he was still being pilloried for the 'flimsy' arguments which he adduced in defence of his veto.[6]

At every Ard Fheis during de Valera's remaining years as leader of the party, an anti-Partition resolution was tabled for debate: in the main, they were ritualistic pledges which promised to pursue by all constitutional means the unification of Ireland.[7] One resolution, in 1955, — if it had been honoured — might have had a salutary effect on party policy. This reminded the delegates that as the national effort 'must be to induce in all sections of the Irish people the desire to restore the political unity of the country', the Ard Fheis should direct 'that policies and actions are to be tested by their probable effect on this primary aim, are to be supported if they are likely to contribute to the achievement and opposed if they are likely to have the contrary result.'[8] But when it came to specific implementation of such a policy, there were always dissident voices at the Ard Fheis, willing for instance, to criticize Lemass for fraternizing with Northern Irish ministers in Dublin.[9]

Such meetings were in connection with the only policy area where any success could be claimed: functional co-operation between north and south in matters of common interest.[10] Here, genuine advances were made by both Fianna Fail and Coalition governments, and, it may be said, by the Unionists who had earlier had considerable misgivings. Always anxious to pursue a 'good neighbour' policy towards the south, the Unionists believed the basis for such a relationship should be southern recognition of the north's constitutional position.[11]

---

[6] McQuillan, DE: 163: 781, 4 July 1957.
[7] See resolutions on agenda, 1950, 1951, 1952, 1953, 1957, 1958.
[8] Agenda, 1955 Ard Fheis.   [9] *Irish Press*, 5 Nov. 1952.
[10] *Keesing's Contemporary Archives*, 13-20 May 1950, p. 10711, 15-22 Aug. 1953, p. 13090.
[11] See Brooke's speech in Canada and de Valera's reply, *Irish Press*, 25 June 1951.

Lemass himself may have been the main advocate of functional co-operation within Fianna Fail; he believed that every such initiative 'would hasten the day' of unity.[12] But de Valera, too, approved. In 1955, he told the Ard Fheis, that if nuclear power were to be developed in Ireland 'it would probably be desirable that there would be cooperation in that also'[13] and in 1957 — the last Ard Fheis at which he was to discuss Partition — he reaffirmed his policy: 'His conclusion grew stronger with the years — that the proper way to try to solve it was to endeavour to have as close relations as possible with the people of the Six Counties and get them to combine with us on matters of common concern.'[14]

There was one fundamental matter of common concern where northern and southern policies had a common purpose but could not — overtly, at any rate — be fully co-ordinated: the suppression of the IRA. Although both Belfast and Dublin governments were totally opposed to the use of force, there were considerable differences in their attitudes. To the first generation of constitutional nationalists in the south, the north looked like 'unfinished business' and while condemning any resort to force as misguided, they were reluctant to regard it as immoral and found it a painful duty to suppress its perpetrators.[15] Whilst a small and diminishing minority of southern politicians supported a resort to force, some others adopted a neutral stance and could be considered 'fellow-travellers': what was politically inadmissible for most of the first generation was concerted action with the northern security forces against the IRA.[16] Indeed the IRA's decision in the 1950s to refrain from any attacks on the southern security forces was clearly designed to invite a reciprocal response from the latter,

---

[12] Lemass, ibid., 5 Nov. 1952; MacEntee was in agreement, ibid.

[13] Ibid., 23 Nov. 1955.

[14] Ibid., 20 Nov. 1957; see also DE: 152: 550, 12 July 1955; DE: 103: 705, 13 Nov. 1946, *Irish Press*, 25 June 1951.

[15] *Irish Press*, 23 Nov. 1955; DE: 112: 964; 21 July 1948.

[16] See Clann na Poblachta statement, *The Times*, 29 Jan. 1957; Costello, ibid., 1 Dec. 1955; Liam Cosgrave (Minister for External Affairs) informed the government that 'combined police activity and extradition, would be 'impossible'. Cosgrave, 'Memo for the Government: a solution of Partition by peaceful means', 29 Jan. 1956, McGilligan papers, P35C/198.

thereby providing the IRA with a safe territorial base for their sporadic raids on Northern Ireland.[17]

Occasional statements by maverick politicians in the Dail and by some judges, combined with condolences by county councils for IRA casualties, all illustrated the ambivalence of southern opinion.[18] The obvious military response to the IRA border raids was cross-border security co-operation, but this left the southern government open to the charge of using the police and army to defend Partition.[19] For many republicans, constitutionalism was merely a strategy which could legitimately be resorted to, but only for as long as it proved promising. Clearly, many of those originally recruited to Fianna Fail could be termed conditional constitutionalists. While many of them would have subsequently become convinced of the futility of force in any circumstances, at least a small minority of the party could still be classified as having an 'each way bet' on force.[20] It is this political sub-culture, peculiar to Fianna Fail, which should be remembered in judging de Valera's speeches on the Partition issue.

Many had warned that the constant propaganda campaigns of the late forties would inevitably set up expectations which, if not met, would lead to a recrudesence of violence. Maffey, in particular, as early as 1946, warned London of 'the dangerous incitement . . . for an indoctrinated and frustrated generation of Irishmen';[21] Ulster Unionists too believed that 'a monster' had been created by the anti-Partition propaganda;[22] nationalist critics such as Blythe, believed it 'one of the root causes' of the subsequent violence.[23]

In the 1954 general election campaign, Fianna Fail could point to no achievements on the Partition question since

---

[17] Bell (1971: 245-6).

[18] DE: 107: 48-62, 24 June 1947; O'Leary (1979: 44-5); see also Alexis Fitz-Gerald, 'Irish democracy', *University Review*, vol. 2, no. 2, 1958, pp. 31-46.

[19] *The Times*, 27 Dec. 1956.

[20] *Irish Press*, 7 Nov. 1951; David Harkness, 'Unionist reaction: bitterness and hostility', *Irish Times*, 19 May 1976.

[21] Maffey, report of talk with de Valera 18 May 1946, PRO CAB 129/10 CP (46) 212.

[22] W. A. Carson, *Ulster and the Irish Republic* (Belfast: n.d. (1956)), p. 2.

[23] Ernest Blythe, 'The significance of the Irish language for the future of the nation', *University Review*, vol. 2, no. 2, 1958, p. 17.

inheriting power from the Coalition three years before. Their
speeches differed little from 1951:[24] again, they put themselves forward as the inheritors of the republican tradition of
1916–23, with a leader who was the most likely of all available
politicians to keep the 'nation on the march'.[25] Statesmanship,
argued de Valera in an election broadcast, 'should surely concern itself with the practicable and the possible. We might all
agree that it would be worth while to get to the moon or
Mars. It is how to get there is the problem.'[26] On Partition,
while emphasizing that unity was inevitable, he made no
promises: 'I wish I could point out to you directly how this is
going to be achieved. I do not want to pretend to have any
certain plan which would definitely secure that end. Neither
has anyone else.'[27] Lemass asked his audience at the final
rally at the GPO to 'come along with us and although we
might not reach the end of the road, we will build the bridges
for the future generations to cross.'[28]

For the third time in as many elections, power changed
hands in this election, with Costello again forming a Coalition
government; although it depended on MacBride's depleted
Clann na Poblachta deputies for its majority, the latter did
not on this occasion accept cabinet office. This second period
of Coalition government was marked by a renewal of an IRA
campaign against Partition which took the form of sporadic
guerrilla-type attacks on military and economic targets in
Northern Ireland by IRA units based in the south.[29] Bell, the
historian of the IRA, suggests that 'Ireland seemed', at this
period, 'to hover on the brink of a deep emotional commitment to a desperate crusade';[30] whilst his rather romanticized
account of the period may be treated cautiously, there is little
doubt that — as the funerals of the IRA martyrs and the voting
in the 1957 election both demonstrated — there was significant
public ambivalence and sympathy for the IRA campaign.[31]
Such a campaign was anticipated by de Valera who clearly

[24] Based on total *Irish Press* coverage of both election campaigns.
[25] De Valera, *Irish Press*, 28 Apr., 11 May; Lemass, ibid., 12 May 1954.
[26] De Valera, election broadcast *Radio Eireann*, 14 May 1954.
[27] *Irish Press*, 6 May 1954.   [28] Ibid., 18 May 1954.
[29] Bell (1971: chs. 14–15, *passim*).   [30] Ibid., p. 300.
[31] Ibid., 303–4; Murphy (1975: 138).

did his best to avert it. There is — during this period — a
missionary zeal in his lectures to the Dail and to the annual
Ard Fheis concerning the impracticality of force.[32] He feared
that 'the generous young people' who recognized the injustice,
might 'be led away to try to pursue courses which in the end
will be more harmful than helpful';[33] he feared that 'precious
lives' might be lost in a violent campaign.[34] Sympathizing in
particular with those northern nationalists in border areas, he
told the 1954 Ard Fheis that there would always be 'sympathy
for those who tried to assert their national rights against
force.' He himself was not a pacifist; he was not against force
in principle, but because it could not succeed: 'If you brought
about the unity of this country by force, you are condemning
the government and parliament of this country to govern that
area by police methods.' The measures necessary for effective
control of such an Ulster would be comparable to those
which the Ulster Unionists had been 'practically compelled'
to adopt following the tragedy of Partition.[35]

For their part, the IRA — not for the first time — misunderstood de Valera, their leadership believing 'the illusion that
their simple promise to remain quiescent in the South would
be sufficient surety' for the southern authorities to ignore
their presence.[36] In a clandestine meeting in 1956, an IRA
group met de Valera — the intermediaries were Fianna Fail
TDs[37] — and asked him

to assist in their attacks or at least connive at them. De Valera gave them
not the slightest encouragement. He was indeed extremely forthright
with them and impressed upon them his belief, often stated publicly,
that partition could not be solved by force of arms. Their movement,
he said, was bound to fail; it would cause great suffering without any
visible weakening of partition.[38]

[32] Among many speeches, see *Irish Press*, 13 Oct. 1954; ibid., 23 Nov. 1955;
ibid., 20 Nov. 1957; DE: 152:549, 12 July 1955.

[33] *Irish Press*, 13 Oct. 1954.

[34] Ibid., 23 Nov. 1955. This note was typical of Fianna Fail criticism of the
IRA in those years, Gray, memo of conversation with de Valera 19 Aug. 1942,
NA, R.G. 59, 841E.00/39.

[35] *Irish Press*, 13 Oct. 1954.

[36] Bell (1971: 305-7).

[37] I am indebted to T. P. O'Neill for this information.

[38] Longford and O'Neill (1970: 444).

While insisting that no task was 'more hateful' to an Irish government than 'having to deal severely with any section of the Irish people', de Valera was the leading advocate in the Dail of strong legal measures to suppress the campaign.[39] With Costello's government possibly reticent because of its electoral dependence on Clann na Poblachta, de Valera was the first to condemn this resort to force:[40] even the Ulster Unionists invoked his condemnation, in appealing to Costello to suppress the violence.[41] When the Costello government introduced tougher measures to deal with the continuing IRA campaign, Clann na Poblachta objected to what they termed the government's undertaking of 'the role of Britain's policemen against a section of the Irish people.' The party, unconsciously revealing a partitionist, twenty-six-county view — added that such government policies resulted in a drift 'towards a tragic situation of internal strife'.[42]

The note struck by Fianna Fail speakers in this election was that the IRA's resort to force was understandable but counter-productive. The party believed that the young men of the IRA needed 'friendly sympathy and advice' to desist from violence:[43] the Coalition had been guilty of 'delay and vacillation';[44] they had failed to take 'firm and prompt action to quell this menace' until it had threatened the state and 'gravely set back' the cause of Irish unity.[45] In contrast to Coalition governments, a Fianna Fail government had the unity, capacity, and will to curb the IRA.[46]

In what was to be de Valera's last general election as leader of Fianna Fail, many speeches were made which differed little from the appeal made by the party in their first contested election thirty years before. To Fianna Fail it was important to be accepted as the republican standard-bearers, hence their emphasis on this occasion on working for 'the ideals of 1916

[39] DE: 112: 964: 21 July 1948.
[40] Gallagher papers, MS 18,375(3); DE: 170: 1073, 17 July 1958.
[41] *The Times*, 29 Nov. 1955.   [42] Ibid., 29 Jan. 1957.
[43] Speeches by de Valera, 15 Feb., Sean Moore, 18 Feb., Gerald Boland, 19 Feb. 1957, ibid.
[44] Vivion de Valera, ibid., 15 Feb. 1957.
[45] Sean MacEntee, ibid., 28 Feb. 1957.
[46] MacEntee, ibid., 4 Mar. 1957.

and of 1917 to 1921';[47] in fact, de Valera stated that Fianna Fail 'had stood by its principles, the same principles to which they subscribed between 1917 and 1921 when they were the Sinn Fein party.'[48] This was a ritualistic claim by Fianna Fail but may have been given particular emphasis on this occasion because of the presence of two rival republican parties, Clann na Poblachta and the abstentionist candidates of Sinn Fein. Fianna Fail speakers did not lack confidence in their party's past or future role; it was 'the greatest party' in Irish parliamentary history,[49] the 'finest national movement ever established';[50] its record on Partition, claimed MacEntee, was 'unblemished', it truly represented 'the idealism, the realism, the intelligence and the commonsense of the great mass of all classes of the Irish people.' In voting Fianna Fail, electors would be 'voting for . . . Ireland'.[51] De Valera told a meeting in Bandon that 'there was no single day he was in office that the idea of a united Ireland was not fully before his mind.' Fianna Fail's goal was the achievement of Pearse's ideal — an Ireland, free and Gaelic. 'If we make sure that this five-sixths is made really Irish we will have the preservation of the Irish nation in our hands. Time will settle the other thing.'[52]

Yet again, this election effected a change in government, de Valera forming his eighth and last administration in March 1957. In a television interview, he was asked if he thought the fact that Sinn Fein abstentionist candidates had won four seats was an indication of a growth in support for violence. He replied:

I do not know. I would not like to be definite about that. As long as you have a problem and peaceful methods to solve it that are not very effective then you always have people who think that force ought to be used. My own view is that the peaceful line or approach is best, in fact, the only one.[53]

Questioned on the IRA campaign at his press conference the following day, he regretted that no steps were being taken 'to

[47] De Valera, ibid., 4 Mar. 1957.
[48] Ibid., 2 Mar. 1957.   [49] Matt Feehan, ibid., 5 Mar. 1957.
[50] J. O'Toole, ibid.   [51] *Irish Press*, 5 Mar. 1957.
[52] Ibid., 4 Mar. 1957.
[53] *BBC* Television, 7 Mar., reported *Irish News*, 8 Mar. 1957.

remove the cause' of violence, Partition. Force, however, would not be effective 'and cannot get the right solution'; abstentionist Sinn Fein TDs were 'living in the past'; private armies would not be tolerated by his government.[54] Significantly, editorial opinion in Belfast's unionist press welcomed de Valera's return to power,[55] as, in contrast to Costello's 'tardy action' against the IRA, he was certain to be 'master in his own house'.[56]

One proposal current on de Valera's resumption as Taoiseach in 1957, was a suggestion by the Roman Catholic Primate, Cardinal D'Alton for a united Ireland within the Commonwealth. Asked about such a solution six years before, de Valera, while refusing to exclude the option of 'free association with other states', had stated that he did 'not think the Irish people would even think about it'.[57] By 1957, he seems to have had a more open mind. There was 'no use' in making proposals in the south unless they were 'met with sympathy' in the north; he himself had put forward proposals which were 'not dissimilar' but to no avail.[58] Again in 1958, at a London press conference, he was asked if a united Ireland would rejoin the Commonwealth; his reply was that 'adjustments would have to be made when the six counties joined the twenty-six. A conference would be necessary to settle this question and at such a conference the question of a new relationship with Britain would have to be settled.'[59] *The Times* made the complaint that even 'the most diligent questioning' had not led de Valera 'to break new ground'. In fact, his reply — making allowances for the ratchet pulling in the opposite direction — was a significantly open one.[60]

Another dimension to the Partition question after the war was the complications which it entailed for the defence strategy of the North Atlantic states. The coming of peace in 1945 had not resulted in any diminution in the strategic importance of Ireland; while Belfast and London reassured each other of

---

[54] Press conference, *Irish News*, 9 Mar. 1957.
[55] Editorials, *Belfast Telegraph*, 7 Mar., *Northern Whig, Belfast Newsletter*, 8 Mar. 1957.
[56] Editorial, *Northern Whig*, 8 Mar. 1957.   [57] *Irish Press*, 17 Mar. 1951.
[58] Ibid., 9 Mar. 1957.   [59] Ibid., 19 Mar. 1958.
[60] *The Times*, 19 Mar. 1958.

their mutual interdependence, Dublin continued to emphasize the overall instability which resulted from Partition. The Coalition government expressed a positive interest in NATO, MacBride informing Pearson that if Partition were to be solved, 'we are willing and anxious' to join.[61]

De Valera, himself pessimistic about the prospects of another war, appreciated that this dimension was one of the few on which the south could offer concessions coveted by London, but he was unwilling to barter neutrality for Irish unity, contenting himself with the comment that whereas a divided Ireland would have no option but to remain neutral in another war, it would be 'difficult to say what a free Ireland would do.' He refused to consider as a condition of unity that the Allies would be guaranteed bases on Irish soil — there would be no 'bargaining of that sort'.[62]

By his last term as Taoiseach, de Valera was again parrying Dail questions about his lack of agitation on Partition, Irish membership of the UN being possibly an embarrassment in this regard, since to his critics it seemed that he was ignoring an ideal forum in which to raise the question. One course of action which he emphatically rejected was any call for international arbitration: the dispute was essentially an Irish problem and it would be 'foolish' if 'in desperation' an Irish government was to put its solution at the disposal of any outside body.[63] In general de Valera was disenchanted with the possibility of progress through international agencies. He was no enthusiast for the European Community, although one of his ministers, Gerald Boland, as early as 1957 thought that when the Common Market 'became a reality, it would go a long way to removing the border'.[64] Later that year, de Valera told the Ard Fheis that 'the nations of Europe could

[61] Copy, MacBride to Lester Pearson, 7 Feb. 1949, DEA Ottawa, 50021-40.
[62] *Irish Times*, 17 Mar. 1951.
[63] *Irish Press*, 20 Nov. 1957.
[64] Ibid., 19 Feb. 1957. Gerald Boland (1885-1973); veteran of 1916 Rising; TD, 1923-61; founder member and among chief organizers of Fianna Fail; Minister in all de Valera governments, 1933-54; his own republican credentials helped him as Minister for Justice (1939-48, 1951-4) to curb IRA; resigned as vice-president and trustee of Fianna Fail in 1970 in sympathy with his son, Kevin's protests against party's then northern policy.

not lend much ear to our problems. They believed that our problems were very small indeed.'[65]

Nor — although the fact that government records are still closed for the period must be borne in mind — does the nineteen-fifties seem to have been a particularly creative period in diplomatic initiatives on Partition. British ministers declined to discuss it,[66] de Valera admitting publicly that he had not much opportunity of discussing it during these years.[67] There was one courtesy lunch with Churchill in September 1953 when both men were in power, but this was in the nature of a sentimental meeting between old adversaries, not an Anglo-Irish summit to discuss Partition.[68] While Gallagher presumed that 'the opportunity was wisely used to further, somehow, the compelling dream of de Valera's life — the reunification of Ireland',[69] Rugby's verdict to Gray — they remained correspondents in their retirement — showed more judgement: 'I wonder how Winston and Dev. got on! No warmth, I'll bet.'[70] The brevity of de Valera's own note of the meeting reveals the entrenched positions of both men:

I spoke first of a possible unification of the country. To this he replied that they could never put out of the United Kingdom the people of the Six Counties so long as the majority wished to remain with them. There were also political factors which no Conservative would ignore.[71]

Meanwhile de Valera claimed he was 'constantly making approaches' to the Ulster Unionists but without success.[72] Until there was 'some response' from Belfast, there was 'no use us saying we will do this or that.'[73] He continued to advocate his federal proposals throughout the 1950s although, clearly, he was all too aware of unionist lack of interest.[74] He seems to have been as preoccupied by the other 'national aim' — the restoration of the language.[75] Here was a policy-area

[65] Ibid., 20 Nov. 1957.
[66] Interview, F. H. Boland.
[67] Press conference, London, *Irish Press*, 19 Mar. 1958.
[68] *The Times*, 16 and 17 Sept., 1953.
[69] Gallagher papers, MS 18,375(3).
[70] Rugby to Gray, 22 Sept. 1953, Gray papers, box 4.
[71] Longford and O'Neill (1970: 442-3).
[72] *Irish Press*, 19 Mar. 1958.   [73] Ibid., 9 Mar. 1957.
[74] Ibid., 19 Mar. 1958.   [75] Ibid., 19 Mar. 1958.

where success depended on the collective national will in the south. But de Valera's own enthusiasm for this goal was not shared by his party colleagues who displayed cynicism on the subject.[76]

De Valera's final address to the Fianna Fail Ard Fheis, at the 1958 Ard Fheis, demonstrated this preoccupation.[77] On this occasion — it should be remembered that he may not have known that this was to be his final speech to this particular assembly — he did not mention Partition. At the previous year's Ard Fheis he had confided to the delegates that he had 'lived with this problem' of Partition for forty years; he had 'done everything humanly possible ... to try and solve this problem.' Delegates who, consistently since the party's foundation, had argued that only de Valera could solve the question, now hoped that he would live to see a united Ireland. De Valera replied:

I pray to Heaven that I will see this problem solved before I die (prolonged cheering). I don't want any of you to think that it is more than a prayer to the Almighty. The Almighty has been very good to this nation. We have achieved wondrous things in the last forty years. We have seen wondrous things happen and, in God's mercy we may see the rest. But I cannot promise it to you and nobody else in this country can.

The delegates then 'stood and cheered for several minutes.'[78] To the Dail, during the last debate on the estimates for his department he repeated a challenge which he had first issued on the eve of his election victory in 1932;[79] its repetition now at the close of the de Valera era merely underlined the central disappointment of his career. While having no blueprint for unity himself, he stated that 'anybody who would get the solution would be regarded as one of the greatest men in Irish history.'[80]

[76] See emphasis in last general election campaign, ibid., 4, and 5 Mar. 1957.
[77] Ard Fheis, ibid., 29 and 30 Oct. 1958.
[78] Ibid., 20 Nov. 1957.   [79] Ibid., 28 Oct. 1931.
[80] DE: 170: 1072, 17 July 1958.

PART III
CONCLUSION: DE VALERA'S IMPACT ON PARTITION, 1917–1959: HIS LEGACY TO HIS SUCCESSORS, 1959–1982

' . . . the two barriers to a united Ireland at the moment are Eire and Northern Ireland.' (Malcolm MacDonald, minute, 21 Aug. 1938, PRO DO 35/893/X.11/234.)

'Dev knows in his heart that he did more than any man to create Partition. That responsibility now dominates his thoughts. He will not fit mathematically into his grave in a section of Ireland.' (Rugby to Liesching, 2 May 1949, PRO DO 130/99/277/49.)

8. 'The First Thing in My mind'

'. . . but until I die, Partition will be the first thing in
my mind.' (Eamon de Valera, April 1938.)[1]

(i) THE GREEN CARD

In 1924, Eamon de Valera was the victim of a 'Watergate'. His
political opponents, then in power, authorized the planting
of hidden microphones to overhear his discussion of political
strategy. That de Valera was a prisoner at the time — interned
by the Cosgrave government at the conclusion of the Civil
War — offered the authorities their opportunity to overhear
his prediction of their own inevitable failure in Irish politics.
The 'vital weakness' of the Cumann na nGaedheal government,
de Valera was recorded as saying, was that 'it knew nothing
of the psychology of the people. It was too passive. The
people now didn't care about politics as such. They ceased to
do so with the disappearance of the old Irish Party. Nationality
was the only thing that mattered.' He believed the Cosgrave
government 'incapable of feeling the nation's pulse',[2] a failing
from which he himself was immune: had he not told the Dail
during the Treaty debate that 'whenever I wanted to know
what the Irish people wanted I had only to examine my own
heart and it told me straight off'?[3] This claim that *nationality*
rather than *politics* was what mattered in Ireland suggests the
key to de Valera's subsequent success; his playing of the
'Green card' arguably ensured the dominance of Fianna Fail
in southern politics, even if it also ensured that the 'Orange

[1] *The Times*, 30 Apr. 1938.
[2] Intelligence report of de Valera's prison conversations in Arbour Hill prison,
3 and 4 Jan. 1924, Mulcahy papers, P7/B/286/1-5.
[3] DE: 6 Jan. 1922, p. 274, during Treaty debate.

card' would be all the more effective in the north.[4] The temptation to play the Green card was difficult to resist given the aspirations of the Fianna Fail party and the nature of its support; de Valera's Ulster policy had to be shaped with due regard to the state of nationalist opinion. A consummate reader of the nationalist mind, his rhetoric was intended, not to alienate the unionists — although it often had this effect — but rather to curb republican extremism and maintain his position as the leader of anti-Partitionism. This pragmatic, pacific, constructive side to de Valera was rarely evident to his contemporary detractors; not only because he lapsed into bellicose extremist phases, but also because to them — whether pro-Treaty or pro-Union — he was a hate-figure, the butt of their propaganda, and a bogeyman held responsible for the Civil War. Outside Ireland, being the only widely reported politician on the republican side, de Valera could appear to be an extremist or a fellow-traveller to those who lacked sympathy for his position, or insight into his political strategy.

(ii) DE VALERA AND THE NATIONALIST MYTHS CONCERNING PARTITION[5]

(a) *Myth 1: one nation*

That the Irish self-evidently formed a single nation was the most central tenet of Irish nationalism. Never subjected to searching analysis, there was considerable confusion among nationalists on this point, the Ulster unionists being excluded or included in the Irish nation depending on the argument in hand. De Valera wavered between the view that the Ulster unionists were 'fundamentally Irish'[6] and that their preference for British citizenship should logically lead them to 'go over to Britain'.[7] He was firmly opposed to any 'two nations' theory;

---

[4] For a discussion of de Valera's playing of the Green card, see Ronan Fanning, *Irish Times*, 19 May 1976.

[5] For a listing of nationalist myths on Partition, see pp. 29–30 above; these myths varied in importance, and the amount of evidence on each, in the case of de Valera, also varies; this explains the clustering of myths 4–6 below, and the lengthier treatment of myth 3.

[6] *Irish Press*, 13 Oct. 1954.   [7] Ibid., 23 June 1948.

there was no 'racial difference' between the inhabitants south and north of the border.[8] To him, geography was the final arbiter in determining the Irish nation, and throughout his public life, he gave visitors to his office a lecture on Partition and the 'map treatment'.[9] From a scrutiny of his anti-Partition speeches, from the cartographical propaganda which he originated, and from the cumulative testimony of numerous witnesses, including journalists, politicians, and diplomats, it is possible to delineate de Valera's detailed map-image of 'the Ulster question'. 'This Ulster', he told an American audience in 1920 before Partition was enacted, 'is a thing of the mind only, non-existent in the world of reality.'[10] Such a statement taken along with his selective analysis of the Ulster results in the general election of 1918, demonstrates de Valera's highly subjective imagining of the geographical data, a common phenomenon among nationalists who often hold 'illusory or deceptive conceptions' conforming to what they 'would like rather than necessarily to the truth'.[11] Fairly, he insisted that the border as drawn discriminated against nationalists, an argument, the logic of which suggested the rectification rather than the abolition of the boundary. He also considered Ireland to be too small an island to be partitioned.[12] Fundamental to his anti-Partition stance was his belief in natural boundaries: the exclusion of the six counties from the Irish polity was akin to 'cutting out Ireland's heart'.[13] He did admit that there was 'a certain amount of truth' in the arguments of those — such as political geographers and theorists of nationality — who argued that the boundaries of individual nationalisms were subject to change over time, but in his reply to such theorists — he was speaking in 1939 — he quoted with approval from a recent statement by Mussolini:

[8] DE: 112: 931-2, 20 July and ibid., col. 948, 21 July 1948; 'De Valera makes appeal for reunification of Ireland', 3 Apr. 1948, read into record of US House of Representatives, 28 Apr. 1948.
[9] Cudahy to SS, 14 Jan. 1938, NA, R.G. 59, 741.41D/48; Maffey to DO, 20 Sept. 1939, PRO DO 35/1109/W.X.1/5; Gray to Roosevelt, 6 June 1940, Roosevelt papers, PSF 56; Menzies (1967: 40).
[10] Gaelic American, 24 Jan. 1920.
[11] John K. Wright, 'Terrae Incognitae: the place of the imagination in Geography', Annals of the Association of American Geographers, vol. 37, no. 1, Mar. 1947, pp. 1-15.   [12] Irish Press, 30 May 1938.
[13] Interview US news agency, quoted Belfast Newsletter, 9 Feb. 1938.

There is something about the boundaries that seem to be drawn by the hand of the Almighty which is very different from the boundaries that are drawn by ink upon a map:- Frontiers traced by inks on other inks can be modified. It is quite another thing when the frontiers were traced by Providence.[14]

(b) Myth 2: Perfidious Albion again

The conventional nationalist complaint was that 'Providence [had] arranged the geography of Ireland' but that Lloyd George had 'changed it.'[15] De Valera often spoke in this sense[16] although he also claimed that were it not for the concentration of unionists in the north-east of the island, Britain could not have effected her purpose. At the start of his political career, his view was that Britain had deliberately fomented Partition, her motive being strategic security.[17] By 1939, de Valera suggested that he had never thought Britain 'wholly responsible' and to a heckler at that year's Ard Fheis, he replied that there was 'no use in saying this matter can be solved altogether with Britain. It cannot.'[18] He became appreciably more critical of Britain's responsibility in the wake of the 1949 Ireland Act, claiming that Westminster, which had created and maintained Partition, now intended to consolidate it. From 1921 it remained his fixed view that the problem could only be resolved in 'the larger general play of English interest',[19] and his own policy was invariably directed to London, not Belfast. He had little empathy with the Ulster unionists and this was reciprocated, the Unionist party monolith being implacably opposed to any thaw in north–south relations during de Valera's years in power. That hostility, combined with the latent Anglophobia of the Fianna Fail party, would have circumscribed de Valera's policy options had he wished to make serious overtures to the north. In general the emphasis he placed on Britain's culpability for Partition was not remarkable. Many others, under fewer pressures, did likewise.[20]

---

[14] SE: 22: 980, 7 Feb. 1939.   [15] Quoted, Mansergh (1965: 216–7).
[16] Heslinga (1962: 67).   [17] MacEntee (1975).
[18] SE: 22: 982, 7 Feb. 1939.   [19] Longford and O'Neill (1970: 123).
[20] For instance, (Eoin MacNeill) typescript, 'Memoirs dictated: 1932-3', McGilligan papers, P35/B/144; Mackenzie King, diary 9 June 1940, Mackenzie King papers, M.G. 26, J13, box 174, vol. 37.

(c) Myths 4, 5, 6: that Britain could effect Irish unity

Myths 4 and 6 are concerned with nationalist expectations of British policy; they suggest that a united, politically stable Ireland would result if only Britain used her available resources to coerce the Ulster unionists into acceptance of such an outcome. Pre-war, the British had claimed to be a disinterested party and this was repeatedly stressed to de Valera between 1932 and 1939.[21] De Valera, for his part, was again relatively moderate on this question: the purpose of the government's anti-Partition campaign in Britain, he told the Senate in 1939, was 'not to beg the British people to do anything in the way of coercing those in the north-east who do not want to come with us but to cease actively encouraging that section to keep out.'[22] He was not only opposed to the use of force by Irish nationalists to coerce Ulster, but rejected any use of force by Britain to compel the unionists into an allegiance which they did not voluntarily espouse. In fact, he suggested that he would fight alongside the Ulster unionists to resist any such coercion.[23] What de Valera expected of Britain was a public declaration of their commitment to Irish unity, the cessation of what he saw as the military coercion of the border nationalists, and the ending of British economic support for Partition. He told Cudahy that the northern economy could not survive the withdrawal of British economic support.[24] De Valera received his most sympathetic hearing in London during the Chamberlain–MacDonald era in Anglo-Irish relations in the late 1930s. Then, the Unionists' record on civil rights was questioned in Whitehall, where there was scant sympathy for special financial supports for Northern Ireland. As for Dublin's suggestion that Britain publicly declare her support for any united Ireland which might be agreed between north and south, MacDonald assiduously pressed for such a declaration from his colleagues during the 1938 negotiations, finally persuaded them to agree a draft being sent to Dublin, where it

[21] Harding, note of a discussion with Dulanty 19 Feb. 1934, PRO DO 35/398/11111A/55.

[22] SE: 22: 985-6; 7 Feb. 1939.

[23] Conference between representatives of UK and Eire, 17 Jan. 1938, PRO CAB 27/642, IN(38)1.

[24] Cudahy to SS, 4 Nov. 1938, NA, R.G. 59, 841D.01/161.

was considered to be unsatisfactory and was dropped because of the south's unwillingness to agree trade concessions to Northern Ireland in return. The declaration was no advance on what successive British ministers had privately insisted was the case, but it would have marked a serious reversal for the Ulster Unionists and a gain for Fianna Fail had the latter felt able to accept the terms on which it had been offered.

Not only was de Valera privately assured that the British government would 'welcome the ending of Partition' if he could secure the 'willing consent' of Northern Ireland[25] but, during this period, London specifically rejected Ulster Unionist suggestions that it would be 'most helpful' if Britain affirmed its positive commitment to Partition as an imperial interest. The Chamberlain administration rejected this as putting the British government 'in a position to which they have never aspired and do not aspire.'[26] Yet within ten years, Westminster, motivated by positive support for Northern Ireland, passed the Ireland Act of 1949, starkly revealing the deterioration in Dublin's bargaining position caused by wartime neutrality and the south's severing of the last link with the British Commonwealth. The switching of the veto on Irish unity from London to Belfast must have represented for de Valera the most serious reversal in his anti-Partition campaign. It was the 'contrary assertion' to that for which he had been patiently lobbying for the previous sixteen years.[27] In 1951 de Valera dismissed as 'political hypocrisy' attempts by London 'unctuously to suggest' that Irish unity depended on agreement between north and south.[28] Nevertheless, rejecting myth 6, de Valera did not believe that British military force could be used to effect a united Ireland.[29] Myth 5 suggests that if the British withdrew from Northern Ireland, unionist opposition to Dublin would fade, their second option being some form of Irish unity rather than a state centred on their own nationalism. This myth was widely believed in Fianna Fail.[30] De Valera while claiming that a British withdrawal

[25] Devonshire, note 21 Aug. 1938, PRO DO 35/893/X.11/234.
[26] See discussion of the Andrews/Chamberlain/Londonderry correspondence, pp. 196–7 above.
[27] DE: 115: 813, 10 May 1949.   [28] *Irish Press*, 15 Sept. 1951.
[29] Gray to Roosevelt, 28 June 1940, Roosevelt papers, PSF 56.
[30] Interviews, C. J. Haughey, Neil Blaney.

would be 'most persuasive' in bringing the Ulster unionists 'to a reasonable viewpoint',[31] was again comparatively realistic on this subject, since, more than most southern politicians he emphasized the intractability of Partition, and, as will be shown presently, warned of the probability of instability and anarchy in the north if the unity issue were forced.

(iii) DE VALERA'S ULSTER POLICY

(a) Unity — inevitable but postponable

The most widely accepted myth among Irish nationalists — myth 3 in this book — is that Partition cannot last since it is inherently absurd. Indeed de Valera suggested that 'all the misery of the intervening years' could be avoided if Ulster would accept the inevitability of unity.[32] It is also true that de Valera came to doubt this myth as he admitted in his last public speech in 1973,[33] but throughout his career the prevailing presumption in his speeches was that Partition could not be a permanent solution to the Ulster question.[34] Unity, however, along with being inevitable, was also postponable.[35]

If Fianna Fail supporters could not be told *when* to expect Irish unity, what did de Valera say on *how* Partition might be ended? In short, what was his Ulster policy? His central tenet was that any attempt to end Partition by force would fail. He had, in the 1917–18 period, threatened coercion against Ulster, but although these speeches were recalled by his political opponents in later years, they no longer represented de Valera's views.[36] His was not a pacifist position; if he thought force could unite the island, he would support it.[37] His essential strategy was to convert all Irish nationalists to his conviction that any attempt to unite the people of the island through the use of force would, not only, in all probability, fail, but

---

[31] Cudahy to SS, 24 Jan. 1938, NA, R.G. 59, 741.41D/51.
[32] DE: 147: 200, 28 Oct. 1954.   [33] *Irish Times*, 25 June 1973.
[34] He impressed this twice on Cudahy in the spring of 1938, Cudahy to SS, 28 Feb., NA, R.G. 59, 741.41D/60, ibid., 19 Mar. 1938, —/65.
[35] See speeches by de Valera, *Irish Press*, 12 Oct. 1944; by Aiken, ibid., 31 May 1938, 14 May 1949; by Derrig, DE: 68: 393, 14 June 1937.
[36] DE: 30: 878-81, 5 June 1929.
[37] Cudahy to SS, 14 Jan. 1938, NA, R.G. 59, 741.41D/48.

that even if it were to result in unity, this would be intrinsically unstable and probably transient. On hundreds of occasions he spelt out this fundamental belief.[38] In February 1939 after the outbreak of the IRA's bombing campaign in Britain, de Valera told the Senate that he considered the 1921 decision to rule out force as 'a wise one', adding that he had 'never retreated from that position in public yet nor in private.' However, he would, if he could see a way of doing it effectively, 'rescue' the border nationalists 'from the coercion which they are suffering at the present time.' But this, he added, would not solve the problem of Partition.[39] The conclusion which de Valera drew from this consideration of the use of force to annex border areas was probably his central motive for thus thinking aloud; the message that force might push the border northwards but not solve Partition may have been intended for those republicans then advocating the use of force to gain control of border areas.[40] There was some perplexity in the Dominions Office when de Valera made a similar speech at his first post-war Ard Fheis in 1945. But again, his purpose was pacific; any resort to force in such minority disputes, he concluded, would mean that 'civilisation, as we know it, will come to an end.'[41] Maffey's summary in 1946 was fair, that whereas de Valera's government was 'sane and sound' on the issue of force, the 'blood-sacrifice tradition in Ireland is strong.'[42]

Although opting for political rather than military means to undo Partition, it cannot be presumed that all members of Fianna Fail disapproved of force. As has been shown throughout this book, there were always some extremists in the party who advocated it and many more who would be reluctant to become Britain's 'policemen' in preventing the south being used by others as a safe haven.[43] The thrust of de Valera's

---

[38] This was also emphasized in Irish diplomatic lobbying, *aide-memoire* to O. D. Skelton, 22 Dec. 1939, Skelton papers, R.G. 25, vol. 781, file 398; Gray, 'Memorandum on the state of Ireland', 8 Sept. 1942, Roosevelt papers, PSF 56.

[39] SE: 22: 979–80, 7 Feb. 1939.

[40] Plan advocated by Tom Barry, ex-IRA leader, Coogan (1970: 116).

[41] Tory to Stephenson, 9 Nov. 1945, PRO DO 35/1228/W.X.101/106.

[42] Maffey, note of talk with de Valera 18 May 1946, PRO CAB 129/10, CP(46)212.

[43] DE: 273: 1613–14, 26 June 1974; interview Martin Corry, former Fianna Fail TD.

entire career was to discourage any resort to force. As he confided to Maffey, in July 1940 — 'with all emphasis', his government would never attack the north: 'No solution there can come by force. There we must wait and let the solution come with time and patience.'[44]

De Valera did share the conviction of nationalists that for as long as Partition remained, sporadic violence was inevitable. And he was willing to exploit this factor as a lever in attempting to erode British confidence in Partition. Occasionally, he seemed to use this argument in a threatening way but as his record in government shows, he was not only implacably opposed to the IRA, but specifically rejected in the thirties and again in the fifties their suggestions that his government could reap the political benefits of an IRA campaign which obliged the British to negotiate with Dublin on Irish unity. It remained his conviction that the political stability and strategic interests of the two islands would be best served by some amelioration of Partition, but although this strategic dimension remained a potential catalyst,[45] de Valera's attempts to link the defence and Partition issues in the 1938 negotiations proved unsuccessful and when Britain attempted to strike a bargain in June 1940, de Valera felt in no position to accept. This decision remained, for London, the test case of this question whenever it was considered after the war.

Although he was his own foreign minister throughout the 1932–48 period, diplomacy did not prove for de Valera a fruitful means of making progress on Partition. His most creative period in Anglo-Irish relations was from 1932 to 1939; his concentration was on issues other than Partition until the very close of this period, when, with republican extremists forcing him into a position of intransigence, he merely exacerbated an already hopeless situation. Thereafter, the war and the decline in his electoral fortunes which followed it, together with unsympathetic governments in London, precluded any useful attempts to make progress through

[44] Maffey to DO, 17 July 1940, PRO CAB 66/10 WP(40)274; Hempel to Foreign Ministry, 21 June 1940, *DGFP*: D: 9: doc. 506.

[45] That Britain was likely to subsidize Northern Ireland for as long as Irish defence policy was not 'closely co-ordinated with hers' was MacEntee's conclusion after fifty years in anti-Partition politics, *Irish Press*, 20 Jan. 1970.

diplomacy. One of the most senior Irish diplomats with long experience of de Valera's attempts to interest London in the issue concluded that de Valera's error was that he believed that Partition 'could be solved by logical argument'.[46]

Although always a believer in propaganda, it was not until after the war and in particular his loss of power in 1948 that de Valera decided fully to explore the potential of this approach. It, too, proved futile: no worse moment could have been chosen to attempt to interest the world in what were, relatively, the insignificant grievances of the northern minority.[47]

Yet another approach which proved unavailing was Fianna Fail's protectionist economic policy. This had enough leverage to alienate the unionists but not sufficient to divide their ranks or oblige them to prefer unity.

One faction within Fianna Fail, of whom Lemass seems to have been the earliest and strongest proponent, advocated functional co-operation with the north as useful in itself and at least not harmful to the anti-Partitionist cause. Although there was greater emphasis on this policy in the Lemass years, some progress was also made by de Valera.[48]

Compared with his successors as leader of Fianna Fail, de Valera placed great emphasis on the injustice of the boundary *as drawn*. This may have hidden a personal conviction on his part that a readjustment of the border, while not a solution, would have represented an improvement. This was a point on which there were genuine differences between nationalists. One school believed that the 'absurd and ridiculous' border was 'better a hundred-fold' than 'an effective and workable one';[49] de Valera, on the other hand, laid such stress on how truncated the northern state would be if there were to be a plebiscite among border nationalists that he was sometimes

---

[46] Confidential source.

[47] This did not deter nationalist propagandists, some of whom even compared the fate of northern nationalists to that of 'the Jews in Hitler's Germany', Henry Harrison, leaflet 'The Ireland Bill: one amendment obviously indispensable', Henry Harrison papers, 8,755(2).

[48] *Irish Press*, 23 Nov. 1955; Longford and O'Neill (1970: 471).

[49] O'Shiel to cabinet (Nov. 1922), Mulcahy papers, P7/B/288.

presumed to be calling for a redrawing of the boundary.[50] His
private conversations reveal him as wavering on this question.
In January 1938, Cudahy records him as having 'no desire to
coerce anybody' and of being willing to accept a fair referendum to determine the boundary:

> He said he would be entirely satisfied if these north counties, which he
> seemed sanguine would express their desire to become a part of Ireland,
> were allowed to do so, voicing the thought that the remaining counties
> could not, during the course of time, resist the majority of the Irish
> people.[51]

Yet some months later, Chamberlain records him as not seeking
any readjustment of the border,[52] and, by 1940, Downing
Street believed that 'all the information' suggested that de
Valera 'would not in any way be satisfied by a suggestion
that the boundary should be revised; nothing less than the
whole would content him finally.'[53]

(b) De Valera's federal policy

From early in 1921, de Valera had advocated a federal solution
to the Ulster question. His political difficulty was not in
selling this to the Ulster Unionists — they had no interest
whatever — but in convincing his supporters that local autonomy and external association were consistent with the proclaimed goals of republicans at Easter 1916. To rally support
for a unitary republic was a simpler proposition than to
persuade those opposed to the Treaty to believe that their
forlorn sacrifices in the Civil War had been in defence of
Document No. 2. Yet this, in fact, was de Valera's programme
and, indeed, with the establishment of Fianna Fail, his achievement. At the conclusion of the Civil War, in a letter of clarification to the *Irish Independent*, he again put on record his
proposed federal solution to the Ulster question. This had the
effect of reminding the defeated republicans of some of the
'small print' in what de Valera hoped would once again
become their political programme. That he forwarded a copy

[50] DE: 109: 1-6, 26 Nov. 1947.
[51] Cudahy to SS, 14 Jan. 1938, NA, R.G. 59, 741.41D/48.
[52] Chamberlain, note of talk with de Valera 4 Oct. 1938, PRO DO 35/893/
X.11/247.
[53] J. J. Garner to J. Peck, 22 Nov. 1940, PRO PREM 4/53/6.

to McGarrity in American was a further indication of the essential importance he attached to keeping his political programme before those whose proclaimed intention was to revert to force at the first opportunity.

In his letter to the *Independent*, de Valera stressed what the republican cabinet of 1921 had agreed as their Ulster policy: in 'an earnest desire to be just and fair', they had proposed

> that the fullest measure of local autonomy consistent with the unity of Ireland as a whole should be granted to the aggregate of those areas in which by a majority vote the residents demanded a separate Parliament. We were prepared to take as the unit of area for the plebiscite either the constituencies prior to the Act of 1920, or any smaller unit, such as the Poor Law Guardian or the District Council areas.
>
> By that proposal, Derry City and the greater parts of the Counties of Tyrone and Fermanagh, as well as South Armagh and South Down, would be represented directly in the National Parliament.

On no plea, added de Valera, could the Ulster unionists 'demand anything more'.[54] But by 1938 more was being offered, when, in his final version of the federal solution, he envisaged local autonomy being devolved to a Belfast parliament controlling all six counties. Such a concession was not popular with all northern nationalists. Healy believed de Valera had gone 'to the limit';[55] there was republican dissent too, MacSwiney believing it was yet another inadmissable compromise.[56] This federal policy was constantly rejected by the Unionists — which may indeed have rendered it all the more tolerable to his party — and de Valera never succeeded in even placing it on the agenda in any Anglo-Irish talks. In F. H. Boland's view this federal offer had another purpose; he believed that de Valera had come to the conclusion that there was 'no chance' of unity 'without a fight and that he certainly didn't want'; his federal offer was 'a prophylaxis against a clash'.[57]

Another factor may here be considered. De Valera had a missionary zeal to effect fundamental societal changes in

[54] De Valera to editor, *Irish Independent*, typescript copy, 20 July 1923, McGarrity papers, MS 18,375(10).
[55] NIHC: 32: 3649; 30 Nov. 1948.
[56] MacSwiney to Cardinal MacRory, 27 June 1940, MacSwiney papers, P48/C/32.
[57] Interview, F. H. Boland.

Ireland. That not all members of his governments shared his vision of an ideal Ireland is manifest from their testimony and indeed his.[58] In February 1939, for instance, he told the Senate that he was speaking for himself when he said that he would 'not tomorrow for the sake of a united Ireland give up the policy of trying to make this a really Irish-Ireland — not by any means.' He instanced the language restoration policy as one which he would not abandon even if that resulted in a united Ireland:

I do not know how many would agree with me. I would say no, and I would say it for this reason: that I believe that as long as the language remains you have a distinguishing characteristic of nationality which will enable the nation to persist. If you lose the language the danger is that there would be absorption.[59]

Although his twenty-six-county emphasis can be understood in terms of making the best of his limited political options, given his overall 'Irish-Ireland' goal, his speeches would also be consistent with a belief that a federal solution with local autonomy for Ulster was preferable as an interim measure, to a unitary state in which his emphasis on Gaelic, Catholic, and republican values would prove unacceptable. His belief was that the restoration of the language was the most urgent political priority; his claim that, once restored, it would cross the border, indicates that the assimilation of the Ulster unionists was his ultimate ideal. Unionists however, had no wish to 'live in a so-called paradise',[60] seeing the south's language policy as 'a sort of awful insanity'.[61] Longford and O'Neill record de Valera, at the end of his life, as having

no fear that his dream of restoring Irish would run counter in any way to his other dream — the reuniting of the country. His view would be that the Northern Unionists were, at bottom, proud of being Irish; that the history, tradition and culture of the historic Irish nation could not fail to attract them.[62]

In short, de Valera's avowed *state-idea*, the establishment of an Irish-speaking, autarkical, neutral, independent, united

[58] MacEntee, *Irish Times*, 19 May 1976.
[59] SE: 22: 988-9, 7 Feb. 1939.   [60] *The Times*, 18 Mar. 1947.
[61] Hugh Shearman, *Anglo-Irish relations* (London: 1948), p. 241.
[62] Longford and O'Neill (1970: 459-60).

Ireland was an implausible scenario from the outset; but even he must have appreciated that its chances of being realized were greater if it were to be attempted in two stages.[63] In February 1940 he claimed that as long as 'they had five-sixths of the national territory and three-quarters of the Irish nation safe, they had a seed from which unity must grow.'[64] In his last election campaign in 1957 he claimed that if 'we make sure that this five-sixths is made really Irish we will have the preservation of the Irish nation in our hands. Time will settle the other thing';[65] and after he had retired from party politics, he claimed that 'France was France without Alsace and Lorraine . . . Ireland is Ireland without the North.'[66]

(c) No solution?

Another dimension to de Valera's approach to Partition was an emphasis on opportunism. Gallagher outlined de Valera's duty as preparing for the disappearance of Partition 'which he must be ever ready to aid when the right moment comes and the right combination of circumstances arises'.[67] In 1951 de Valera told the Dail that 'circumstances may come our way again — we cannot create them, we can only avail of them'.[68] In 1938 he told the Senate that in the consideration of political choices, he had always posed one question to himself: 'Are we making towards ultimately having one State — one national State, or not? Are the things that we are doing going ultimately to mean a national State or not?'[69] He was also on record as never having believed in a 'policy of trying to coax' the Ulster unionists. They deserved justice, but no special privileges and he claimed in 1938 that a policy based on their conversion was likely to succeed.[70] Stressing that all in the south were agreed on the desirability of unity, de Valera told the Ard Fheis that year:

[63] Sterling to SS, 27 May 1933, NA, R.G. 59, 841.00/1029; Owsley to SS, 7 July 1936, ibid., 841D. 00/1103.
[64] *Irish Press*, 19 Feb. 1940.
[65] Ibid., 5 Mar. 1957.
[66] Interview, *New York Times*, 1963, reprinted, *Profile*, May 1973.
[67] Gallagher papers, MS 18,375(3).
[68] DE: 126: 2022, 19 July 1951.
[69] SE: 22: 978, 7 Feb. 1939.   [70] *Irish Press*, 7 June 1938.

We have a third of the people in the six counties with us. The difference between one third and one half is only one sixth, so that if we win one sixth of the population in that area we will have a majority there.

When we have that majority we can listen to people talking about plebiscites. I believe it will not take long to get that majority.[71]

This claim must be considered in the context of the higher birth-rate among the north's Roman Catholics. Even Unionists acknowledged that their future hegemony was insecure in this respect. As Maffey put it to London in 1945, the Unionists were 'fighting an insidious enemy who is gaining upon them. Their ballot box is not safe over a period against the Catholic birth-rate.'[72] De Valera shared this belief; he stated in a news agency interview in 1939 that 'We shall have to let time and the natural forces do their work',[73] and he confided to an American diplomat during the war that Partition 'would be solved by the natural increase of the Catholics . . . who would, at a propitious time, call for a plebiscite to end partition and British occupation in the North.'[74]

An associated fear for unionists was that migrant workers from the south would in time become residents and then voters.[75] There is also some evidence that northern nationalists attempted systematically to organize the financing of land purchase schemes whereby Catholics could borrow finance to enable them to buy Protestant farms. Although attempts may have been made to interest the Dublin government in supporting such schemes, there is no evidence that this was tried on any substantial scale.[76] However, any hopes of an anti-Partition majority within Northern Ireland, whether through 'peaceful penetration' from the south, the purchase of Protestant farms, the higher Catholic birth-rate, or the conversion of unionists, proved ill-founded.

Given how fundamental the expectation of unity was to Fianna Fail supporters, it is not surprising that, with so little progress to report, de Valera placed such emphasis on the

[71] Ibid., 24 Nov. 1938.

[72] Maffey, 'The Irish Question in 1945', 21 Aug. 1945, PRO CAB 129/2 CP (45) 152 annex I.

[73] Typescript, Associated Press, interview 17 Mar. (1939).

[74] See Carter (1977: 68).   [75] *Irish News*, editorials 4 and 20 May 1937.

[76] See Healy papers, D2991/A/148.

inevitability of unity: Partition, being 'inherently absurd' could not last; it was 'on a rotten foundation and it will totter and end.' Nationalists needed merely to make up their minds 'to make the proper assault'.[77] De Valera, however, never spelt out what he believed the 'proper assault' to be. Although never admitting that the problem was insoluble, he did accept that Fianna Fail, in the absence of any help from London and Belfast, had no solution.[78] During the post-war election campaigns, in his last address to the Dail on the Taoiseach's estimate, and in his last speech on Partition to the Ard Fheis, he repeated that he could make no promises on unity, adding that 'nobody else in this country can.'[79] Nor was this merely a pessimism which derived from three decades of failure on the issue. To the 1931 Ard Fheis — before Fianna Fail had ever reached office — he had attempted to dampen expectations by insisting that it was not possible to show how Partition could be ended.[80]

On his retirement from party politics at the close of the 1950s, he could point to no success in what had been over forty years of political opposition to Partition: diplomacy, propaganda, economic coercion had all proved unavailing. Nor did the south prove to be the political or economic utopia which he had sometimes predicted would attract sufficient unionists to create a northern majority against Partition. In fact — as had so often been predicted by northern-born members of Fianna Fail — conversions in the north were from nationalist to unionist ranks, many of them presumably due to the economic attractions of the north's membership of the United Kingdom. Far from undermining Partition, de Valera's years in politics marked its entrenchment.[81] Positively, in Fianna Fail's book, he had undone the Treaty settlement and through Articles 2 and 3 formally disputed the south's acceptance of the boundary in 1925. He had indeed 'subverted the Free State' as was Fianna Fail's initial purpose,[82] but the

[77] Interview, *New York Times*, reported *Irish Press* 20 Mar. 1940; *Irish Press*, 23 June 1948.   [78] Cudahy to SS, 31 Jan. 1938, NA, R.G. 59, 741.41D/54.
[79] *Irish Press*, 30 May 1951; ibid., 20 Nov. 1957; DE: 170: 1072, 17 July 1958.
[80] *Irish Press*, 28 Oct. 1931.
[81] Once boundaries are established, no matter how arbitrary they may be, they tend to 'harden', Mitchel (1971: 58), Orme (1970: 249-50).
[82] Interview, Kevin Boland.

Republic which had finally resulted was confined to twenty-six counties with less support than ever within Northern Ireland for Irish unity.

(iv) RESPONSIBLE 'IN ANY WAY AT ALL'?

(a) ' . . . inside a temperamentally different state'

De Valera's biographers state that after the Civil War, the 'lack of progress towards Irish unity was . . . the great tragedy in his political life'. It would, however, they add, 'be grossly and manifestly unfair to hold him responsible in any way at all for the continuance of partition.'[83] One of his most senior political colleagues, MacEntee, retrospectively took a more critical view of Fianna Fail's approach to Partition. Although he credits de Valera with being 'a great man, a Moses even, who led a small people out of bondage',[84] he also accepted that the south's approach to the Partition issue had been a failure. Writing in January 1970 he admitted:

We elders have failed to find a solution for the problem; and after fifty years we may be forgiven for thinking that perhaps we went the wrong way about it. Maybe we were too rigid in our approach, too tenacious of our own point of view, too proud to temporise or placate. Whatever may have been the reason, we made no headway; so our successors must start from 'square one'.[85]

Whereas MacEntee is prepared to admit that his generation of politicians was unrealistic in its approach, opposition politicians tend to reserve this criticism for de Valera.[86] Dillon's verdict is that he was 'quite remote from reality . . . his mind was quite closed' on the Partition issue; in MacDermot's view, on this central goal in his career, he achieved 'nothing'.[87] It is true that, judged from his public record, de Valera's lack of understanding of the Ulster unionists seems manifest, but privately he is recorded as having a more sophisticated view. His experience at the League of Nations, he confided to

---

[83] Longford and O'Neill (1970: 470)   [84] MacEntee (1975).
[85] *Irish Press*, 22 Jan. 1970.
[86] Interview, Patrick McGilligan; John Kelly, 'FF on the North: crooked talk on a breathtaking scale', *Hibernia*, 4 Oct. 1979.
[87] Interviews, James Dillon, Frank MacDermot.

Devonshire, had 'taught him how stubborn and difficult this minority problem was, and that it needed endless patience and goodwill to deal with it.'[88] More revealingly, in December 1939, Gallagher recorded de Valera's analysis of the Ulster question:

Discussed Partition with the Chief and what makes it so grievous a wound. He felt that the thing that made the deepest wound was not the division of a territory but the separation of the people — the division of the personnel of the nation.

Gallagher then added a recollection of an earlier conversation in which de Valera had outlined his perception of the Ulster unionist viewpoint:

the problem . . . was on[e] of a group now in power fearing to become a minority inside a temperamentally different state. That was the essence of the persistence of Partition and it should be approached from that point of view.[89]

Given these insights, how does one explain the *naivete* of de Valera's scenario for his 'ideal Ireland'? He can scarcely have believed that the Ulster unionists, already alienated by the 'temperamentally different state' which he had inherited from Cosgrave, could be coaxed into accepting the even more alien Ireland he was determined to shape. There was, of course, a minimum republican core of Fianna Fail's programme which was non-negotiable. Unless de Valera achieved or continued to aspire to these goals, he could not sustain his support or satisfy his own conscience. Already, with local autonomy and external association, he was straining both; in these policy areas, given his commitments, he had no option but to pursue his programme of substituting Document No. 2 for the Treaty. But what was also true, was that there were optional 'extras' in de Valera's programme to which he was personally committed, but to which many of his cabinet colleagues and voters were indifferent, ambivalent, or hostile, and which served

---

[88] Devonshire, note 4 Oct. 1938, PRO DO 35/893/X.11/247.

[89] Gallagher, note 20 Dec. 1939, of two conversations with de Valera, Gallagher papers, MS 18,375 (11). De Valera claimed, as early as the summer of 1921, that within his cabinet 'the political conditions in Antrim' were 'understood and sympathized with'. De Valera, holograph notes, Kathleen Napoli McKenna papers, MS 22,608.

further to alienate the Ulster unionists. Examples would include the priority he gave to the restoration of the Irish language, his extraordinary reference in a Constitution avowedly shaped for a united Ireland to the 'special position' of the Catholic Church, and his protectionist economic policies. The point is, perhaps, best made by comparing his approach to all of these questions with that of his successor as Fianna Fail leader, Lemass. Moreover, de Valera's ideal Ireland proved not to be feasible even south of the border which is an indication of how unrealistic it was as a long-term programme for the entire island. There is indirect evidence that at the end of his life, de Valera may have been conscious of this failure.[90]

Cobban's verdict seems fair when he suggests that 'the gulf dug between the Ulster Orangemen and Eire became almost impassable after the treaty, though not necessarily as a result of it.' He suggests that de Valera's decision to opt for 'a uni-national state' inevitably resulted in Partition being entrenched.[91] However conciliatory and generous de Valera believed his policy towards the Ulster unionists to be, they perceived him as belonging to what Herz epitomizes as 'the exclusivist, xenophobic, expansionist, oppressive' school of nationalists.[92] However overstated this might be, the significant point is that it was the unionist *perception* of de Valera.[93]

(b) Who are the Irish?

Pre-Treaty alone, the futures which de Valera envisaged for the Ulster unionists included expulsion, coercion, assimilation, accommodation and even, briefly in August 1921, self-determination, based on the right of counties to opt for exclusion from the republic.[94] His biographers assert, in a

[90] Rita Childers, letter *Irish Times*, 29 Jan. 1981.

[91] Cobban (1969: 164).

[92] John H. Herz, 'The territorial state revisited: reflections on the future of the nation-state', reprinted J. N. Rosenau, *International politics and foreign policy* (New York: 1969 edn.), p. 89.

[93] David Harkness, 'Unionist reaction: bitterness and hostility', *Irish Times*, 19 May 1976.

[94] See pp. 30–56 *passim*, above.

concluding chapter obviously based on interviews with their subject, that de Valera 'has given conclusive proof by his actions and by his public assertion that to him a Northern Irishman is as Irish as one from any other part of Ireland.'[95] This may represent de Valera's preferred rationalization at the end of his career, but it is an incomplete and misleading summary of his position. He is indeed on record as saying that the Ulster unionists were 'fundamentally Irish'[96] and that 'no matter how the world goes, these people and ourselves are going to live on one island here.'[97] However, his deepest belief was that Ulster unionists were only entitled to remain in Ireland on the condition that they renounced their unionism and opted for Irish citizenship. Consistently he argued in this sense, suggesting to the 1939 Ard Fheis that a sponsored scheme of population exchange between the emigrant Irish in Britain and Ulster unionists would, while costly, prove worth while in the long term.[98] In 1943 he told the American Minister, Gray, that a statesmanlike settlement was available '"especially since the precedent for the exchange of populations has been established."'[99] After the war, de Valera repeatedly suggested that the eventual choice for the unionists was either assimilation or emigration with compensation.[1] Later as President, after he had retired from party politics, he told the *New York Times* that if 'in the North there are people who spiritually want to be English [*sic*] rather than Irish, they can go and we will see that they get the adequate, right compensation for their property.'[2] The historian, David Harkness, questioned de Valera on this issue in 1964. He asked if it were his view that the north should for 'the sake of cartographical tidiness, be annexed, or forcibly expelled or forcibly integrated or destroyed, or could it be persuaded of the error of its assumptions and led willingly back to its national

[95] Longford and O'Neill (1970: 471).
[96] *Irish Press*, 13 Oct. 1954.   [97] DE: 126: 2027; 19 July 1951.
[98] *Irish Press*, 14 Dec. 1939.
[99] It was Gray's impression that de Valera had in mind the exchange of populations between Greece and Turkey after the First World War, Gray, memorandum on the Irish situation August 1943, NA, R.G. 59, 841D.00/8-1843.
[1] Speech to Massachusetts State Legislature, 'With de Valera in America and Australia: world appeal against Partition', *Irish Press* (Dublin, 1948); *Irish Press*, 23 June 1948; ibid., 19 Mar. 1951.
[2] Interview, *New York Times*, 1962, reprinted *Profile*, May 1973.

membership?' To de Valera, notes Harkness, 'at least in retrospect, the analogy of Cyprus, as it was in the early sixties,
was a helpful analogy'. His belief was that the minority citizen,
be he Turk or Ulster Unionist, 'must decide his priority: land
or allegiance. If the former was more important, then he
must accept subjection to the political will of the majority of
the island; if being Turkish or British was the more important,
then he should return forthwith to the favoured country,
Turkey or Britain. The matter was as cut and dried as that.'
None of this endeared de Valera to the north. In Harkness's
view the Ulster unionists perceived him as a man 'deluded by
notions of British interest' and unaware of how, to them, his
policy was 'unattractively Catholic, unpalatably anti-British,
of unproven political stability and of uncertain economic
viability.'[3]

Moreover, the unionists recognized all too clearly the
ratchet effect — not surprisingly, since they were its intended
victims. De Valera's offer of October 1938, for instance, was
characterized by Craigavon as yet another example of a further
demand from the south 'before the ink [was] dry' on the
Anglo-Irish Agreement of April;[4] and the south's neutrality
was, for Craigavon, the 'culminating point' in the policy of
accepting 'concession after concession' from London, a *'process* which we have foreseen in the North for the past forty
years.'[5] Unionists would have agreed with Dillon's summary
of Fianna Fail's policy that once they 'deluthered' the north
into accepting unity, they would then put them 'in a republican
pocket'.[6] Indeed in his *Evening Standard* interview of October
1938 at which he outlined his federal policy de Valera was
questioned specifically on the ratchet effect. He was asked if
the Ulster unionists could rely on not being victims of a subsequent unilateral initiative, if they were to accept his terms.
He replied that he could not 'guarantee all the tomorrows to
come'.[7] Given such an approach, it is little surprise that the
Unionists never revised Craigavon's initial verdict on de Valera's

---

[3] As note 93 above.   [4] Interview, *Sunday Dispatch*, 23 Oct. 1938.
[5] Lady Craigavon, diary 15 Nov. 1940.   [6] DE: 56: 2192; 4 June 1935.
[7] *Keesing's Contemporary Archives*, 16–17 Oct. 1938, p. 3282; this quotation
is not included in De Valera: speeches: 1980: 358–62, where de Valera is quoted
as saying 'We can deal only with probabilities. I cannot say what the future may
bring.'

attaining power in 1932: 'There is now no question. De Valera has forever destroyed any hopes of a united Ireland.'[8] Whereas de Valera's expulsion with compensation solution is not remembered within the Fianna Fail party, it has been recalled by Ulster loyalists. In May 1981 Ian Paisley stated: 'De Valera made it clear. He meant that all the Protestants that wanted the British connection should get off this island. We're not getting off this island.'[9]

Some political philosophers commenting on the problems posed by minorities have adverted to de Valera's approach to the Ulster unionist minority within Ireland. Field notes that the Irish

refuse to recognise the right of Northern Ireland to vote itself out of the Irish Republic. Mr de Valera is reported as saying in that connection, 'self-determination only applies to nationalities'. He did not explain what practical criterion of nationality there can be except self-determination.

Field understands how 'people belong to a particular nationality because they think they do', but difficult to understand how it can be maintained that 'they belong because someone else thinks they ought to.'[10] A similar point is made by Crick with his dismissal of 'objective criteria to coerce the unilluminated'.[11] Popper suggests that the 'utter absurdity' of the theory of self-determination

must be plain to anybody who devotes a moment's effort to criticizing it. The principle amounts to the demand that each state should be a nation-state: that it should be confined within the natural border, and that this border should coincide with the location of an ethnic group; so that it should be the ethnic group, the 'nation', which should determine and protect the natural limits of the state.

But, argues Popper, 'nation-states of this kind do not exist'; and this is so because 'the so-called "nations" or "peoples" of which the nationalists dream do not exist. There are no, or hardly any, homogeneous ethnic groups long settled in countries with natural borders.' Popper cites the Irish case among examples where the principle of national self-determination

[8] Quoted by Harkness, *Irish Times*, 19 May 1976.
[9] 'Ulster Decides', *Ulster Television*, 18 May 1981.
[10] G. C. Field, *Political theory* (London: 1955), p. 246.
[11] Crick (1964: 77).

has failed. As ethnic minorities are found everywhere, Popper believes that 'the proper aim cannot be to "liberate" all of them; rather, it must be to protect all of them. The oppression of national groups is a great evil; but national self-determination is not a feasible remedy.'[12]

The self-determination principle could not be applied to Ireland *simpliciter*, as de Valera advocated in the United States in 1919–20.[13] The problem in Ireland was that geography determined the putative boundaries of the state while the self-determining majority, by, and for whom, the state was to be created, was not coterminous with the geographical island. This left the custodians of the putative united republic — of whom de Valera was the leading figure in his generation — with a virtually insoluble problem.

However, no matter how inadmissible the natural boundary theory might be to political geographers, they do accept its importance when believed: 'If a people believes in "natural" boundaries, and ascribes to certain features of the physical environment a mystical, irrational function, then this belief becomes an unshakeable basis for national action.'[14] Pounds concludes that

if any principle governing the size of states emerges, it is that they are — or try to be — at least as large as the nations which form them. If a state falls short, and part of its nation lies beyond its borders, it is likely to have an irredentist policy. Since the primary objective of a state is to preserve its own culture and traditions, such aims, pursued with whatever means the state has at its command, must be regarded as normal.[15]

Given the significant nationalist minority contiguous to the border, an irredentist lobby was inevitable in the south. The complicating factor was the fact that the coveted territory included almost one million unionists with no desire to be redeemed.

---

[12] Karl Popper, 'The history of our time: an optimist's view', in *Conjectures and refutations* (London: 1963), p. 368.
[13] Cobban (1969: *passim*, especially, 137, 163–5).
[14] Cohen (1964: 191).
[15] Pounds (1972: 40).

(c) Aspirational politics

Must de Valera's anti-Partitionism be seen then, as merely an example of Frankel's aspirational politics? Was not Irish unity, to de Valera, a long-term aspiration, 'rooted in history', of particular concern to the party extremists, providing purpose, or direction, or 'a sense of hope'; perhaps, even a response to the powerlessness of the south on the issue, an 'escape into day-dreams'?[16] The historian, David Miller, suggested that a great many southern voters took solace from the south's constitutional claim on the north: they 'no longer want the North actually to be incorporated in their country, but . . . still want the law to say that it should be'. For many people in various societies, writes Miller, the law 'symbolically enshrines what ought to be.'[17] Conor Cruise O'Brien, suggests the term 'low intensity aspirations' to describe attitudes south of the border towards unity: 'the aspiration is there: diffuse, elusive, persistent, cryptic, lightly pervasive, a chronic mist.'[18]

That at government level there was an element of hypocrisy concerning unity was asserted by a former British Ambassador to Dublin, Andrew Gilchrist. Perhaps reflecting the London view of the south's irredentist stance, Gilchrist concluded that 'the policy of both Dublin and London is founded on hypocrisy.' Why not? A well understood hypocrisy . . . is a normal aspect of political life; and the demand for Irish unity falls into this category.' Dublin's passionate commitment to Irish unity, was, he argued, 'a mere bogey. Any Irish Government is inescapably the custodian of a myth . . . and the maintenance of the myth, in however tepid a form, is probably helpful rather than otherwise and is in any case unavoidable.'[19]

---

[16] Frankel (1970: 32-3); see pp. 107-8 above.

[17] *Fortnight*, Nov. 1975.

[18] Conor Cruise O'Brien, *The Crane Bag*, vol. 1, no. 2, 1977. Conor Cruise O'Brien (1917-   ), diplomat, writer, historian, journalist, politician; as civil servant involved in south's anti-Partition propaganda, 1949-51; Labour TD, 1969-77; Minister for Posts and Telegraphs, 1973-7; Editor-in-chief, *Observer*, 1978-81; revisionist historian of Irish nationalism; critic of south's unity policy as naive, counterproductive, and an encouragement to the IRA.

[19] Letter, *The Times*, 28 Sept. 1977. Sir Andrew Gilchrist was British Ambassador in Dublin, 1967-70.

(v) DE VALERA'S LEGACY

(a) *Articles 2 and 3*

Articles 2 and 3 of the 1937 Constitution represent de Valera's most formal legacy on the Partition issue. To the fundamentalists within Fianna Fail, these Articles remained sacrosanct, although, as will be shown presently, significant revision of Article 3 was tolerable to senior members of the party during the quiescent decade of the 1960s, when the Partition issue faded,[20] and Lemass's imprint was most deeply felt on the party's anti-Partition strategy.[21] Although de Valera's successors as Fianna Fail leader would always claim that their policies were consistent with the de Valera orthodoxies,[22] there was now no pretence that his Constitution would be suited to a united country. Indeed, it became virtually axiomatic for those advocating constitutional reforms in the sixties and seventies to cite the need to appease the northern Protestants as the appropriate grounds on which to justify change. Some evidence of this approach can also be seen in the report of the 1967 Committee on the Constitution.[23] Initiated by Lemass, who, after his retirement from the party leadership, himself served on this Committee, its recommendation of a change in Article 3 shocked at least Kevin Boland, who saw himself as one of a dwindling group within Fianna Fail who were faithful to the original core of republican doctrine.[24]

---

[20] Lyons (1971: 577); Basil Chubb, *The government and politics of Ireland* (Oxford: 1970), pp. 48-9; Patrick Gormley MP, *Sunday Press*, 31 May 1964.

[21] J. J. Lee, 'Lemass and his two partnerships', *Irish Times*, 19 May 1976, interview, Sean Lemass; interview, Michael McInerney.

[22] 'Following in Dev's footsteps: the north: Haughey takes up the torch', *Donegal election special*, Fianna Fail, Nov. 1980. Biographical notes on de Valera's successors as Fianna Fail leader are on p. 7, no. 30 above.

[23] *Report of the Committee on the Constitution, December 1967* (Dublin: 1967).

[24] Kevin Boland, *'We won't stand (idly) by'*, (Dublin: (1974)), ch. 4 *passim*. Kevin Boland (1917-) TD and member of Fianna Fail governments 1957-70; acerbic critic of Fianna Fail's northern policy since 1969; in 1970-1, resigned from government, Dail and party, in protest against what he believed was the party's apostasy towards northern nationalists and its hypocrisy in being content with its success in a partitioned Ireland; his alternative constitutional republican party, Aontacht Eireann (1971-6) failed to supplant Fianna Fail. Only member of

The working papers of the Committee reveal that a sceptical approach to Article 3 was invited from the outset: a composite list of suggested amendments circulated to each member and used as the basis for discussion, assumed that Article 3 had been naïvely drafted and had proved counter-productive. The drafters of the Article in 1937 were excused on the grounds that to that generation Partition may have seemed 'provisional'; but, by 1967, it was argued, 'so far from looking provisional', Partition had 'hardened to a degree which only the vaguest of optimists can think of as temporary.' The commentary added: 'Where the fault lies for this we need not enquire.'[25]

If the commentary was diplomatic — it was known to have originated from within Fine Gael[26] — it was also pessimistic. The 'only hope — and it is a slim one — of achieving Irish unity' was thought to lie 'in mutual tolerance and a better understanding by each side of the other's aspirations and convictions.' Were not Articles 2 and 3 'too polemical', presenting as 'legalistic claims of right' what, to any outsider, 'would seem highly intricate and doubtful'? Whereas it was not suggested that the legitimate aspiration to unity ought to be renounced,

there ought to be nothing disgraceful in making a gesture to North-South ecumenism by deleting from Article 3 the words "and without prejudice to the right of the Parliament and Government established by this Constitution to exercise jurisdiction over the whole of that territory (the island of Ireland).

Apart from the possible gain in goodwill, the commentary concluded, 'the lack of realism in these words which the experience of the last 45 years has made patent ought to justify their disappearance.'[27] As can be seen from the initial draft of the report, the 'careful consideration' given to Article 3 by the Committee was due to the fact that 'it has been the cause of some friction in North/South relations. Without in any way relinquishing our right to re-integration of the

---

a de Valera government to write memoirs covering Fianna Fail affairs; book cited this reference, and '*Up Dev!*' (Dublin: 1977).

[25] Typescript, 'Composite list of possible changes in Constitution', circulated to the Committee, March 1967. This account is based on a complete file of the minutes and working papers of the committee, confidential source.

[26] Interview, John M. Kelly.   [27] As note 25 above.

national territory, we feel that it would now be appropriate to adopt a new provision to replace Article 3.'[28] With these prefatory remarks omitted from the published report, the Committee recommended changing the wording to read as follows: 'The Irish nation hereby proclaims its firm will that its territory be re-united in harmony and brotherly affection between all Irishmen.'[29] Boland, then a member of Lynch's government, was astonished by this suggestion believing it to be 'the first formal public indication' of Fianna Fail's 'departure from Republican principles'.[30] However, his attempts to exonerate Lemass, while castigating all of his other former colleagues, for signing the completed report is not only unconvincing, but, from the working papers of the Committee, unsustainable.[31] The report was not acted upon, the defenders of de Valera's original wording treating it dismissively: 'It was just published and left there.'[32] Moreover, such 'heresies' as were in the report were presumed to have damaged the party leadership prospects of Colley, the Committee's chairman.[33]

Soon, the entire context of the Partition question was to alter. This was initiated by a significant change of strategy in the late 1960s by northern nationalists. Declaring Partition to be a non-issue, they demanded full civil rights within the United Kingdom. The Unionists' 'too little, too late' response, the continuing civil disturbances, the emergence of the Provisional IRA, and the failure of successive political and security policies to restore stability, led to the proroguement of the Northern Ireland parliament and the implementation of direct rule from London in 1972. All of these developments had their repercussions in southern politics and, most particularly, within Fianna Fail. Two senior Fianna Fail ministers were dismissed by Lynch in May 1970 because of his suspicion that they had been involved in an attempt illegally to import arms for the defence of northern nationalists. The trial, and acquittal, of one ex-minister, Haughey — by 1979 to be Lynch's successor as leader of the party — had a traumatic

---

[28] Preliminary draft of committee's report, confidential source.
[29] As note 23 above.   [30] Boland (1974: 29).
[31] Committee's minutes and working papers, *passim*, confidential source.
[32] Haughey, press conference, Dublin, 7 Nov. 1981, questioned by author.
[33] See Colley's comments, DE: 269: 218–19, 21 Nov. 1973; letter, *Irish Times*, 8 Feb. 1977.

effect within the party. It is beyond the scope of this work to detail this impact but two points can be made: first, de Valera — still President when the crisis broke — again displayed caution and probity when attempts were made to involve him;[34] second, as the instability of Northern Ireland became more manifest and the call for a British withdrawal gained public and political support in Britain, the pull of orthodox separatism became irresistible within Fianna Fail.[35]

The quickening of expectations within the south focused further attention on de Valera's Constitution. Lynch, the third leader of the party, insisted in 1972 that the Constitution was 'not suitable for a new Ireland' and allowed that its critics were fair in seeing it as 'narrower and less generous' than the original principles of Irish nationalism had promised.[36] That the south's politicians had been generally complacent about the Constitution in this regard is clear from Cohen's survey of the Irish political élite in 1969 when 'virtually no respondents' believed the clause in Article 44 mentioning the 'special position' of the Catholic Church was inimical to unity.[37]

In 1972, an Inter-Party Committee on the Implications of Irish Unity was established. Again the politicians scrutinized de Valera's Constitution. Again, no changes resulted from their deliberations. Indeed, on this occasion there was not even a published report, the main difficulty arose from Fianna Fail's insistence on the retention of Articles 2 and 3 and opposition deputies' scepticism and hostility towards the same

[34] Interview, Kevin Boland; Boland (1977: *passim*); Denis Taylor, 'Eamon de Valera: a lifetime at the forefront of his country's history: the courage of Ireland's soldier of destiny', *The Times*, 22 June 1973; account by Peter Berry (Secretary, Department of Justice), of meeting with de Valera during Arms Crisis, 1970, *Magill*, June 1980. Neil Blaney was also dismissed but charges were dropped against him before the Arms Trial; TD, 1948– , expelled from Fianna Fail; hawk on Partition issue.

[35] This is best shown by the significant change in party policy, against the leader's wishes, between the Ard Fheis of 1975 and that of 1976; see reports in *Irish Times* of Fianna Fail's northern policy, 15 Feb., 14, 15, 20, 29, 30, and 31 Oct., 3 Nov., 1 and 15 Dec. 1975, 14 Feb. 1976; confidential sources.

[36] Lynch, 'The Anglo-Irish problem', *Foreign Affairs*, vol. 50, no. 4, July 1972, pp. 601-17.

[37] A. S. Cohen, 'The question of a united Ireland: perspectives of the Irish political elite', *International Affairs*, vol. 53, no. 2, Apr. 1977, pp. 232-54.

Articles.[38] Although the working papers of the Committee[39] are relatively cursory in attributing views to individuals, the known positions of the various members — de Valera's son, Vivion, was among Fianna Fail's representatives — demonstrate the wide divergence of approach among the southern parties towards the irredentist Articles framed a generation before. Discussing their general approach to constitutional change in the context of the south's aspiration to unity, some members argued that any changes should depend on whether they suited the existing twenty-six-county state, while others believed that this 'could be construed as diminishing the claim to a united Ireland'. Fianna Fail members believed that the revision of the Constitution should await 'actual moves towards unity'; others disagreed, arguing that de Valera's Constitution was inimical to 'unity by consent', and suggested its replacement by a 'shorter 26-county constitution' embodying the aspiration to unity but omitting the territorial claim. Clearly there was no consensus. The chairman summarizing this discussion emphasized the Committee's lack of knowledge of northern opinion and proposed that all northern political parties and independent elected representatives should be invited to appear before the Committee.[40]

The only unionist grouping to accept the invitation was the New Ulster Movement, a liberal, centre, non-party grouping in the north. In its submission it accused the Committee of attempting to work with 'narrow, unrealistic terms of reference', of 'playing with words' — something which was 'now endemic in Republican thought and polemics'. In contrast to the 'healing balm of time and diplomacy' which southern leaders had applied to Anglo-Irish relations with considerable success, 'no effort' of a similar kind had been used in dealing 'with fellow Irishmen in Northern Ireland'. In fact southern political leaders, from de Valera to Lynch, had failed to understand the north: the 'significance of this failure by

[38] O'Kennedy, committee chairman, speech,*Irish Times*, 29 Jan. 1977. Michael O'Kennedy (1936–) Foreign Minister, 1977–80, European Community Commissioner (1980–82).

[39] This account is based on a complete file of the minutes and working papers of this committee, confidential source.

[40] Minutes, 2 Nov. 1972, Inter-Party Committee on the Implications of Irish Unity, confidential source.

Republicans to recognize Ulster Unionists for what they are, and not the descendants of Theobald Wolfe Tone, awaiting national baptism' could not be overestimated. Deliberately avoiding other constitutional changes, they called for the abandonment of the 'irredentist claim on which the IRA can call to its aid Article 2 of the 1937 Constitution': this was 'where the major issue lies.'[41]

Among others to criticize Articles 2 and 3 were opposition politicians in the south, notably Conor Cruise O'Brien and Garret FitzGerald.[42] In the north, Ian Paisley believed that de Valera's Constitution was 'the cancer' in the island's politics.[43] Meanwhile the northern nationalists — now represented by the SDLP — took comfort from the south's formal constitutional claim.[44]

As republican orthodoxy became more important within Fianna Fail, there was less willingness by Lynch to query the Constitution.[45] When the Coalition government signed the Sunningdale Agreement in which the south formally recognized that northern consent was a precondition for unity, Boland, on the grounds that this was repugnant to the 1937 Constitution, challenged the Sunningdale settlement through the courts. Although unsuccessful, it remains true that this action further circumscribed the Coalition's policy options,[46] while to Fianna Fail it must have served as a salutary reminder of how vulnerable southern politicians could be if they questioned the old orthodoxies. It was little surprise that the Fianna Fail Ard Fheis which followed Sunningdale suggested that the sovereignty enshrined in the 1937 Constitution and 'achieved by Fianna Fail under the leadership of Eamon de

[41] New Ulster Movement, memorandum to Committee, confidential source.

[42] Cruise O'Brien, *Irish Times*, 1 Feb. 1977; FitzGerald, 'FitzGerald: hamstrung by Articles two and three', *Irish Times*, 29 Dec. 1977. Garret FitzGerald (1926-   ), TD, 1969- , Foreign Minister, 1973-7; leader Fine Gael, 1977- , Taoiseach, 1981-2; committed to reform of south as a precondition to unity.

[43] *Irish Times*, 29 Nov. 1971. Ian Paisley (1926-), MP Westminster, 1970- , elected to NIHC, 1970-2, to NI Assembly, 1973-5, to NI Constitutional Convention, 1975-6, to European Parliament, 1979- ; demagogic leader of Ulster loyalists; a marked egocentric, he has founded his own church, newspaper, political party, and — some critics allege — private army.

[44] Interviews, John Hume, Paddy Devlin.

[45] For Lynch's period of enthusiasm for constitutional change, see *Irish Press*, 22 Feb. 1971.

[46] Interviews, Garret FitzGerald, Brian Faulkner, Kevin Boland.

Valera, will not be altered except by the consent of the people
in a referendum.'[47] When Lynch was asked whether, had he
been negotiating at Sunningdale, he would have insisted on
Articles 2 and 3 being written into the agreement, he contented himself with the assurance that he would have ensured
'that our constitutional position would be maintained as well
as the British constitutional position being maintained and
written into the agreement.'[48] Yet the defenders of the Sunningdale agreement could point to the parallel British declaration in the Agreement that London would support a united
Ireland if it had majority support in the north, the SDLP
claiming that this was 'the precise declaration sought from
the British by Mr de Valera in 1949.'[49] There were misgivings
within Fianna Fail on the Sunningdale Agreement: Vivion de
Valera hinted at his own reservations,[50] and when the power-
sharing Executive collapsed some months later, offered his
analysis of Partition which evoked the accolade from Blaney:
'thanks be to God there is still a de Valera in this House.'[51]

De Valera's legacy on Partition was not confined to Articles
2 and 3. His successors as leaders of Fianna Fail — no matter
how altered the context in which they were working — were
obliged to claim consistency with his policy. But there was
little interest in recalling those aspects of his approach most
vulnerable to republican criticism but which represented his
attempts — no matter how unavailing — to interest London or
Belfast in some movement towards Irish unity. All nationalist
policy on Partition may be subjected to what may be termed
an orthodoxy/heresy test — the orthodox claim being for
Pearse's unitary, separatist, Gaelic republic and the heretical
policies being deviations from this in an attempt to formulate
a realistic policy. De Valera, in his time, had been a leading
heretic, not only with his 'county option' proposals of August
1921, but also with the kernels of his subsequent policy,
external association, and local autonomy for the north. Yet
these latter dimensions to his policy, which he had, with some

[47] Agenda 1974 Ard Fheis.   [48] 'This Week', *RTE Radio*, 17 Feb. 1974.
[49] Hugh Logue, *Irish Times*, 17 Jan. 1974.
[50] DE: 271: 12, 13 Mar. 1974.   [51] DE: 273: 1606-14, *passim*.

difficulty managed to preserve, subsequently proved to be of little interest to the party. They preferred to remember the legend of de Valera as the principal champion of Irish unity, thereby ignoring, for the most part, the creative, essentially political, dimensions to his policy. The choice in short for the leadership of a party such as Fianna Fail was between the comfort of an approach based on Pearse's orthodoxy, or the pursuit of an heretical, but more realistic policy designed to meet the politico-geographic realities of the island of Ireland. While de Valera himself had been a brilliant and indefatigable exploiter of the fact that his former colleagues in his pre-Treaty cabinet had approved his 1921 heresies of external association and local autonomy, his own successors seldom exploited his imprimatur when testing the tolerance for a debatably heretical policy. Although, as has been shown, his own record on Ulster reveals him as predominantly pragmatic and occasionally heretical or revisionist, de Valera was invariably invoked as the test of 'fundamental republicanism' within the party. Indeed, his granddaughter, Sile de Valera TD, in 1979, was among the leading dissidents in the parliamentary party who precipitated the early resignation of the party's third leader, Lynch. There is further irony that her attack on Lynch — 'to demonstrate his Republicanism' — should have been made at a commemorative ceremony for Liam Lynch, leader of the republican forces in the Civil War.[52] In de Valera's last meeting with him, at which he persuaded him to abandon military resistance to the Free State, Liam Lynch was concerned lest the decision reached fell short of fundamental republicanism. Years later, Gallagher recorded de Valera's account of the exchange:

When the meeting broke up, the Chief of Staff, Liam Lynch and de Valera were walking together down from the farm-house where they had come to the agreement when Lynch said: 'I wonder what Tom Clarke [1916 leader] would think of this decision'. De Valera stopped in his tracks. 'Tom Clarke is dead', he said, 'He has not our responsibilities. Nobody will ever know what he would do for this situation did not arise for him. But it has risen for us and we must face it with our intelligence and conscious of our responsibility.'[53]

[52] Sile de Valera, *Irish Times*, 10 Sept. 1979. Sile de Valera (1954–), TD, 1977–8 Member European Parliament, 1979– ; outspoken exponent of republicanism; lost seat 1981 election, failed to regain it 1982.
[53] Gallagher, typescript 'De Valera', Gallagher papers, MS 18,375(6).

On this occasion, at least, de Valera sided with Thomas Paine that 'the most ridiculous and insolent of tyrannies' was the 'vanity and presumption of governing beyond the grave.'[54]

(b) The de Valera card

De Valera's party, after his retirement from the leadership in 1959, and after his death in 1975, continued to cite him as the exponent of party orthodoxy on Partition — this despite the complexity, if not confusion, manifest in his record on the question. Most notably, Haughey, the fourth leader of Fianna Fail, has been projected by the party 'as the spiritual heir to de Valera' in this context.[55] Unveiling the de Valera memorial at Ennis in October 1981, Haughey committed the party of the 1980s to the founder's ideal of Irish unity: 'following in the tradition' established by de Valera, Fianna Fail sought 'no dominance', threatened 'no coercion' of the Ulster unionists; rather did they seek 'a constructive partnership in which any guarantees or undertakings which may be required would be willingly and generously forthcoming'.[56] Haughey's critics read this as posturing:[57] the proffered generous guarantees, combined with assurances that 'we do not want them to change',[58] were conditional on the unionists abandoning their national allegiance and ceasing to be unionists; and while Fianna Fail insisted that unity must be based on the unionists' consent, they dogmatically denied to them any right to refuse that consent.[59]

Such an approach was scorned by northern unionists who charged Fianna Fail with ignorance of the realities of northern politics and of pitching their appeal to the southern electorate.[60] That Haughey's rhetoric could strike a chord consistent with Frankel's aspirational politics was clear from his Ennis speech. De Valera, he claimed, 'would never accept that we

---

[54] Thomas Paine, *Rights of man* (Dublin: 1792), p. 7.
[55] Mary Holland, 'The heir to de Valera', *Sunday Tribune*, 9 Nov. 1980.
[56] *Irish Times*, 12 Oct. 1981.
[57] See letters, 'The Taoiseach's Crusade', *Irish Times*, 19, 21, 23, and 29 Oct. 1981.   [58] Haughey, 'News at 1.30', *RTE Radio*, 28 Sept. 1981.
[59] Haughey, press conference Dublin, 6 Nov. 1981.
[60] Interview, William Craig, *Irish Times*, 7 Nov. 1981; R. L. McCartney, letter, ibid., 23 Oct. 1981.

should not occupy our own separate independent place in the world . . . attaining any goals we set ourselves.'[61] Fianna Fail's failure to achieve its central goals has never embarrassed the party nor prompted much self-criticism; instead the goals are treated consistently with Frankel's typology.[62] As Garvin has noted, Fianna Fail's 'original goals' are now proclaimed in an 'ironic context' — an Ireland largely ruled by Fianna Fail 'but which is far more industrialised, urbanised, English-speaking and probably more partitioned' than it was when the party first dedicated itself to oppose all of these trends. He concludes that the party has 'long outlived its original ideological purposes'.[63]

Such criticism has not cramped Fianna Fail's style. Specializing in being 'greener' than other southern parties, they rarely find difficulty in ignoring evidence which does not fit their preferred analysis. Evidence of this came in their response to the most outspoken criticism of southern attitudes to Partition by any head of an Irish government since Partition was first enacted: the 'constitutional crusade' of FitzGerald, elected Taoiseach in June 1981 at the head of a Fine Gael–Labour Coalition. A veteran critic of southern hypocrisy on Partition, FitzGerald — who has described Ireland as a 'necrocracy'[64] — launched a revisionist assault on de Valera's Constitution. He argued that the Constitution had entrenched Partition, that Articles 2 and 3 were counter-productive, and that any territorial claim should be rephrased as an aspiration to unity. Moreover he believed the question would have to be faced, as to whether the people of the south had 'the will to move away from the partitionist mentality' implicit in the 1937 Constitution. Criticizing some of its provisions as sectarian, he added that Irish law had been 'influenced by the attitudes, interests and religious loyalties' of the majority Catholic Church.[65] Presently, FitzGerald repeated these arguments in a radio interview in which he stated the truly heretical view that northern Protestants ought not to be attracted by the state which had resulted from sixty years of self-government

---

[61] *Irish Times*, 12 Oct. 1981.

[62] See discussion of aspirational politics, above pp. 107–8.

[63] Tom Garvin, *The evolution of Irish nationalist politics* (Dublin: 1981), p. 157.

[64] *Sunday Times*, 1 Nov. 1981. [65] *Cork Examiner*, 22 Sept. 1981.

in the south.[66] Seeking support in the Senate for his constitutional crusade he claimed that 'history is now to be made
by us, the living generation of Irishmen.' He regarded the
debate as fundamental: the issues were 'no less than the
identity, the hopes and the destiny of our people', all brought
into 'critical focus' by the continuing tragedy in Northern
Ireland. FitzGerald believed that 'the acid test of our constitutional provisions' should be their suitability to a united
Ireland; but such tests had never seriously been applied to the
Constitution. He added that it was 'frustration with the sub-
conscious partitionism of this failure that more than anything
else motivated me . . . towards a political career'. FitzGerald
was dismissive of what he termed Fianna Fail's 'No Surrender'
defence of de Valera's Constitution. He believed it was 'a
tragic fallacy' to treat the Constitution as sacrosanct until the
Ulster Unionists were at the negotiating table, implying, as it
did, 'the extraordinary illusion that the Unionists and Loyalists of Northern Ireland are really as eager as we are for Irish
unity.' Implicitly, FitzGerald accused Fianna Fail of adopting
'a cruel, misguided, bargaining strategy, one sure result of
which would be . . . the deeper entrenchment of Partition.'[67]

In his broadcast, when calling for a crusade on constitutional
reform, FitzGerald had called for a Constitution worthy of
the founding fathers of Irish republicanism, Tone and Davis,
to whose pluralist, non-sectarian ideology, Fianna Fail was,
he claimed, antagonistic.[68] This slight on Fianna Fail, along
with a criticism of de Valera for his opposition to a Protestant
being appointed as a county librarian in 1931, exacerbated the
already poor relations with Fianna Fail.[69] Haughey, accusing

[66] 'This Week', *RTE Radio*, 27 Sept. 1981.
[67] SE: 96: 175–201, 9 Oct. 1981, *passim*.   [68] As note 66 above.
[69] No incoming Taoiseach faced such criticism as did Haughey when he was
elected by Fianna Fail to succeed Lynch as party leader in December 1979. Among
many other charges, FitzGerald suggested that his election as Taoiseach 'would be
an obstacle to Irish unity being achieved by agreement.' When FitzGerald became
Taoiseach after the June 1981 election, he inherited what was widely acknowledged
as a historic breakthrough in Anglo-Irish relations credited to Haughey at his
Dublin summit with British Prime Minister, Margaret Thatcher. Whereas Fianna
Fail and Ulster unionist parties both claimed that the joint study by London and
Dublin of 'the totality of relationships within these islands' gave Dublin a voice in
determining Northern Ireland's future, the British were publicly and privately
critical of some Fianna Fail claims, and FitzGerald promised to continue the
initiative but to be less secretive about the details, to involve Northern Ireland

FitzGerald of being defeatist and negative, claimed that he had 'sold the pass as far as the claim for national unity was concerned'.[70] In the national debate which followed, Fitz-Gerald's sin in Fianna Fail's book was clearly heresy on 'the national question'. Meanwhile the old orthodoxies came to the fore in Fianna Fail speeches. They accused FitzGerald of 'foolish and bungling attempts to appease the Unionists',[71] of being 'insecure',[72] and of being an apologist for 'the remnants of that colonial mentality that still linger on in Irish life' and against which de Valera had fought all his life.[73]

Despite the earlier lead given by Lemass and Lynch in calling for regular constitutional reviews,[74] Fianna Fail, in effect, declined to participate in FitzGerald's debate. They also ignored his concern at the growth of partitionism in the south; in fact the Fianna Fail National Executive went so far as 'categorically' to deny this phenomenon.[75] For a party which had historically based its opposition to Partition on the grounds that unity was supported throughout the south and by the nationalist third of the northern population, the opinion polls and attitude surveys on the question should have proved cautionary. Never shy of giving themselves the benefit of any doubt when interpreting electoral or opinion data on the unionist side, Fianna Fail now ignored a wealth of evidence which demonstrably revealed the fallacy of what had once been one of de Valera's preferred projections: that, in time, there would be sufficient conversions from unionist ranks to make effective an anti-Partitionist consensus throughout Ireland.[76]

politicians as far as possible, and to emphasize the necessity of winning the consent of a majority in Northern Ireland for any change in their constitutional position. *Keesing's Contemporary Archives*, Feb. 1980–Aug. 1981, pp. 30110-1, 30314, 30603, 30878, 31040-3; confidential sources.

[70] As note 58 above.   [71] Sile de Valera, *Irish Times*, 30 Nov. 1981.
[72] Brian Lenihan, *Irish Press*, 12 Oct. 1981.   [73] Haughey, ibid.
[74] See FitzGerald's citing of their comments, SE: 96: 175–201, 9 Oct. 1981, *passim.*   [75] 'In defence of the Constitution', *Iris Fianna Fail*, no. 20, 1981.
[76] For an example during the referendum campaign on the Constitution itself, *Irish Press*, 28 June 1937. During the Anglo-Irish negotiations in 1938, de Valera claimed that it 'could be taken for granted that every Catholic (in NI) was in favour of the abolition of partition and that in addition that view was shared by a number of non-Catholics.' Conference between representatives of UK and Eire, 23 Feb. 1938, PRO CAB 27/642, IN(38)6.

Yet all opinion polls and attitude surveys demonstrated the growth in Partitionism. While there was still a majority in the south which favoured Irish unity, the significant trend was the *heretical* drift away from this position.[77] Only 46 per cent of northern catholics in March 1974 found a united Ireland *acceptable*; in March 1976, 45 per cent did; in 1974, 39 per cent of them found 'full integration of Northern Ireland with the rest of the United Kingdom' *acceptable*; by 1976 — when there was another political impasse in Northern Ireland — 55 per cent found such a fate acceptable.[78] In 1981, this figure stood at 39 per cent.[79] That there was significant acquiescence, if not support, within the nationalist community, for unionist solutions was now manifest. There was minimal support among unionists for any form of Irish unity.[80] In an opinion poll on FitzGerald's crusade in the south, 46 per cent of adults disapproved of dropping the claim on the north embodied in the 1937 Constitution, 19 per cent were 'Don't knows', and 35 per cent — the significant, heretical figure — approved the dropping of the claim.[81] Throughout the 1970s, support for a united Ireland in the south was approximately two adults in three, those supporting Partition varying between 29 and 15 per cent, the rest being 'Don't knows'.[82] From these and other surveys, Cruise O'Brien concludes that it 'is now clear that the assumption of overwhelming support for unity is quite untenable and that the population of the island of Ireland is about evenly divided as to whether the island should be united or not.'[83] Fianna Fail, unsure of the public response to their stance decided to disengage from any debate on FitzGerald's crusade[84] and the issue played little part in the 1982 general election. Haughey, returned as Taoiseach in March 1982, again emphasized Britain's responsibility for

[77] This had also been emphasized by FitzGerald's predecessor as Fine Gael leader, Liam Cosgrave, when Taoiseach, 1974–7, interview Liam Cosgrave.

[78] Richard Rose, Ian McAllister, Peter Mair, *Is there a concurring majority about Northern Ireland?* (Glasgow: 1978), table 18, p. 46. See also table 7, p. 19.

[79] MORI, 'Northern Ireland Survey: opinion poll conducted for *Sunday Times*', June 1981, MORI/6986, table NI-8.

[80] Rose: (1978: table 4; pp. 12–13).

[81] *Sunday Tribune*, 18 Oct. 1981.

[82] Rose (1978: table 14; p. 35).

[83] Conor Cruise O'Brien, *Neighbours* (London: 1980), pp. 81–4.

[84] Confidential source.

Partition, declined to initiate changes in the south's constitution, and characterized the outgoing Coalition government's northern policy as 'national sabotage'.[85]

If there has been more apathy,[86] heresy, and hypocrisy on the issue in the south than some have acknowledged, it remains true that the Green card — the claim that Irish unity is the only solution — remains a difficult card to trump in the south's politics. Given Fianna Fail's republican base it was especially difficult for their party leader to resist playing it. This was especially true in Haughey's case since he was less content with aspirational politics than were all his predecessors as party leader. Historically there had always been a tendency in Fianna Fail to see their party as the custodian of the nationalist aspiration to unity. Moreover, there was a tendency for their stridency on the issue to be correlated to how much attention others — whether other Dail parties, northern nationalists, the IRA, or British opinion — were paying to the question. They were especially discomfited by FitzGerald's constitutional crusade since its goal was the revision if not the replacement of what they considered to be one of de Valera's major achievements, the 1937 Constitution. That the crusade was being led in the Dail by parties which, in 1937, had opposed the Constitution and had been tardy in acknowledging their subsequent indebtedness to it, was a further discouragement to rational analytical discourse. In particular, Fianna Fail underestimated the marginal but comparatively significant successes in London and Belfast enjoyed by the Coalition's insistence on adopting a self-critical approach to the south's unification strategy.[87] Ever since Whitehall had

[85] *Irish Times*, 10, 18, 24 Mar. 1982.

[86] A significant level of apathy is manifest in opinion poll and attitudinal survey data only available since the 1960s. That apathy was not unknown in earlier decades is clear from a variety of witnesses: Dr McHugh (Bishop of Derry) to Fr Coyle, 5 Dec. 1925, W. J. Maloney papers, box 22; S. T. O'Kelly to Art O'Brien, 24 Nov. 1925 and reply 17 May 1926, O'Brien papers, MS 8461; Blanché to Briand, 25 Mar. 1926, MAE, Z/282/1 vol. 6.

[87] For unionists' response, as note 60 above; also leaked *UTV* poll, *Sunday Independent*, 22 Nov. 1981. For British opinion, James Prior (NI secretary), 'News at 6.30', *RTE Radio*, 29 Sept., Roy Mason (former NI secretary), 'Scene around Six', *BBC TV (NI)* 28 Sept., Margaret Thatcher, press conference London, 6 Nov. 1981. See also Lord Hailsham to Cearbhall O'Dalaigh, 30 June 1971, O'Dalaigh papers, P51/106(2).

first seen a draft of de Valera's Constitution in May 1937, British politicians had been consistent in telling Dublin that it was far from the blueprint for a united Ireland which de Valera claimed. Although Fianna Fail had long since come to this conclusion themselves, by 1981 they were perplexing London by claiming that the next initiative lay with them — in removing the British guarantee to the northern majority — while being unwilling to call for changes in the south until the Unionists were 'around the negotiating table'. This stance by Fianna Fail ceded to the Fine Gael and Labour parties a monopoly of what had become a consensus between all southern parties by the 1960s: that changes in the south were an obvious precondition if there was to be progress towards Irish unity.

Nor was such an approach merely part of the post-de Valera era. In August 1921, J. J. Horgan had insisted to Childers that 'of course . . . Ireland is permanently partitioned' as was inevitable, in his view, in the wake of recent events: 'That door has been slammed, banged and bolted long ago and can only be opened by an era of constructive politics on this side of the Boyne.'[88] Childers shared this view and he impressed it on de Valera who near his death confided that he had failed to take sufficient heed of this advice. Rita Childers has recorded that at a private meeting with Childers's son — her husband, Erskine Childers II, who was succeeding de Valera as President — de Valera emphasized that he had recently come across the long memorandum written in his death-cell by Childers in November 1922, part of which dealt with future relations with Northern Ireland.

Erskine Childers advocated that never at any time should the Northern Majority, who had a different heritage, be coerced, violently or otherwise, into a United Ireland. But he urged the vital need to get to know, understand and tolerate their point of view by co-operation in every way possible. Mr de Valera at this point explained that because he had been so absorbed in building up the South after Independence he had failed to follow this advice.[89]

---

[88] Horgan to Childers, 24 Aug. 1921, J. J. Horgan papers, P 4645. Horgan (1881-1967), solicitor, author, sometime Irish correspondent, *Round Table*.

[89] Rita Childers, letter *Irish Times*, 29 Jan. 1981. See also, editorial 'Dev's admission', ibid., 2 Feb. 1981.

It may also be said that his own attempts in the decades ahead at 'constructive politics on this side of the Boyne' while securing political stability in the south also stabilized the border. De Valera's politics was based on so limited a notion of Irishness that Stephen Gwynn's private admonition at the very start of his career in 1918 holds good as his epitaph: 'If Ireland as a nation means what de Valera means by it, then Ulster is not part of that nation.'[90] The party which he founded — and which is arguably his greatest achievement — implicitly agrees with Gwynn,[91] but has yet to admit that its guru and one-time headmaster was fallible and deserves the honour of being critically reassessed.

---

[90] Gwynn to Horgan, 20 Aug. 1918, Horgan papers, P 4645. Gwynn (1864–1950), writer, Nationalist MP, 1906–18.

[91] They pay lip-service to de Valera's ideals but pursue, in effect, the Ireland envisaged by Lemass.

Appendices

APPENDIX 1

SECRET. 'North East Ulster Draft Clause' (October 1921), de Valera's revise of Griffith's original draft.*

The following constituencies of North East Ireland, viz: the Boroughs of Belfast and Derry, North, South, East, and Mid Antrim, North, South, and Mid Armagh, North and South Derry, North, South, East, West and Mid Down, North and South Fermanagh, and North-East, North-West and South Tyrone, may by vote of their registered electors (or adult inhabitants) severally elect to be directly represented in the Irish Parliament; provided that if all of them, or a smaller number contiguous and forming a territorially continuous group do not so elect they shall be entitled to maintain a legislature possessed of the local governing powers set out in the Act of the British Parliament known as 'Government of Ireland Act, 1920' (10 and 11 Geo. 5. Ch. 67), and provided they shall be entitled to the same representation relatively to the rest of Ireland in the Irish Parliament as they would have been entitled to in the British Parliament under the provisions of the above mentioned Act.

Should the constituencies enumerated opt to be directly represented in the National Parliament, it is agreed that a Convention be executed with their elected representatives safeguarding any lawful interests peculiar to the area, and for this purpose a Commission shall be appointed consisting of _____ persons nominated by the National Government and _____ persons elected by the representatives of the area mentioned.

To provide adequate and just representation for the political minority, the Irish Government agrees to take into consultation the representatives of this minority with a view to devising a scheme of proportional representation which will secure this object.

* SPO DE 2/304/1.

APPENDIX 2

1937 Constitution: Articles 2 and 3†
Article 2. The national territory consists of the whole island of Ireland, its islands and the territorial seas.

Article 3. Pending the re-integration of the national territory, and without prejudice to the right of the Parliament and Government established by this Constitution to exercise jurisdiction over the whole of that territory, the laws enacted by that Parliament shall have the like area and extent of application as the laws of *Saorstat Eireann* (Irish Free State) and the like extra-territorial effect.

† *Bunreacht na hEireann* (Dublin: 1937).

APPENDIX 3

'Draft Declaration by the Prime Minister of the United Kingdom as communicated to Mr de Valera' (January 1938).†
The attitude of the United Kingdom Government on the question of partition can be briefly defined. They regard any alteration of the present position as a matter which would have to be discussed between the Governments of Northern Ireland and Eire. No development in the direction of ending partition could take place except with the consent of the Northern Ireland Government.

It is no part of the policy or intention of the Government of the United Kingdom to oppose any arrangement which might be freely and voluntarily entered into between the Government of Eire and the Government of Northern Ireland. If, at any time in the future, conditions should change so as to cause Northern Ireland to become favourable to the development of closer relations with Eire, or to the establishment of a United Ireland, the United Kingdom Government, for their part, would welcome such an improvement in their mutual relations and, far from raising any difficulties, would, on the contrary, be ready to take any practicable steps to facilitate any arrangement desired by the two parties.

† PRO DO 35/893/X.11/287

Note on Sources

De Valera confided to his biographer T. P. O'Neill that he 'did not put down on paper what his policies were going to be. He always said: "If you write something down people know what you're going to do . . . are warned and may be in a position to stop you. So always keep your policy under your hat."'[1] That de Valera followed this practice throughout his career is clear from the perfunctory records which mark his approach at every level of his political activity. It was at his suggestion that the fourth meeting of the National Executive of Fianna Fail in December 1926 decided that the results of votes at such meetings should not be recorded.[2] Austin Stack, after a meeting between representatives of Sinn Fein and Fianna Fail in August 1927, complained to de Valera that the Fianna Fail negotiators would 'put nothing in writing'.[3] During the Second World War, de Valera informed Mulcahy that it was his government's policy to do their work orally as far as was possible.[4] In 1947 he informed a prominent Irish-American politician that 'As a rule I didn't keep any diary or notes of conversations, so I have nothing now to which I can refer.'[5]

The minutes of de Valera's cabinet meetings provide the most striking evidence on this point: making no attempt to record the contribution of individual ministers, they are merely a record of decisions taken and, on crucial occasions, are not even that. For instance, vital discussions on the strategy to be adopted during the protracted Anglo-Irish negotiations of January to April 1938 are not even mentioned in the *agenda.*[6] It is no exaggeration to conclude that for this and other vital periods no known record exists of the deliberations of de Valera's government meetings; all that is recorded is the attendance, venue, date, and duration of the meetings.[7] Nor were there any diarists in his cabinets, certainly

---

[1] Interview, T. P. O'Neill.
[2] Minutes, Fianna Fail National Executive, 16 Dec. 1926.
[3] Stack to de Valera, 27 Aug. 1927, Austin Stack papers, MS 17,092.
[4] De Valera to Mulcahy, 12 Feb. 1941, Mulcahy papers, P7a/215.
[5] De Valera to J. C. Walsh, 8 Jan. 1947, J. C. Walsh papers, box 3.
[6] Minutes, cabinet meetings, Jan.-Apr. 1938, SPO CAB G1/1-31.
[7] There is no trace in the cabinet minutes of any deliberations on the MacDonald-de Valera talks of June 1940, SPO G2/155-170 *passim.*

none who subsequently published his account or made his private papers
available for research. Only one member of a de Valera cabinet has ever
written a book about his period in government and he, Kevin Boland,
only served in de Valera's last administration and was prompted to go
into print only when he had severed all connections with Fianna Fail. If
secrecy and silence were a condition of accepting a ministerial portfolio
from de Valera, it would come as no surprise to this researcher. In
addition to this, his own extensive collection of private papers, on
which the Longford and O'Neill biography is based, remain closed to
research until ten years after his death (August 1985).

One consequence of this is that the researcher is often obliged
to rely solely on the evidence of Malcolm MacDonald, Neville Chamberlain, Richard Mulcahy, David Gray, or Sir John Maffey for a particular
episode; two other witnesses, Erskine Childers and Frank Gallagher,
come as it were from within de Valera's 'circle' and may be considered
more sympathetic witnesses. But it is extraordinary that a political
career such as de Valera's which spanned such a considerable period of
time must now be studied for so many important episodes through the
perspective of opposition politicians or the politicians and diplomats of
Britain, the United States, Canada, and Germany.

Sources

PRIMARY SOURCES

State Paper Office, Dublin
Irish cabinet minutes
Dail Eireann papers
Anglo-Irish Treaty Negotiations papers, 1921
North-East Boundary Bureau papers
Departmental papers

Public Record Office of Ireland, Dublin
Correspondence between Eamon de Valera, Eamonn Donnelly, and
others concerning the organization of Cumann na Poblachta and Sinn
Fein, 1919–23

Public Record Office of Northern Ireland, Belfast
Northern Ireland cabinet minutes
Departmental papers

Public Record Office, London
British cabinet minutes
Cabinet memoranda
Cabinet Committee papers:
   Irish Situation Committee, minutes and memoranda
   Anglo-Irish Negotiations, 1938
Prime Minister's Office papers
Dominions Office (later, Commonwealth Relations Office), original correspondence; confidential prints; office papers
British Ministry, Dublin papers
Foreign Office papers
Treasury papers

National Archives, Washington
General records of the Department of State
American Legation Dublin papers

Public Archives of Canada, Ottawa
Canadian cabinet papers
Prime Ministers' papers
Department of External Affairs papers
Governor-General's Office papers

Department of External Affairs, Ottawa
Department of External Affairs papers

Ministère des Affaires Etrangères, Paris
Archives Diplomatiques: Europe, 1918–29: Irlande Vols. 1–6, microfilm of original records, National Library of Ireland, Dublin, P 7398–9

PRIVATE PAPERS

C. W. Ackerman papers
Manuscript Division, Library of Congress, Washington

Clement Attlee papers
Department of Western Manuscripts, Bodleian Library, Oxford

Earl of Avon papers
Public Record Office, London

Stanley Baldwin papers
Department of Western Manuscripts, University Library, Cambridge

R. B. Bennett papers
Public Archives of Canada, Ottawa

Ernest Blythe papers
Archives Department, University College Dublin

Thomas Bodkin papers
Manuscripts Department, Trinity College Library, Dublin

Austin Chamberlain papers
Birmingham University Library, Birmingham

Neville Chamberlain papers
Birmingham University Library, Birmingham

Erskine Childers papers
Manuscripts Department, Trinity College Library, Dublin

Daniel F. Cohalan papers
American Irish Historical Society, New York, photostat of original
papers, National Library of Ireland, Dublin

Sir James Craig papers, see Craigavon papers below

Lord Craigavon papers
Public Record Office of Northern Ireland, Belfast

Lionel Curtis papers
Department of Western Manuscripts, Bodleian Library, Oxford

John Devoy papers
National Library of Ireland, Dublin

John Dillon papers
Manuscripts Department, Trinity College Library, Dublin

Adam Duffin papers
Public Record Office of Northern Ireland, Belfast

George Gavan Duffy papers
National Library of Ireland, Dublin

Sir Anthony Eden papers, see Avon papers above

Fianna Fail records
Fianna Fail headquarters, Dublin

Desmond FitzGerald papers
In private possession of Dr. Garret FitzGerald, Dublin

Frank Gallagher papers
National Library of Ireland, Dublin

Peter Golden papers
National Library of Ireland, Dublin

David Gray papers
Franklyn D. Roosevelt Library, Hyde Park, New York State

Earl Halifax papers
Public Record Office, London.

Maurice Hankey papers
Public Record Office, London

Henry Harrison papers
National Library of Ireland, Dublin

Cahir Healy papers
Deposited and calendared at the Public Record Office of Northern Ireland, Belfast, but not available while this research was being undertaken. All references in the footnotes are to Eamonn Phoenix's calendar which includes extensive quotations of the politically important letters. The PRONI reference numbers have been used in anticipation of this collection being opened to researchers.

Tim Healy papers
Archives Department, University College Dublin

J. J. Hearn papers
National Library of Ireland, Dublin

Sir Samuel Hoare papers, see Templewood papers below

J. J. Horgan papers
National Library of Ireland, Dublin

Cordell Hull papers
Manuscripts Division, Library of Congress, Washington

Harold Ickes papers
Manuscripts Division, Library of Congress, Washington

Irish Race Convention (New York) August 1932, minutes and papers
Manuscripts Department, Trinity College Library, Dublin

Thomas Johnson papers
National Library of Ireland, Dublin

Hugh Kennedy papers
Archives Department, University College Dublin

David Lloyd George papers
House of Lords Record Office, London

Patrick McCartan papers
National Library of Ireland

Frank MacDermot papers
Public Record Office of Ireland, Dublin

Ramsay MacDonald papers
Public Record Office, London

Joseph McGarrity papers
National Library of Ireland, Dublin

W. J. Mackenzie King papers
Public Archives of Canada, Ottawa

Mary MacSwiney papers
Archives Department, University College Dublin

W J. M. Maloney papers
New York Public Library, New York

H. J. Maloney papers
Public Record Office of Northern Ireland, Belfast

Lord Midleton papers
Public Record Office, London

Maurice Moore papers
National Library of Ireland, Dublin

Richard Mulcahy papers
Archives Department, University College Dublin

Kathleeen Napoli McKenna papers
National Library of Ireland, Dublin

Art O'Brien papers
National Library of Ireland, Dublin

William O'Brien papers
National Library of Ireland, Dublin

Cearbhall O Dalaigh papers
Archives Department, University College Dublin

James O'Donovan papers
National Library of Ireland, Dublin

Sean T. O'Kelly papers
National Library of Ireland, Dublin

Ernie O'Malley papers
Archives Department, University College Dublin

Patrick Quinn papers
Kindly loaned by Mr Brian Quinn

John Redmond papers
National Library of Ireland, Dublin

Franklyn D. Roosevelt papers
Franklyn D. Roosevelt Library, Hyde Park, New York State

Desmond Ryan papers
Archives Department, University College Dublin

Frank Ryan letters
A series of letters from Ryan to the Irish Minister in Madrid, Leopold Kerney, June 1940–August 1942, archives of the Department of Foreign Affairs, Dublin. I am grateful to the former Minister for Foreign Affairs, Mr Brian Lenihan for permission to read and quote from these letters.

Hannah Sheehy Skeffington papers
National Library of Ireland, Dublin

J. C. Smuts papers
Department of Western Manuscripts, University Library, Cambridge holds a microfilm of the Smuts papers

W. B. Spender papers
Public Record Office of Northern Ireland, Belfast

Lord Templewood papers (Sir Samuel Hoare)
Department of Western Manuscripts, University Library, Cambridge

Lord Sankey papers
Department of Western Manuscripts, Bodleian Library, Oxford

O. D. Skelton papers
Public Archives of Canada, Ottawa

Austin Stack papers
National Library of Ireland, Dublin

Mark Sturgis papers
Public Record Office, London

F. P. Walsh papers
New York Public Library, New York

J. C. Walsh papers
New York Public Library, New York

Interviews

Frank Aiken
Neil Blaney
Ernest Blythe
F. H. Boland
Kevin Boland
Lord Brookeborough
Neol Browne
Cornelius Cremin
James Dillon
George Gilmore
Joseph Groome
Charles Haughey
Sean Lemass
Lord Longford
Eddie MacAteer
Sean MacBride
Frank MacDermot
Malcolm MacDonald
Sean MacEntee
Liam MacGabhann
Patrick McGilligan
Patrick MacGill
Michael McInerney
Maurice Moynihan
Sean Nunan
Conor Cruise O'Brien
Peadar O'Donnell
Michael O Morain
T. P. O'Neill

Published Sources

Canada: Documents on External Affairs (CDEA)
Documents on German Foreign Policy (DGFP)
Peace and War: speeches by Mr de Valera on international affairs
Maurice Moynihan (ed.) *Speeches and statements by Eamon de Valera:
1917–1973* (Dublin: 1980)
Foreign Relations of the United States (FRUS)

Parliamentary Sources

Dail Eireann debates (DE)

Seenad Eireann debates (SE)
House of Commons, Westminster, debates (HC)
Northern Ireland, House of Commons debates (NIHC)

SECONDARY SOURCES

Works of Reference

Dictionary of National Biography
W. J. Flynn's Parliamentary Companions
Keesing's Contemporary Archives
Magill Book of Irish Politics, 1981
New York Times Index
The Times Index

General Histories

Lyons: 1971 — F. S. L. Lyons, *Ireland since the famine* (London: 1971)
Murphy: 1975 — J. A. Murphy, *Ireland in the twentiety century* (Dublin: 1975)

Works of history, politics, biography

Bell: 1971 — J. Bowyer Bell, *The secret army* (London: 1971)
Boland: 1974 — Kevin Boland *'We won't stand (idly) by'* (Dublin: 1974)
Boland: 1977 — Kevin Boland, *'Up Dev!'* (Dublin: 1977)
Bowman: 1979 — John Bowman, 'De Valera on Ulster: what he told America: 1919-20', *Irish Studies in International Affairs*, vol. 1, no. 1, 1979, pp. 3–18
Bowman: 1980 — John Bowman, 'Sinn Fein's perception of the Ulster Question: autumn 1921', *Crane Bag*, vol. 4, no. 2, pp. 50–6
Buckland: 1979 — Patrick Buckland, *The factory of grievances: devolved government in Northern Ireland: 1921–1939* (Dublin: 1979)
Carroll: 1975 — J. T. Carroll, *Ireland in the war years* (Newton Abbot: 1975)
Carson: 1957 — W. A. Carson, *Ulster and the Irish Republic* Belfast: n.d.)
Carter: 1977 — Carolle J. Carter, *The shamrock and the swastika* (Palo Alta: 1977)
Chubb: 1970 — Basil Chubb, *The government and politics of Ireland* (Oxford: 1970)
Cohen: 1977 — A. S. Cohen, 'The question of a united Ireland', *International Affairs*, vol. 53, no. 2, April 1977
Coogan: 1970 — T. P. Coogan, *The IRA* (London: 1970)

Crozier: 1973 — W. P. Crozier, *Off the record: political interviews, 1933-1943*, (ed.) A. J. P. Taylor (London: 1973)

Dwyer; 1977 — T. Ryle Dwyer, *Irish neutrality and the USA, 1939-1947* (Dublin: 1977)

Ervine: 1949 — St John Ervine, *Craigavon: Ulsterman* (London: 1949)

Farrell: 1971 — Brian Farrell, *Chairman or chief?: the role of Taoiseach in Irish government* (Dublin: 1971)

Fanning: 1976 — Ronan Fanning, 'De Valera plays the Green card', *Irish Times*, 19 May 1976

Fanning: 1978 — Ronan Fanning, *The Irish department of finance, 1922-1958* (Dublin: 1978)

Gallagher: 1957 — Frank Gallagher, *The indivisible island* (London: 1957)

Garner: 1978 — Joseph Garner, *The Commonwealth Office* (London: 1978)

Gilbert: 1975 — Martin Gilbert, *Winston S. Churchill: iv: 1916-1922* (London: 1975)

Hancock: 1937 — W. K. Hancock, *Survey of British Commonwealth affairs, vol. 1, problems of nationality, 1918-1936* (London: 1937)

Hancock: 1968 — W. K. Hancock, *Smuts: fields of force* (London: 1968)

Harbinson: 1973 — J. F. Harbinson, *The Ulster Unionist Party* (Belfast: 1973)

Harkness: 1969 — David Harkness, *The restless Dominion* (Dublin: 1969)

Harkness: 1970 — David Harkness, 'Mr de Valera's Dominion: Irish relations with Britain and the Commonwealth, 1932-1938', *Journal of Commonwealth Political Studies*, vol. 8, no. 3, 1970.

Harkness: 1976 — David Harkness, 'The Unionist reaction: bitterness and hostility', *Irish Times*, 19 May 1976.

Irish Press: 1948 — *With de Valera in America and Australia: world appeal against Partition, Irish Press* supplement (Dublin: 1948).

Jones: 1971 — Thomas Jones, *Whitehall diary, vol. 3: Ireland, 1918-1925*, K. Middlemas (ed.) (London: 1971).

Keatinge: 1978 — Patrick Keatinge, *A place among the nations: issues in Irish foreign policy* (Dublin: 1978).

Kelly: 1979 — John M. Kelly, 'Fianna Fail on the north: crooked talk on a breathtaking scale', *Hibernia*, 4 Oct. 1979.

Lee: 1976 — J. J. Lee, 'Lemass and his two partnerships', *Irish Times*, 19 May 1976.

Lynch: 1971 — John Lynch, *Speeches and statements on Irish unity, Northern Ireland, Anglo-Irish relations* (Dublin: 1971)

Lynch: 1972 — John Lynch, 'The Anglo-Irish problem', *Foreign Affairs*, vol. 50, no. 4, July 1972, pp. 601-17.

Longford and O'Neill: 1970 — Earl of Longford and T. P. O'Neill, *Eamon de Valera* (Dublin: 1970).

Longford: 1972 — Earl of Longford, *Peace by ordeal* (London: 1972).

Longford and McHardy: 1981 — Earl of Longford and Anne McHardy, *Ulster* (London: 1981).

Macardle: 1968 — Dorothy Macardle, *The Irish republic* (London: 1968 edn.).

MacDonald: 1972 — Malcolm MacDonald, *Titans and others* (London: 1972).

MacEntee: 1975 — Sean MacEntee, 'De Valera: the man I knew', *Iris Fianna Fail*, Winter, 1975.

MacMahon: 1975 — Deirdre MacMahon, 'Malcolm MacDonald and Anglo-Irish relations: 1935–38', MA thesis, UCD, 1975.

MacMahon: 1979 — Deirdre MacMahon, 'Anglo-Irish Relations: 1932–38', Ph.D. thesis, Cambridge University, 1979.

Mansergh: 1952 — Nicholas Mansergh, *Survey of British Commonwealth affairs: problems of external policy, 1931–1939* (London: 1952).

Mansergh: 1958 — Nicholas Mansergh, *Survey of British Commonwealth affairs: problems of wartime co-operation and post-war change, 1939–1952* (London: 1958).

Mansergh: 1965 — Nicholas Mansergh, *The Irish question: 1840–1921* (London: 1965).

Menzies: 1967 — Robert Menzies, *Afternoon light* (London: 1967).

Moody: 1974 — T. W. Moody, *The Ulster question: 1603–1973* (Cork: 1974).

Murphy: 1969 — J. A. Murphy, 'The Irish party system, 1938–51', in K. B. Nowlan and T. D. Williams (eds.), *Ireland in the War years and after, 1939–51* (London: 1969).

Murphy: 1973 — J. A. Murphy, 'The New IRA: 1925–62', in T. D. Williams (ed.), *Secret societies in Ireland* (Dublin: 1973).

Murphy: 1975 — J. A. Murphy, 'Eamon de Valera: the politician', *Bulletin of the Department of Foreign Affairs*, no. 872, 26 Sept. 1975.

O'Brien: 1972 — Conor Cruise O'Brien, *States of Ireland* (London: 1972).

O'Neill: 1975 — T. P. O'Neill, 'Eamon de Valera: 1882–1975', *Bulletin of the Department of Foreign Affairs*, no. 872, 26 Sept. 1975.

O'Neill: 1976 — T. P. O'Neill, 'In search of a political path: Irish Republicanism, 1922–1927', *Historical Studies*: X, G. A. Hayes-McCoy (ed.), (Dublin: 1976), pp. 147–71.

Rose: 1971 — Richard Rose, *Governing without consensus* (London: 1971).

Rose: 1976 — Richard Rose, *Northern Ireland: a time of choice* (London: 1976).

Stephan: 1963 — E. Stephan, *Spies in Ireland* (London: 1963).
Stewart: 1977 — A. T. Q. Stewart, *The narrow ground* (London: 1977).
Whyte: 1970 — John H. Whyte, *Church and state in modern Ireland, 1923-1970* (Dublin: 1970).
Williams: 1975 — T. D. Williams, 'Irish foreign policy, 1949-69', in J. J. Lee (ed.), *Ireland: 1945-1970* (Dublin: 1979).
Williams: 1979 — T. D. Williams, 'Eamon de Valera: international affairs', *Bulletin of the Department of Foreign Affairs*, no. 872, 26 Sept. 1975.

Works of political science, and political geography

Boulding: 1959 — K. E. Boulding, 'National images and international systems', in J. N. Rosenau, *International politics and foreign policy* (New York: 1969).
Cobban: 1969 — Alfred Cobban, *The nation-state and national self-determination* (London: 1969).
Cohen: 1964 — S. B. Cohen, *Geography and politics in a divided world* (London: 1964).
Crick: 1964 — Bernard Crick, *In defence of politics* (London: 1964).
Frankel: 1970 — Joseph Frankel, *National Interest* (London: 1970).
Gilfillan: 1924 — S. Columb Gilfillan, 'European political boundaries', *Political Science Quarterly*, vol. 39, 1924, pp. 458-84.
Hartshorne: 1968 — Richard Hartshorne, 'Morphology of the state area: significance for the state', in C. A. Fisher, *Essays in political geography*, (London: 1968).
Herz: 1968 — J. H. Herz, 'The territorial state re-visited: reflections on the future of the nation-state', in J. N. Rosenau, *International politics and foreign policy* (New York: 1969).
Heslinga: 1962 — M. W. Heslinga, *The Irish border as a cultural divide* (Assen: 1962).
Johnson: 1962 — James H. Johnson, 'The political distinctiveness of Northern Ireland', *The Geographical Review*, vol. 52, no. 1, Jan. 1962, pp. 78-91.
Jones: 1959 — S. B. Jones, 'Boundary concepts in the setting of place and time', in H. J. de Blij, *Systematic political geography* (New York: 1973).
Kristof: 1959 — L. K. D. Kristof, 'The nature of frontiers and boundaries', in R. E. Kasperson and J. V. Minghi, *The structure of political geography* (London: 1970).
Kristof: 1968 — L. K. D. Kristof, 'The Russian image of Russia: an applied study in geopolitical methodology', in C. A. Fisher, *Essays in political geography* (London: 1968).

Minghi: 1963 — J. V. Minghi, 'Boundary studies in political geography', in R. E. Kasperson and J. V. Minghi, *The structure of political geography* (London: 1970).

Mitchel: 1971 — N. C. Mitchel, 'Ireland: divided island', *Geoforum*, vol. 8, 1971, pp. 58–60.

Orme: 1970 — A. R. Orme, *The world's landscapes: Ireland* (London: 1970).

Pounds: 1964 — N. J. G. Pounds, 'History and geography: a perspective on partition', *Journal of International Affairs*, vol. 18, 1964, pp. 161–72.

Pounds and Ball: 1964 — N. J. G. Pounds and S. S. Ball, 'Core-areas and the development of the European States System', in H. J. de Blij, *Systematic political geography* (New York: 1973).

Prescott: 1965 — J. R. V. Prescott, *The geography of frontiers and boundaries* (London: 1965).

Smith: 1971 — A. D. Smith, *Theories of nationalism* (London: 1971).

Newspapers, periodicals, etc.

Anglo-Celt
Belfast Newsletter
Belfast Telegraph
Clare Champion
Cork Examiner
Derry Standard
Freeman's Journal
Fianna Fail Bulletin
Gaelic American (New York)
Hibernia
Iris Fianna Fail
Irish Freedom
Irish Independent
Irish News
Irish Press

Irish Times
Irish World (New York)
Magill
Manchester Guardian
The Nation (Dublin)
The Nation (New York)
New Statesman
New York Times
Northern Whig
Sligo Champion
Sunday Independent
Sunday Press
Sunday Tribune
The Times

Index

The following abbreviations are used in addition to those given
in the List of Abbreviations.

A–I	Anglo-Irish	FF	Fianna Fail
AIA38	Anglo-Irish Agreement (1938).	IBC	Irish Boundary Commission
AIN38	Anglo-Irish negotiations, 1938.	PND	partition-neutrality-defence
Cn37	1937 Constitution		talks, June 1940
de V	Eamon de Valera	SF	Sinn Fein
Doc2	Document No. 2	WW2	World War II.
ERA	External Relations Act		

Note that whereas in the text, Sir John Maffey is called Rugby once he becomes
Lord Rugby, in the index he is named as Maffey throughout; likewise, Craigavon
and Brookeborough are cited throughout the index under their original names,
Craig and Brooke.